Human Development Indices and Indicators

2018 Statistical Update

Published for the
United Nations
Development
Programme
(UNDP)

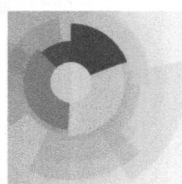

Human Development Indicators and Indices: 2018 Statistical Update Team

Director
Selim Jahan

Deputy director
Thangavel Palanivel

Research, writing and statistics
Milorad Kovacevic (Chief Statistician), Jacob Assa, Astra Bonini, Cecilia Calderon, Yu-Chieh Hsu, Christina Lengfelder, Tanni Mukhopadhyay, Shivani Nayyar, Carolina Rivera and Heriberto Tapia

Production, online and digital
Admir Jahic and Dharshani Seneviratne

Communications and advocacy
Jon Hall, Anna Ortubia and Elodie Turchi

Operations
Sarantuya Mend (Operations Manager), Botagoz Abdreyeva, Fe Juarez Shanahan, May Wint Than and Nu Nu Win

Foreword: the state of global human development in 2018

We are living in a complex world. People, nations and economies are more connected than ever, and so are the global development issues we are facing. These issues span borders, straddle social, economic and environmental realms, and can be persisting or recurring.

From urbanization to the creation of jobs for millions of people, the world's challenges will only be solved using approaches that take both complexity and local context into account. For almost thirty years, UNDP's human development approach—with its emphasis on enlarging people's freedoms and opportunities rather than economic growth—has inspired and informed solutions and policies across the world.

I am pleased to present *Human Development Indices and Indicators: 2018 Statistical Update*. With its comprehensive statistical annex, our data gives an overview of the state of development across the world, looking at long-term trends in human development indicators across multiple dimensions and for every nation.

Human development data, analysis and reporting have been at the heart of that paradigm. UNDP's Human Development Index (HDI) has captured human progress, combining information on people's health, education and income in just one number. Over the years, the HDI has served as a comparative tool of excellence, and as a reliable platform for vigorous public debates on national priorities.

Yet the simplicity of the HDI's story leaves much unsaid. Despite overall progress, large pockets of poverty and exclusion persist. Inequality and conflict are on the rise in many places. Climate change and other environmental concerns are undercutting development now and for future generations. Because our planet seems to be getting more unequal, more unstable and more unsustainable, offering detailed and reliable data has never been so important.

Consider inequality, which has become a defining issue of our time and in many places a cause of entrenched uncertainty and vulnerability. Inequality decreases the global HDI by one fifth. And it deals the hardest blow to countries in the low and medium development categories.

Gender inequality remains one of the greatest barriers to human development. The average HDI for women is 6 percent lower than that of men, with countries in the low development category suffering the widest gaps. Given current rates of progress it could take over 200 years to close the economic gender gap across the planet.

Further, conflicts in many parts of the world remain the norm rather than the exception. Violence not only threatens human security but also erodes development progress. Between 2012 and 2017, the conflicts in Syria, Libya and Yemen contributed to these countries' slipping down the HDI, due to significant declines in their life expectancy or economic setbacks. It will take years, if not decades for them to return to pre-violence levels of development.

Finally, as our environmental indicators show, today's progress is coming at the expense of our children. A changing climate, massive declines in biodiversity, and the depletion of land and freshwater resources pose serious threats to humankind. They require an immediate and ambitious change in production and consumption patterns.

While evidence remains the lifeblood of informed decisions, many policy-makers understandably struggle to know where to turn to for reliable and readily understandable information amidst the current avalanche of new indices, indicators and statistics. Collecting, integrating and filtering new data are needed to see the bigger picture and develop better solutions. This is an exciting period for human development reporting.

The Human Development Report will remain UNDP's premier vehicle to advance development thinking. Our mission to capture the state of global human development and inform development policy across the globe has never been more crucial.

Still, the Sustainable Development Goals (SDGs) require new indicators for assessing the many faces of inequality, the impact of the global environmental crisis on people now and tomorrow, the importance of voice, and the ways in which communities rather than individuals are progressing.

These and many other topics should be reexamined with a human development lens, resulting in a new generation of Human Development Reports. As we work to embrace new data, new ideas and new partners, we will continue to ensure human progress is monitored continuously, analyzed regularly and presented globally.

Achim Steiner
Administrator
United Nations Development Programme

Acknowledgements

Human Development Indices and Indicators: 2018 Statistical Update is the product of the Human Development Report Office (HDRO) at the United Nations Development Programme (UNDP).

The composite indices, indicators and data of the Update are those of the HDRO alone and cannot be attributed to UNDP or to its Executive Board. The UN General Assembly has officially recognized the *Human Development Report* as "an independent intellectual exercise" that has become "an important tool for raising awareness about human development around the world."

The Update's composite indices and other statistical resources rely on the expertise of the leading international data providers in their specialized fields, and we express our gratitude for their continued collegial collaboration with the HDRO.

A group of talented young people contributed to the Update as interns and deserve recognition for their dedication and contributions: Grace Chen, Rashik Alam Chowdhury, Drilona Emrullahu and Shangchao Liu.

We are grateful for the highly professional work of our editors and layout artists at Communications Development Incorporated—led by Bruce Ross-Larson, with Joe Caponio, Nick Moschovakis, Christopher Trott and Elaine Wilson.

Most of all, on a personal note, I am profoundly grateful to UNDP Administrator Achim Steiner for his leadership and vision as well as his commitment to the cause of human development. My thanks also go to all my HDRO colleagues, particularly the statistical team, for their dedication in producing statistical updates that strive to advance human development.

Selim Jahan
Director
Human Development Report Office

Contents

HUMAN DEVELOPMENT INDICES AND INDICATORS: 2018 STATISTICAL UPDATE

Trends in the Human Development Index and its key components—progress not linear, and still far to go	2
Inequalities in human development—a grave challenge to progress	4
Gender inequality—close the gaps to empower half the world's people	5
Human deprivations high despite overall progress	7
Moving beyond quantity to the quality of human development	8
Environmental degradation puts human development gains at risk	11
Conclusion	12
Notes	13
References	13

STATISTICAL ANNEX

Readers guide	17
Statistical tables	

Human development composite indices

1.	Human Development Index and its components	22
2.	Human Development Index trends, 1990–2017	26
3.	Inequality-adjusted Human Development Index	30
4.	Gender Development Index	34
5.	Gender Inequality Index	38
6.	Multidimensional Poverty Index: developing countries	—*

Human development indicators

7.	Population trends	44
8.	Health outcomes	48
9.	Education achievements	52
10.	National income and composition of resources	56
11.	Work and employment	60
12.	Human security	64
13.	Human and capital mobility	68
14.	Supplementary indicators: perceptions of well-being	72
15.	Status of fundamental human rights treaties	76

Human development dashboards

1.	Quality of human development	81
2.	Life-course gender gap	86
3.	Women's empowerment	91
4.	Environmental sustainability	96
5.	Socioeconomic sustainability	101

Developing regions	106
Index to Sustainable Development Goal indicators	107
Statistical references	110

BOXES

1	Measuring human development	1
2	Income inequality within countries	4
3	The Multidimensional Poverty Index	9

FIGURES

1	Evolution of human development composite indices	1
2	Human development dashboards	2
3	Human Development Index values, by country grouping, 1990–2017	3
4	Change in Human Development Index rank in conflict-affected countries, 2012–2017	3
5	Loss in Human Development Index value due to inequality, by human development group, 2017	5
6	Inequalities in human development outcomes around the world, 2017	5
7	Life expectancy at birth, by human development group, 2017	6
8	Human Development Index by gender, gender gap and Gender Development Index, by developing region, 2017	7
9	Gender Inequality Index, by developing region, 2017	8
10	Life-course gender gap, 2017	9
11	Healthy life expectancy and overall life expectancy, by human development group, 2017	10
12	Impressive progress in expected years of schooling and mean years of schooling, 1990–2017	11
13	Number of primary school pupils per teacher, by human development group, 2012–2017	11
14	Carbon dioxide emissions per capita, by human development group, 2014 (tonnes)	12
15	Change in forest area, by human development group, 1990–2015	12

* This table, based on a revised methodology developed jointly with the Oxford Poverty and Human Development Initiative, will be available in due course.

Human development indices and indicators
2018 statistical update

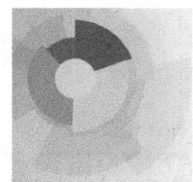

Human development is about human freedoms. It is about building human capabilities—not just for a few, not even for most, but for everyone. In 1990 UNDP published the first Human Development Report (HDR). Since then, it has produced more than 800 global, regional, national and subnational HDRs and organized hundreds of workshops, conferences and other outreach initiatives to foster human development. These activities have extended the frontiers of analytical thinking about human progress beyond economic growth, firmly placing people and human well-being at the centre of development policies and strategies.

The greatest innovations of the HDRs have been new measurement tools—notably the Human Development Index (HDI), launched in the first HDR (box 1). The underlying principle of the HDI, considered pathbreaking in 1990, was elegantly simple: National development should be measured not only by income per capita, as had long been the practice, but also by health and education achievements. Ranking countries by their HDI value transformed the development discourse and dethroned income per capita as the sole indicator of development progress.

Over the years additional indices have been developed to capture other dimensions of human development to identify groups falling behind in human progress and to monitor the distribution of human development (figure 1). In 2010 three indices were launched to monitor poverty, inequality and gender empowerment across multiple human development dimensions: the Multidimensional Poverty Index (MPI), the Inequality-adjusted Human Development Index (IHDI) and the Gender Inequality Index (GII). In 2014 the Gender Development Index (GDI) was introduced.

It is 28 years since the launch of the first HDR, and new challenges to human development, especially inequality and sustainability, require concerted measurement and analytical attention. Data availability is expanding with new opportunities for measurement innovation and disaggregation and possibilities for new partnerships growing out of the 2030 Agenda for Sustainable Development. Technologies are introducing new ways of communicating key report messages. These are all opportunities to strengthen the analysis, insights, relevance and reach of future HDRs.

Reflecting on the next generation of HDRs that give full consideration to new challenges and opportunities for analysis and innovation takes time. *Human Development Indices and Indicators: 2018 Statistical Update* is being

FIGURE 1

Evolution of human development composite indices

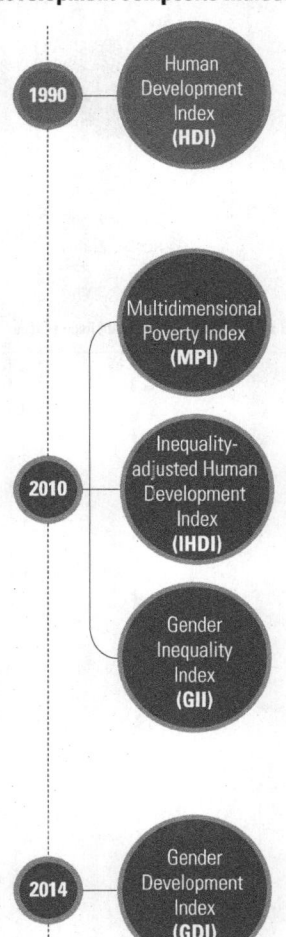

Source: Human Development Report Office.

BOX 1

Measuring human development

The Human Development Index (HDI) is a composite index focusing on three basic dimensions of human development: the ability to lead a long and healthy life, measured by life expectancy at birth; the ability to acquire knowledge, measured by mean years of schooling and expected years of schooling; and the ability to achieve a decent standard of living, measured by gross national income per capita.

To measure human development more comprehensively, the Human Development Report presents four other composite indices. The Inequality-adjusted HDI discounts the HDI according to the extent of inequality. The Gender Development Index compares female and male HDI values. The Gender Inequality Index highlights women's empowerment. And the Multidimensional Poverty Index measures nonincome dimensions of poverty.

Source: Human Development Report Office.

FIGURE 2

Human development dashboards

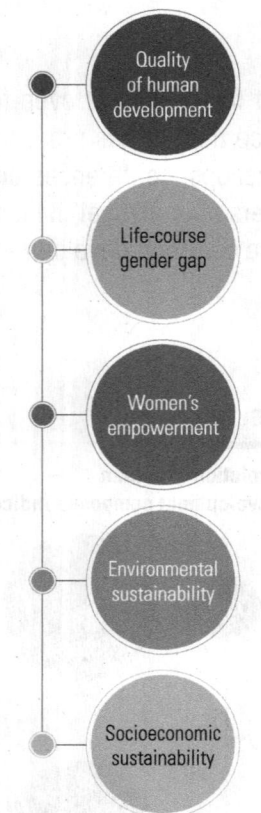

Source: Human Development Report Office.

released to ensure consistency in reporting on key human development indices and statistics. It provides a brief overview of the state of human development—snapshots of current conditions as well as long-term trends in human development indicators. And it includes a full statistical annex of human development composite indices and indicators across their various dimensions.

This update includes the 2017 values for the HDI and other composite indices as well as current statistics in key areas of human development for use by policymakers, researchers and others in their analytical, planning and policy work. In addition to the standard HDR tables, statistical dashboards are included to draw attention to the relationship between human well-being and five topics: quality of human development, life-course gender gaps, women's empowerment, environmental sustainability and socioeconomic sustainability (figure 2). Accompanying the statistical annex is an overview of trends in human development, highlighting the considerable progress, but also the persistent deprivations and disparities.

Trends in the Human Development Index and its key components—progress not linear, and still far to go

The 2018 Update presents HDI values for 189 countries and territories with the most recent data for 2017.[1] Of these countries, 59 are in the very high human development group, 53 in the high, 39 in the medium and only 38 in the low. In 2010, 49 countries were in the low human development group.

The top five countries in the global HDI ranking are Norway (0.953), Switzerland (0.944), Australia (0.939), Ireland (0.938) and Germany (0.936) (see statistical table 1). The bottom five are Burundi (0.417), Chad (0.404), South Sudan (0.388), the Central African Republic (0.367) and Niger (0.354). The largest increases in HDI rank between 2012 and 2017 were for Ireland, which moved up 13 places, and for Botswana, the Dominican Republic and Turkey, which each moved up 8. The largest declines were for the Syrian Arab Republic (down 27), Libya (26) and Yemen (20).

Looking back over almost three decades, all regions and human development groups have made substantial progress. The global HDI value in 2017 was 0.728, up about 21.7 percent from 0.598 in 1990. Across the world, people are living longer, are more educated and have greater livelihood opportunities. The average lifespan is seven years longer than it was in 1990, and more than 130 countries have universal enrolment in primary education.

Although HDI values have been rising across all regions and human development groups, the rates vary significantly (see statistical table 2). South Asia was the fastest growing region over 1990–2017, at 45.3 percent, followed by East Asia and the Pacific at 41.8 percent and Sub-Saharan Africa at 34.9 percent (figure 3). The Organisation for Economic Co-operation and Development (OECD) countries, by contrast, grew 14.0 percent. The trends hold promise for reducing gaps in human development across regions.

But HDI growth has also slowed in all regions, particularly in the last decade. Part of the reason lies in the 2008–2009 global food, financial and economic crises. But part is simply that as human progress advances, slower HDI growth is inevitable, given the growth ceilings of different components of the HDI—as seen with OECD countries. There is a biological limit to life expectancy, and years of schooling and rates of enrolment cannot grow indefinitely. Income is the only component of the HDI that could continue to grow; but even income growth slows as economies mature.[2] As more countries reach the upper limits of HDI dimensions, measures of the quality of human development become more central.

Progress since 1990 has not always been steady. Some countries suffered reversals due to conflicts, epidemics or economic crises. For example, many countries in Eastern Europe and Central Asia saw their HDI values fall in the 1990s due to the collapse of the Soviet Union and to military conflict, hyperinflation and a painful introduction (or expansion) of market mechanisms. Sub-Saharan Africa also had losses in the 1990s, when conflict and the HIV/AIDS epidemic caused life expectancy to drop dramatically. Despite these challenges,

FIGURE 3

Human Development Index values, by country grouping, 1990–2017

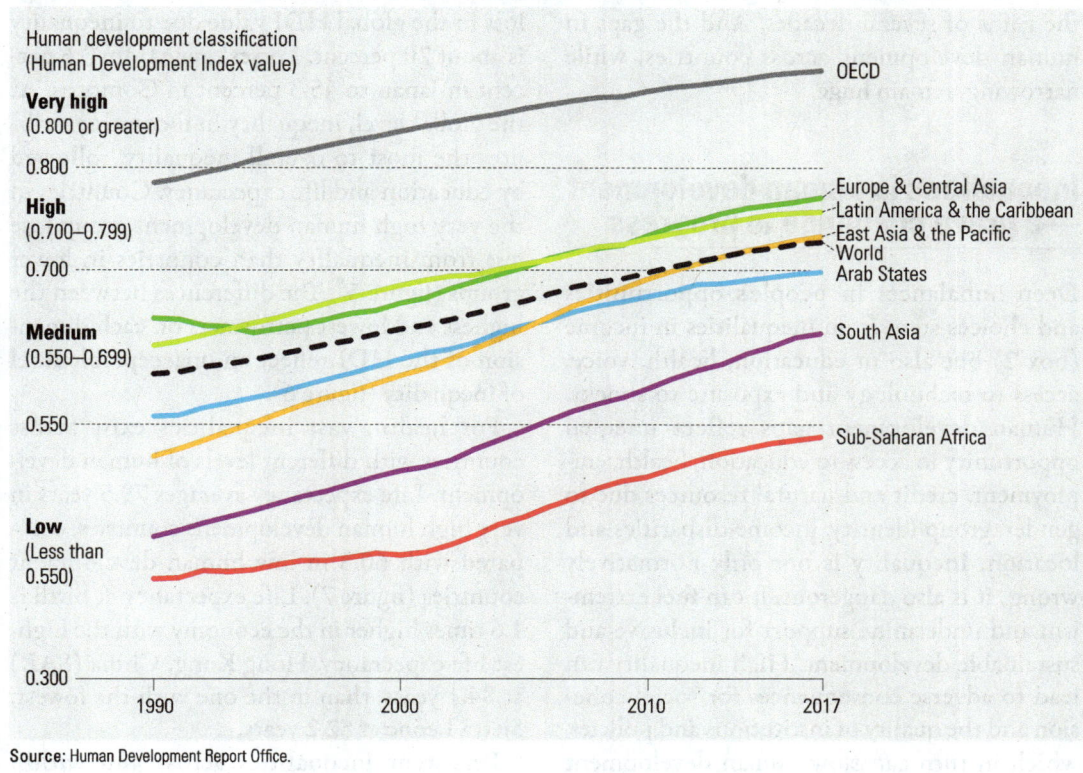

Source: Human Development Report Office.

> Progress on the HDI since 1990 has not always been steady. Some countries suffered reversals due to conflicts, epidemics or economic crises

countries in these regions recovered their losses on the HDI and grew over the last two decades. For example, Sub-Saharan Africa went from the second slowest growing region on the HDI in the 1990s to the fastest growing between 2000 and 2010.

In recent years other countries had setbacks as new challenges emerged and conflicts erupted. Between 2012 and 2017 Libya, the Syrian Arab Republic and Yemen had falling HDI values and ranks—the direct effect of violent conflict (figure 4). Although Lebanon is not directly involved in violent conflict, it has suffered spillovers from the conflict in the Syrian Arab Republic, hosting more than a million Syrian refugees.[3] In 2012 the Syrian Arab Republic ranked 128 on the HDI, in the medium human development group. But after years of conflict it dropped to 155 in 2017, in the low human development group, due mainly to lower life expectancy.

In sum, there have been significant advances in human development over the past few decades, especially in low human development

FIGURE 4

Change in Human Development Index rank in conflict-affected countries, 2012–2017

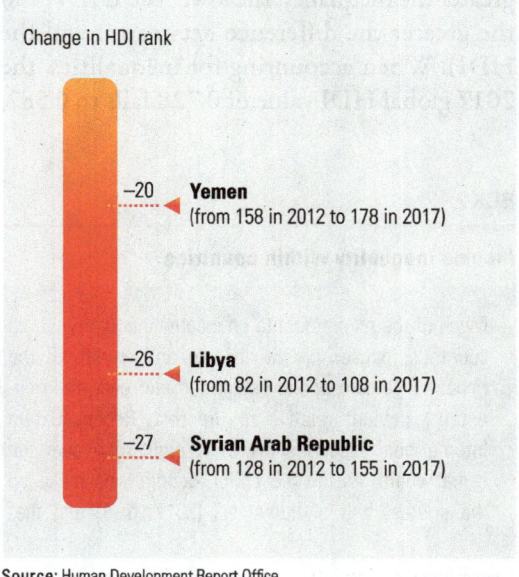

Source: Human Development Report Office.

> The average loss in the global HDI value due to inequality is about 20 percent

countries, up 46.6 percent on the HDI since 1990. But some countries have suffered serious setbacks—sometimes erasing in a few years the gains of several decades. And the gaps in human development across countries, while narrowing, remain huge.

Inequalities in human development—a grave challenge to progress

Deep imbalances in people's opportunities and choices stem from inequalities in income (box 2) but also in education, health, voice, access to technology and exposure to shocks. Human development gaps reflect unequal opportunity in access to education, health, employment, credit and natural resources due to gender, group identity, income disparities and location. Inequality is not only normatively wrong; it is also dangerous. It can fuel extremism and undermine support for inclusive and sustainable development. High inequality can lead to adverse consequences for social cohesion and the quality of institutions and policies, which in turn can slow human development progress.

Since 2010 the IHDI has been published in an effort to capture the distribution of human development within countries. With perfect equality the HDI and the IHDI are equal. When there is inequality in the distribution of health, education and income, the HDI in a society is less than the aggregate HDI. The greater the inequality, the lower the IHDI (and the greater the difference between it and the HDI). When accounting for inequalities, the 2017 global HDI value of 0.728 falls to 0.582, which represents a drop from the high human development category to the medium (see statistical table 3). In other words, the average loss in the global HDI value due to inequality is about 20 percent. Losses range from 3.6 percent in Japan to 45.3 percent in Comoros. At the global level, inequality in income contributes the most to overall inequality, followed by education and life expectancy. Countries in the very high human development group lose less from inequality than countries in lower groups (figure 5). The differences between the highest and lowest performers on each dimension of the HDI reflect an unacceptable level of inequality (figure 6).

For health, vast inequalities exist across countries with different levels of human development. Life expectancy averages 79.5 years in very high human development countries, compared with 60.8 in low human development countries (figure 7). Life expectancy at birth is 1.6 times higher in the economy with the highest life expectancy, Hong Kong, China (SAR) at 84.1 years, than in the one with the lowest, Sierra Leone at 52.2 years.

Persistent inequalities across and within countries also exist in education. Adults in very high human development countries average 7.5 more years of schooling than those in low human development countries, and children of school entrance age in very high human development countries can expect to be in school for about 7 more years than those in low human development countries. Low human development countries see a large drop in the gross enrolment ratio between primary school (98 percent) and secondary school (43 percent).

BOX 2

Income inequality within countries

Much of the recent debate on income inequality within countries focuses on the income and wealth of the richest 1 percent of the population and even the richest 0.1 percent relative to the rest. Recent Oxfam International reports show that "eight men own the same wealth as the 3.6 billion people who make up the poorest half of humanity" (2017, p. 1) and that "82 percent of all global wealth in the last year went to the top 1 percent, while the bottom half of humanity saw no increase at all" (2018, p. 10). While the share of the richest 1 percent and 0.1 percent is eye catching, focusing on these groups risks obscuring another growing concern in inequality—the decline and stagnation in the livelihood conditions of middle-income households.

Source: Oxfam International (2017, 2018) and Human Development Report Office.

FIGURE 5

Loss in Human Development Index value due to inequality, by human development group, 2017

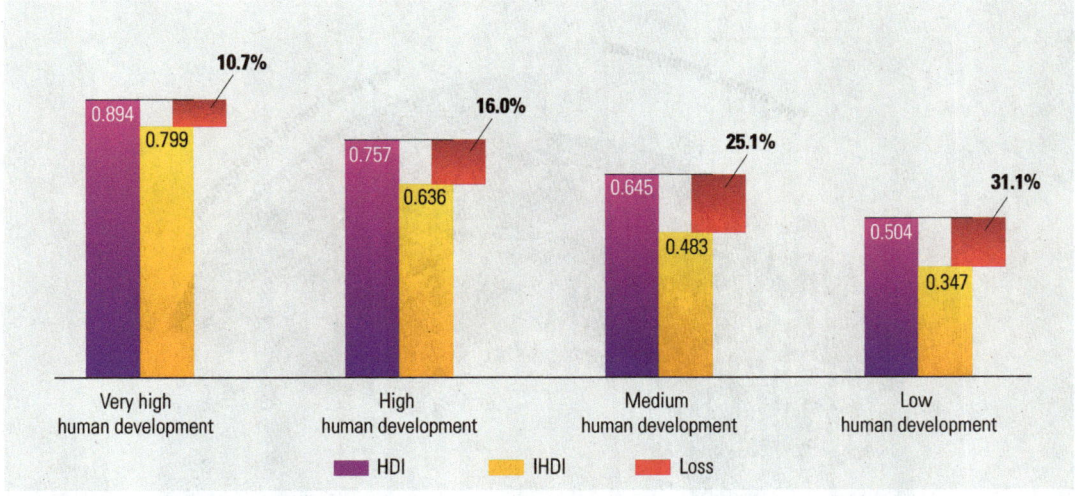

Source: Human Development Report Office.

FIGURE 6

Inequalities in human development outcomes around the world, 2017

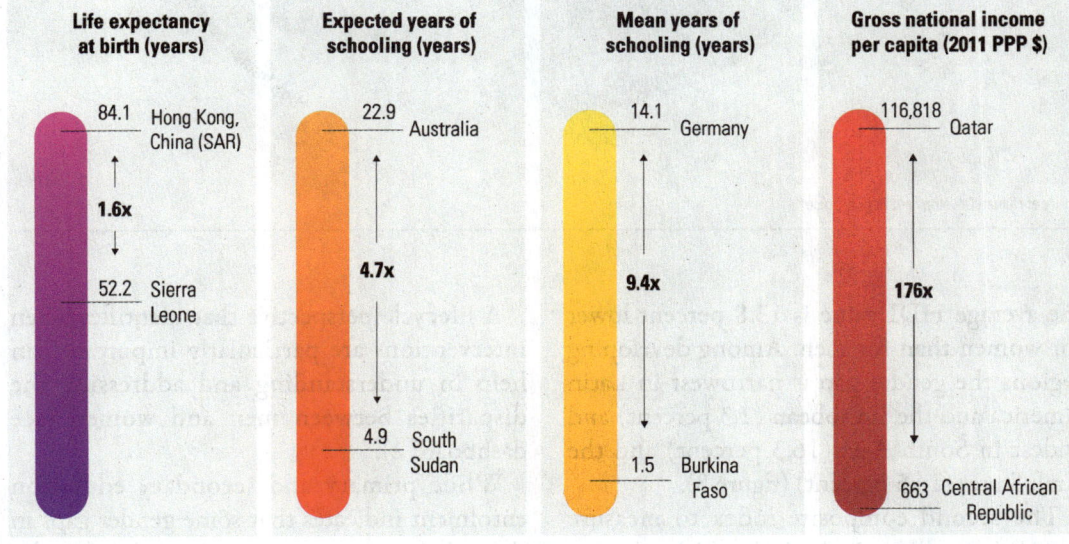

Source: Human Development Report Office.

Gender inequality—close the gaps to empower half the world's people

The disadvantages facing women and girls are a major source of inequality and one of the greatest barriers to human development progress. Two composite indices and two statistical dashboards capture the disparities between men and women.

First is the GDI, which reports female and male achievements in the basic dimensions of human development. Worldwide, the average HDI value for women (0.705) is 5.9 percent lower than that for men (0.749) (see statistical table 4). Much of the gap is due to women's lower income and educational attainment in many countries. The gender gap is widest in low human development countries, where

> Worldwide, the average HDI value for women (0.705) is 5.9 percent lower than that for men

FIGURE 7

Life expectancy at birth, by human development group, 2017

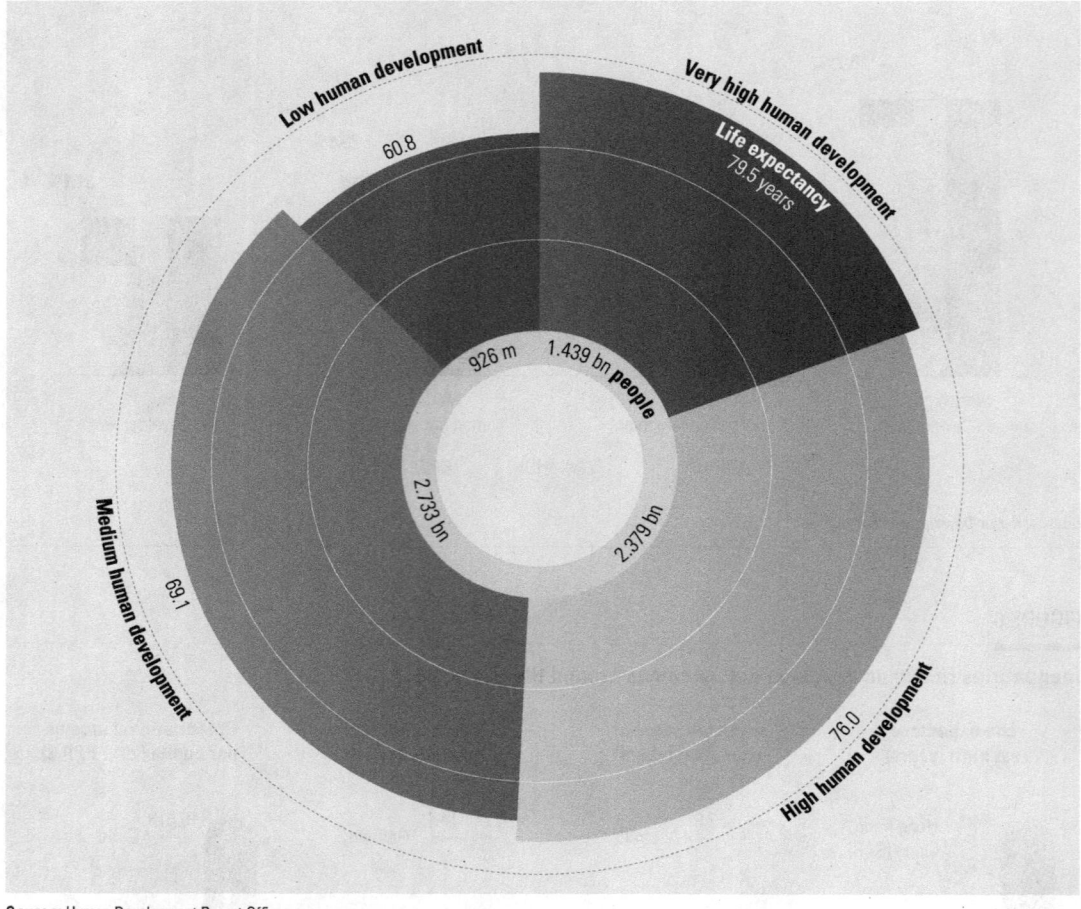

Source: Human Development Report Office.

> Among developing regions the gender gap is narrowest in Latin America and the Caribbean (2.3 percent) and widest in South Asia (16.3 percent) and the Arab States (14.5 percent)

the average HDI value is 13.8 percent lower for women than for men. Among developing regions the gender gap is narrowest in Latin America and the Caribbean (2.3 percent) and widest in South Asia (16.3 percent) and the Arab States (14.5 percent) (figure 8).

The second composite index to measure gender inequalities is the GII, which captures the inequalities women face in reproductive health, education, political representation and the labour market. The higher the GII value, the greater the gender inequality—which occurs in all countries. The global GII value in 2017 was 0.441 (see statistical table 5). Among developing regions the GII value ranges from 0.270 for Europe and Central Asia to 0.531 for the Arab States to 0.569 in Sub-Saharan Africa (figure 9). The value for OECD countries is 0.186.

A lifecycle perspective that identifies when interventions are particularly important can help in understanding and addressing the disparities between men and women (see dashboard 2).

While primary and secondary education enrolment indicates that some gender gaps in the early formative years are closing, the gender gaps in adulthood remain high (figure 10). Women hold only 23.5 percent of seats in parliament, and among women unemployment rates are higher and labour force participation rates lower. Yet women provide most unpaid care work in the home—limiting their choices in paid work.

A wide gap between men and women is also seen in old age. Even though on average women live longer than men, the proportion of men receiving a pension is 2.9 percentage

FIGURE 8

Human Development Index by gender, gender gap and Gender Development Index, by developing region, 2017

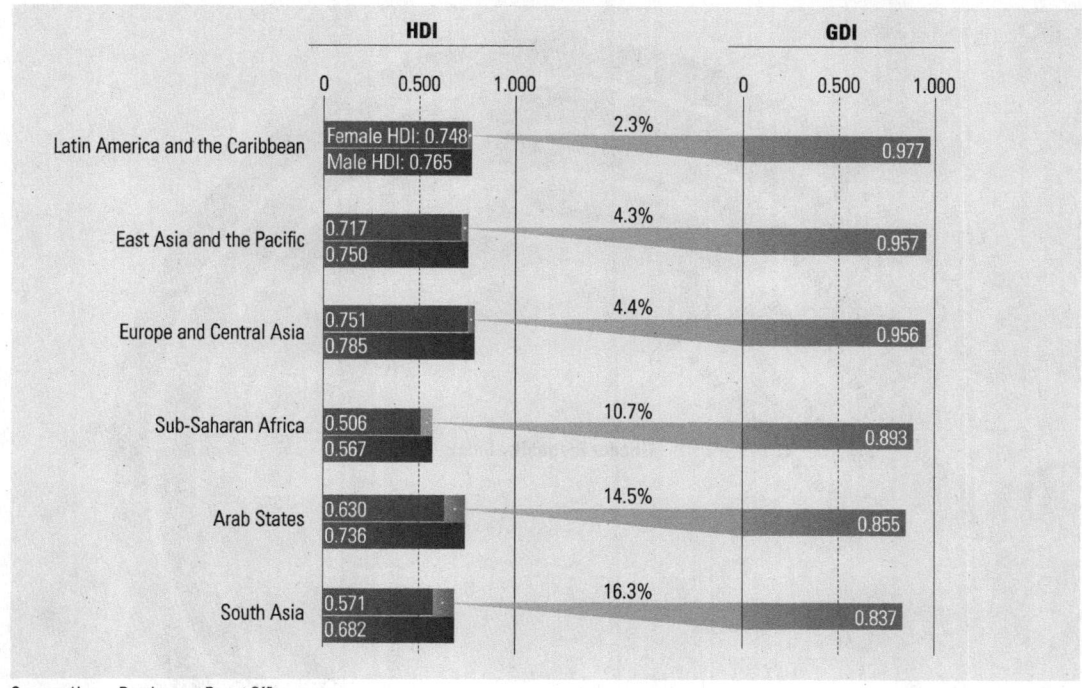

Source: Human Development Report Office.

points higher than the proportion of women (90.4 percent versus 87.5 percent). This reflects deficient social security schemes and, for women who do primarily unpaid care work, insufficient noncontributory pension benefits.

Lack of women's empowerment is a critical aspect of gender inequality. While empowerment barriers exist in many forms, girls and women are especially vulnerable to deprivations of physical integrity. Some 31.7 percent of women in South Asia, 31.5 percent in Sub-Saharan Africa and 26.3 percent in Europe and Central Asia have experienced intimate partner violence (other regions lack data). At the global level data are available for only about half the countries (see dashboard 3).

In low human development countries 39 percent of women ages 20–24 were married before their 18th birthday. Childhood marriage determines their way of life and—more often than not—undermines their opportunities for education, income and independence. High adolescent birth rates also undermine young women's opportunities, especially when pregnancies are by chance and not choice. Worldwide, the adolescent birth rate is 44.0 per 1,000 women ages 15–19 and highest in Sub-Saharan Africa, at 101.3.

Human deprivations high despite overall progress

The MPI, calculated primarily for developing countries since 2010, captures some human deprivations, lingering in all countries. It measures nonincome dimensions of poverty and shows how human deprivations overlap.

The most recent global estimates will be published in due course in a separate publication with the Oxford Poverty and Human Development Initiative, based on a new joint methodology (box 3).

The MPI does not capture all deprivations, so a more detailed analysis of poverty requires assessing additional indicators. Today 26.5 percent of adults who are employed are part of the working poor—making less than $3.10 a day in purchasing power parity terms (see statistical table 11). In low human development countries 47.5 percent of adults are illiterate, and only 17.1 percent of the population has access to the Internet.

> In low human development countries 47.5 percent of adults are illiterate, and only 17.1 percent of the population has access to the Internet.

FIGURE 9

Gender Inequality Index, by developing region, 2017

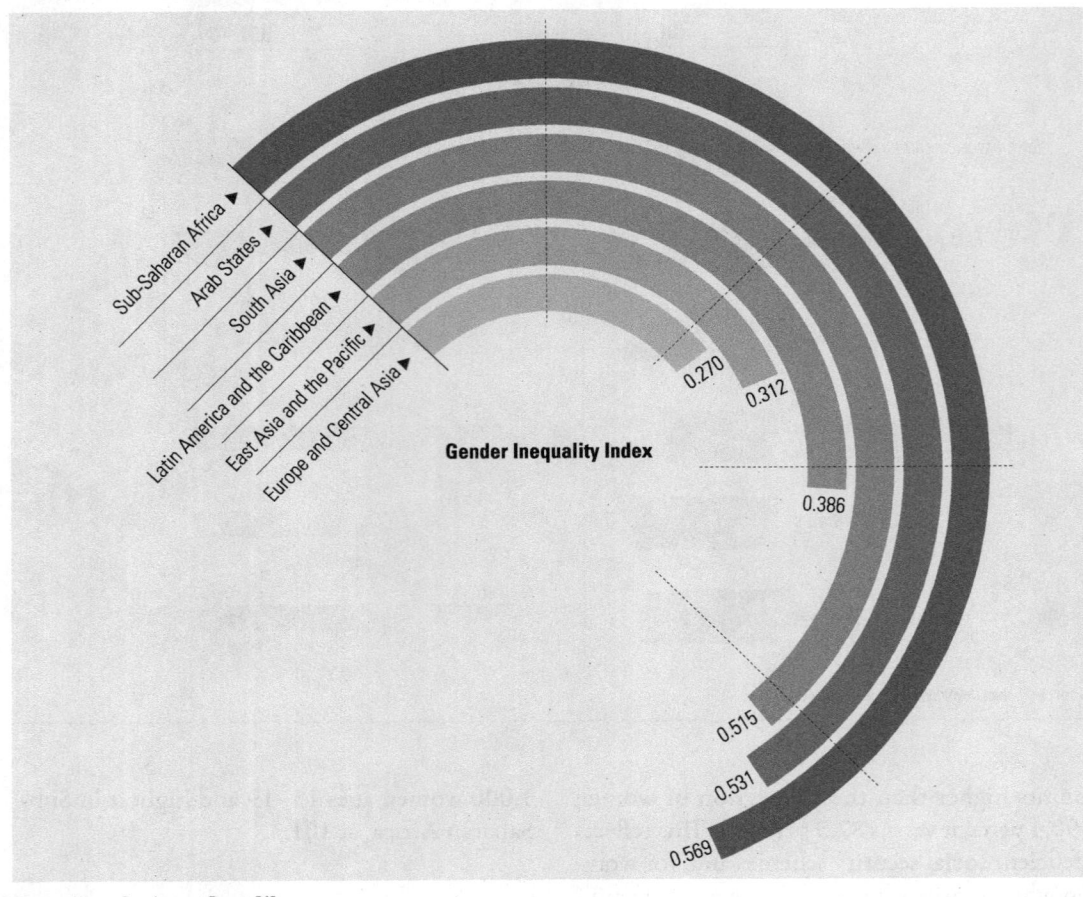

Source: Human Development Report Office.

Moving beyond quantity to the quality of human development

Achievements in human development should be expressed not only in terms of quantity, such as life expectancy or years of schooling, but also in terms of quality. Were the years lived really enjoyable or plagued by illness? Have children merely attended school, or did they gain the skills and knowledge that will equip them to lead a meaningful life? Is work allowing people to thrive, or are most people toiling in insecure and unsafe work? Are people shaping things that influence their lives or excluded from participating? From a human development viewpoint, true progress can be achieved only by ensuring quality—in education, health and beyond.

> From a human development viewpoint, true progress can be achieved only by ensuring quality—in education, health and beyond

Quality of health

Although life expectancy has increased substantially in most countries over the past three decades, the measure does not reveal whether the years lived are healthy and enjoyable. Several proxies for the quality of health exist and can be divided into input and output indicators. Consider the differences in access to physicians and hospital beds, both input indicators. Europe and Central Asia has 24.7 physicians per 10,000 people, South Asia 7.8 and Sub-Saharan Africa 1.9 (see dashboard 1). The average number of hospital beds per 10,000 people is 58 in high human development countries, compared with 9 in medium human development countries and 13 in low human development countries.

Another way to assess the quality of health is to look at output indicators such as healthy life expectancy, which provides information on

FIGURE 10

Life-course gender gap, 2017

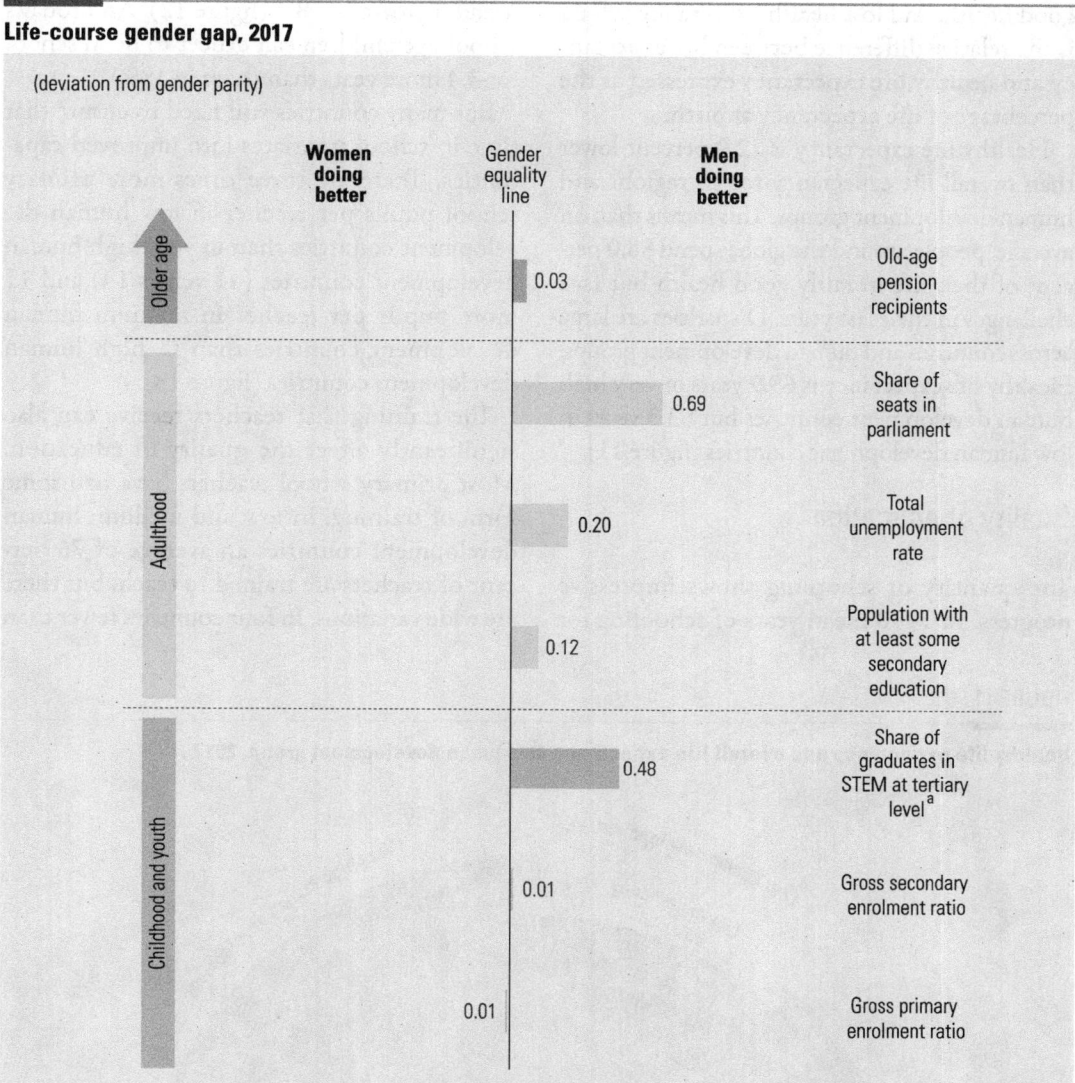

a. STEM includes science, mathematics, engineering, manufacturing and construction.

Source: Human Development Report Office.

BOX 3

The Multidimensional Poverty Index

The Multidimensional Poverty Index (MPI), developed by the Oxford Poverty and Human Development Initiative (OPHI) for HDRO, was added to the suite of composite human development indices in 2010. This year, an MPI with a modified methodology, jointly developed by HDRO and OPHI, is being launched.

The modified MPI identifies overlapping deprivations at the household level across the same three dimensions as the HDI (health, education and living standards). It shows the proportion of people who are multidimensionally poor and the average number of deprivations that each poor person experiences. It is calculated as a weighted average of 10 deprivation indicators, including school attainment and attendance, nutrition, child mortality, assets and access to some basic services.

Source: Human Development Report Office.

whether the years lived are expected to be in good health, and lost health expectancy, which is the relative difference between life expectancy and healthy life expectancy expressed as the percentage of life expectancy at birth.

Healthy life expectancy is 12.0 percent lower than overall life expectancy for all regions and human development groups. This means that, on average, people around the globe spend 88.0 percent of their life in fairly good health but face challenges in their last years. Disparities are large across countries and human development groups. Healthy life expectancy is 69.9 years in very high human development countries but 53.3 years in low human development countries (figure 11).

Quality of education

The quantity of schooling shows impressive progress. In 1990 mean years of schooling for the global adult population was 5.8; by 2017 it had increased to 8.4 (figure 12). And today's school-age children can expect to be in school for 3.4 more years than those in 1990.

But many countries still need to ensure that time in school translates into improved capabilities. There are three times more primary school pupils per teacher in low human development countries than in very high human development countries (41 versus 14) and 11 more pupils per teacher in medium human development countries than in high human development countries (figure 13).

The training that teachers receive can also significantly affect the quality of education. Most primary school teachers have had some form of training. In low and medium human development countries an average of 76 percent of teachers are trained to teach, but there are wide variations. In four countries fewer than

> Healthy life expectancy is 12 percent lower than overall life expectancy

FIGURE 11

Healthy life expectancy and overall life expectancy, by human development group, 2017

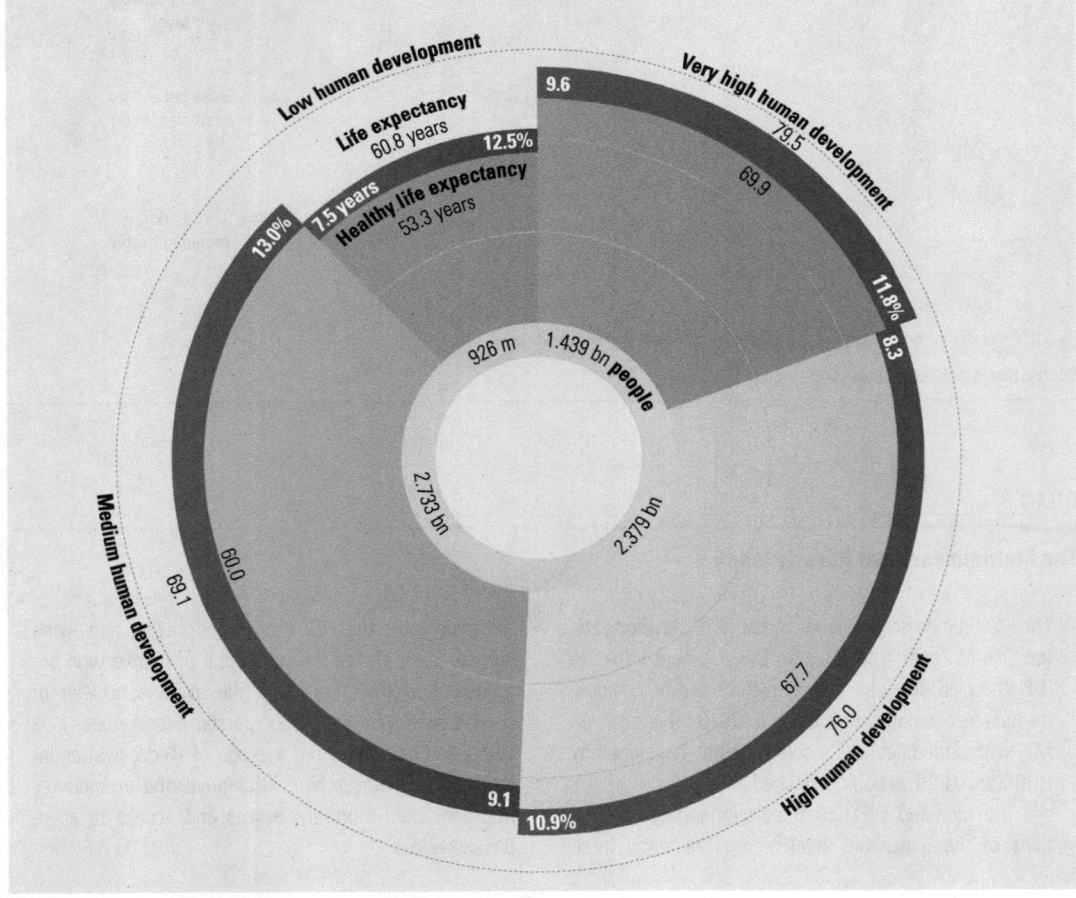

Source: Human Development Report Office.

FIGURE 12

Impressive progress in expected years of schooling and mean years of schooling, 1990–2017

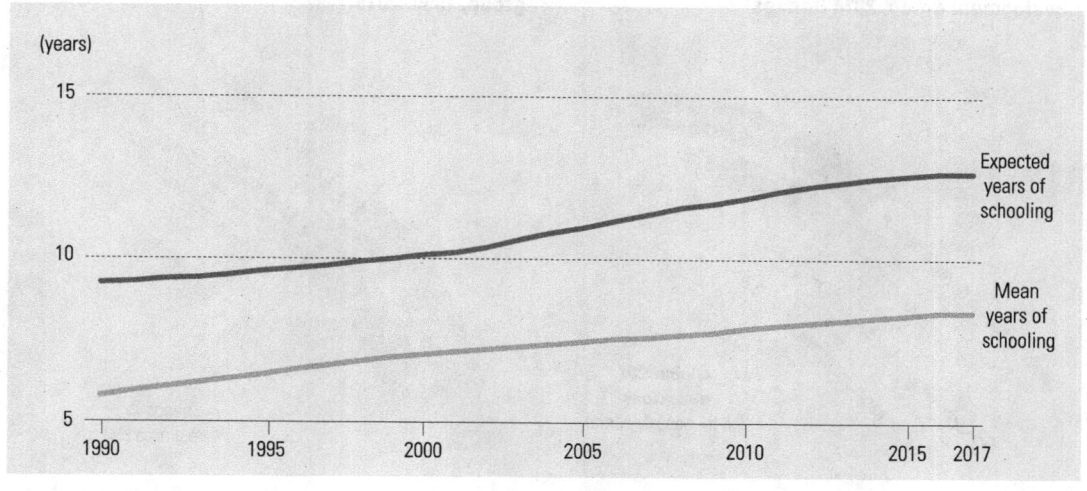

Source: Human Development Report Office.

FIGURE 13

Number of primary school pupils per teacher, by human development group, 2012–2017

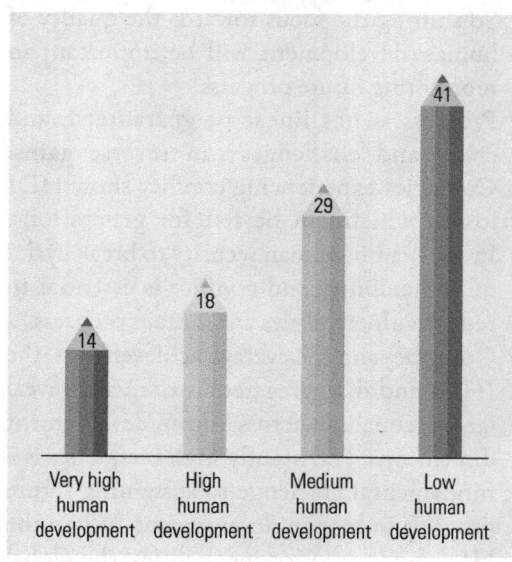

Source: Human Development Report Office.

30 percent of teachers are trained: Madagascar (15 percent), Kyrgyzstan (21 percent), Sao Tome and Principe (27 percent) and Vanuatu (28 percent). The availability of communications technologies also has implications for the quality of education. But modernizing schools requires substantial investments, a challenge in most developing regions.

Environmental degradation puts human development gains at risk

The degradation of the environment and atmosphere, coupled with significant declines in biodiversity, is linked to other development concerns ranging from declining food and water supplies to losses of livelihood and to losses of life from extreme weather events. This profoundly serious crisis threatens the human development of current and future generations.

Business-as-usual approaches must change, with countries at different levels of human development exposed to and contributing to environmental degradation in different ways (see dashboard 4). Very high human development countries are the biggest contributors to climate change, with average carbon dioxide emissions per capita of 10.7 tonnes, compared with 0.3 tonne in low human development countries (figure 14). These averages mask considerable variation: Qatar had the highest carbon dioxide emissions per capita in 2014, releasing more than 45 tonnes per person, while Uruguay, also a very high human development country, released only 2 tonnes per person. Countries with lower levels of human development, especially small island developing states, generally have the lowest emissions but are often the most vulnerable to climate change.

> The degradation of the environment and atmosphere, coupled with significant declines in biodiversity, threatens the human development of current and future generations

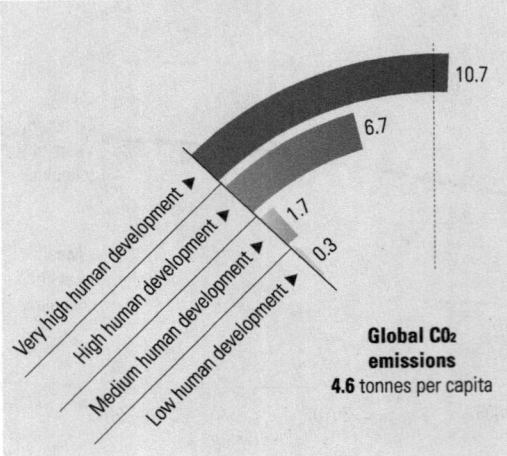

FIGURE 14

Carbon dioxide emissions per capita, by human development group, 2014 (tonnes)

Global CO₂ emissions **4.6** tonnes per capita

Source: Human Development Report Office.

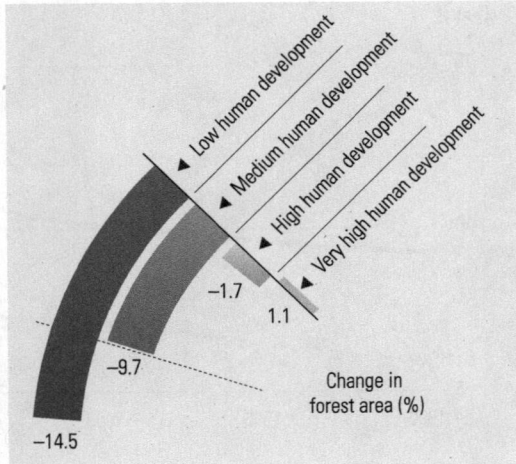

FIGURE 15

Change in forest area, by human development group, 1990–2015

Source: Human Development Report Office.

> Every human being counts, and every human life is equally valuable. That universalism is at the core of the human development concept

Linked to climate change and biodiversity loss, deforestation also degrades land and reduces the quantity and quality of freshwater. The overall pace of forest loss has slowed in recent years, but the planet still lost 3.2 percent of its forests between 1990 and 2015. And low human development countries, many of them reservoirs of global biodiversity, lost 14.5 percent (figure 15).

Freshwater withdrawals stand at 7.2 percent of the global supply, with vast differences across countries and regions. In South Asia annual withdrawals stand at 23.8 percent of total renewable supplies. Unsustainable water withdrawals and inadequate treatment of waste contaminate drinking water, with cascading impacts on health, employment and gender inequality.

Conclusion

This Update has shown a snapshot of conditions today as well as key trends in human development indices and indicators. Five key findings emerge from the analysis:
- Most people today live longer, are more educated and have more access to goods and services than ever before. Even in low human development countries people's human development has improved significantly. But the quality of human development reveals large deficits. Living longer does not automatically mean more years spent enjoying life. Being in school longer does not automatically translate into equivalent capabilities and skills. So shifting the focus towards the quality of human development will be important in monitoring future progress.
- Progress is not linear or guaranteed, and crises and challenges can reverse gains. Countries experiencing conflict show HDI losses, which can be felt for generations. Investment in human security to break cycles of vulnerability and conflict is essential to reduce vulnerabilities and sustain progress.
- Going beyond the average achievements, the IHDI and disaggregated assessments reveal large inequalities across human development dimensions. Persistently high inequality is a fundamental challenge to sustaining future progress in human development. When the HDI is adjusted for inequalities, the global HDI value falls 20 percent.
- Disparities between women and men in realizing their full potential stand as a great barrier to human development progress, holding back half the world's population. Women have a lower HDI value than men across regions and face particular barriers to empowerment all through life.
- Progress in human development cannot be sustained without addressing environmental degradation and climate change, which the

recent progress on the HDI has exacerbated. For human development to become truly sustainable, the world needs to break with business-as-usual approaches and adopt sustainable production and consumption patterns.

* * *

Every human being counts, and every human life is equally valuable. That universalism is at the core of the human development concept. With the 2030 Agenda for Sustainable Development, the Sustainable Development Goals and the promises to leave no one behind, this universal perspective is more critical than ever, particularly in a world that is increasingly unequal, unstable and unsustainable.

Notes

1. The Marshall Islands was added this year.
2. In calculating the HDI, income per capita is capped at $75,000.
3. http://www.unhcr.org/en-us/syria-emergency.html.

References

Oxfam International. 2017. "An Economy for the 99%." Oxfam Briefing Paper. Oxford, UK.

———. 2018. "Reward Work, Not Wealth. Oxfam Briefing Paper. Oxford, UK.

Statistical annex

Readers guide	17

Statistical tables

Human development composite indices

1	Human Development Index and its components	22
2	Human Development Index trends, 1990–2017	26
3	Inequality-adjusted Human Development Index	30
4	Gender Development Index	34
5	Gender Inequality Index	38
6	Multidimensional Poverty Index: developing countries	—*

Human development indicators

7	Population trends	44
8	Health outcomes	48
9	Education achievements	52
10	National income and composition of resources	56
11	Work and employment	60
12	Human security	64
13	Human and capital mobility	68
14	Supplementary indicators: perceptions of well-being	72
15	Status of fundamental human rights treaties	76

Human development dashboards

1	Quality of human development	81
2	Life-course gender gap	86
3	Women's empowerment	91
4	Environmental sustainability	96
5	Socioeconomic sustainability	101

Developing regions	106
Index to Sustainable Development Goal indicators	107
Statistical references	110

* This table, based on a revised methodology developed jointly with the Oxford Poverty and Human Development Initiative, will be available in due course.

Readers guide

The 20 statistical tables in this annex provide an overview of key aspects of human development. The first five tables contain the family of composite human development indices and their components estimated by the Human Development Report Office (HDRO). The sixth table is produced in partnership with the Oxford Poverty and Human Development Initiative (OPHI) and will be added in due course. Remaining tables present a broader set of indicators related to human development. The five dashboards use colour coding to visualize partial groupings of countries according to performance on each indicator.

Unless otherwise noted, tables use data available to the HDRO as of 15 July 2018. All indices and indicators, along with technical notes on the calculation of composite indices and additional source information, are available at http://hdr.undp.org/en/data.

Countries and territories are ranked by 2017 Human Development Index (HDI) value. Robustness and reliability analysis has shown that for most countries differences in HDI are not statistically significant at the fourth decimal place. For this reason countries with the same HDI value at three decimal places are listed with tied ranks.

Sources and definitions

Unless otherwise noted, the HDRO uses data from international data agencies with the mandate, resources and expertise to collect national data on specific indicators.

Definitions of indicators and sources for original data components are given at the end of each table, with full source details in *Statistical references*.

Methodology updates

The 2018 Statistical Update retains all the composite indices from the family of human development indices—the HDI, the Inequality-adjusted Human Development Index (IHDI), the Gender Development Index (GDI), the Gender Inequality Index (GII) and the Multidimensional Poverty Index (MPI). The methodology used to compute the first four indices is the same as the one used in the 2016 Report. For details, see *Technical notes 1–4* at http://hdr.undp.org/sites/default/files/hdr2018_technical_notes.pdf. The methodology used to compute the MPI has been revised jointly with OPHI. For details, see *Technical note 5* at http://hdr.undp.org/sites/default/files/hdr2018_technical_notes.pdf.

The 2018 Statistical Update expands the number of colour-coded dashboards to five (quality of human development, life-course gender gap, women's empowerment, environmental sustainability and socioeconomic sustainability). For details on the methodology used to create them, see *Technical note 6* at http://hdr.undp.org/sites/default/files/hdr2018_technical_notes.pdf.

Comparisons over time and across editions

Because national and international agencies continually improve their data series, the data—including the HDI values and ranks—presented in this report are not comparable to those published in earlier editions. For HDI comparability across years and countries, see table 2, which presents trends using consistent data, or http://hdr.undp.org/en/data, which presents interpolated consistent data.

Discrepancies between national and international estimates

National and international data can differ because international agencies harmonize national data using a consistent methodology and occasionally produce estimates of missing data to allow comparability across countries. In other cases international agencies might not have access to the most recent national data. When HDRO becomes aware of discrepancies, it brings them to the attention of national and international data authorities.

Country groupings and aggregates

The tables present weighted aggregates for several country groupings. In general, an aggregate is shown only when data are available for at least half the countries and represent at least two-thirds of the population in that grouping. Aggregates for each grouping cover only the countries for which data are available.

Human development classification

HDI classifications are based on HDI fixed cutoff points, which are derived from the quartiles of distributions of the component indicators. The cutoff points are HDI of less than 0.550 for low human development, 0.550–0.699 for medium human development, 0.700–0.799 for high human development and 0.800 or greater for very high human development.

Regional groupings

Regional groupings are based on United Nations Development Programme regional classifications. Least Developed Countries and Small Island Developing States are defined according to UN classifications (see www.unohrlls.org).

Developing countries

The developing countries aggregates include all countries that are included in a regional grouping.

Organisation for Economic Co-operation and Development

Of the 35 Organisation for Economic Co-operation and Development members, 32 are considered developed countries and 3 (Chile, Mexico and Turkey) are considered developing countries. Aggregates refer to all countries from the group for which data are available.

Country notes

Data for China do not include Hong Kong Special Administrative Region of China, Macao Special Administrative Region of China or Taiwan Province of China.

As of 2 May 2016, Czechia is the short name to be used for the Czech Republic.

As of 1 June 2018, the Kingdom of Eswatini is the name of the country formerly known as Swaziland.

Symbols

A dash between two years, as in 2011–2017, indicates that the data are from the most recent year available during the period specified. A slash between years, as in 2012/2017, indicates that the data are the average for the years shown. Growth rates are usually average annual rates of growth between the first and last years of the period shown.

The following symbols are used in the tables:
..   Not available
0 or 0.0   Nil or negligible
—   Not applicable

Statistical acknowledgements

The 2018 Statistical Update's composite indices and other statistical resources draw on a wide variety of the most respected international data providers in their specialized fields. HDRO is particularly grateful to the Centre for Research on the Epidemiology of Disasters; Economic Commission for Latin America and the Caribbean; Eurostat; Food and Agriculture Organization; Gallup; ICF Macro; Institute for Criminal Policy Research; Internal Displacement Monitoring Centre; International Labour Organization; International Monetary Fund; International Telecommunication Union; Inter-Parliamentary Union; Luxembourg Income Study; Office of the United Nations High Commissioner for Human Rights; Office of the United Nations High Commissioner for Refugees; Organisation for Economic Co-operation and Development; Socio-Economic Database for Latin America and the Caribbean; Syrian Center for Policy Research; United Nations Children's Fund; United Nations Conference on Trade and Development; United Nations Department of Economic and Social Affairs; United Nations Economic and Social Commission for West Asia; United Nations Educational, Scientific and Cultural Organization Institute for Statistics; United Nations Entity for Gender Equality and the Empowerment of Women; United Nations Office on Drugs and Crime; United Nations World Tourism Organization; World Bank; and World Health Organization. The international education database maintained by Robert Barro (Harvard University) and Jong-Wha Lee (Korea University) was another invaluable source for the calculation of the 2018 Statistical Update's indices.

Statistical tables

The first six tables relate to the five composite human development indices and their components. Since the 2010 Human Development Report, four composite human development indices—the HDI, the IHDI, the GII and the MPI for developing countries—have been calculated. The 2014 Report introduced the GDI, which compares the HDI calculated separately for women and men. A table with the MPI calculated based on a revised methodology developed jointly by OPHI and UNDP will be available in due course.

The remaining tables present a broader set of human development indicators and provide a more comprehensive picture of a country's human development.

For indicators that are global Sustainable Development Goals indicators or can be used in monitoring progress towards specific goals, the table headers include the relevant goals and targets.

Table 1, Human Development Index and its components, ranks countries by 2017 HDI value and details the values of the three HDI components: longevity, education (with two indicators) and income per capita. The table also presents the difference in rankings by HDI value and gross national income per capita, as well as the rank on the 2016 HDI, calculated using the most recently revised historical data available in 2018.

Table 2, Human Development Index trends, 1990–2017, provides a time series of HDI values allowing 2017 HDI values to be compared with those for previous years. The table uses the most recently revised historical data available in 2018 and the same methodology applied to compute 2017 HDI values. The table also includes the change in HDI rank over the last five years and the average annual HDI growth rate across four time intervals: 1990–2000, 2000–2010, 2010–2017 and 1990–2017.

Table 3, Inequality-adjusted Human Development Index, contains two related measures of inequality—the IHDI and the loss in HDI due to inequality. The IHDI looks beyond the average achievements of a country in longevity, education and income to show how these achievements are distributed among its residents. The IHDI value can be interpreted as the level of human development when inequality is accounted for. The relative difference between IHDI and HDI values is the loss due to inequality in distribution of the HDI within the country. The table presents the coefficient of human inequality, which is the unweighted average of inequalities in the three dimensions. In addition, the table shows each country's difference in rank on the HDI and the IHDI. A negative value means that taking inequality into account lowers a country's rank on the HDI. The table also presents three standard measures of income inequality: the ratio of the top and the bottom quintiles; the Palma ratio, which is the ratio of income of the top 10 percent and the bottom 40 percent; and the Gini coefficient.

Table 4, Gender Development Index, measures disparities on the HDI by gender. The table contains HDI values estimated separately for women and men; the ratio of which is the GDI value. The closer the ratio is to 1, the smaller the gap between women and men. Values for the three HDI components—longevity, education (with two indicators) and income per capita—are also presented by gender. The table includes five country groupings by absolute deviation from gender parity in HDI values.

Table 5, Gender Inequality Index, presents a composite measure of gender inequality using three dimensions: reproductive health, empowerment and the labour market. The reproductive health indicators are the maternal mortality ratio and the adolescent birth rate. The empowerment indicators are the share of parliamentary seats held by women and the share of population with at least some secondary education by gender. The labour market indicator is participation in the labour force by gender. A low GII value indicates low inequality between women and men, and vice-versa.

Table 6, Multidimensional Poverty Index, captures the multiple overlapping deprivations that people in developing countries face in their health, education and standard of living. The MPI shows both the incidence of nonincome multidimensional poverty (a headcount of those in multidimensional poverty) and its intensity (the average deprivation score experienced by poor people). Based on deprivation score thresholds, people are classified as near multidimensional poverty, multidimensionally poor or in severe poverty. The table includes the contribution of deprivation in each dimension to overall multidimensional poverty. It also presents measures of income poverty—population living below the national poverty line and population living on less than $1.90 in purchasing power parity terms per day. MPI values are based on a revised methodology developed in partnership with OPHI. For details, see *Technical note 5* at http://hdr.undp.org/sites/default/files/hdr2018_technical_notes.pdf and OPHI's website (http://ophi.org.uk/multidimensional-poverty-index/).

Table 7, Population trends, contains major population indicators, including total population, median age, dependency ratios and total fertility rates, which can help assess the burden of support that falls on the labour force in a country.

Table 8, Health outcomes, presents indicators of infant health (percentage of infants who are exclusively breastfed in the 24 hours prior to the survey, percentage of infants who lack immunization for DPT and measles and infant mortality rate) and of child health (percentage of children under age 5 who are stunted and under-five mortality rates). The table also contains indicators of adult health (adult mortality rates by gender, incidence of malaria and tuberculosis and HIV prevalence rates). Finally, it includes healthy life expectancy at birth and current health expenditure as a percentage of GDP.

Table 9, Education achievements, presents standard education indicators. The table provides indicators of educational attainment—adult and youth literacy rates and the share of the adult population with at least some secondary education. Gross enrolment ratios at each level of education are complemented by primary school dropout rate and survival rate to the last grade of lower secondary general education. The table also presents government expenditure on education as a percentage of GDP.

Table 10, National income and composition of resources, covers several macroeconomic indicators such as gross domestic product (GDP), gross fixed capital formation, and taxes on income, profit and capital gains as a percentage of total tax revenue. Gross fixed capital formation is a rough indicator of national income that is invested rather than consumed. In times of economic uncertainty or recession, gross fixed capital formation typically declines. General government final consumption expenditure (presented as a share of GDP and as average annual growth) is an indicator of public spending. In addition, the table presents two indicators of debt—domestic credit provided by the financial sector and total debt service, both measured as a percentage of GDP or GNI. The consumer price index, a measure of inflation, is also presented.

Table 11, Work and employment, contains indicators on four topics: employment, unemployment, work that is a risk to human development and employment-related social security. The employment indicators are the employment to population ratio, the labour force participation rate, employment in agriculture and employment in services. The unemployment indicators are total unemployment, youth unemployment and youth not in school or employment. The indicators on work that is a risk to human development are child labour and the working poor. And the indicator on employment-related social security is the percentage of the eligible population that receives an old-age pension.

Table 12, Human security, reflects the extent to which the population is secure. The table begins with the percentage of births that are registered, followed by the number of refugees by country of origin and the number of internally displaced people. It then shows the size of the homeless population due to natural disasters, the population of orphaned children and the prison population. It also provides homicide and suicide rates (by gender) and includes an indicator on justification of wife beating and an indicator on the depth of food deficit.

Table 13, Human and capital mobility, provides indicators of several aspects of globalization. International trade is captured by measuring exports and imports as a share of GDP. Financial flows are represented by net inflows of foreign direct investment and flows of private capital, net official development assistance and inflows of remittances. Human mobility is captured by the net migration rate, the stock of immigrants, the net number of tertiary students from abroad (expressed as a percentage of total tertiary enrolment in the country) and the number of international inbound tourists. International communication is represented by the percentages of the total and female populations that use the Internet, the number of mobile phone subscriptions per 100 people and the percentage change in mobile phone subscriptions between 2010 and 2016.

Table 14, Supplementary indicators: perceptions of well-being, includes indicators that reflect individuals' perceptions of relevant dimensions of human development—education quality, health care quality, standard of living, personal safety, freedom of choice and overall life satisfaction. The table also presents indicators reflecting perceptions about community and government.

Table 15, Status of fundamental human rights treaties, shows when countries ratified key human rights conventions. The 11 selected conventions cover basic human rights and freedoms related to elimination of all forms of racial and gender discrimination and violence, protection of children's rights, rights of migrant workers and persons with disabilities. They also cover torture and other cruel, inhuman and degrading treatment as well as protection from enforced disappearance.

Dashboard 1, Quality of human development, contains a selection of indicators associated with the quality of health, education and standard of living. The indicators on quality of health are lost health expectancy, number of physicians and number of hospital beds. The indicators on quality of education are pupil–teacher ratio in primary schools; primary school teachers trained to teach; proportion of schools with access to the Internet; and Programme for International Student Assessment (PISA) scores in mathematics, reading and science. The indicators on quality of standard of living are the proportion of employment that is in vulnerable employment, the proportion of rural population with access to electricity, the proportion of population using improved drinking-water sources and the proportion of population using improved sanitation facilities. A country in the top third of an indicator distribution has performed better than at least two-thirds of countries. A country that is in the top third group on all indicators can be considered a country with the highest quality of human development. The dashboard shows that not all countries in the very high human development group have the highest quality of human development and that many countries in the low human development group are in the bottom third of all quality indicators in the table.

Dashboard 2, Life-course gender gap, contains a selection of indicators that indicate gender gaps in choices and opportunities over the life course—childhood and youth, adulthood and older age. The indicators refer to health, education, labour market and work, seats in parliament, time use and social protection. Most indicators are presented as a ratio of female to male values. Sex ratio at birth is an exception to grouping by tercile—countries are divided into two groups: the natural group (countries with a value of 1.04–1.07, inclusive) and the gender-biased group (all other countries). Deviations from the natural sex ratio at birth have implications for population replacement levels, suggest possible future social and economic problems and may indicate gender bias. Countries with values of a parity index concentrated around 1 form the group with the best achievements in that indicator. Deviations from parity are treated equally regardless of which gender is overachieving.

Dashboard 3, Women's empowerment, contains a selection of woman-specific empowerment indicators that allows empowerment to be compared across three dimensions: reproductive health and family planning, violence against girls and women and socioeconomic empowerment. Most countries have at least one indicator in each tercile, which implies that women's empowerment is unequal across indicators and countries.

Dashboard 4, Environmental sustainability, contains a selection of indicators that cover environmental sustainability and environmental threats. The environmental sustainability indicators present levels of or changes in energy consumption, carbon dioxide emissions, forest area and fresh water withdrawals. The environmental threats indicators are mortality rates attributed to household and ambient air pollution and to unsafe water, sanitation and hygiene services and the International Union for Conservation of Nature Red List Index value, which measures aggregate extinction risk across groups of species.

Dashboard 5, Socioeconomic sustainability, contains a selection of indicators that cover economic and social sustainability. The economic sustainability indicators are adjusted net savings, total debt service, gross capital formation, skilled labour force, diversity of exports and expenditure on research and development. The social sustainability indicators are the ratio of education and health expenditure to military expenditure, change in overall loss in HDI value due to inequality and changes in gender and income inequality.

Human development composite indices

TABLE 1

Human Development Index and its components

		SDG 3	SDG 4.3	SDG 4.6	SDG 8.5		
	Human Development Index (HDI)	Life expectancy at birth	Expected years of schooling	Mean years of schooling	Gross national income (GNI) per capita	GNI per capita rank minus HDI rank	HDI rank
	Value	(years)	(years)	(years)	(2011 PPP $)		
HDI rank	2017	2017	2017[a]	2017[a]	2017	2017	2016
VERY HIGH HUMAN DEVELOPMENT							
1 Norway	0.953	82.3	17.9	12.6	68,012	5	1
2 Switzerland	0.944	83.5	16.2	13.4	57,625	8	2
3 Australia	0.939	83.1	22.9[b]	12.9	43,560	18	3
4 Ireland	0.938	81.6	19.6[b]	12.5[c]	53,754	8	4
5 Germany	0.936	81.2	17.0	14.1	46,136	13	4
6 Iceland	0.935	82.9	19.3[b]	12.4[c]	45,810	13	6
7 Hong Kong, China (SAR)	0.933	84.1	16.3	12.0	58,420	2	8
7 Sweden	0.933	82.6	17.6	12.4	47,766	9	7
9 Singapore	0.932	83.2	16.2[d]	11.5	82,503[e]	−6	8
10 Netherlands	0.931	82.0	18.0	12.2	47,900	5	10
11 Denmark	0.929	80.9	19.1[b]	12.6[f]	47,918	3	10
12 Canada	0.926	82.5	16.4[c]	13.3	43,433	10	12
13 United States	0.924	79.5	16.5	13.4	54,941	−2	12
14 United Kingdom	0.922	81.7	17.4	12.9[f]	39,116	13	14
15 Finland	0.920	81.5	17.6	12.4	41,002	10	15
16 New Zealand	0.917	82.0	18.9[b]	12.5	33,970	18	16
17 Belgium	0.916	81.3	19.8[b]	11.8	42,156	6	16
17 Liechtenstein	0.916	80.4[g]	14.7	12.5[h]	97,336[e,i]	−15	16
19 Japan	0.909	83.9	15.2	12.8[j]	38,986	9	19
20 Austria	0.908	81.8	16.1	12.1	45,415	0	20
21 Luxembourg	0.904	82.0	14.0	12.1[f]	65,016[k]	−13	26
22 Israel	0.903	82.7	15.9	13.0	32,711	13	21
22 Korea (Republic of)	0.903	82.4	16.5	12.1	35,945	8	22
24 France	0.901	82.7	16.4	11.5	39,254	2	23
25 Slovenia	0.896	81.1	17.2	12.2	30,594	12	24
26 Spain	0.891	83.3	17.9	9.8	34,258	7	25
27 Czechia	0.888	78.9	16.9	12.7	30,588	11	27
28 Italy	0.880	83.2	16.3	10.2[f]	35,299	3	28
29 Malta	0.878	81.0	15.9	11.3	34,396	3	29
30 Estonia	0.871	77.7	16.1	12.7	28,993	10	30
31 Greece	0.870	81.4	17.3	10.8	24,648	20	30
32 Cyprus	0.869	80.7	14.6	12.1	31,568	4	32
33 Poland	0.865	77.8	16.4	12.3	26,150	12	34
34 United Arab Emirates	0.863	77.4	13.6	10.8[l]	67,805	−27	33
35 Andorra	0.858	81.7[g]	13.5[d]	10.2	47,574[m]	−18	35
35 Lithuania	0.858	74.8	16.1	13.0	28,314	7	36
37 Qatar	0.856	78.3	13.4	9.8	116,818[e]	−36	36
38 Slovakia	0.855	77.0	15.0	12.5	29,467	1	39
39 Brunei Darussalam	0.853	77.4	14.5	9.1[j]	76,427[e]	−35	40
39 Saudi Arabia	0.853	74.7	16.9	9.5[f]	49,680	−26	38
41 Latvia	0.847	74.7	15.8	12.8[f]	25,002	8	43
41 Portugal	0.847	81.4	16.3	9.2	27,315	2	42
43 Bahrain	0.846	77.0	16.0	9.4[l]	41,580	−19	41
44 Chile	0.843	79.7	16.4	10.3	21,910	13	44
45 Hungary	0.838	76.1	15.1	11.9	25,393	3	45
46 Croatia	0.831	77.8	15.0	11.3[l]	22,162	10	46
47 Argentina	0.825	76.7	17.4	9.9[l]	18,461	19	47
48 Oman	0.821	77.3	13.9	9.5	36,290	−19	47
49 Russian Federation	0.816	71.2	15.5	12.0[f]	24,233	3	49
50 Montenegro	0.814	77.3	14.9	11.3[f]	16,779	19	50
51 Bulgaria	0.813	74.9	14.8	11.8	18,740	13	50
52 Romania	0.811	75.6	14.3	11.0	22,646	2	52
53 Belarus	0.808	73.1	15.5	12.3	16,323	18	54
54 Bahamas	0.807	75.8	12.8[n]	11.1[f]	26,681	−10	53
55 Uruguay	0.804	77.6	15.9	8.7	19,930	5	56
56 Kuwait	0.803	74.8	13.6	7.3	70,524	−51	55
57 Malaysia	0.802	75.5	13.7	10.2[f]	26,107	−11	57
58 Barbados	0.800	76.1	15.3	10.6[o]	15,843[k]	14	57
58 Kazakhstan	0.800	70.0	15.1	11.8[j]	22,626	−3	60

HUMAN DEVELOPMENT INDICES AND INDICATORS: **2018 STATISTICAL UPDATE**

TABLE 1

		Human Development Index (HDI)	SDG 3 Life expectancy at birth	SDG 4.3 Expected years of schooling	SDG 4.6 Mean years of schooling	SDG 8.5 Gross national income (GNI) per capita	GNI per capita rank minus HDI rank	HDI rank
		Value	(years)	(years)	(years)	(2011 PPP $)		
HDI rank		2017	2017	2017[a]	2017[a]	2017	2017	2016
HIGH HUMAN DEVELOPMENT								
60	Iran (Islamic Republic of)	0.798	76.2	14.9	9.8	19,130	3	61
60	Palau	0.798	73.4[g]	15.6	12.3	12,831	28	59
62	Seychelles	0.797	73.7	14.8	9.5[d]	26,077[k]	−15	62
63	Costa Rica	0.794	80.0	15.4	8.8	14,636	15	63
64	Turkey	0.791	76.0	15.2	8.0	24,804	−14	65
65	Mauritius	0.790	74.9	15.1	9.3[j]	20,189	−6	64
66	Panama	0.789	78.2	12.7	10.2[j]	19,178	−4	66
67	Serbia	0.787	75.3	14.6	11.1	13,019	18	66
68	Albania	0.785	78.5	14.8	10.0	11,886	23	69
69	Trinidad and Tobago	0.784	70.8	12.9[n]	10.9[f]	28,622[k]	−28	66
70	Antigua and Barbuda	0.780	76.5	13.2[f]	9.2[d]	20,764[k]	−12	70
70	Georgia	0.780	73.4	15.0	12.8	9,186	35	71
72	Saint Kitts and Nevis	0.778	74.4[g]	14.4	8.4[n]	23,978[k]	−19	72
73	Cuba	0.777	79.9	14.0	11.8[f]	7,524[p]	43	72
74	Mexico	0.774	77.3	14.1	8.6	16,944	−6	74
75	Grenada	0.772	73.8	16.9	8.7[n]	12,864[k]	12	75
76	Sri Lanka	0.770	75.5	13.9	10.9[f]	11,326	19	76
77	Bosnia and Herzegovina	0.768	77.1	14.2[o]	9.7	11,716	16	77
78	Venezuela (Bolivarian Republic of)	0.761	74.7	14.3	10.3	10,672[k]	20	77
79	Brazil	0.759	75.7	15.4	7.8[f]	13,755[k]	2	79
80	Azerbaijan	0.757	72.1	12.7[q]	10.7	15,600[k]	−7	80
80	Lebanon	0.757	79.8	12.5	8.7[f]	13,378	3	82
80	The former Yugoslav Republic of Macedonia	0.757	75.9	13.3	9.6[o]	12,505	9	81
83	Armenia	0.755	74.8	13.0	11.7	9,144	24	84
83	Thailand	0.755	75.5	14.7	7.6	15,516	−7	86
85	Algeria	0.754	76.3	14.4	8.0[f]	13,802	−5	83
86	China	0.752	76.4	13.8	7.8[l]	15,270	−9	86
86	Ecuador	0.752	76.6	14.7	8.7	10,347	15	84
88	Ukraine	0.751	72.1	15.0	11.3[l]	8,130	24	90
89	Peru	0.750	75.2	13.8	9.2	11,789	3	86
90	Colombia	0.747	74.6	14.4	8.3	12,938	−4	89
90	Saint Lucia	0.747	75.7	13.6[q]	8.9[f]	11,695	4	91
92	Fiji	0.741	70.4	15.3[f]	10.8[j]	8,324[k]	18	93
92	Mongolia	0.741	69.5	15.5	10.1	10,103	11	92
94	Dominican Republic	0.736	74.0	13.7	7.8	13,921	−15	95
95	Jordan	0.735	74.5	13.1[f]	10.4[j]	8,288	16	94
95	Tunisia	0.735	75.9	15.1	7.2[l]	10,275[k]	7	96
97	Jamaica	0.732	76.1	13.1[f]	9.8[f]	7,846	17	96
98	Tonga	0.726	73.2	14.3[n]	11.2[f]	5,547[k]	37	98
99	Saint Vincent and the Grenadines	0.723	73.3	13.3	8.6	10,499[k]	0	99
100	Suriname	0.720	71.5	12.7[q]	8.5[f]	13,306[k]	−16	100
101	Botswana	0.717	67.6	12.6[f]	9.3[l]	15,534	−26	102
101	Maldives	0.717	77.6	12.6	6.3[j]	13,567[k]	−19	102
103	Dominica	0.715	78.0[g]	12.7[n]	7.8[d]	8,344[k]	6	101
104	Samoa	0.713	75.2	12.5[d]	10.3[d]	5,909[k]	24	104
105	Uzbekistan	0.710	71.4	12.0	11.5	6,470	19	107
106	Belize	0.708	70.6	12.8	10.5[f]	7,166	14	105
106	Marshall Islands	0.708	73.6[g]	13.0[d]	10.9	5,125	33	..
108	Libya	0.706	72.1	13.4[n]	7.3[l]	11,100[k]	−12	114
108	Turkmenistan	0.706	68.0	10.8	9.8[q]	15,594[k]	−34	106
110	Gabon	0.702	66.5	12.8[q]	8.2[q]	16,431	−40	109
110	Paraguay	0.702	73.2	12.7	8.4	8,380	−2	108
112	Moldova (Republic of)	0.700	71.7	11.6	11.6	5,554	22	110
MEDIUM HUMAN DEVELOPMENT								
113	Philippines	0.699	69.2	12.6	9.3[f]	9,154	−7	111
113	South Africa	0.699	63.4	13.3	10.1	11,923	−23	111
115	Egypt	0.696	71.7	13.1	7.2[j]	10,355	−15	113
116	Indonesia	0.694	69.4	12.8	8.0	10,846	−19	115
116	Viet Nam	0.694	76.5	12.7[o]	8.2[o]	5,859	14	116

TABLE 1 Human Development Index and its components

TABLE 1 HUMAN DEVELOPMENT INDEX AND ITS COMPONENTS

		SDG 3	SDG 4.3	SDG 4.6	SDG 8.5		
	Human Development Index (HDI)	Life expectancy at birth	Expected years of schooling	Mean years of schooling	Gross national income (GNI) per capita	GNI per capita rank minus HDI rank	HDI rank
	Value	(years)	(years)	(years)	(2011 PPP $)		
HDI rank	2017	2017	2017[a]	2017[a]	2017	2017	2016
118 Bolivia (Plurinational State of)	0.693	69.5	14.0	8.9	6,714	5	116
119 Palestine, State of	0.686	73.6	12.8	9.1	5,055	21	116
120 Iraq	0.685	70.0	11.0[q]	6.8[f]	17,789[k]	−53	120
121 El Salvador	0.674	73.8	12.6	6.9	6,868	0	119
122 Kyrgyzstan	0.672	71.1	13.4	10.9[q]	3,255	32	121
123 Morocco	0.667	76.1	12.4	5.5[j]	7,340	−5	122
124 Nicaragua	0.658	75.7	12.1	6.7[j]	5,157	14	123
125 Cabo Verde	0.654	73.0	12.6	6.1	5,983	2	124
125 Guyana	0.654	66.8	11.4	8.4[o]	7,447[k]	−8	124
127 Guatemala	0.650	73.7	10.8	6.5[f]	7,278	−8	126
127 Tajikistan	0.650	71.2	11.2	10.4[j]	3,317[k]	25	127
129 Namibia	0.647	64.9	12.3[q]	6.8[j]	9,387	−25	128
130 India	0.640	68.8	12.3	6.4[f]	6,353	−5	129
131 Micronesia (Federated States of)	0.627	69.3	11.7[d]	8.0[d]	3,843[k]	13	131
132 Timor-Leste	0.625	69.2	12.8	4.5[q]	6,846	−10	130
133 Honduras	0.617	73.8	10.2	6.5	4,215	8	132
134 Bhutan	0.612	70.6	12.3	3.1[o]	8,065	−21	135
134 Kiribati	0.612	66.5	12.9	7.9[d]	3,042[k]	22	134
136 Bangladesh	0.608	72.8	11.4[f]	5.8[l]	3,677	9	138
137 Congo	0.606	65.1	11.4	6.3[l]	5,694	−5	133
138 Vanuatu	0.603	72.3	10.9[n]	6.8[o]	2,995	19	136
139 Lao People's Democratic Republic	0.601	67.0	11.2	5.2[j]	6,070	−13	137
140 Ghana	0.592	63.0	11.6	7.1[j]	4,096	3	140
141 Equatorial Guinea	0.591	57.9	9.3[n]	5.5[q]	19,513	−80	139
142 Kenya	0.590	67.3	12.1[q]	6.5[j]	2,961	16	143
143 Sao Tome and Principe	0.589	66.8	12.5	6.3[f]	2,941[k]	16	144
144 Eswatini (Kingdom of)	0.588	58.3	11.2	6.5[o]	7,620	−29	141
144 Zambia	0.588	62.3	12.5[q]	7.0[q]	3,557[k]	3	141
146 Cambodia	0.582	69.3	11.7[f]	4.8[j]	3,413	3	146
147 Angola	0.581	61.8	11.8[q]	5.1[q]	5,790	−16	145
148 Myanmar	0.578	66.7	10.0	4.9[q]	5,567[k]	−15	147
149 Nepal	0.574	70.6	12.2	4.9[j]	2,471	12	148
150 Pakistan	0.562	66.6	8.6	5.2	5,311	−14	149
151 Cameroon	0.556	58.6	12.2	6.3[l]	3,315	2	150
LOW HUMAN DEVELOPMENT							
152 Solomon Islands	0.546	71.0	10.2[d]	5.5[q]	1,872[k]	15	151
153 Papua New Guinea	0.544	65.7	10.0[n]	4.6[j]	3,403[k]	−3	151
154 Tanzania (United Republic of)	0.538	66.3	8.9[q]	5.8[j]	2,655	6	154
155 Syrian Arab Republic	0.536	71.0	8.8	5.1[f]	2,337[s]	8	153
156 Zimbabwe	0.535	61.7	10.3	8.1	1,683	17	155
157 Nigeria	0.532	53.9	10.0[q]	6.2[q]	5,231	−20	156
158 Rwanda	0.524	67.5	11.2	4.1[f]	1,811	11	157
159 Lesotho	0.520	54.6	10.6	6.3[j]	3,255	−4	159
159 Mauritania	0.520	63.4	8.6	4.5[j]	3,592	−13	159
161 Madagascar	0.519	66.3	10.6	6.1[j]	1,358	20	158
162 Uganda	0.516	60.2	11.6[q]	6.1[q]	1,658	13	162
163 Benin	0.515	61.2	12.6	3.6[o]	2,061	2	161
164 Senegal	0.505	67.5	9.7	3.0	2,384	−2	165
165 Comoros	0.503	63.9	11.2	4.8[q]	1,399	15	163
165 Togo	0.503	60.5	12.4[q]	4.8[q]	1,453	14	164
167 Sudan	0.502	64.7	7.4	3.7[j]	4,119	−25	165
168 Afghanistan	0.498	64.0	10.4	3.8[j]	1,824	0	168
168 Haiti	0.498	63.6	9.3[n]	5.3[q]	1,665	6	167
170 Côte d'Ivoire	0.492	54.1	9.0	5.2[j]	3,481	−22	169
171 Malawi	0.477	63.7	10.8	4.5[j]	1,064	14	170
172 Djibouti	0.476	62.6	6.2	4.1[o]	3,392	−21	170
173 Ethiopia	0.463	65.9	8.5[f]	2.7[q]	1,719	−1	173
174 Gambia	0.460	61.4	9.2	3.5[j]	1,516	4	173
175 Guinea	0.459	60.6	9.1	2.6[q]	2,067	−11	177
176 Congo (Democratic Republic of the)	0.457	60.0	9.8	6.8[f]	796	12	176
177 Guinea-Bissau	0.455	57.8	10.5[o]	3.0[o]	1,552	0	175
178 Yemen	0.452	65.2	9.0[f]	3.0[l]	1,239	5	172

HUMAN DEVELOPMENT INDICES AND INDICATORS: 2018 STATISTICAL UPDATE

TABLE 1

HDI rank		Human Development Index (HDI)	SDG 3 Life expectancy at birth	SDG 4.3 Expected years of schooling	SDG 4.6 Mean years of schooling	SDG 8.5 Gross national income (GNI) per capita	GNI per capita rank minus HDI rank	HDI rank
		Value	(years)	(years)	(years)	(2011 PPP $)		
		2017	2017	2017[a]	2017[a]	2017	2017	2016
179	Eritrea	0.440	65.5	5.4	4.0[n]	1,750[k]	−9	178
180	Mozambique	0.437	58.9	9.7	3.5[f]	1,093	4	179
181	Liberia	0.435	63.0	10.0[q]	4.7[j]	667	9	180
182	Mali	0.427	58.5	7.7	2.3[f]	1,953	−16	181
183	Burkina Faso	0.423	60.8	8.5	1.5[q]	1,650	−7	182
184	Sierra Leone	0.419	52.2	9.8[q]	3.5[j]	1,240	−2	184
185	Burundi	0.417	57.9	11.7	3.0[q]	702	4	183
186	Chad	0.404	53.2	8.0	2.3[q]	1,750	−15	185
187	South Sudan	0.388	57.3	4.9[q]	4.8	963[k]	−1	186
188	Central African Republic	0.367	52.9	7.2[f]	4.3[j]	663	3	187
189	Niger	0.354	60.4	5.4	2.0[j]	906	−2	188
OTHER COUNTRIES OR TERRITORIES								
..	Korea (Democratic People's Rep. of)	..	71.9	12.0	..	..	..	..
..	Monaco	..	..	..	..	..	..	..
..	Nauru	..	..	10.3	..	18,573[k]	..	..
..	San Marino	..	..	15.1	..	..	..	..
..	Somalia	..	56.7	..	..	..	..	..
..	Tuvalu	..	..	..	..	5,888[k]	..	..
Human development groups								
	Very high human development	0.894	79.5	16.4	12.2	40,041	—	—
	High human development	0.757	76.0	14.1	8.2	14,999	—	—
	Medium human development	0.645	69.1	12.0	6.7	6,849	—	—
	Low human development	0.504	60.8	9.4	4.7	2,521	—	—
Developing countries		0.681	70.7	12.2	7.3	10,055	—	—
Regions								
	Arab States	0.699	71.5	11.9	7.0	15,837	—	—
	East Asia and the Pacific	0.733	74.7	13.3	7.9	13,688	—	—
	Europe and Central Asia	0.771	73.4	14.1	10.3	15,331	—	—
	Latin America and the Caribbean	0.758	75.7	14.4	8.5	13,671	—	—
	South Asia	0.638	69.3	11.9	6.4	6,473	—	—
	Sub-Saharan Africa	0.537	60.7	10.1	5.6	3,399	—	—
Least developed countries		0.524	64.8	9.8	4.7	2,506	—	—
Small island developing states		0.676	71.0	11.8	8.2	7,721	—	—
Organisation for Economic Co-operation and Development		0.895	80.6	16.2	12.0	39,595	—	—
World		**0.728**	**72.2**	**12.7**	**8.4**	**15,295**	—	—

NOTES

a Data refer to 2017 or the most recent year available.
b In calculating the HDI value, expected years of schooling is capped at 18 years.
c Based on data from OECD (2017a).
d Based on data from the national statistical office.
e In calculating the HDI value, GNI per capita is capped at $75,000.
f Updated by HDRO based on data from UNESCO Institute for Statistics (2018).
g Value from UNDESA (2011).
h Imputed mean years of schooling for Austria.
i Estimated using the purchasing power parity (PPP) rate and projected growth rate of Switzerland.
j Based on Barro and Lee (2016).
k HDRO estimate based on data from World Bank (2018b) and United Nations Statistics Division (2018b).
l Updated by HDRO using Barro and Lee (2016) estimates.
m Estimated using the PPP rate and projected growth rate of Spain.
n Based on cross-country regression.
o Updated by HDRO based on data from United Nations Children's Fund (UNICEF) Multiple Indicator Cluster Surveys for 2006–2017.
p Based on a cross-country regression and the projected growth rate from UNECLAC (2018).
q Updated by HDRO based on data from ICF Macro Demographic and Health Surveys for 2006–2017.
r Updated by HDRO based on Syrian Center for Policy Research (2017).
s HDRO estimate based on data from World Bank (2018b), United Nations Statistics Division (2018b) and projected growth rates from UNESCWA (2018).

DEFINITIONS

Human Development Index (HDI): A composite index measuring average achievement in three basic dimensions of human development—a long and healthy life, knowledge and a decent standard of living. See *Technical note 1* at http://hdr.undp.org/sites/default/files/hdr2018_technical_notes.pdf for details on how the HDI is calculated.

Life expectancy at birth: Number of years a newborn infant could expect to live if prevailing patterns of age-specific mortality rates at the time of birth stay the same throughout the infant's life.

Expected years of schooling: Number of years of schooling that a child of school entrance age can expect to receive if prevailing patterns of age-specific enrolment rates persist throughout the child's life.

Mean years of schooling: Average number of years of education received by people ages 25 and older, converted from education attainment levels using official durations of each level.

Gross national income (GNI) per capita: Aggregate income of an economy generated by its production and its ownership of factors of production, less the incomes paid for the use of factors of production owned by the rest of the world, converted to international dollars using PPP rates, divided by midyear population.

GNI per capita rank minus HDI rank: Difference in ranking by GNI per capita and by HDI value. A negative value means that the country is better ranked by GNI than by HDI value.

HDI rank for 2016: Ranking by HDI value for 2016, which was calculated using the same most recently revised data available in 2018 that were used to calculate HDI values for 2017.

MAIN DATA SOURCES

Columns 1 and 7: HDRO calculations based on data from UNDESA (2017a), UNESCO Institute for Statistics (2018), United Nations Statistics Division (2018b), World Bank (2018b), Barro and Lee (2016) and IMF (2018).

Column 2: UNDESA (2017a).

Column 3: UNESCO Institute for Statistics (2018), ICF Macro Demographic and Health Surveys, UNICEF Multiple Indicator Cluster Surveys and OECD (2017a).

Column 4: UNESCO Institute for Statistics (2018), Barro and Lee (2016), ICF Macro Demographic and Health Surveys, UNICEF Multiple Indicator Cluster Surveys and OECD (2017a).

Column 5: World Bank (2018b), IMF (2018) and United Nations Statistics Division (2018b).

Column 6: Calculated based on data in columns 1 and 5.

TABLE 2

Human Development Index trends, 1990–2017

HDI rank		Human Development Index (HDI) Value							Change in HDI rank	Average annual HDI growth (%)		
		1990	2000	2010	2012	2014	2015	2016	2017	2012–2017[a]	1990–2000	2000–2010	2010–2017	1990–2017
VERY HIGH HUMAN DEVELOPMENT													
1	Norway	0.850	0.917	0.942	0.942	0.946	0.948	0.951	0.953	0	0.76	0.27	0.17	0.42
2	Switzerland	0.832	0.889	0.932	0.935	0.939	0.942	0.943	0.944	0	0.67	0.47	0.18	0.47
3	Australia	0.866	0.898	0.923	0.929	0.933	0.936	0.938	0.939	0	0.36	0.27	0.24	0.30
4	Ireland	0.763	0.857	0.909	0.902	0.921	0.929	0.934	0.938	13	1.16	0.60	0.45	0.77
5	Germany	0.801	0.868	0.921	0.928	0.930	0.933	0.934	0.936	–1	0.81	0.59	0.24	0.58
6	Iceland	0.802	0.860	0.891	0.909	0.925	0.927	0.933	0.935	5	0.71	0.36	0.68	0.57
7	Hong Kong, China (SAR)	0.781	0.827	0.901	0.911	0.923	0.927	0.930	0.933	3	0.58	0.87	0.49	0.66
7	Sweden	0.816	0.897	0.905	0.908	0.920	0.929	0.932	0.933	5	0.96	0.09	0.43	0.50
9	Singapore	0.718	0.819	0.909	0.920	0.928	0.929	0.930	0.932	–2	1.33	1.05	0.36	0.97
10	Netherlands	0.829	0.876	0.910	0.921	0.924	0.926	0.928	0.931	–4	0.55	0.39	0.32	0.43
11	Denmark	0.799	0.863	0.910	0.924	0.928	0.926	0.928	0.929	–6	0.77	0.53	0.30	0.56
12	Canada	0.849	0.867	0.902	0.908	0.918	0.920	0.922	0.926	0	0.21	0.39	0.38	0.32
13	United States	0.860	0.885	0.914	0.918	0.918	0.920	0.922	0.924	–5	0.28	0.32	0.16	0.27
14	United Kingdom	0.775	0.867	0.905	0.898	0.919	0.918	0.920	0.922	5	1.13	0.43	0.25	0.64
15	Finland	0.784	0.858	0.903	0.908	0.914	0.915	0.918	0.920	–3	0.90	0.52	0.25	0.59
16	New Zealand	0.818	0.869	0.899	0.905	0.910	0.914	0.915	0.917	–1	0.61	0.35	0.28	0.42
17	Belgium	0.806	0.873	0.903	0.905	0.909	0.913	0.915	0.916	–2	0.80	0.33	0.21	0.47
17	Liechtenstein	..	0.862	0.904	0.913	0.911	0.912	0.915	0.916	–8	..	0.48	0.19	..
19	Japan	0.816	0.855	0.885	0.895	0.903	0.905	0.907	0.909	1	0.48	0.34	0.39	0.40
20	Austria	0.795	0.838	0.895	0.899	0.901	0.903	0.906	0.908	–2	0.53	0.66	0.20	0.49
21	Luxembourg	0.782	0.855	0.889	0.892	0.895	0.899	0.903	0.904	1	0.89	0.39	0.24	0.54
22	Israel	0.792	0.853	0.887	0.893	0.899	0.901	0.902	0.903	–1	0.75	0.39	0.26	0.49
22	Korea (Republic of)	0.728	0.817	0.884	0.890	0.896	0.898	0.900	0.903	1	1.17	0.79	0.30	0.80
24	France	0.779	0.849	0.882	0.886	0.894	0.898	0.899	0.901	0	0.86	0.38	0.31	0.54
25	Slovenia	0.767	0.825	0.882	0.877	0.887	0.889	0.894	0.896	0	0.73	0.68	0.23	0.58
26	Spain	0.754	0.825	0.865	0.873	0.880	0.885	0.889	0.891	1	0.90	0.47	0.43	0.62
27	Czechia	0.730	0.796	0.862	0.865	0.879	0.882	0.885	0.888	1	0.86	0.80	0.42	0.72
28	Italy	0.769	0.830	0.870	0.874	0.874	0.876	0.878	0.880	–2	0.76	0.48	0.15	0.50
29	Malta	0.740	0.783	0.843	0.849	0.862	0.871	0.875	0.878	4	0.56	0.74	0.59	0.64
30	Estonia	0.733	0.780	0.845	0.859	0.864	0.866	0.868	0.871	–1	0.63	0.79	0.44	0.64
31	Greece	0.753	0.796	0.856	0.854	0.864	0.866	0.868	0.870	–1	0.56	0.72	0.24	0.54
32	Cyprus	0.732	0.802	0.850	0.852	0.856	0.860	0.867	0.869	–1	0.91	0.59	0.31	0.64
33	Poland	0.712	0.785	0.835	0.836	0.842	0.855	0.860	0.865	5	0.98	0.62	0.50	0.72
34	United Arab Emirates	0.727	0.798	0.836	0.846	0.855	0.860	0.862	0.863	1	0.94	0.47	0.45	0.64
35	Andorra	..	0.759	0.828	0.849	0.853	0.854	0.856	0.858	–2	..	0.88	0.51	..
35	Lithuania	0.732	0.756	0.824	0.831	0.851	0.852	0.855	0.858	5	0.33	0.87	0.58	0.59
37	Qatar	0.754	0.810	0.825	0.844	0.853	0.854	0.855	0.856	–1	0.72	0.19	0.52	0.47
38	Slovakia	0.739	0.764	0.829	0.842	0.845	0.851	0.853	0.855	–1	0.33	0.83	0.44	0.54
39	Brunei Darussalam	0.782	0.819	0.842	0.852	0.853	0.852	0.852	0.853	–8	0.46	0.28	0.19	0.32
39	Saudi Arabia	0.697	0.743	0.808	0.835	0.852	0.854	0.854	0.853	0	0.64	0.84	0.78	0.75
41	Latvia	0.704	0.728	0.816	0.824	0.838	0.841	0.844	0.847	2	0.33	1.15	0.53	0.69
41	Portugal	0.711	0.785	0.822	0.829	0.839	0.842	0.845	0.847	1	0.98	0.46	0.44	0.65
43	Bahrain	0.746	0.792	0.796	0.800	0.810	0.832	0.846	0.846	7	0.60	0.06	0.87	0.47
44	Chile	0.701	0.759	0.808	0.819	0.833	0.840	0.842	0.843	0	0.80	0.62	0.61	0.68
45	Hungary	0.704	0.769	0.823	0.830	0.833	0.834	0.835	0.838	–4	0.89	0.68	0.26	0.65
46	Croatia	0.670	0.750	0.808	0.816	0.824	0.827	0.828	0.831	0	1.14	0.75	0.40	0.80
47	Argentina	0.704	0.771	0.813	0.818	0.820	0.822	0.822	0.825	–2	0.91	0.54	0.20	0.59
48	Oman	..	0.704	0.793	0.804	0.815	0.822	0.822	0.821	0	..	1.19	0.50	..
49	Russian Federation	0.734	0.720	0.780	0.798	0.807	0.813	0.815	0.816	3	–0.18	0.80	0.66	0.40
50	Montenegro	..	..	0.793	0.800	0.805	0.809	0.810	0.814	0	..	..	0.36	..
51	Bulgaria	0.694	0.712	0.779	0.786	0.797	0.807	0.810	0.813	6	0.26	0.90	0.61	0.59
52	Romania	0.701	0.709	0.797	0.795	0.802	0.805	0.807	0.811	2	0.11	1.18	0.25	0.54
53	Belarus	..	0.683	0.792	0.803	0.807	0.805	0.805	0.808	–4	..	1.49	0.29	..
54	Bahamas	..	0.776	0.789	0.807	0.807	0.807	0.806	0.807	–7	..	0.17	0.32	..
55	Uruguay	0.692	0.742	0.773	0.790	0.801	0.800	0.802	0.804	1	0.70	0.40	0.57	0.56
56	Kuwait	0.713	0.786	0.792	0.796	0.799	0.802	0.804	0.803	–3	0.99	0.07	0.20	0.44
57	Malaysia	0.643	0.725	0.772	0.781	0.790	0.795	0.799	0.802	1	1.20	0.63	0.54	0.82
58	Barbados	0.716	0.752	0.782	0.795	0.796	0.797	0.799	0.800	–4	0.49	0.39	0.34	0.41
58	Kazakhstan	0.690	0.685	0.765	0.781	0.793	0.797	0.797	0.800	0	–0.07	1.12	0.64	0.55

HUMAN DEVELOPMENT INDICES AND INDICATORS: **2018 STATISTICAL UPDATE**

TABLE 2

		Human Development Index (HDI)							Change in HDI rank	Average annual HDI growth			
		Value								(%)			
HDI rank		1990	2000	2010	2012	2014	2015	2016	2017	2012–2017[a]	1990–2000	2000–2010	2010–2017	1990–2017
HIGH HUMAN DEVELOPMENT														
60	Iran (Islamic Republic of)	0.577	0.670	0.755	0.781	0.788	0.789	0.796	0.798	−2	1.52	1.20	0.79	1.21
60	Palau	..	0.743	0.769	0.778	0.786	0.793	0.798	0.798	1	..	0.34	0.54	..
62	Seychelles	..	0.718	0.747	0.770	0.786	0.791	0.793	0.797	4	..	0.39	0.92	..
63	Costa Rica	0.656	0.711	0.754	0.772	0.780	0.788	0.791	0.794	1	0.81	0.59	0.74	0.71
64	Turkey	0.579	0.655	0.734	0.760	0.778	0.783	0.787	0.791	8	1.26	1.14	1.06	1.16
65	Mauritius	0.619	0.673	0.749	0.767	0.782	0.782	0.788	0.790	3	0.84	1.06	0.78	0.91
66	Panama	0.659	0.719	0.758	0.771	0.781	0.781	0.785	0.789	−1	0.87	0.53	0.58	0.67
67	Serbia	0.718	0.711	0.759	0.768	0.775	0.780	0.785	0.787	0	−0.11	0.66	0.52	0.34
68	Albania	0.645	0.669	0.741	0.767	0.773	0.776	0.782	0.785	0	0.37	1.02	0.83	0.73
69	Trinidad and Tobago	0.672	0.716	0.775	0.774	0.779	0.783	0.785	0.784	−7	0.64	0.80	0.16	0.57
70	Antigua and Barbuda	..	..	0.766	0.765	0.770	0.775	0.778	0.780	1	..	..	0.25	..
70	Georgia	..	0.673	0.735	0.750	0.765	0.771	0.776	0.780	7	..	0.88	0.85	..
72	Saint Kitts and Nevis	..	..	0.745	0.756	0.770	0.773	0.774	0.778	3	..	..	0.62	..
73	Cuba	0.676	0.686	0.779	0.767	0.768	0.772	0.774	0.777	−5	0.15	1.28	−0.03	0.52
74	Mexico	0.650	0.702	0.743	0.757	0.761	0.767	0.772	0.774	−1	0.78	0.57	0.58	0.65
75	Grenada	..	..	0.743	0.749	0.761	0.767	0.770	0.772	3	..	..	0.55	..
76	Sri Lanka	0.625	0.685	0.745	0.757	0.763	0.766	0.768	0.770	−3	0.93	0.84	0.47	0.78
77	Bosnia and Herzegovina	..	0.672	0.713	0.739	0.754	0.755	0.766	0.768	7	..	0.60	1.07	..
78	Venezuela (Bolivarian Republic of)	0.634	0.672	0.759	0.774	0.778	0.775	0.766	0.761	−16	0.58	1.22	0.04	0.68
79	Brazil	0.611	0.684	0.727	0.736	0.752	0.757	0.758	0.759	7	1.14	0.60	0.63	0.81
80	Azerbaijan	..	0.640	0.740	0.745	0.758	0.758	0.757	0.757	−1	..	1.47	0.32	..
80	Lebanon	..	..	0.758	0.751	0.751	0.752	0.753	0.757	−4	..	..	−0.03	..
80	The former Yugoslav Republic of Macedonia	..	0.669	0.735	0.740	0.747	0.754	0.756	0.757	2	..	0.94	0.42	..
83	Armenia	0.631	0.647	0.728	0.737	0.745	0.748	0.749	0.755	2	0.26	1.17	0.53	0.67
83	Thailand	0.574	0.649	0.724	0.731	0.735	0.741	0.748	0.755	4	1.24	1.10	0.59	1.02
85	Algeria	0.577	0.644	0.729	0.740	0.747	0.749	0.752	0.754	−3	1.10	1.24	0.49	0.99
86	China	0.502	0.594	0.706	0.722	0.738	0.743	0.748	0.752	7	1.69	1.75	0.90	1.51
86	Ecuador	0.643	0.670	0.715	0.726	0.742	0.743	0.749	0.752	4	0.41	0.66	0.72	0.58
88	Ukraine	0.705	0.671	0.733	0.743	0.748	0.743	0.746	0.751	−8	−0.50	0.88	0.34	0.23
89	Peru	0.611	0.678	0.717	0.729	0.746	0.745	0.748	0.750	0	1.04	0.56	0.64	0.76
90	Colombia	0.592	0.653	0.719	0.725	0.738	0.742	0.747	0.747	2	0.98	0.96	0.55	0.86
90	Saint Lucia	..	0.690	0.731	0.730	0.737	0.744	0.745	0.747	−2	..	0.57	0.32	..
92	Fiji	0.643	0.683	0.711	0.719	0.730	0.738	0.738	0.741	5	0.61	0.40	0.59	0.53
92	Mongolia	0.579	0.589	0.697	0.720	0.734	0.737	0.743	0.741	4	0.17	1.70	0.87	0.92
94	Dominican Republic	0.598	0.657	0.702	0.710	0.718	0.729	0.733	0.736	8	0.94	0.68	0.66	0.77
95	Jordan	0.617	0.702	0.728	0.726	0.730	0.733	0.735	0.735	−5	1.31	0.36	0.14	0.65
95	Tunisia	0.569	0.653	0.716	0.719	0.725	0.728	0.732	0.735	2	1.39	0.91	0.38	0.95
97	Jamaica	0.638	0.662	0.712	0.721	0.728	0.730	0.732	0.732	−3	0.37	0.74	0.40	0.51
98	Tonga	0.648	0.673	0.712	0.717	0.717	0.721	0.724	0.726	2	0.38	0.56	0.28	0.42
99	Saint Vincent and the Grenadines	..	0.673	0.715	0.718	0.720	0.720	0.721	0.723	0	..	0.60	0.15	..
100	Suriname	..	..	0.703	0.711	0.718	0.721	0.719	0.720	1	..	..	0.33	..
101	Botswana	0.581	0.565	0.660	0.683	0.701	0.706	0.712	0.717	8	−0.28	1.57	1.18	0.78
101	Maldives	..	0.606	0.671	0.688	0.705	0.710	0.712	0.717	4	..	1.03	0.96	..
103	Dominica	..	0.693	0.722	0.721	0.724	0.721	0.718	0.715	−9	..	0.41	−0.13	..
104	Samoa	0.620	0.647	0.693	0.697	0.703	0.706	0.711	0.713	0	0.42	0.69	0.41	0.52
105	Uzbekistan	..	0.595	0.666	0.683	0.695	0.698	0.703	0.710	4	..	1.14	0.91	..
106	Belize	0.644	0.677	0.699	0.706	0.706	0.709	0.709	0.708	−3	0.51	0.31	0.18	0.35
106	Marshall Islands	..	..	..	..	..	..	..	0.708	..	..	..	..	..
108	Libya	0.677	0.727	0.755	0.741	0.695	0.694	0.693	0.706	−26	0.72	0.38	−0.97	0.15
108	Turkmenistan	..	..	0.673	0.686	0.697	0.701	0.705	0.706	0	..	..	0.68	..
110	Gabon	0.620	0.633	0.665	0.678	0.693	0.694	0.698	0.702	3	0.20	0.51	0.77	0.46
110	Paraguay	0.580	0.624	0.675	0.680	0.698	0.702	0.702	0.702	2	0.73	0.79	0.57	0.71
112	Moldova (Republic of)	0.651	0.597	0.670	0.684	0.696	0.693	0.697	0.700	−3	−0.86	1.15	0.62	0.27
MEDIUM HUMAN DEVELOPMENT														
113	Philippines	0.586	0.624	0.665	0.677	0.689	0.693	0.696	0.699	1	0.64	0.64	0.71	0.66
113	South Africa	0.618	0.630	0.649	0.664	0.685	0.692	0.696	0.699	6	0.19	0.30	1.06	0.46
115	Egypt	0.546	0.611	0.665	0.675	0.683	0.691	0.694	0.696	0	1.12	0.86	0.64	0.90
116	Indonesia	0.528	0.606	0.661	0.675	0.683	0.686	0.691	0.694	−1	1.39	0.88	0.69	1.02
116	Viet Nam	0.475	0.579	0.654	0.670	0.678	0.684	0.689	0.694	1	1.99	1.23	0.85	1.41

TABLE 2 Human Development Index trends, 1990–2017

TABLE 2 HUMAN DEVELOPMENT INDEX TRENDS, 1990–2017

HDI rank		Human Development Index (HDI) Value							Change in HDI rank	Average annual HDI growth (%)			
		1990	2000	2010	2012	2014	2015	2016	2017	2012–2017[a]	1990–2000	2000–2010	2010–2017	1990–2017
118	Bolivia (Plurinational State of)	0.536	0.608	0.649	0.662	0.675	0.681	0.689	0.693	2	1.27	0.66	0.94	0.96
119	Palestine, State of	..	..	0.672	0.687	0.679	0.687	0.689	0.686	–12	..	..	0.30	..
120	Iraq	0.572	0.607	0.649	0.659	0.666	0.668	0.672	0.685	1	0.60	0.67	0.77	0.67
121	El Salvador	0.529	0.615	0.671	0.670	0.670	0.674	0.679	0.674	–4	1.52	0.88	0.07	0.90
122	Kyrgyzstan	0.618	0.594	0.636	0.649	0.663	0.666	0.669	0.672	0	–0.39	0.69	0.79	0.31
123	Morocco	0.458	0.530	0.616	0.635	0.650	0.655	0.662	0.667	3	1.47	1.51	1.13	1.40
124	Nicaragua	0.489	0.570	0.621	0.633	0.649	0.652	0.657	0.658	3	1.54	0.87	0.82	1.10
125	Cabo Verde	..	0.570	0.629	0.636	0.644	0.647	0.652	0.654	0	..	0.99	0.56	..
125	Guyana	0.538	0.604	0.630	0.642	0.648	0.651	0.652	0.654	–2	1.18	0.42	0.52	0.73
127	Guatemala	0.478	0.546	0.611	0.613	0.643	0.645	0.649	0.650	4	1.35	1.13	0.89	1.15
127	Tajikistan	0.623	0.550	0.634	0.642	0.645	0.645	0.647	0.650	–4	–1.23	1.43	0.36	0.16
129	Namibia	0.579	0.558	0.594	0.617	0.636	0.642	0.645	0.647	0	–0.37	0.63	1.21	0.41
130	India	0.427	0.493	0.581	0.600	0.618	0.627	0.636	0.640	2	1.45	1.64	1.40	1.51
131	Micronesia (Federated States of)	..	0.552	0.608	0.616	0.618	0.627	0.627	0.627	–1	..	0.98	0.44	..
132	Timor-Leste	..	0.507	0.619	0.599	0.610	0.630	0.631	0.625	1	..	2.02	0.13	..
133	Honduras	0.506	0.554	0.596	0.597	0.603	0.609	0.614	0.617	2	0.92	0.72	0.50	0.74
134	Bhutan	..	..	0.566	0.585	0.599	0.603	0.609	0.612	4	..	..	1.14	..
134	Kiribati	..	0.552	0.590	0.598	0.616	0.621	0.610	0.612	0	..	0.67	0.53	..
136	Bangladesh	0.387	0.468	0.545	0.566	0.583	0.592	0.597	0.608	7	1.93	1.54	1.57	1.69
137	Congo	0.536	0.490	0.557	0.573	0.595	0.613	0.612	0.606	2	–0.91	1.30	1.21	0.46
138	Vanuatu	..	..	0.591	0.592	0.598	0.599	0.600	0.603	–2	..	..	0.28	..
139	Lao People's Democratic Republic	0.400	0.466	0.546	0.569	0.586	0.593	0.598	0.601	2	1.53	1.59	1.39	1.52
140	Ghana	0.455	0.484	0.554	0.570	0.576	0.585	0.588	0.592	0	0.62	1.36	0.94	0.98
141	Equatorial Guinea	..	0.516	0.581	0.589	0.590	0.593	0.592	0.591	–4	..	1.19	0.23	..
142	Kenya	0.468	0.451	0.543	0.559	0.572	0.578	0.585	0.590	3	–0.38	1.88	1.18	0.86
143	Sao Tome and Principe	0.452	0.490	0.542	0.551	0.567	0.580	0.584	0.589	4	0.80	1.01	1.21	0.98
144	Eswatini (Kingdom of)	0.536	0.471	0.538	0.561	0.580	0.584	0.586	0.588	0	–1.28	1.34	1.28	0.35
144	Zambia	0.401	0.432	0.544	0.569	0.580	0.583	0.586	0.588	–3	0.76	2.34	1.11	1.43
146	Cambodia	0.364	0.420	0.537	0.553	0.566	0.571	0.576	0.582	0	1.44	2.49	1.15	1.75
147	Angola	..	0.387	0.520	0.543	0.564	0.572	0.577	0.581	3	..	3.00	1.59	..
148	Myanmar	0.358	0.431	0.530	0.549	0.564	0.569	0.574	0.578	0	1.86	2.09	1.25	1.79
149	Nepal	0.378	0.446	0.529	0.548	0.560	0.566	0.569	0.574	0	1.66	1.72	1.19	1.56
150	Pakistan	0.404	0.450	0.526	0.535	0.548	0.551	0.560	0.562	1	1.08	1.57	0.95	1.23
151	Cameroon	0.440	0.431	0.506	0.526	0.543	0.548	0.553	0.556	3	–0.21	1.61	1.35	0.87
LOW HUMAN DEVELOPMENT														
152	Solomon Islands	..	0.450	0.507	0.529	0.539	0.546	0.543	0.546	1	..	1.19	1.07	..
153	Papua New Guinea	0.380	0.449	0.520	0.530	0.536	0.542	0.543	0.544	–1	1.70	1.48	0.64	1.34
154	Tanzania (United Republic of)	0.370	0.395	0.493	0.506	0.515	0.528	0.533	0.538	3	0.65	2.24	1.25	1.39
155	Syrian Arab Republic	..	0.590	0.644	0.631	0.550	0.538	0.536	0.536	–27	..	0.88	–2.60	..
156	Zimbabwe	0.491	0.440	0.467	0.505	0.525	0.529	0.532	0.535	2	–1.07	0.59	1.95	0.32
157	Nigeria	..	..	0.484	0.512	0.524	0.527	0.530	0.532	–2	..	..	1.36	..
158	Rwanda	0.250	0.335	0.485	0.500	0.509	0.510	0.520	0.524	3	2.98	3.77	1.11	2.78
159	Lesotho	0.499	0.467	0.493	0.505	0.509	0.511	0.516	0.520	–1	–0.66	0.54	0.77	0.15
159	Mauritania	0.374	0.442	0.486	0.499	0.514	0.514	0.516	0.520	3	1.69	0.96	0.95	1.22
161	Madagascar	..	0.456	0.504	0.507	0.512	0.514	0.517	0.519	–5	..	1.01	0.43	..
162	Uganda	0.311	0.398	0.486	0.492	0.500	0.505	0.508	0.516	2	2.51	2.02	0.86	1.90
163	Benin	0.348	0.398	0.473	0.489	0.505	0.508	0.512	0.515	2	1.36	1.74	1.22	1.46
164	Senegal	0.367	0.380	0.456	0.476	0.486	0.492	0.499	0.505	5	0.36	1.84	1.47	1.20
165	Comoros	..	..	0.482	0.493	0.501	0.502	0.502	0.503	–2	..	..	0.63	..
165	Togo	0.405	0.425	0.456	0.466	0.481	0.495	0.500	0.503	5	0.50	0.71	1.41	0.81
167	Sudan	0.331	0.402	0.470	0.485	0.492	0.497	0.499	0.502	–1	1.96	1.58	0.95	1.56
168	Afghanistan	..	..	0.463	0.482	0.491	0.493	0.494	0.498	–1	..	..	1.05	..
168	Haiti	0.409	0.442	0.470	0.481	0.490	0.493	0.496	0.498	0	0.78	0.61	0.83	0.73
170	Côte d'Ivoire	0.388	0.394	0.442	0.454	0.465	0.478	0.486	0.492	3	0.16	1.16	1.55	0.89
171	Malawi	0.340	0.399	0.441	0.455	0.468	0.470	0.474	0.477	1	1.62	1.01	1.11	1.26
172	Djibouti	..	0.363	0.449	0.459	0.467	0.470	0.474	0.476	–1	..	2.15	0.82	..
173	Ethiopia	..	0.283	0.412	0.430	0.445	0.451	0.457	0.463	3	..	3.82	1.67	..
174	Gambia	0.333	0.385	0.441	0.445	0.454	0.457	0.457	0.460	0	1.47	1.36	0.61	1.20
175	Guinea	0.276	0.329	0.404	0.428	0.440	0.443	0.449	0.459	2	1.75	2.09	1.83	1.90
176	Congo (Democratic Republic of the)	0.356	0.333	0.407	0.420	0.436	0.444	0.452	0.457	3	–0.68	2.02	1.70	0.93
177	Guinea-Bissau	..	..	0.426	0.437	0.445	0.449	0.453	0.455	–2	..	..	0.95	..
178	Yemen	0.399	0.443	0.498	0.505	0.505	0.483	0.462	0.452	–20	1.03	1.18	–1.37	0.46
179	Eritrea	..	..	0.416	0.422	0.428	0.433	0.436	0.440	–1	..	..	0.79	..

HUMAN DEVELOPMENT INDICES AND INDICATORS: 2018 STATISTICAL UPDATE

TABLE 2

	Human Development Index (HDI)								Change in HDI rank	Average annual HDI growth (%)			
	Value												
HDI rank	1990	2000	2010	2012	2014	2015	2016	2017	2012–2017[a]	1990–2000	2000–2010	2010–2017	1990–2017
180 Mozambique	0.209	0.298	0.403	0.412	0.427	0.432	0.435	0.437	1	3.61	3.09	1.13	2.77
181 Liberia	..	0.387	0.407	0.420	0.431	0.432	0.432	0.435	−2	..	0.50	0.97	..
182 Mali	0.231	0.308	0.403	0.408	0.414	0.418	0.421	0.427	0	2.92	2.72	0.81	2.30
183 Burkina Faso	..	0.286	0.375	0.394	0.405	0.412	0.420	0.423	2	..	2.74	1.76	..
184 Sierra Leone	0.275	0.284	0.385	0.407	0.423	0.413	0.413	0.419	0	0.32	3.10	1.20	1.57
185 Burundi	0.297	0.303	0.395	0.408	0.421	0.418	0.418	0.417	−3	0.23	2.68	0.77	1.27
186 Chad	..	0.299	0.371	0.391	0.403	0.407	0.405	0.404	0	..	2.20	1.22	..
187 South Sudan	..	..	0.413	0.388	0.397	0.399	0.394	0.388	0	..	..	−0.91	..
188 Central African Republic	0.317	0.309	0.351	0.365	0.349	0.357	0.362	0.367	0	−0.26	1.27	0.64	0.54
189 Niger	0.210	0.252	0.318	0.336	0.345	0.347	0.351	0.354	0	1.82	2.35	1.54	1.95
OTHER COUNTRIES OR TERRITORIES													
.. Korea (Democratic People's Rep. of)	..	..	..	..	..	..	..	..	..	..	..	..	..
.. Monaco	..	..	..	..	..	..	..	..	..	..	..	..	..
.. Nauru	..	..	..	..	..	..	..	..	..	..	..	..	..
.. San Marino	..	..	..	..	..	..	..	..	..	..	..	..	..
.. Somalia	..	..	..	..	..	..	..	..	..	..	..	..	..
.. Tuvalu	..	..	..	..	..	..	..	..	..	..	..	..	..
Human development groups													
Very high human development	0.787	0.831	0.873	0.880	0.887	0.890	0.892	0.894	—	0.55	0.50	0.34	0.48
High human development	0.571	0.635	0.718	0.732	0.745	0.750	0.754	0.757	—	1.06	1.24	0.76	1.05
Medium human development	0.462	0.523	0.596	0.613	0.627	0.634	0.641	0.645	—	1.25	1.32	1.13	1.24
Low human development	0.351	0.387	0.472	0.486	0.495	0.498	0.501	0.504	—	1.00	1.99	0.93	1.35
Developing countries	0.515	0.570	0.642	0.657	0.669	0.673	0.678	0.681	—	1.03	1.20	0.84	1.04
Regions													
Arab States	0.557	0.613	0.675	0.686	0.690	0.694	0.697	0.699	—	0.95	0.96	0.51	0.84
East Asia and the Pacific	0.517	0.597	0.692	0.707	0.720	0.725	0.730	0.733	—	1.45	1.48	0.83	1.30
Europe and Central Asia	0.653	0.668	0.733	0.749	0.761	0.764	0.767	0.771	—	0.23	0.94	0.71	0.62
Latin America and the Caribbean	0.626	0.686	0.731	0.740	0.751	0.754	0.757	0.758	—	0.92	0.65	0.51	0.71
South Asia	0.439	0.503	0.584	0.602	0.618	0.625	0.634	0.638	—	1.38	1.51	1.26	1.39
Sub-Saharan Africa	0.398	0.421	0.498	0.514	0.526	0.531	0.534	0.537	—	0.57	1.70	1.09	1.12
Least developed countries	0.346	0.400	0.484	0.499	0.511	0.515	0.519	0.524	—	1.47	1.93	1.14	1.55
Small island developing states	0.572	0.606	0.659	0.661	0.667	0.673	0.674	0.676	—	0.58	0.84	0.38	0.62
Organisation for Economic Co-operation and Development	0.785	0.835	0.874	0.880	0.886	0.890	0.893	0.895	—	0.62	0.45	0.33	0.49
World	**0.598**	**0.642**	**0.698**	**0.709**	**0.718**	**0.722**	**0.726**	**0.728**	—	**0.72**	**0.84**	**0.60**	**0.73**

NOTES

For HDI values that are comparable across years and countries, use this table or the interpolated data at http://hdr.undp.org/en/data, which present trends using consistent data.

a A positive value indicates an improvement in rank.

DEFINITIONS

Human Development Index (HDI): A composite index measuring average achievement in three basic dimensions of human development—a long and healthy life, knowledge and a decent standard of living. See *Technical note 1* at http://hdr.undp.org/sites/default/files/hdr2018_technical_notes.pdf for details on how the HDI is calculated.

Average annual HDI growth: A smoothed annualized growth of the HDI in a given period, calculated as the annual compound growth rate.

MAIN DATA SOURCES

Columns 1–8: HDRO calculations based on data from UNDESA (2017a), UNESCO Institute for Statistics (2018), United Nations Statistics Division (2018b), World Bank (2018b), Barro and Lee (2016) and IMF (2018).

Column 9: Calculated based on data in columns 4 and 8.

Columns 10–13: Calculated based on data in columns 1, 2, 3 and 8.

TABLE 3

Inequality-adjusted Human Development Index

	Human Development Index (HDI)	Inequality-adjusted HDI (IHDI)			Coefficient of human inequality	Inequality in life expectancy	Inequality-adjusted life expectancy index	Inequality in education[a]	Inequality-adjusted education index	Inequality in income[a]	Inequality-adjusted income index	Income inequality		
		Value	Overall loss (%)	Difference from HDI rank[b]		(%)	Value	(%)	Value	(%)	Value	Quintile ratio	Palma ratio	Gini coefficient
HDI rank	2017	2017	2017	2017	2017	2015–2020[c]	2017	2017[d]	2017	2017[d]	2017	2010–2017[e]	2010–2017[e]	2010–2017[e]
VERY HIGH HUMAN DEVELOPMENT														
1 Norway	0.953	0.876	8.0	−1	7.9	2.7	0.933	6.1	0.859	14.9	0.839	4.1	1.0	27.5
2 Switzerland	0.944	0.871	7.8	−2	7.5	3.5	0.942	2.4	0.876	16.8	0.799	5.2	1.3	32.5
3 Australia	0.939	0.861	8.2	−4	8.0	3.6	0.935	2.6	0.904	17.7	0.755	5.8	1.4	34.7
4 Ireland	0.938	0.854	9.0	−7	8.6	2.8	0.922	2.9	0.891	20.1	0.759	5.1	1.2	31.9[f]
5 Germany	0.936	0.861	8.1	−2	7.8	3.0	0.913	2.7	0.915	17.7	0.763	5.1	1.2	31.7
6 Iceland	0.935	0.878	6.0	5	5.9	2.4	0.945	2.6	0.889	12.8	0.807	3.6	0.9	25.6
7 Hong Kong, China (SAR)	0.933	0.809	13.3	−14	12.7	2.5	0.961	10.2	0.768	25.6	0.716	..	..	..
7 Sweden	0.933	0.864	7.4	1	7.2	2.7	0.937	3.7	0.870	15.3	0.789	4.6	1.0	29.2
9 Singapore	0.932	0.816	12.5	−10	11.9	2.6	0.947	8.2	0.764	25.0	0.750	..	..	..
10 Netherlands	0.931	0.857	7.9	0	7.8	3.0	0.925	5.3	0.858	15.0	0.792	4.4	1.1	29.3[f]
11 Denmark	0.929	0.860	7.5	2	7.4	3.4	0.905	4.3	0.880	14.4	0.798	4.0	1.0	28.2
12 Canada	0.926	0.852	8.0	0	7.7	4.3	0.921	1.4	0.887	17.4	0.758	6.2	1.3	34.0
13 United States	0.924	0.797	13.8	−11	13.1	5.6	0.865	5.5	0.853	28.1	0.685	9.4	2.0	41.5
14 United Kingdom	0.922	0.835	9.4	−3	9.1	4.0	0.912	3.7	0.880	19.5	0.726	5.4	1.3	33.2
15 Finland	0.920	0.868	5.6	10	5.5	2.8	0.920	1.9	0.887	11.7	0.802	3.9	1.0	27.1
16 New Zealand	0.917	0.846	7.7	3	7.5	4.3	0.913	1.7	0.901	16.4	0.736	..	..	..
17 Belgium	0.916	0.836	8.7	1	8.7	3.6	0.909	8.7	0.815	13.7	0.788	4.2	1.0	27.7
17 Liechtenstein	0.916	..	..	..	..	..	..	..	..	..	..	..	..	..
19 Japan	0.909	0.876	3.6	16	3.6	2.9	0.955	1.6	0.835	6.3	0.844	5.4[f]	1.2[f]	32.1[f]
20 Austria	0.908	0.835	8.0	2	7.8	3.0	0.922	2.6	0.830	17.7	0.760	4.9	1.1[f]	30.5
21 Luxembourg	0.904	0.811	10.3	0	10.1	3.4	0.921	9.4	0.718	17.7	0.805	5.0	1.2	31.2[f]
22 Israel	0.903	0.787	12.8	−6	12.2	3.3	0.932	7.0	0.813	26.4	0.644	9.8	2.0	41.4
22 Korea (Republic of)	0.903	0.773	14.3	−8	14.0	3.2	0.929	18.5	0.702	20.2	0.709	5.3	1.2	31.6
24 France	0.901	0.808	10.3	1	10.1	3.6	0.930	8.6	0.768	18.1	0.739	5.2	1.3	32.7[f]
25 Slovenia	0.896	0.846	5.6	11	5.5	3.0	0.912	2.2	0.866	11.4	0.766	3.7	0.9	25.4
26 Spain	0.891	0.754	15.4	−12	14.9	3.0	0.945	18.6	0.671	23.3	0.676	7.3	1.5	36.2
27 Czechia	0.888	0.840	5.3	11	5.2	3.3	0.876	1.6	0.879	10.8	0.771	3.7	0.9	25.9
28 Italy	0.880	0.771	12.3	−4	11.9	2.9	0.944	10.5	0.708	22.5	0.687	6.6	1.4	34.7
29 Malta	0.878	0.805	8.3	5	8.2	4.0	0.901	6.9	0.762	13.7	0.761	4.4[f]	1.1	29.0[f]
30 Estonia	0.871	0.794	8.8	3	8.5	4.3	0.850	2.3	0.849	18.9	0.694	5.4	1.2	32.7
31 Greece	0.870	0.753	13.5	−8	13.1	3.5	0.912	13.1	0.728	22.8	0.642	7.1	1.5	36.0
32 Cyprus	0.869	0.769	11.5	−1	11.3	3.6	0.900	11.7	0.714	18.7	0.707	5.3	1.4	34.0
33 Poland	0.865	0.787	9.0	5	8.8	4.7	0.847	4.7	0.825	17.1	0.697	5.0	1.2	31.8
34 United Arab Emirates	0.863	..	..	..	..	5.2	0.837	..	..	..	..	..	..	..
35 Andorra	0.858	..	..	..	..	..	..	9.4	0.647	..	..	..	..	..
35 Lithuania	0.858	0.757	11.7	−1	11.3	5.4	0.797	4.5	0.840	23.9	0.649	7.2	1.6	37.4
37 Qatar	0.856	..	..	..	..	5.9	0.844	11.4	0.619	..	..	..	..	..
38 Slovakia	0.855	0.797	6.8	10	6.7	5.2	0.831	1.4	0.819	13.4	0.744	4.1	0.9	26.5
39 Brunei Darussalam	0.853	..	..	..	..	5.5	0.834	..	..	..	..	..	..	..
39 Saudi Arabia	0.853	..	..	..	..	8.9	0.767	16.2	0.660	..	..	..	..	..
41 Latvia	0.847	0.759	10.4	2	10.1	5.9	0.792	3.7	0.834	20.7	0.661	5.9	1.4	34.2
41 Portugal	0.847	0.732	13.6	−7	13.2	2.9	0.918	16.3	0.635	20.5	0.674	6.4	1.5	35.5
43 Bahrain	0.846	..	..	..	..	5.6	0.828	19.0	0.614	..	..	..	..	..
44 Chile	0.843	0.710	15.7	−7	14.9	6.1	0.863	7.5	0.741	31.1	0.561	11.2	2.8	47.7
45 Hungary	0.838	0.772	7.8	8	7.7	4.7	0.822	3.2	0.789	15.2	0.710	4.9	1.1	30.4
46 Croatia	0.831	0.756	9.0	4	8.8	4.1	0.853	5.0	0.752	17.3	0.675	5.2	1.1	30.8
47 Argentina	0.825	0.707	14.3	−6	13.9	9.5	0.790	6.2	0.765	25.8	0.585	9.5	2.1	42.4
48 Oman	0.821	..	..	..	..	7.1	0.818	..	..	..	..	..	..	..
49 Russian Federation	0.816	0.738	9.5	1	9.3	8.0	0.725	2.2	0.814	17.7	0.683	6.6	1.7	37.7
50 Montenegro	0.814	0.741	8.9	3	8.8	4.4	0.842	7.4	0.732	14.6	0.661	4.8	1.2	31.9
51 Bulgaria	0.813	0.710	12.7	−1	12.3	6.7	0.788	6.5	0.753	23.6	0.604	7.3	1.6	37.4
52 Romania	0.811	0.717	11.7	1	11.4	6.8	0.797	6.3	0.714	21.0	0.647	4.3	1.0	28.3
53 Belarus	0.808	0.755	6.5	9	6.5	4.9	0.776	3.7	0.807	10.8	0.686	3.8	1.0	27.0
54 Bahamas	0.807	..	..	..	..	8.7	0.784	6.3	0.680	..	..	..	..	..
55 Uruguay	0.804	0.689	14.3	−4	13.9	9.0	0.807	7.4	0.679	25.3	0.598	7.9	1.8	39.7
56 Kuwait	0.803	..	..	..	..	6.3	0.790	17.8	0.510	..	..	..	..	..
57 Malaysia	0.802	..	..	..	..	5.9	0.803	15.6	0.607	..	..	11.2[f]	2.6[f]	46.3[f]
58 Barbados	0.800	0.669	16.4	−8	15.4	7.0	0.802	5.5	0.734	33.6	0.508	..	..	..
58 Kazakhstan	0.800	0.737	7.9	6	7.9	10.1	0.692	3.2	0.788	10.3	0.734	3.7	1.0	26.9

HUMAN DEVELOPMENT INDICES AND INDICATORS: 2018 STATISTICAL UPDATE

TABLE 3 Inequality-adjusted Human Development Index

	Human Development Index (HDI)	Inequality-adjusted HDI (IHDI)			Coefficient of human inequality	Inequality in life expectancy	Inequality-adjusted life expectancy index	Inequality in education[a]	Inequality-adjusted education index	Inequality in income[a]	Inequality-adjusted income index	Income inequality		
	Value	Value	Overall loss (%)	Difference from HDI rank[b]		(%)	Value	(%)	Value	(%)	Value	Quintile ratio	Palma ratio	Gini coefficient
HDI rank	2017	2017	2017	2017	2017	2015–2020[c]	2017	2017[d]	2017	2017[d]	2017	2010–2017[e]	2010–2017[e]	2010–2017[e]
HIGH HUMAN DEVELOPMENT														
60 Iran (Islamic Republic of)	0.798	0.707	11.4	3	11.2	9.0	0.786	4.9	0.705	19.7	0.637	7.2	1.7	38.8
60 Palau	0.798	..	..	..	..	..	..	1.9	0.828	..	..	..	..	..
62 Seychelles	0.797	..	..	..	..	7.7	0.763	..	..	29.3	0.594	9.8	2.6	46.8
63 Costa Rica	0.794	0.651	18.0	−10	17.3	7.5	0.854	11.9	0.634	32.4	0.509	12.9	3.0	48.7[f]
64 Turkey	0.791	0.669	15.4	−4	15.3	9.6	0.779	13.5	0.595	22.6	0.644	8.5	2.1	41.9
65 Mauritius	0.790	0.683	13.5	1	13.4	8.9	0.769	13.2	0.633	18.2	0.656	5.9	1.5	35.8
66 Panama	0.789	0.623	21.1	−14	20.2	11.5	0.792	12.5	0.605	36.5	0.504	16.6	3.4	50.4
67 Serbia	0.787	0.667	15.2	−3	14.6	7.1	0.791	8.1	0.714	28.7	0.525	4.2	1.0	28.5
68 Albania	0.785	0.706	10.0	7	10.0	9.2	0.817	8.5	0.681	12.2	0.633	4.3	1.0	29.0
69 Trinidad and Tobago	0.784	..	..	..	..	15.6	0.659	..	..	21.9	0.667	..	..	..
70 Antigua and Barbuda	0.780	..	..	..	..	7.5	0.804	..	..	..	..	..	..	..
70 Georgia	0.780	0.682	12.6	4	12.0	8.1	0.756	2.2	0.826	25.7	0.508	6.5	1.5	36.5
72 Saint Kitts and Nevis	0.778	..	..	..	..	..	..	..	..	..	..	..	..	..
73 Cuba	0.777	..	..	..	..	5.3	0.873	10.9	0.695	..	..	..	..	..
74 Mexico	0.774	0.609	21.3	−13	20.8	12.3	0.773	17.1	0.562	32.8	0.521	8.8	2.3	43.4
75 Grenada	0.772	..	..	..	..	8.0	0.761	..	..	..	..	..	..	..
76 Sri Lanka	0.770	0.664	13.8	0	13.6	7.1	0.793	12.8	0.653	21.0	0.564	6.8	1.9	39.8
77 Bosnia and Herzegovina	0.768	0.649	15.5	−2	15.3	5.9	0.826	19.8	0.576	20.2	0.574	5.3	1.3	32.7
78 Venezuela (Bolivarian Republic of)	0.761	0.636	16.5	−4	16.2	10.5	0.754	12.9	0.645	25.2	0.528	15.8[f]	2.8[f]	46.9[f]
79 Brazil	0.759	0.578	23.9	−17	23.2	10.8	0.765	22.0	0.535	36.7	0.471	15.6	3.5	51.3
80 Azerbaijan	0.757	0.681	10.0	9	9.9	17.0	0.666	3.8	0.682	8.9	0.695	2.3[f]	0.6[f]	16.6[f]
80 Lebanon	0.757	..	..	..	..	6.7	0.858	6.2	0.598	..	..	5.1	1.2	31.8
80 The former Yugoslav Republic of Macedonia	0.757	0.661	12.6	3	12.4	6.5	0.803	10.5	0.618	20.3	0.582	7.3	1.4	35.6
83 Armenia	0.755	0.680	10.0	10	9.8	9.0	0.767	2.9	0.727	17.4	0.563	5.1	1.3	32.5
83 Thailand	0.755	0.636	15.7	0	15.5	9.3	0.774	13.3	0.573	23.8	0.581	6.5	1.7	37.8
85 Algeria	0.754	0.598	20.7	−9	20.1	15.1	0.735	33.7	0.441	11.4	0.660	4.0	1.0	27.6
86 China	0.752	0.643	14.5	5	14.2	7.9	0.799	11.5	0.571	23.3	0.582	9.2	2.1	42.2
86 Ecuador	0.752	0.603	19.8	−7	19.4	13.9	0.749	13.8	0.601	30.5	0.487	10.7	2.4	45.0
88 Ukraine	0.751	0.701	6.6	20	6.5	7.5	0.742	3.6	0.766	8.5	0.608	3.5	0.9	25.0
89 Peru	0.750	0.606	19.2	−2	18.9	13.2	0.737	15.3	0.583	28.3	0.517	10.6	2.3	43.8
90 Colombia	0.747	0.571	23.6	−12	22.9	13.2	0.729	19.4	0.545	36.2	0.468	14.3	3.4	50.8
90 Saint Lucia	0.747	0.622	16.7	3	16.3	9.0	0.780	12.6	0.591	27.4	0.522	..	..	..
92 Fiji	0.741	..	..	..	..	10.9	0.691	..	..	..	..	5.8	1.6	36.4
92 Mongolia	0.741	0.639	13.7	10	13.7	13.4	0.659	11.9	0.675	15.7	0.589	5.1	1.3	32.3
94 Dominican Republic	0.736	0.581	21.0	−3	20.8	15.4	0.703	19.1	0.520	28.1	0.536	10.4	2.5	45.3
95 Jordan	0.735	0.617	16.1	6	16.0	10.7	0.748	16.9	0.591	20.5	0.531	5.2	1.4	33.7
95 Tunisia	0.735	0.573	22.0	−7	21.4	10.7	0.769	34.6	0.431	18.9	0.568	6.4	1.5	35.8
97 Jamaica	0.732	0.608	17.0	6	16.2	11.0	0.768	5.6	0.652	32.0	0.448	..	..	..
98 Tonga	0.726	..	..	..	..	13.0	0.712	4.5	0.736	..	..	6.7[f]	1.6[f]	37.5[f]
99 Saint Vincent and the Grenadines	0.723	..	..	..	..	11.9	0.722	..	..	..	..	..	..	..
100 Suriname	0.720	0.557	22.6	−8	21.8	12.4	0.694	15.6	0.537	37.3	0.463	..	..	..
101 Botswana	0.717	..	..	..	..	18.6	0.596	..	..	..	..	23.2[f]	5.8[f]	60.5[f]
101 Maldives	0.717	0.549	23.4	−9	22.0	5.7	0.836	40.0	0.336	20.5	0.590	7.0[f]	1.7[f]	38.4[f]
103 Dominica	0.715	..	..	..	..	..	..	..	..	..	..	..	..	..
104 Samoa	0.713	..	..	..	..	11.4	0.753	4.9	0.658	..	..	7.7[f]	2.1[f]	42.0[f]
105 Uzbekistan	0.710	..	..	..	..	17.0	0.657	0.8	0.712	..	..	..	..	..
106 Belize	0.708	0.550	22.3	−7	21.3	10.1	0.700	15.9	0.593	37.9	0.401	..	..	..
106 Marshall Islands	0.708	..	..	..	..	..	..	..	..	..	..	..	..	..
108 Libya	0.706	..	..	..	..	14.1	0.689	..	..	..	..	..	..	..
108 Turkmenistan	0.706	0.575	18.5	2	17.9	23.4	0.565	3.6	0.604	26.8	0.558	..	..	..
110 Gabon	0.702	0.545	22.3	−8	22.3	23.1	0.550	23.5	0.481	20.4	0.613	8.4[f]	2.1[f]	42.2[f]
110 Paraguay	0.702	0.522	25.5	−11	24.8	18.0	0.671	16.7	0.525	39.5	0.404	11.8	2.9	47.9
112 Moldova (Republic of)	0.700	0.627	10.4	18	10.3	9.6	0.719	7.3	0.658	14.0	0.522	3.7	0.9	26.3
MEDIUM HUMAN DEVELOPMENT														
113 Philippines	0.699	0.574	17.9	5	17.6	14.4	0.648	11.6	0.584	26.8	0.500	7.2	1.9	40.1
113 South Africa	0.699	0.467	33.2	−17	30.3	20.3	0.532	14.3	0.607	56.4	0.315	28.4	7.0	63.0[f]
115 Egypt	0.696	0.493	29.2	−10	28.3	11.6	0.703	36.9	0.381	36.3	0.446	4.6	1.3	31.8
116 Indonesia	0.694	0.563	18.8	4	18.7	14.8	0.647	16.5	0.520	24.9	0.532	6.6	1.8	39.5
116 Viet Nam	0.694	0.574	17.3	8	17.3	12.7	0.758	17.6	0.515	21.4	0.483	5.9	1.4	34.8

TABLE 3 INEQUALITY-ADJUSTED HUMAN DEVELOPMENT INDEX

	Human Development Index (HDI)	Inequality-adjusted HDI (IHDI)			Coefficient of human inequality	Inequality in life expectancy	Inequality-adjusted life expectancy index	Inequality in education[a]	Inequality-adjusted education index	Inequality in income[a]	Inequality-adjusted income index	Income inequality		
			Overall loss (%)	Difference from HDI rank[b]								Quintile ratio	Palma ratio	Gini coefficient
	Value	Value				(%)	Value	(%)	Value	(%)	Value			
HDI rank	2017	2017	2017	2017	2017	2015–2020[c]	2017	2017[d]	2017	2017[d]	2017	2010–2017[e]	2010–2017[e]	2010–2017[e]
118 Bolivia (Plurinational State of)	0.693	0.514	25.8	−4	25.7	25.2	0.569	20.0	0.549	31.8	0.434	12.6	2.4	44.6
119 Palestine, State of	0.686	0.583	15.0	15	14.9	12.2	0.725	14.1	0.566	18.5	0.483	5.5	1.4	34.4
120 Iraq	0.685	0.546	20.4	3	20.2	17.3	0.637	27.2	0.389	16.1	0.656	4.4	1.1	29.5
121 El Salvador	0.674	0.524	22.3	1	21.9	12.2	0.726	30.3	0.404	23.2	0.490	7.9	1.9	40.0
122 Kyrgyzstan	0.672	0.606	9.8	22	9.8	12.1	0.691	5.0	0.698	12.2	0.462	3.7	1.0	26.8
123 Morocco	0.667	..	..	..	..	14.0	0.742	..	..	..	..	7.4[f]	2.0[f]	40.7[f]
124 Nicaragua	0.658	0.507	22.9	0	22.6	12.9	0.746	25.7	0.415	29.2	0.421	10.2	2.6	46.2
125 Cabo Verde	0.654	..	..	..	..	13.3	0.707	23.7	0.423	..	..	10.7[f]	2.7[f]	47.2[f]
125 Guyana	0.654	0.532	18.6	5	18.4	19.5	0.579	10.7	0.532	25.1	0.488	..	..	..
127 Guatemala	0.650	0.467	28.2	−5	27.7	16.0	0.693	35.0	0.335	32.2	0.439	11.9	2.9	48.3
127 Tajikistan	0.650	0.562	13.6	12	13.4	20.1	0.630	6.5	0.616	13.5	0.457	5.6	1.4	34.0
129 Namibia	0.647	0.422	34.8	−13	32.9	20.2	0.551	25.0	0.428	53.6	0.318	20.1[f]	5.8[f]	61.0[f]
130 India	0.640	0.468	26.8	−1	26.3	21.4	0.590	38.7	0.341	18.8	0.509	5.3	1.5	35.1
131 Micronesia (Federated States of)	0.627	..	..	..	..	19.0	0.615	..	..	26.4	0.406	8.4	1.8	40.1
132 Timor-Leste	0.625	0.452	27.7	−6	26.4	20.6	0.601	44.9	0.278	13.6	0.552	4.1	1.1	28.7
133 Honduras	0.617	0.459	25.6	−4	25.2	18.1	0.678	22.7	0.388	34.9	0.368	16.9	3.4	50.0
134 Bhutan	0.612	0.446	27.2	−5	26.4	17.8	0.639	41.7	0.259	19.6	0.533	6.9	1.8	38.8
134 Kiribati	0.612	..	..	..	..	24.5	0.540	21.4	0.488	..	..	6.7[f]	1.6[f]	37.0[f]
136 Bangladesh	0.608	0.462	24.1	−1	23.4	17.3	0.672	37.3	0.319	15.7	0.459	4.8	1.3	32.4
137 Congo	0.606	0.469	22.6	6	22.6	25.1	0.520	21.5	0.413	21.2	0.481	12.8	3.1	48.9
138 Vanuatu	0.603	0.499	17.1	10	17.1	14.1	0.692	17.5	0.437	19.7	0.412	6.7	1.7	37.6
139 Lao People's Democratic Republic	0.601	0.445	26.1	−2	25.8	23.1	0.556	34.1	0.320	20.3	0.494	5.9	1.6	36.4
140 Ghana	0.592	0.420	28.9	−5	28.8	26.2	0.489	34.9	0.363	25.3	0.419	8.9	2.1	42.4
141 Equatorial Guinea	0.591	..	..	..	..	35.0	0.379	..	..	..	..	..	..	..
142 Kenya	0.590	0.434	26.4	−1	26.3	22.8	0.562	22.9	0.425	33.1	0.342	11.5[f]	2.9[f]	48.5[f]
143 Sao Tome and Principe	0.589	0.473	19.8	12	19.7	25.9	0.533	18.3	0.455	14.9	0.435	4.7	1.2	30.8
144 Eswatini (Kingdom of)	0.588	0.414	29.7	−3	29.4	26.2	0.434	24.1	0.401	37.9	0.406	14.2[f]	3.5[f]	51.5[f]
144 Zambia	0.588	0.388	34.1	−6	33.0	28.8	0.463	21.7	0.454	48.6	0.278	21.1	5.0	57.1
146 Cambodia	0.582	0.469	19.4	14	19.2	16.0	0.638	27.3	0.354	14.3	0.457	..	..	..
147 Angola	0.581	0.393	32.4	−2	32.3	33.8	0.426	34.3	0.327	28.9	0.436	9.0[f]	2.2[f]	42.7[f]
148 Myanmar	0.578	0.466	19.4	11	18.9	24.0	0.547	26.9	0.324	5.8	0.572	6.3	1.7	38.1
149 Nepal	0.574	0.427	25.6	5	24.6	16.6	0.649	40.9	0.296	16.3	0.405	5.0	1.3	32.8
150 Pakistan	0.562	0.387	31.0	−1	29.6	31.0	0.495	46.2	0.221	11.6	0.531	4.4	1.2	30.7
151 Cameroon	0.556	0.366	34.2	−4	34.2	33.7	0.393	33.0	0.367	35.9	0.339	11.5	2.7	46.6
LOW HUMAN DEVELOPMENT														
152 Solomon Islands	0.546	..	..	..	..	15.9	0.660	..	..	..	..	6.4	1.6	37.1
153 Papua New Guinea	0.544	..	..	..	..	25.3	0.525	11.5	0.381	..	..	9.3[f]	2.1[f]	41.9[f]
154 Tanzania (United Republic of)	0.538	0.404	24.8	4	24.8	24.9	0.535	27.0	0.322	22.4	0.384	6.2	1.7	37.8
155 Syrian Arab Republic	0.536	..	..	..	..	13.0	0.682	..	..	..	..	..	..	..
156 Zimbabwe	0.535	..	..	..	..	26.6	0.471	16.8	0.464	..	..	8.6	2.2	43.2
157 Nigeria	0.532	0.347	34.7	−6	34.6	37.4	0.326	38.1	0.299	28.2	0.429	9.1[f]	2.2[f]	43.0[f]
158 Rwanda	0.524	0.367	30.0	0	29.8	23.8	0.557	29.3	0.318	36.4	0.278	11.0	3.2	50.4
159 Lesotho	0.520	0.359	31.0	−1	30.5	28.5	0.380	21.9	0.392	41.1	0.310	20.8	4.3	54.2
159 Mauritania	0.520	0.348	33.0	−3	32.7	32.6	0.450	40.8	0.230	24.6	0.408	5.4	1.3	32.6
161 Madagascar	0.519	0.385	25.9	5	25.6	21.3	0.561	35.0	0.324	20.4	0.313	8.7	2.1	42.6
162 Uganda	0.516	0.370	28.3	5	28.2	32.5	0.417	27.9	0.378	24.2	0.321	7.6	2.0	41.0
163 Benin	0.515	0.326	36.6	−6	36.3	35.0	0.412	43.7	0.265	30.3	0.319	16.3	2.9	47.8
164 Senegal	0.505	0.340	32.6	−1	31.7	21.1	0.576	46.5	0.197	27.7	0.347	7.7	1.9	40.3
165 Comoros	0.503	0.275	45.3	−18	44.2	28.9	0.480	47.6	0.248	56.0	0.175	11.2	2.5	45.3
165 Togo	0.503	0.344	31.7	1	31.5	30.5	0.433	38.9	0.309	25.1	0.303	9.7	2.2	43.1
167 Sudan	0.502	0.328	34.7	−1	34.5	27.9	0.496	42.5	0.189	33.0	0.376	6.2[f]	1.4[f]	35.4[f]
168 Afghanistan	0.498	0.350	29.6	7	28.2	28.4	0.485	45.4	0.227	10.8	0.391	..	..	..
168 Haiti	0.498	0.304	39.0	−7	38.4	28.6	0.479	38.3	0.267	48.4	0.219	8.6	2.0	41.1
170 Côte d'Ivoire	0.492	0.311	36.9	−1	36.3	34.2	0.345	47.4	0.223	27.4	0.389	8.4	2.0	41.5
171 Malawi	0.477	0.332	30.4	5	30.4	30.3	0.468	28.4	0.323	32.4	0.242	9.4	2.5	45.5
172 Djibouti	0.476	0.306	35.8	−1	35.2	30.8	0.454	47.0	0.164	27.7	0.385	10.2	2.3	44.1
173 Ethiopia	0.463	0.331	28.4	6	27.3	24.9	0.530	43.5	0.185	13.4	0.372	7.1	1.8	39.1
174 Gambia	0.460	0.289	37.2	−4	36.4	28.5	0.456	49.3	0.189	31.5	0.281	5.9	1.5	35.9
175 Guinea	0.459	0.306	33.4	2	32.2	31.2	0.430	48.3	0.175	17.1	0.379	5.5	1.3	33.7
176 Congo (Democratic Republic of the)	0.457	0.319	30.3	6	30.2	36.1	0.394	26.3	0.365	28.2	0.225	8.8	2.1	42.1
177 Guinea-Bissau	0.455	0.276	39.4	−5	39.4	38.4	0.358	41.9	0.228	37.9	0.257	12.6	3.3	50.7

HUMAN DEVELOPMENT INDICES AND INDICATORS: **2018 STATISTICAL UPDATE**

TABLE 3

		Human Development Index (HDI)	Inequality-adjusted HDI (IHDI)			Coefficient of human inequality	Inequality in life expectancy	Inequality-adjusted life expectancy index	Inequality in education[a]	Inequality-adjusted education index	Inequality in income[a]	Inequality-adjusted income index	Income inequality		
		Value	Value	Overall loss (%)	Difference from HDI rank[b]		(%)	Value	(%)	Value	(%)	Value	Quintile ratio	Palma ratio	Gini coefficient
HDI rank		2017	2017	2017	2017	2017	2015–2020[c]	2017	2017[d]	2017	2017[d]	2017	2010–2017[e]	2010–2017[e]	2010–2017[e]
178	Yemen	0.452	0.308	31.9	6	30.9	24.9	0.522	46.1	0.188	21.8	0.297	6.1	1.6	36.7
179	Eritrea	0.440	..	..	..	..	21.4	0.551	..	..	..	..	..	..	..
180	Mozambique	0.437	0.294	32.7	2	32.6	35.6	0.385	33.8	0.255	28.4	0.259	14.2	3.9	54.0
181	Liberia	0.435	0.298	31.6	4	31.0	27.5	0.480	42.9	0.248	22.7	0.221	5.4	1.3	33.2
182	Mali	0.427	0.282	34.0	1	32.8	36.8	0.374	46.2	0.158	15.4	0.380	5.2[f]	1.3[f]	33.0[f]
183	Burkina Faso	0.423	0.288	32.1	3	31.8	32.0	0.427	39.2	0.174	24.2	0.321	5.3	1.5	35.3
184	Sierra Leone	0.419	0.266	36.5	–1	35.4	39.8	0.298	47.3	0.206	19.2	0.307	5.4	1.4	34.0
185	Burundi	0.417	0.278	33.3	3	32.8	38.1	0.361	39.5	0.256	20.9	0.233	6.7	1.7	38.6
186	Chad	0.404	0.249	38.3	–1	37.9	42.4	0.294	43.0	0.170	28.4	0.310	10.0	2.2	43.3
187	South Sudan	0.388	0.247	36.3	–1	36.3	37.0	0.361	39.6	0.180	32.3	0.232	13.0[f]	2.7[f]	46.3[f]
188	Central African Republic	0.367	0.212	42.1	–1	41.8	41.7	0.295	34.5	0.223	49.2	0.145	18.5[f]	4.5[f]	56.2[f]
189	Niger	0.354	0.250	29.3	3	28.8	34.9	0.405	35.0	0.139	16.4	0.278	5.4	1.4	34.3
OTHER COUNTRIES OR TERRITORIES															
..	Korea (Democratic People's Rep. of)	..	..	..	..	..	11.6	0.706	..	..	..	..	..	..	..
..	Monaco	..	..	..	..	..	..	..	..	..	..	..	..	..	..
..	Nauru	..	..	..	..	..	..	..	..	..	..	..	..	..	..
..	San Marino	..	..	..	..	..	..	..	..	..	..	..	..	..	..
..	Somalia	..	..	..	..	..	38.9	0.345	..	..	..	..	..	..	..
..	Tuvalu	..	..	..	..	..	..	..	10.5	..	23.4	0.472	7.0	1.8	39.1
Human development groups															
	Very high human development	0.894	0.799	10.7	—	10.4	5.0	0.870	6.3	0.810	20.1	0.723	—	—	—
	High human development	0.757	0.636	16.0	—	15.7	9.2	0.782	13.1	0.579	24.8	0.569	—	—	—
	Medium human development	0.645	0.483	25.1	—	24.9	20.3	0.602	33.1	0.372	21.2	0.503	—	—	—
	Low human development	0.504	0.347	31.1	—	30.9	31.2	0.431	37.0	0.263	24.6	0.368	—	—	—
Developing countries		0.681	0.531	22.0	—	21.9	17.4	0.644	25.3	0.435	23.1	0.535	—	—	—
Regions															
	Arab States	0.699	0.523	25.1	—	24.8	15.7	0.668	32.6	0.381	26.1	0.564	—	—	—
	East Asia and the Pacific	0.733	0.619	15.6	—	15.4	10.0	0.757	13.1	0.548	23.1	0.572	—	—	—
	Europe and Central Asia	0.771	0.681	11.7	—	11.6	10.9	0.732	7.2	0.680	16.7	0.633	—	—	—
	Latin America and the Caribbean	0.758	0.593	21.8	—	21.2	12.1	0.753	18.4	0.558	33.2	0.496	—	—	—
	South Asia	0.638	0.471	26.1	—	25.6	21.4	0.596	37.7	0.338	17.6	0.519	—	—	—
	Sub-Saharan Africa	0.537	0.372	30.8	—	30.7	30.8	0.434	33.7	0.308	27.7	0.385	—	—	—
Least developed countries		0.524	0.375	28.5	—	28.2	27.1	0.502	36.2	0.274	21.4	0.382	—	—	—
Small island developing states		0.676	0.508	24.9	—	24.5	17.8	0.646	20.9	0.475	34.9	0.427	—	—	—
Organisation for Economic Co-operation and Development		0.895	0.788	11.9	—	11.6	5.3	0.883	7.7	0.785	21.7	0.708	—	—	—
World		0.728	0.582	20.0	—	19.9	15.2	0.681	22.0	0.493	22.6	0.588	—	—	—

NOTES

a See http://hdr.undp.org/en/composite/IHDI for the list of surveys used to estimate inequalities.

b Based on countries for which an Inequality-adjusted Human Development Index value is calculated.

c Calculated by HDRO from the 2015–2020 period life tables from UNDESA (2017a).

d Data refer to 2017 or the most recent year available.

e Data refer to the most recent year available during the period specified.

f Data refer to a year earlier than 2010.

DEFINITIONS

Human Development Index (HDI): A composite index measuring average achievement in three basic dimensions of human development—a long and healthy life, knowledge and a decent standard of living. See Technical note 1 at http://hdr.undp.org/sites/default/files/hdr2018_technical_notes.pdf for details on how the HDI is calculated.

Inequality-adjusted HDI (IHDI): HDI value adjusted for inequalities in the three basic dimensions of human development. See Technical note 2 at http://hdr.undp.org/sites/default/files/hdr2018_technical_notes.pdf for details on how the IHDI is calculated.

Overall loss: Percentage difference between the IHDI value and the HDI value.

Difference from HDI rank: Difference in ranks on the IHDI and the HDI, calculated only for countries for which an IHDI value is calculated.

Coefficient of human inequality: Average inequality in three basic dimensions of human development.

Inequality in life expectancy: Inequality in distribution of expected length of life based on data from life tables estimated using the Atkinson inequality index.

Inequality-adjusted life expectancy index: HDI life expectancy index value adjusted for inequality in distribution of expected length of life based on data from life tables listed in Main data sources.

Inequality in education: Inequality in distribution of years of schooling based on data from household surveys estimated using the Atkinson inequality index.

Inequality-adjusted education index: HDI education index value adjusted for inequality in distribution of years of schooling based on data from household surveys listed in Main data sources.

Inequality in income: Inequality in income distribution based on data from household surveys estimated using the Atkinson inequality index.

Inequality-adjusted income index: HDI income index value adjusted for inequality in income distribution based on data from household surveys listed in Main data sources.

Quintile ratio: Ratio of the average income of the richest 20 percent of the population to the average income of the poorest 20 percent of the population.

Palma ratio: Ratio of the richest 10 percent of the population's share of gross national income (GNI) divided by the poorest 40 percent's share. It is based on the work of Palma (2011).

Gini coefficient: Measure of the deviation of the distribution of income among individuals or households within a country from a perfectly equal distribution. A value of 0 represents absolute equality, a value of 100 absolute inequality.

MAIN DATA SOURCES

Column 1: HDRO calculations based on data from UNDESA (2017a), UNESCO Institute for Statistics (2018), United Nations Statistics Division (2018b), World Bank (2018b), Barro and Lee (2016) and IMF (2018).

Column 2: Calculated as the geometric mean of the values in inequality-adjusted life expectancy index, inequality-adjusted education index and inequality-adjusted income index using the methodology in Technical note 2 (available at http://hdr.undp.org/sites/default/files/hdr2018_technical_notes.pdf).

Column 3: Calculated based on data in columns 1 and 2.

Column 4: Calculated based on IHDI values and recalculated HDI ranks for countries for which an IHDI value is calculated.

Column 5: Calculated as the arithmetic mean of the values in inequality in life expectancy, inequality in education and inequality in income using the methodology in Technical note 2 (available at http://hdr.undp.org/sites/default/files/hdr2018_technical_notes.pdf).

Column 6: Calculated based on abridged life tables from UNDESA (2017a).

Column 7: Calculated based on inequality in life expectancy and the HDI life expectancy index.

Columns 8 and 10: Calculated based on data from the Luxembourg Income Study database, Eurostat's European Union Statistics on Income and Living Conditions, the World Bank's International Income Distribution Database, the Center for Distributive, Labor and Social Studies and the World Bank's Socio-Economic Database for Latin America and the Caribbean, ICF Macro Demographic and Health Surveys and United Nations Children's Fund Multiple Indicator Cluster Surveys using the methodology in Technical note 2 (available at http://hdr.undp.org/sites/default/files/hdr2018_technical_notes.pdf).

Column 9: Calculated based on inequality in education and the HDI education index.

Column 11: Calculated based on inequality in income and the HDI income index.

Columns 12 and 13: HDRO calculations based on data from World Bank (2018a).

Column 14: World Bank (2018a).

TABLE 3 Inequality-adjusted Human Development Index

TABLE 4

Gender Development Index

		Gender Development Index		Human Development Index (HDI)		SDG 3 Life expectancy at birth		SDG 4.3 Expected years of schooling		SDG 4.6 Mean years of schooling		SDG 8.5 Estimated gross national income per capita[a]	
				Value		(years)		(years)		(years)		(2011 PPP $)	
		Value	Group[b]	Female	Male	Female	Male	Female	Male	Female	Male	Female	Male
HDI rank		2017	2017	2017	2017	2017	2017	2017[c]	2017[c]	2017[c]	2017[c]	2017	2017
VERY HIGH HUMAN DEVELOPMENT													
1	Norway	0.991	1	0.945	0.953	84.2	80.5	18.6[d]	17.2	12.6	12.5	60,153	75,731[e]
2	Switzerland	0.987	1	0.937	0.949	85.3	81.5	16.1	16.3	13.9	12.9	47,938	67,490
3	Australia	0.975	2	0.926	0.950	85.0	81.2	23.3[d]	22.5[d]	12.9	12.8	35,323	51,857
4	Ireland	0.979	1	0.926	0.946	83.6	79.7	19.7[d]	19.5[d]	12.7[f]	12.1[f]	42,771	64,916
5	Germany	0.967	2	0.919	0.951	83.5	78.9	16.9	17.0	13.6	14.5	37,689	54,843
6	Iceland	0.966	2	0.920	0.952	84.4	81.5	20.5[d]	18.2[d]	12.3[f]	12.7[f]	38,004	53,562
7	Hong Kong, China (SAR)	0.965	2	0.916	0.949	87.1	81.2	16.3	16.4	11.6	12.5	43,813	75,577[e]
7	Sweden	0.992	1	0.927	0.934	84.3	80.9	18.4[d]	16.9	12.5	12.3	41,743	53,777
9	Singapore	0.982	1	0.922	0.939	85.2	81.1	16.4[g]	16.0[g]	11.0	12.1	69,508	95,809[e]
10	Netherlands	0.966	2	0.913	0.944	83.7	80.3	18.3[d]	17.8	11.9	12.5	38,767	57,123
11	Denmark	0.980	1	0.919	0.938	82.8	79.0	19.8[d]	18.4[d]	12.7[h]	12.4[h]	40,293	55,624
12	Canada	0.986	1	0.916	0.930	84.4	80.7	16.9[f]	16.0[f]	13.3	12.9	34,928	52,070
13	United States	0.992	1	0.919	0.926	81.8	77.3	17.2	15.7	13.4	13.3	43,899	66,208
14	United Kingdom	0.960	2	0.903	0.941	83.4	79.9	17.9	17.0	12.8[h]	13.5[h]	28,043	50,485
15	Finland	1.000	1	0.917	0.917	84.3	78.7	18.4[d]	16.9	12.6	12.3	34,504	47,691
16	New Zealand	0.966	2	0.900	0.932	83.7	80.4	19.7[d]	18.0	12.7	12.5	25,872	42,339
17	Belgium	0.971	2	0.901	0.928	83.6	78.9	20.8[d]	18.8[d]	11.6	11.9	33,260	51,302
17	Liechtenstein	..	..	..	..	..	..	..	..	13.4	16.1	..	..
19	Japan	0.975	1	0.894	0.917	87.1	80.7	15.2	15.3	12.9[i]	12.5[i]	27,209	51,326
20	Austria	0.971	2	0.893	0.920	84.1	79.4	16.4	15.8	11.8	12.6	35,626	55,591
21	Luxembourg	0.969	2	0.888	0.916	84.1	79.8	14.1	13.9	11.7[h]	12.4[h]	51,154	78,737[e]
22	Israel	0.975	2	0.890	0.913	84.3	80.9	16.5	15.3	13.0	13.0	24,620	40,910
22	Korea (Republic of)	0.932	3	0.866	0.929	85.3	79.2	15.9	17.1	11.4	12.9	22,572	49,297
24	France	0.987	1	0.894	0.906	85.6	79.8	16.8	16.0	11.3	11.8	32,518	46,218
25	Slovenia	1.003	1	0.898	0.895	83.9	78.3	18.0	16.5	12.2	12.3	26,898	34,341
26	Spain	0.979	1	0.879	0.898	86.0	80.5	18.2[d]	17.5	9.7	10.0	26,954	41,850
27	Czechia	0.986	1	0.881	0.894	81.7	76.0	17.6	16.1	12.6	13.1	23,224	38,206
28	Italy	0.967	2	0.863	0.893	85.3	80.9	16.6	15.9	10.0[h]	10.4[h]	25,767	45,326
29	Malta	0.960	2	0.858	0.893	82.6	79.4	16.4	15.4	11.0	11.6	24,255	44,446
30	Estonia	1.019	1	0.876	0.860	82.0	73.0	16.5	15.3	13.0	12.2	21,896	37,043
31	Greece	0.964	2	0.853	0.885	83.9	78.9	17.0	17.5	10.5	11.0	19,658	29,796
32	Cyprus	0.984	1	0.861	0.875	82.8	78.5	15.0	14.2	12.0	12.2	26,580	36,543
33	Poland	1.006	1	0.866	0.861	81.6	73.9	17.3	15.6	12.3	12.3	20,367	32,343
34	United Arab Emirates	0.968	2	0.832	0.859	78.9	76.7	14.3	13.4	11.9[j]	9.7[j]	24,973	84,130[e]
35	Andorra	..	..	..	..	..	..	..	..	10.1	10.2	..	..
35	Lithuania	1.026	2	0.868	0.846	80.0	69.4	16.6	15.7	13.0	13.0	24,366	32,934
37	Qatar	1.031	2	0.870	0.843	80.0	77.6	14.8	12.0	10.8	9.5	59,164	135,961[e]
38	Slovakia	0.991	1	0.850	0.858	80.4	73.4	15.5	14.4	12.3	12.6	22,600	36,726
39	Brunei Darussalam	0.990	1	0.846	0.854	79.1	75.8	14.8	14.1	9.0[i]	9.1[i]	63,939	88,204[e]
39	Saudi Arabia	0.877	5	0.782	0.892	76.5	73.4	16.0	17.8	8.8[h]	9.9[h]	17,422	73,945
41	Latvia	1.030	2	0.858	0.834	79.4	69.7	16.5	15.1	13.2[h]	12.5[h]	20,822	29,924
41	Portugal	0.983	1	0.839	0.853	84.2	78.4	16.2	16.4	9.2	9.2	23,095	32,013
43	Bahrain	0.931	3	0.805	0.865	78.1	76.2	16.6	15.6	9.3[j]	9.5[j]	18,774	55,130
44	Chile	0.961	2	0.823	0.856	82.1	77.2	16.7	16.2	10.2	10.5	15,137	28,809
45	Hungary	0.985	1	0.830	0.843	79.4	72.5	15.4	14.8	11.7	12.1	19,931	31,413
46	Croatia	0.991	1	0.828	0.835	81.0	74.5	15.7	14.3	11.2[j]	11.7[j]	17,507	27,164
47	Argentina	0.997	1	0.816	0.819	80.4	73.0	18.7	16.2	10.1[j]	9.7[j]	12,395	24,789
48	Oman	0.942	3	0.781	0.829	79.7	75.6	14.7	13.4	10.4	9.2	11,246	49,282
49	Russian Federation	1.019	1	0.823	0.808	76.8	65.6	15.9	15.2	12.0[h]	12.1[h]	19,510	29,671
50	Montenegro	0.956	2	0.794	0.831	79.6	74.9	15.2	14.7	10.7[h]	12.0[h]	12,967	20,692
51	Bulgaria	0.990	1	0.808	0.816	78.4	71.5	15.0	14.6	11.9	11.8	14,777	22,930
52	Romania	0.985	1	0.804	0.817	79.0	72.1	14.6	13.9	10.6	11.3	18,217	27,358
53	Belarus	1.020	1	0.814	0.799	78.5	67.5	15.9	15.1	12.2	12.4	13,479	19,592
54	Bahamas	..	..	..	..	78.8	72.7	..	..	11.5[h]	10.5[h]	22,156	31,397
55	Uruguay	1.014	1	0.807	0.796	81.0	74.0	16.9	15.0	9.0	8.4	15,282	24,905
56	Kuwait	0.990	1	0.791	0.799	76.1	73.9	14.3	12.9	8.0	6.9	39,570	93,476[e]
57	Malaysia	0.976	1	0.791	0.810	77.9	73.3	14.1	13.3	10.0[h]	10.3[h]	20,004	31,826
58	Barbados	1.015	1	0.805	0.792	78.4	73.6	16.7	13.9	10.6[k]	10.4[k]	13,509	18,384
58	Kazakhstan	1.007	1	0.801	0.795	74.8	65.3	15.5	14.8	11.8[i]	11.7[i]	16,814	28,815

HUMAN DEVELOPMENT INDICES AND INDICATORS: 2018 STATISTICAL UPDATE

TABLE 4 Gender Development Index

		Gender Development Index		Human Development Index (HDI)		SDG 3 Life expectancy at birth (years)		SDG 4.3 Expected years of schooling (years)		SDG 4.6 Mean years of schooling (years)		SDG 8.5 Estimated gross national income per capita[a] (2011 PPP $)	
		Value	Group[b]	Value									
				Female	Male	Female	Male	Female	Male	Female	Male	Female	Male
HDI rank		2017	2017	2017	2017	2017	2017	2017[c]	2017[c]	2017[c]	2017[c]	2017	2017
HIGH HUMAN DEVELOPMENT													
60	Iran (Islamic Republic of)	0.871	5	0.726	0.834	77.3	75.1	14.6	15.1	9.7[i]	9.9[i]	6,094	32,017
60	Palau	..	..	..	..	..	..	17.8	16.5	..	..	..	..
62	Seychelles	..	..	..	..	78.6	69.5	15.3	14.3	..	..	..	..
63	Costa Rica	0.974	2	0.779	0.800	82.4	77.7	15.8	14.9	8.8	8.5	10,419	18,851
64	Turkey	0.922	4	0.755	0.819	79.2	72.8	14.7	15.7	7.1	8.8	15,576	34,313
65	Mauritius	0.968	2	0.773	0.799	78.4	71.4	15.5	14.6	9.1[i]	9.5[i]	12,558	27,986
66	Panama	0.988	1	0.782	0.791	81.3	75.3	13.3	12.1	10.4[i]	9.9[i]	13,229	25,102
67	Serbia	0.976	1	0.777	0.796	78.2	72.5	15.1	14.2	10.7	11.6	10,672	15,474
68	Albania	0.970	2	0.772	0.796	80.6	76.5	15.0	14.4	9.8	10.2	9,702	14,028
69	Trinidad and Tobago	1.013	1	0.794	0.784	74.4	67.4	14.4[l]	12.5[l]	11.0[h]	10.8[h]	22,008	35,435
70	Antigua and Barbuda	..	..	..	..	78.9	74.0	13.9[h]	12.6[h]	..	..	..	..
70	Georgia	0.975	1	0.766	0.786	77.6	69.2	15.3	14.8	12.8	12.8	6,177	12,481
72	Saint Kitts and Nevis	..	..	..	..	..	..	14.6	14.3	..	..	..	..
73	Cuba	0.942	3	0.751	0.797	81.9	78.0	14.3	13.7	11.6[h]	12.1[h]	5,001	10,045
74	Mexico	0.954	2	0.752	0.789	79.7	74.9	14.4	13.8	8.4	8.8	11,065	22,873
75	Grenada	..	..	..	..	76.3	71.4	17.4	16.3	..	..	..	..
76	Sri Lanka	0.935	3	0.738	0.789	78.8	72.1	14.1	13.6	10.3[h]	11.4[h]	6,462	16,581
77	Bosnia and Herzegovina	0.924	4	0.739	0.800	79.6	74.6	14.9[k]	14.5[k]	8.6	10.9	7,723	15,856
78	Venezuela (Bolivarian Republic of)	1.011	1	0.762	0.754	78.9	70.8	15.4	13.2	10.7	10.0	7,401	13,976
79	Brazil	0.992	1	0.755	0.761	79.3	72.1	15.9	14.9	8.0[h]	7.7[h]	10,073	17,566
80	Azerbaijan	0.949	3	0.734	0.773	75.2	69.1	12.6[m]	12.7[m]	10.5	11.0	10,089	21,152
80	Lebanon	0.889	5	0.701	0.788	81.6	78.2	12.4	12.7	8.5[h]	8.9[h]	5,523	21,182
80	The former Yugoslav Republic of Macedonia	0.946	3	0.731	0.773	77.9	73.9	13.5	13.2	8.9[k]	9.9[k]	9,114	15,897
83	Armenia	0.969	2	0.740	0.764	77.8	71.4	13.4	12.6	11.7	11.7	6,358	12,281
83	Thailand	0.996	1	0.753	0.756	79.3	71.8	14.8	14.5	7.4[h]	7.8[h]	13,793	17,327
85	Algeria	0.861	5	0.680	0.791	77.6	75.1	14.6	14.1	7.6[h]	8.6[h]	4,232	23,181
86	China	0.955	2	0.735	0.769	78.0	74.9	14.0	13.6	7.6[j]	8.3[j]	12,053	18,295
86	Ecuador	0.978	1	0.741	0.757	79.3	73.9	15.4	13.9	8.6	8.8	7,388	13,307
88	Ukraine	0.993	1	0.746	0.751	76.9	67.1	15.2	14.8	11.3[j]	11.3[j]	6,082	10,513
89	Peru	0.950	3	0.728	0.766	77.9	72.6	13.9	13.6	8.7	9.7	8,446	15,140
90	Colombia	0.997	1	0.747	0.749	78.2	71.0	14.9	14.3	8.5	8.1	10,271	15,692
90	Saint Lucia	0.993	1	0.744	0.749	78.4	73.0	13.9[m]	13.3[m]	9.4[h]	8.7[h]	9,388	14,101
92	Fiji	..	..	..	..	73.6	67.5	..	..	10.9[i]	10.7[i]	5,604	10,963
92	Mongolia	1.023	1	0.750	0.733	73.7	65.4	15.9	15.0	10.6	9.8	8,482	11,759
94	Dominican Republic	0.989	1	0.728	0.736	77.3	71.0	14.5	13.0	8.1	7.5	8,909	18,975
95	Jordan	0.857	5	0.658	0.767	76.3	72.8	13.4[h]	12.9[h]	10.1[i]	10.6[i]	2,459	13,971
95	Tunisia	0.897	5	0.684	0.762	78.0	73.9	15.8	14.4	6.4[j]	7.9[j]	4,537	16,152
97	Jamaica	0.988	1	0.731	0.739	78.5	73.7	14.4[h]	12.8[h]	10.0[h]	9.5[h]	5,898	9,812
98	Tonga	0.960	2	0.707	0.736	76.2	70.2	14.6[l]	14.0[l]	11.2[h]	11.1[h]	3,769	7,314
99	Saint Vincent and the Grenadines	..	..	..	..	75.6	71.2	13.4	13.1	..	..	7,643	13,306
100	Suriname	0.975	2	0.705	0.723	74.9	68.4	13.0[m]	12.0[m]	8.3[h]	8.6[h]	9,132	17,449
101	Botswana	0.976	1	0.707	0.725	70.2	64.9	12.8[h]	12.5[h]	9.2[j]	9.5[j]	12,613	18,521
101	Maldives	0.919	4	0.679	0.739	78.8	76.7	12.7[m]	12.6[m]	6.2[i]	6.4[i]	7,064	18,501
103	Dominica	..	..	..	..	..	..	..	..	..	..	..	..
104	Samoa	..	..	..	..	78.5	72.3	12.9[g]	12.1[g]	..	..	3,778	7,909
105	Uzbekistan	0.945	3	0.687	0.726	74.2	68.6	11.8	12.2	11.2	11.8	4,687	8,264
106	Belize	0.979	1	0.699	0.714	73.6	67.9	13.0	12.7	10.5[h]	10.4[h]	5,689	8,655
106	Marshall Islands	..	..	..	..	..	..	..	..	10.7	11.1	..	..
108	Libya	0.929	3	0.668	0.719	75.1	69.3	13.6[l]	13.2[l]	7.7[j]	7.0[j]	4,623	17,472
108	Turkmenistan	..	..	..	..	71.4	64.5	10.5	11.1	..	..	11,240	20,083
110	Gabon	0.911	4	0.670	0.735	68.2	64.9	12.5[m]	13.4[m]	7.4[m]	9.1[m]	11,789	20,825
110	Paraguay	0.972	2	0.690	0.710	75.5	71.1	13.2	12.2	8.4	8.3	6,212	10,486
112	Moldova (Republic of)	1.005	1	0.701	0.698	76.0	67.4	11.9	11.4	11.5	11.7	4,849	6,318
MEDIUM HUMAN DEVELOPMENT													
113	Philippines	1.000	1	0.699	0.698	72.8	65.9	12.9	12.3	9.5[h]	9.2[h]	7,582	10,705
113	South Africa	0.984	1	0.692	0.704	67.0	59.9	13.7	13.1	9.9	10.4	9,060	14,894
115	Egypt	0.872	5	0.636	0.729	74.0	69.5	13.1	13.1	6.5[i]	7.9[i]	4,081	16,489
116	Indonesia	0.932	3	0.666	0.715	71.6	67.3	12.8	12.8	7.5	8.4	7,259	14,385
116	Viet Nam	1.005	1	0.696	0.692	81.0	71.8	12.9[k]	12.5[k]	7.9[k]	8.5[k]	5,345	6,383

TABLE 4 GENDER DEVELOPMENT INDEX

	Gender Development Index		Human Development Index (HDI)		SDG 3 Life expectancy at birth		SDG 4.3 Expected years of schooling		SDG 4.6 Mean years of schooling		SDG 8.5 Estimated gross national income per capita[a]	
	Value	Group[b]	Female	Male	Female	Male	Female	Male	Female	Male	Female	Male
			Value		(years)		(years)		(years)		(2011 PPP $)	
HDI rank	2017	2017	2017	2017	2017	2017	2017[c]	2017[c]	2017[c]	2017[c]	2017	2017
118 Bolivia (Plurinational State of)	0.929	3	0.665	0.716	72.1	67.0	14.0	14.0	8.2	9.7	4,686	8,737
119 Palestine, State of	0.877	5	0.623	0.710	75.6	71.8	13.7	12.0	8.9	9.3	1,802	8,216
120 Iraq	0.823	5	0.603	0.733	72.3	67.8	10.1[m]	12.0[m]	5.4[h]	7.8[h]	6,039	29,250
121 El Salvador	0.969	2	0.663	0.684	78.1	69.1	12.5	12.0	6.7	7.3	5,226	8,722
122 Kyrgyzstan	0.960	2	0.654	0.681	75.1	67.1	13.7	13.2	10.9[m]	10.8[m]	2,159	4,369
123 Morocco	0.838	5	0.598	0.713	77.2	74.9	12.0	12.8	4.5[i]	6.5[i]	3,197	11,561
124 Nicaragua	0.966	2	0.642	0.665	78.6	72.6	12.3	11.8	6.9[i]	6.4[i]	3,434	6,930
125 Cabo Verde	0.949	3	0.632	0.666	74.9	70.9	12.8	12.1	5.9	6.4	4,295	7,683
125 Guyana	0.948	3	0.631	0.666	69.2	64.5	11.7	11.0	8.5[k]	8.4[k]	4,543	10,295
127 Guatemala	0.948	3	0.630	0.665	76.8	70.4	10.7	10.9	6.4[h]	6.5[h]	4,768	9,869
127 Tajikistan	0.933	3	0.624	0.669	74.4	68.4	10.5	11.9	10.7[i]	10.2[i]	2,233	4,392
129 Namibia	1.014	1	0.651	0.642	67.7	61.8	12.4[m]	12.2[m]	7.2[i]	6.6[i]	8,895	9,907
130 India	0.841	5	0.575	0.683	70.4	67.3	12.9	11.9	4.8[h]	8.2[h]	2,722	9,729
131 Micronesia (Federated States of)	..	..	..	..	70.5	68.1	..	..	..	..	..	..
132 Timor-Leste	0.855	5	0.567	0.663	71.1	67.4	12.3	13.2	3.6[m]	5.3[m]	3,301	10,282
133 Honduras	0.978	1	0.608	0.622	76.3	71.2	10.7	9.8	6.6	6.5	3,277	5,159
134 Bhutan	0.893	5	0.576	0.645	70.9	70.3	12.4	12.2	2.1[k]	4.2[k]	6,002	9,889
134 Kiribati	..	..	..	..	69.8	63.2	13.4	12.6	..	..	..	..
136 Bangladesh	0.881	5	0.567	0.644	74.6	71.2	11.7[h]	11.3[h]	5.2[j]	6.7[j]	2,041	5,285
137 Congo	0.934	3	0.583	0.624	66.7	63.5	11.2	11.5	5.5[i]	6.7[i]	4,905	6,483
138 Vanuatu	..	..	..	..	74.7	70.2	10.4[l]	11.1[l]	..	..	2,340	3,635
139 Lao People's Democratic Republic	0.934	3	0.579	0.621	68.6	65.4	10.9	11.5	4.6[i]	5.7[i]	5,354	6,789
140 Ghana	0.910	4	0.563	0.619	64.1	62.0	11.5	11.8	6.3[i]	7.9[i]	3,349	4,849
141 Equatorial Guinea	..	..	..	..	59.4	56.7	..	..	4.0[m]	7.3[m]	14,869	23,258
142 Kenya	0.931	3	0.568	0.610	69.7	64.9	11.7[m]	12.5[m]	5.7[i]	7.1[i]	2,529	3,398
143 Sao Tome and Principe	0.892	5	0.550	0.617	68.9	64.6	12.6	12.4	5.6[h]	7.1[h]	1,780	4,112
144 Eswatini (Kingdom of)	0.943	3	0.568	0.603	61.3	54.9	10.8	11.6	6.1[k]	6.9[k]	5,722	9,641
144 Zambia	0.941	3	0.569	0.605	65.0	59.6	12.0[m]	13.0[m]	6.5[m]	7.4[m]	2,986	4,138
146 Cambodia	0.914	4	0.553	0.605	71.3	67.1	11.2[h]	12.2[h]	3.8[i]	5.6[i]	2,970	3,878
147 Angola	..	..	..	..	64.7	59.0	11.0	12.7	..	..	5,063	6,546
148 Myanmar	0.959	2	0.563	0.586	69.1	64.4	10.3	9.8	4.9[m]	4.8[m]	3,860	7,355
149 Nepal	0.925	4	0.552	0.598	72.2	69.0	12.6	11.8	3.6[i]	6.4[i]	2,219	2,738
150 Pakistan	0.750	5	0.465	0.620	67.7	65.6	7.8	9.3	3.8	6.5	1,642	8,786
151 Cameroon	0.866	5	0.513	0.593	59.7	57.5	11.3	13.0	4.7[j]	7.6[j]	2,751	3,878
LOW HUMAN DEVELOPMENT												
152 Solomon Islands	..	..	..	..	72.6	69.5	9.7[g]	10.7[g]	..	..	1,450	2,281
153 Papua New Guinea	..	..	..	..	68.3	63.3	..	..	3.8[i]	5.3[i]	3,002	3,789
154 Tanzania (United Republic of)	0.928	3	0.517	0.557	68.1	64.6	8.6[m]	9.3[m]	5.4[i]	6.2[i]	2,282	3,037
155 Syrian Arab Republic	0.788	5	0.443	0.563	77.4	65.4	8.7	8.8	4.6[n]	5.6[n]	561	4,077
156 Zimbabwe	0.924	4	0.513	0.555	63.5	59.8	10.2	10.5	7.5	8.9	1,431	1,948
157 Nigeria	0.868	5	0.494	0.569	54.7	53.1	9.2[m]	10.8[m]	5.0[m]	7.3[m]	4,433	6,008
158 Rwanda	0.941	3	0.508	0.540	69.6	65.3	11.2	11.2	3.7[h]	4.7[h]	1,568	2,064
159 Lesotho	1.004	1	0.519	0.516	56.7	52.2	11.0	10.2	7.0[i]	5.5[i]	2,608	3,940
159 Mauritania	0.845	5	0.470	0.556	64.9	61.9	8.5	8.6	3.5[i]	5.5[i]	1,936	5,221
161 Madagascar	0.962	2	0.511	0.531	67.9	64.7	10.5	10.6	6.7[m]	6.1[m]	1,173	1,544
162 Uganda	0.865	5	0.475	0.550	62.4	58.0	11.0	12.2	4.7[m]	7.2[m]	1,212	2,109
163 Benin	0.875	5	0.479	0.547	62.7	59.6	11.1	14.0	3.0[k]	4.3[k]	1,795	2,329
164 Senegal	0.911	4	0.481	0.528	69.4	65.4	10.0	9.3	2.4	3.8	1,691	3,101
165 Comoros	0.876	5	0.465	0.531	65.7	62.2	11.1	11.4	3.7[m]	5.6[m]	1,027	1,764
165 Togo	0.822	5	0.446	0.542	61.3	59.6	10.0	13.2[m]	3.3[m]	6.5[m]	1,265	1,643
167 Sudan	0.831	5	0.446	0.537	66.3	63.1	7.2	7.7	3.1[i]	4.1[i]	1,785	6,455
168 Afghanistan	0.625	5	0.364	0.583	65.4	62.8	8.0	12.7	1.9[i]	6.0[i]	541	3,030
168 Haiti	..	..	..	..	65.8	61.4	..	..	4.3[m]	6.6[m]	1,400	1,937
170 Côte d'Ivoire	0.841	5	0.446	0.531	55.7	52.7	8.1	10.0	4.0[i]	6.2[i]	2,529	4,409
171 Malawi	0.936	3	0.460	0.492	66.2	61.0	10.9	10.8	4.0[i]	5.1[i]	897	1,235
172 Djibouti	..	..	..	..	64.4	61.0	5.8	6.7	..	..	2,491	4,286
173 Ethiopia	0.846	5	0.424	0.501	67.8	64.0	8.2[h]	9.1[h]	1.6[m]	3.8[m]	1,304	2,136
174 Gambia	0.890	5	0.434	0.487	62.8	60.1	9.3	9.2	2.9[i]	4.3[i]	1,168	1,870
175 Guinea	0.810	5	0.411	0.507	61.2	60.1	7.8	10.4	1.5[m]	3.9[m]	1,804	2,328
176 Congo (Democratic Republic of the)	0.852	5	0.420	0.493	61.5	58.5	8.7	10.6	5.3[h]	8.4[h]	703	889
177 Guinea-Bissau	..	..	..	..	59.5	56.0	..	..	..	..	1,269	1,843

HUMAN DEVELOPMENT INDICES AND INDICATORS: **2018 STATISTICAL UPDATE**

TABLE 4 Gender Development Index

		Gender Development Index		Human Development Index (HDI)		SDG 3 Life expectancy at birth		SDG 4.3 Expected years of schooling		SDG 4.6 Mean years of schooling		SDG 8.5 Estimated gross national income per capita[a]	
		Value	Group[b]	Value		(years)		(years)		(years)		(2011 PPP $)	
				Female	Male	Female	Male	Female	Male	Female	Male	Female	Male
HDI rank		2017	2017	2017	2017	2017	2017	2017[c]	2017[c]	2017[c]	2017[c]	2017	2017
178	Yemen	0.425	5	0.223	0.524	66.6	63.7	7.6[h]	10.3[h]	1.9[j]	4.2[j]	149	2,308
179	Eritrea	..	..	..	..	67.7	63.4	4.9	5.8	..	..	1,451	2,048
180	Mozambique	0.904	4	0.414	0.458	61.0	56.7	9.2	10.2	2.5[h]	4.6[h]	1,052	1,135
181	Liberia	0.846	5	0.398	0.470	64.0	62.0	9.3[m]	10.6[m]	3.5[i]	6.1[i]	577	755
182	Mali	0.811	5	0.380	0.469	59.2	57.7	6.8	8.6	1.7[h]	3.0[h]	1,345	2,560
183	Burkina Faso	0.870	5	0.393	0.452	61.4	60.0	8.3	8.8	1.0[m]	2.0[m]	1,289	2,014
184	Sierra Leone	0.872	5	0.389	0.446	52.8	51.6	9.3[m]	10.2[m]	2.7[i]	4.3[i]	1,096	1,387
185	Burundi	1.002	1	0.419	0.418	59.9	55.9	11.3	12.1	2.7[m]	3.7[m]	807	594
186	Chad	0.775	5	0.350	0.452	54.5	52.0	6.4	9.5	1.2[m]	3.4[m]	1,412	2,088
187	South Sudan	0.826	5	0.348	0.422	58.3	56.3	3.8[m]	6.3[m]	4.0	5.3	843	1,083
188	Central African Republic	0.780	5	0.319	0.409	54.8	51.0	5.9[h]	8.5[h]	3.0[i]	5.6[i]	521	809
189	Niger	0.812	5	0.317	0.391	61.5	59.4	4.7	6.0	1.5[i]	2.6[i]	691	1,119
OTHER COUNTRIES OR TERRITORIES													
..	Korea (Democratic People's Rep. of)	..	..	..	..	75.3	68.3	..	..	..	..	..	..
..	Monaco	..	..	..	..	..	..	..	..	..	..	..	..
..	Nauru	..	..	..	..	..	..	10.8	9.9	..	..	..	..
..	San Marino	..	..	..	..	..	..	15.6	14.6	..	..	..	..
..	Somalia	..	..	..	..	58.4	55.1	..	..	..	..	..	..
..	Tuvalu	..	..	..	..	..	..	..	..	..	..	..	..
Human development groups													
	Very high human development	0.983	—	0.884	0.899	82.4	76.7	16.9	16.0	12.2	12.3	30,276	50,033
	High human development	0.957	—	0.740	0.773	78.2	74.0	14.3	13.9	8.0	8.6	10,945	18,948
	Medium human development	0.878	—	0.598	0.680	71.1	67.2	12.2	11.8	5.6	7.9	3,673	9,906
	Low human development	0.862	—	0.465	0.540	62.3	59.2	8.7	10.1	3.8	5.7	1,915	3,126
Developing countries		0.917	—	0.649	0.708	72.7	68.8	12.2	12.2	6.7	8.1	6,562	13,441
Regions													
	Arab States	0.855	—	0.630	0.736	73.4	69.8	11.6	12.2	6.2	7.7	5,380	25,533
	East Asia and the Pacific	0.957	—	0.717	0.750	76.7	72.8	13.5	13.2	7.6	8.3	10,689	16,568
	Europe and Central Asia	0.956	—	0.751	0.785	77.0	69.7	13.9	14.2	9.9	10.6	10,413	20,529
	Latin America and the Caribbean	0.977	—	0.748	0.765	78.9	72.6	15.0	14.1	8.5	8.5	9,622	17,809
	South Asia	0.837	—	0.571	0.682	70.9	67.8	12.1	11.7	5.0	8.0	2,694	10,035
	Sub-Saharan Africa	0.893	—	0.506	0.567	62.4	59.0	9.5	10.6	4.7	6.5	2,763	4,034
Least developed countries		0.868	—	0.486	0.559	66.5	63.1	9.4	10.4	3.9	5.6	1,744	3,272
Small island developing states		0.953	—	0.675	0.708	73.5	68.6	..	..	8.1	8.7	5,298	10,012
Organisation for Economic Co-operation and Development		0.976	—	0.881	0.903	83.1	78.0	16.6	15.9	11.8	12.1	30,325	49,125
World		**0.941**	—	**0.705**	**0.749**	**74.4**	**70.1**	**12.8**	**12.7**	**7.9**	**9.0**	**10,986**	**19,525**

NOTES

a Because disaggregated income data are not available, data are crudely estimated. See Definitions and Technical note 3 at http://hdr.undp.org/sites/default/files/hdr2018_technical_notes.pdf for details on how the Gender Development Index is calculated.

b Countries are divided into five groups by absolute deviation from gender parity in HDI values.

c Data refer to 2017 or the most recent year available.

d In calculating the HDI value, expected years of schooling is capped at 18 years.

e In calculating the male HDI value, estimated gross national income per capita is capped at $75,000.

f Based on data from OECD (2017a).

g Based on data from national statistical office.

h Updated by HDRO based on data from UNESCO Institute for Statistics (2018).

i Based on Barro and Lee (2016).

j Updated by HDRO using Barro and Lee (2016) estimates.

k Based on data from United Nations Children's Fund (UNICEF) Multiple Indicator Cluster Surveys for 2006–2017.

l Based on cross-country regression.

m Updated by HDRO based on data from ICF Macro Demographic and Health Surveys for 2006–2017.

n Updated by HDRO based on Syrian Center for Policy Research (2017).

DEFINITIONS

Gender Development Index: Ratio of female to male HDI values. See Technical note 3 at http://hdr.undp.org/sites/default/files/hdr2018_technical_notes.pdf for details on how the Gender Development Index is calculated.

Gender Development Index groups: Countries are divided into five groups by absolute deviation from gender parity in HDI values. Group 1 comprises countries with high equality in HDI achievements between women and men (absolute deviation of less than 2.5 percent), group 2 comprises countries with medium to high equality in HDI achievements between women and men (absolute deviation of 2.5–5 percent), group 3 comprises countries with medium equality in HDI achievements between women and men (absolute deviation of 5–7.5 percent), group 4 comprises countries with medium to low equality in HDI achievements between women and men (absolute deviation of 7.5–10 percent) and group 5 comprises countries with low equality in HDI achievements between women and men (absolute deviation from gender parity of more than 10 percent).

Human Development Index (HDI): A composite index measuring average achievement in three basic dimensions of human development—a long and healthy life, knowledge and a decent standard of living. See Technical note 1 at http://hdr.undp.org/sites/default/files/hdr2018_technical_notes.pdf for details on how the HDI is calculated.

Life expectancy at birth: Number of years a newborn infant could expect to live if prevailing patterns of age-specific mortality rates at the time of birth stay the same throughout the infant's life.

Expected years of schooling: Number of years of schooling that a child of school entrance age can expect to receive if prevailing patterns of age-specific enrolment rates persist throughout the child's life.

Mean years of schooling: Average number of years of education received by people ages 25 and older, converted from educational attainment levels using official durations of each level.

Estimated gross national income per capita: Derived from the ratio of female to male wages, female and male shares of economically active population and gross national income (in 2011 purchasing power parity terms). See Technical note 3 at http://hdr.undp.org/sites/default/files/hdr2018_technical_notes.pdf for details.

MAIN DATA SOURCES

Column 1: Calculated based on data in columns 3 and 4.

Column 2: Calculated based on data in column 1.

Columns 3 and 4: HDRO calculations based on data from UNDESA (2017a), UNESCO Institute for Statistics (2018), Barro and Lee (2016), World Bank (2018b), ILO (2018a) and IMF (2018).

Columns 5 and 6: UNDESA (2017a).

Columns 7 and 8: UNESCO Institute for Statistics (2018), ICF Macro Demographic and Health Surveys, UNICEF Multiple Indicator Cluster Surveys and OECD (2017a).

Columns 9 and 10: UNESCO Institute for Statistics (2018), Barro and Lee (2016), ICF Macro Demographic and Health Surveys, UNICEF Multiple Indicator Cluster Surveys and OECD (2017a).

Columns 11 and 12: HDRO calculations based on ILO (2018a), UNDESA (2017a), World Bank (2018b) and IMF (2018).

TABLE 5

Gender Inequality Index

			SDG 3.1	SDG 3.7	SDG 5.5	SDG 4.6		Labour force	
	Gender Inequality Index		Maternal mortality ratio	Adolescent birth rate	Share of seats in parliament	Population with at least some secondary education		participation rate[a]	
			(deaths per 100,000 live births)	(births per 1,000 women ages 15–19)	(% held by women)	(% ages 25 and older)		(% ages 15 and older)	
	Value	Rank				Female	Male	Female	Male
HDI rank	2017	2017	2015	2015–2020[b]	2017	2010–2017[c]	2010–2017[c]	2017	2017
VERY HIGH HUMAN DEVELOPMENT									
1 Norway	0.048	5	5	5.6	41.4	96.3	95.1	60.8	67.6
2 Switzerland	0.039	1	5	3.0	29.3	96.4	97.2	62.9	74.1
3 Australia	0.109	23	6	12.9	32.7	90.0	89.9	59.2	70.5
4 Ireland	0.109	23	8	9.7	24.3	90.2	86.3	53.0	67.3
5 Germany	0.072	14	6	6.5	31.5	96.2	96.8	55.0	66.2
6 Iceland	0.062	9	3	6.8	38.1	100.0	100.0	72.8	81.8
7 Hong Kong, China (SAR)	..	..	..	2.7	..	75.7	81.8	54.0	68.1
7 Sweden	0.044	3	4	5.2	43.6	88.4	88.7	60.8	67.4
9 Singapore	0.067	12	10	3.7	23.0	76.1	82.9	60.5	76.8
10 Netherlands	0.044	3	7	4.0	35.6	86.4	90.4	58.0	69.2
11 Denmark	0.040	2	6	4.1	37.4	90.1	91.3	59.2	67.2
12 Canada	0.092	20	7	9.4	30.1	100.0	100.0	60.7	69.8
13 United States	0.189	41	14	18.8	19.7	95.5	95.2	55.7	68.3
14 United Kingdom	0.116	25	9	12.5	28.5	82.4	85.2	56.8	68.1
15 Finland	0.058	8	3	6.8	42.0	100.0	100.0	54.8	61.9
16 New Zealand	0.136	34	11	20.0	38.3	99.0	98.8	63.9	74.9
17 Belgium	0.048	5	7	4.9	41.4	82.2	86.7	47.8	58.7
17 Liechtenstein	..	..	..	..	12.0	..	..	..	..
19 Japan	0.103	22	5	4.1	13.7	94.8	91.9	50.5	70.6
20 Austria	0.071	13	4	6.9	33.6	100.0	100.0	55.0	66.0
21 Luxembourg	0.066	11	10	5.2	28.3	100.0	100.0	52.3	63.5
22 Israel	0.098	21	5	9.2	27.5	87.8	90.5	59.3	69.2
22 Korea (Republic of)	0.063	10	11	1.6	17.0	89.8	95.6	52.2	73.2
24 France	0.083	16	8	8.6	35.4	80.6	85.6	50.6	60.1
25 Slovenia	0.054	7	9	4.2	28.7	97.4	98.9	51.7	60.9
26 Spain	0.080	15	5	8.6	38.6	72.2	77.6	52.2	63.8
27 Czechia	0.124	29	4	10.0	21.1	99.8	99.8	52.0	68.3
28 Italy	0.087	18	4	6.1	30.1	75.6	83.0	39.5	58.3
29 Malta	0.216	45	9	16.6	11.9	73.2	82.0	42.3	66.6
30 Estonia	0.122	27	9	12.6	26.7	100.0	100.0	56.4	70.3
31 Greece	0.120	26	3	7.2	18.3	65.4	73.2	45.5	60.6
32 Cyprus	0.085	17	7	4.6	17.9	76.8	80.7	58.1	67.5
33 Poland	0.132	32	3	12.7	25.5	81.1	86.9	48.8	65.1
34 United Arab Emirates	0.232	49	6	28.4	22.5	78.8[d]	65.7[d]	40.9	92.0
35 Andorra	..	..	..	..	32.1	71.7	73.3	..	..
35 Lithuania	0.123	28	10	10.7	21.3	91.8	96.4	55.9	66.2
37 Qatar	0.206	44	13	9.9	9.8	70.9	68.0	58.1	94.6
38 Slovakia	0.180	39	6	22.0	20.0	99.1	100.0	52.5	67.7
39 Brunei Darussalam	0.236	51	23	10.3	9.1	69.1[d]	70.3[d]	59.0	74.7
39 Saudi Arabia	0.234	50	12	7.8	19.9	67.8	75.5	22.3	79.5
41 Latvia	0.196	42	18	13.5	16.0	99.4	99.1	55.2	67.3
41 Portugal	0.088	19	10	9.4	34.8	52.1	53.4	53.3	63.8
43 Bahrain	0.222	47	15	13.4	15.0	63.7	57.1	44.0	87.0
44 Chile	0.319	72	22	45.6	15.8[e]	79.0	80.9	50.6	74.4
45 Hungary	0.259	54	17	19.7	10.1	95.7	98.0	47.9	64.2
46 Croatia	0.124	29	8	8.9	18.5	94.5	96.9	45.5	57.7
47 Argentina	0.358	81	52	62.8	38.9	65.9[d]	62.8[d]	47.3	73.2
48 Oman	0.264	56	17	7.1	8.8	73.4	63.7	30.2	87.3
49 Russian Federation	0.257	53	25	21.6	16.1	95.8	95.3	56.6	71.8
50 Montenegro	0.132	32	7	11.8	23.5	87.0	96.4	42.2	55.0
51 Bulgaria	0.217	46	11	39.5	23.8	93.7	96.1	47.8	59.6
52 Romania	0.311	68	31	33.1	18.7	86.5	92.7	44.1	63.1
53 Belarus	0.130	31	4	17.2	33.1	87.0	92.2	58.4	70.7
54 Bahamas	0.340	75	80	26.7	21.8	87.4	87.6	70.0	82.0
55 Uruguay	0.270	57	15	54.7	22.3	55.8	52.1	56.1	74.4
56 Kuwait	0.270	57	4	9.0	3.1	54.8	49.3	47.4	84.1
57 Malaysia	0.287	62	40	13.4	13.1	78.9	81.3	50.8	77.4
58 Barbados	0.284	60	27	37.3	19.6	94.2[d]	91.6[d]	62.3	70.0
58 Kazakhstan	0.197	43	12	27.5	22.1	98.5	99.1	65.4	77.3

38 | HUMAN DEVELOPMENT INDICES AND INDICATORS: **2018 STATISTICAL UPDATE**

HUMAN DEVELOPMENT INDICES AND INDICATORS: **2018 STATISTICAL UPDATE**

TABLE 5

		Gender Inequality Index		SDG 3.1 Maternal mortality ratio	SDG 3.7 Adolescent birth rate	SDG 5.5 Share of seats in parliament	SDG 4.6 Population with at least some secondary education		Labour force participation rate[a]	
		Value	Rank	(deaths per 100,000 live births)	(births per 1,000 women ages 15–19)	(% held by women)	(% ages 25 and older)		(% ages 15 and older)	
							Female	Male	Female	Male
HDI rank		2017	2017	2015	2015–2020[b]	2017	2010–2017[c]	2010–2017[c]	2017	2017
HIGH HUMAN DEVELOPMENT										
60	Iran (Islamic Republic of)	0.461	109	25	25.0	5.9	65.8	70.9	16.8	71.4
60	Palau	..	..	..	..	13.8	96.9	97.3	..	..
62	Seychelles	..	..	..	56.9	21.2	..	..	..	..
63	Costa Rica	0.300	64	25	53.5	35.1	53.8	51.9	45.3	73.9
64	Turkey	0.317	69	16	25.8	14.6	44.9	66.0	32.4	71.9
65	Mauritius	0.373	84	53	26.6	11.6	64.3	67.3	45.1	72.7
66	Panama	0.461	109	94	81.8	18.3	72.7	68.4	52.8	81.2
67	Serbia	0.181	40	17	18.9	34.4	84.6	93.0	45.9	61.7
68	Albania	0.238	52	29	20.7	27.9	93.1	92.8	47.2	64.9
69	Trinidad and Tobago	0.324	73	63	30.1	30.1	74.4	69.1	51.0	73.7
70	Antigua and Barbuda	..	..	..	43.5	20.0	..	..	..	..
70	Georgia	0.350	78	36	45.9	16.0	95.1	96.0	57.9	78.8
72	Saint Kitts and Nevis	..	..	..	..	13.3	..	..	..	..
73	Cuba	0.301	65	39	43.6	48.9	86.7	88.9	41.5	67.3
74	Mexico	0.343	76	38	60.3	41.4	57.8	61.0	44.1	79.0
75	Grenada	..	..	27	29.2	25.0	..	..	..	..
76	Sri Lanka	0.354	80	30	14.1	5.8	82.6	83.1	35.1	74.1
77	Bosnia and Herzegovina	0.166	37	11	10.0	19.3	71.7	88.7	35.2	58.7
78	Venezuela (Bolivarian Republic of)	0.454	105	95	85.3	22.2	71.7	66.6	50.2	77.4
79	Brazil	0.407	94	44	61.6	11.3	61.0	57.7	53.2	74.7
80	Azerbaijan	0.318	71	25	53.5	16.8	93.8	97.5	62.9	69.5
80	Lebanon	0.381	85	15	11.8	3.1	53.0	55.4	23.2	71.1
80	The former Yugoslav Republic of Macedonia	0.149	35	8	16.2	37.5	40.5	56.0	42.5	67.6
83	Armenia	0.262	55	25	23.2	18.1	96.9	97.6	51.4	70.6
83	Thailand	0.393	93	20	51.9	4.8	42.4	47.5	60.5	77.3
85	Algeria	0.442	100	140	10.1	21.3	37.5[d]	37.9[d]	15.2	67.3
86	China	0.152	36	27	6.4	24.2	74.0	82.0	61.5	76.1
86	Ecuador	0.385	88	64	73.9	38.0	52.1	52.2	55.4	81.3
88	Ukraine	0.285	61	24	23.8	12.3	94.5[d]	95.6[d]	46.9	63.0
89	Peru	0.368	83	68	47.5	27.7	57.1	67.5	69.0	84.5
90	Colombia	0.383	87	64	47.5	19.8	51.1	49.2	58.8	82.6
90	Saint Lucia	0.333	74	48	40.5	20.7	48.2	42.0	61.2	75.9
92	Fiji	0.352	79	30	43.9	16.0	77.3[d]	68.3[d]	40.8	75.4
92	Mongolia	0.301	65	44	23.6	17.1	91.2	86.3	52.7	66.2
94	Dominican Republic	0.451	103	92	95.0	24.3	58.6	54.4	54.4	79.5
95	Jordan	0.460	108	58	22.4	15.4	81.4	85.8	14.0	63.7
95	Tunisia	0.298	63	62	7.7	31.3	41.2	52.7	24.3	70.6
97	Jamaica	0.412	95	89	52.8	19.0	69.9	62.4	57.3	77.4
98	Tonga	0.416	96	124	14.7	7.7	92.7	92.3	45.2	74.2
99	Saint Vincent and the Grenadines	..	..	45	49.0	13.0	..	..	58.6	80.3
100	Suriname	0.441	99	155	46.0	25.5	58.7	57.8	41.8	65.3
101	Botswana	0.434	98	129	30.0	9.5	88.8[d]	89.6[d]	65.6	78.4
101	Maldives	0.343	76	68	5.8	5.9	44.9[d]	49.3[d]	42.9	82.1
103	Dominica	..	..	..	..	25.0	..	..	..	..
104	Samoa	0.365	82	51	23.9	10.0	79.1	71.6	23.7	38.9
105	Uzbekistan	0.274	59	36	16.5	16.4	99.9	99.9	53.8	77.9
106	Belize	0.386	89	28	63.5	11.1	78.9	78.4	53.2	81.3
106	Marshall Islands	..	..	..	..	9.1	91.6	92.5	..	..
108	Libya	0.170	38	9	5.7	16.0	69.4[d]	45.0[d]	25.8	79.0
108	Turkmenistan	..	..	42	24.4	25.8	..	..	53.4	78.2
110	Gabon	0.534	128	291	95.3	17.4	65.6[d]	49.8[d]	42.9	59.4
110	Paraguay	0.467	113	132	55.7	16.0	47.0	49.2	56.6	83.9
112	Moldova (Republic of)	0.226	48	23	22.0	22.8	95.5	97.4	39.5	45.8
MEDIUM HUMAN DEVELOPMENT										
113	Philippines	0.427	97	114	60.5	29.1	76.6	72.4	49.6	75.1
113	South Africa	0.389	90	138	42.8	41.0[f]	74.2	77.4	47.9	62.0
115	Egypt	0.449	101	33	50.0	14.9	58.2[d]	70.7[d]	22.2	73.7
116	Indonesia	0.453	104	126	47.4	19.8	44.5	53.2	50.7	81.8
116	Viet Nam	0.304	67	54	27.3	26.7	66.2	77.7	73.2	83.5

TABLE 5 Gender Inequality Index | 39

TABLE 5 GENDER INEQUALITY INDEX

		Gender Inequality Index		SDG 3.1 Maternal mortality ratio	SDG 3.7 Adolescent birth rate	SDG 5.5 Share of seats in parliament	SDG 4.6 Population with at least some secondary education (% ages 25 and older)		Labour force participation rate[a] (% ages 15 and older)	
		Value	Rank	(deaths per 100,000 live births)	(births per 1,000 women ages 15–19)	(% held by women)	Female	Male	Female	Male
HDI rank		2017	2017	2015	2015–2020[b]	2017	2010–2017[c]	2010–2017[c]	2017	2017
118	Bolivia (Plurinational State of)	0.450	102	206	68.1	51.8	50.5	59.5	55.2	79.9
119	Palestine, State of	..	..	45	56.2	..	58.5	62.3	19.5	71.8
120	Iraq	0.506	123	50	80.1	25.3	38.7	56.7	18.7	74.1
121	El Salvador	0.392	91	54	69.5	32.1	42.2	47.9	47.0	78.8
122	Kyrgyzstan	0.392	91	76	38.1	19.2	98.6	98.3	48.2	75.7
123	Morocco	0.482	119	121	31.1	18.4	28.0[d]	34.8[d]	25.0	74.1
124	Nicaragua	0.456	106	150	85.4	45.7	48.3[d]	46.6[d]	50.3	84.0
125	Cabo Verde	..	..	42	73.8	20.8[g]	..	..	49.6	71.5
125	Guyana	0.504	122	229	85.8	31.9	70.9[d]	55.5[d]	40.7	74.6
127	Guatemala	0.493	120	88	70.9	12.7	38.4	37.2	40.6	85.0
127	Tajikistan	0.317	69	32	36.4	20.0	98.9[d]	87.0[d]	45.5	73.3
129	Namibia	0.472	115	265	73.8	36.3	39.9[d]	41.0[d]	58.5	65.2
130	India	0.524	127	174	23.1	11.6	39.0	63.5	27.2	78.8
131	Micronesia (Federated States of)	..	..	100	13.9	0.0[h]	..	..	..	..
132	Timor-Leste	..	..	215	44.0	32.3	..	..	24.9	52.3
133	Honduras	0.461	109	129	70.8	25.8[e]	36.8	33.5	50.9	85.8
134	Bhutan	0.476	117	148	20.3	8.3	6.0	13.7	58.0	74.3
134	Kiribati	..	..	90	16.2	6.5	..	..	..	..
136	Bangladesh	0.542	134	176	83.5	20.3	44.0[d]	48.2[d]	33.0	79.8
137	Congo	0.578	143	442	111.8	14.0	46.7[d]	51.0[d]	67.4	72.0
138	Vanuatu	..	..	78	41.9	0.0[h]	..	..	61.5	79.6
139	Lao People's Democratic Republic	0.461	109	197	62.6	27.5	33.6[d]	45.2[d]	76.9	79.7
140	Ghana	0.538	131	319	66.6	12.7	54.6	70.4	74.8	79.2
141	Equatorial Guinea	..	..	342	155.6	19.7[e]	..	..	55.7	61.8
142	Kenya	0.549	137	510	80.5	23.3	29.2	36.6	62.4	68.5
143	Sao Tome and Principe	0.538	131	156	94.8	18.2	31.1	45.2	41.3	75.4
144	Eswatini (Kingdom of)	0.569	141	389	77.0	14.7	30.0[d]	32.7[d]	42.7	67.2
144	Zambia	0.517	125	224	82.8	18.0	39.2[d]	52.4[d]	70.1	79.7
146	Cambodia	0.473	116	161	50.2	18.5	15.1	28.1	80.9	88.7
147	Angola	..	..	477	151.6	30.5	..	..	75.3	80.1
148	Myanmar	0.456	106	178	28.7	10.2	28.7[d]	22.3	51.3	79.9
149	Nepal	0.480	118	258	60.5	29.6	27.3	43.1	82.7	85.9
150	Pakistan	0.541	133	178	36.9	20.0	27.0	47.3	24.9	82.7
151	Cameroon	0.569	141	596	105.8	27.1	32.5	39.2	71.2	81.2
LOW HUMAN DEVELOPMENT										
152	Solomon Islands	..	..	114	46.4	2.0	..	..	62.5	80.3
153	Papua New Guinea	0.741	159	215	52.7	0.0[h]	9.5[d]	15.0[d]	69.0	70.8
154	Tanzania (United Republic of)	0.537	130	398	115.1	37.2	11.9	16.9	79.5	87.4
155	Syrian Arab Republic	0.547	136	68	38.6	13.2	37.1	42.6	11.9	70.2
156	Zimbabwe	0.534	128	443	104.1	36.2	55.9	66.3	78.5	89.1
157	Nigeria	..	..	814	107.3	5.8	..	..	50.4	59.8
158	Rwanda	0.381	85	290	25.7	55.7	12.6	17.0	86.0	86.3
159	Lesotho	0.544	135	487	89.5	22.7	31.8[d]	24.2[d]	59.3	74.4
159	Mauritania	0.617	147	602	79.2	25.2	12.2[d]	24.5[d]	31.0	67.7
161	Madagascar	..	..	353	109.6	19.6	..	..	83.6	89.4
162	Uganda	0.523	126	343	106.5	34.3	26.7	32.4	66.6	74.9
163	Benin	0.611	146	405	86.1	7.2	18.2[d]	32.7[d]	68.7	73.1
164	Senegal	0.515	124	315	72.7	41.8	11.1	20.1	45.5	69.9
165	Comoros	..	..	335	65.4	6.1	..	..	36.0	50.2
165	Togo	0.567	140	368	89.1	17.6	26.3	52.5	75.8	79.4
167	Sudan	0.564	139	311	64.0	31.0	14.7[d]	19.3[d]	23.6	69.9
168	Afghanistan	0.653	153	396	64.5	27.4	11.4[d]	36.9[d]	19.5	86.7
168	Haiti	0.601	144	359	37.5	2.7	26.9[d]	39.9[d]	63.8	72.6
170	Côte d'Ivoire	0.663	155	645	132.7	9.2[i]	17.8	34.1	48.1	66.2
171	Malawi	0.619	148	634	140.2	16.7	16.7[d]	25.4[d]	72.3	81.9
172	Djibouti	..	..	229	18.8	10.8	..	..	49.5	68.5
173	Ethiopia	0.502	121	353	62.5	37.3	11.2	21.4	77.2	87.8
174	Gambia	0.623	149	706	79.2	10.3	29.0[d]	42.3[d]	51.2	67.7
175	Guinea	..	..	679	135.3	21.9	..	..	63.0	65.4

HUMAN DEVELOPMENT INDICES AND INDICATORS: **2018 STATISTICAL UPDATE**

TABLE 5

Gender Inequality Index

		Gender Inequality Index		SDG 3.1 Maternal mortality ratio	SDG 3.7 Adolescent birth rate	SDG 5.5 Share of seats in parliament	SDG 4.6 Population with at least some secondary education		Labour force participation rate[a]	
							(% ages 25 and older)		(% ages 15 and older)	
		Value	Rank	(deaths per 100,000 live births)	(births per 1,000 women ages 15–19)	(% held by women)	Female	Male	Female	Male
HDI rank		2017	2017	2015	2015–2020[b]	2017	2010–2017[c]	2010–2017[c]	2017	2017
176	Congo (Democratic Republic of the)	0.652	152	693	124.2	8.2	36.7	65.8	71.4	73.5
177	Guinea-Bissau	..	..	549	84.5	13.7	..	..	65.6	78.1
178	Yemen	0.834	160	385	60.4	0.5	18.7[d]	34.8[d]	6.0	69.6
179	Eritrea	..	..	501	51.6	22.0	..	..	75.4	87.4
180	Mozambique	0.552	138	489	135.2	39.6	16.1	27.3	82.5	74.6
181	Liberia	0.656	154	725	127.5	9.9	18.5[d]	39.6[d]	53.9	57.4
182	Mali	0.678	157	587	169.1	8.8	7.3	16.4	60.8	82.5
183	Burkina Faso	0.610	145	371	104.3	11.0	6.0	11.7	58.2	75.2
184	Sierra Leone	0.645	150	1,360	112.8	12.4	19.2[d]	32.3[d]	57.1	58.7
185	Burundi	0.471	114	712	26.8	37.8	7.5	10.5	80.2	77.5
186	Chad	0.708	158	856	161.1	12.8	1.7	10.0	64.8	77.6
187	South Sudan	..	..	789	62.0	26.6	..	..	70.8	73.9
188	Central African Republic	0.673	156	882	103.8	8.6	13.2[d]	30.8[d]	63.3	80.0
189	Niger	0.649	151	553	192.0	17.0	4.3[d]	8.9[d]	67.5	90.7
OTHER COUNTRIES OR TERRITORIES										
..	Korea (Democratic People's Rep. of)	..	..	82	0.3	16.3	..	..	74.4	86.9
..	Monaco	..	..	..	..	20.8	..	..	..	..
..	Nauru	..	..	..	..	10.5	..	..	..	..
..	San Marino	..	..	..	..	26.7	..	..	..	..
..	Somalia	..	..	732	100.1	24.3	..	..	18.6	74.3
..	Tuvalu	..	..	..	..	6.7	..	..	..	..
Human development groups										
	Very high human development	0.170	—	15	15.9	26.7	88.8	89.5	52.9	68.9
	High human development	0.289	—	38	26.6	22.3	69.5	75.7	55.0	75.5
	Medium human development	0.489	—	176	41.3	21.8	42.9	59.4	36.8	78.9
	Low human development	0.586	—	554	98.4	21.7	18.5	30.7	59.3	74.7
Developing countries		0.468	—	232	48.0	21.9	54.6	65.5	47.5	77.0
Regions										
	Arab States	0.531	—	149	46.3	18.0	45.1	54.6	20.7	74.2
	East Asia and the Pacific	0.312	—	62	22.4	19.8	67.8	75.5	60.1	77.3
	Europe and Central Asia	0.270	—	24	25.5	20.7	78.4	85.9	45.5	70.3
	Latin America and the Caribbean	0.386	—	67	61.5	28.8	59.5	59.1	51.6	77.5
	South Asia	0.515	—	176	32.1	17.5	39.8	60.6	27.9	79.1
	Sub-Saharan Africa	0.569	—	549	101.3	23.5	28.8	39.2	65.2	74.0
Least developed countries		0.559	—	434[T]	91.0	22.4	25.0	34.3	57.4	79.6
Small island developing states		0.459	—	202	56.5	23.4	56.7	58.8	53.8	72.4
Organisation for Economic Co-operation and Development		0.186	—	15	20.7	28.9	84.6	87.3	51.3	68.6
World		0.441	—	216[T]	44.0	23.5	62.5	70.9	48.7	75.3

NOTES

a Estimates modelled by the International Labour Organization.
b Data are the annual average of projected values for 2015–2020.
c Data refer to the most recent year available during the period specified.
d Based on Barro and Lee (2016).
e Refers to 2016.
f Excludes the 36 special rotating delegates appointed on an ad hoc basis.
g Refers to 2013.
h In calculating the Gender Inequality Index, a value of 0.1 percent was used.
i Refers to 2015.
T From original data source.

DEFINITIONS

Gender Inequality Index: A composite measure reflecting inequality in achievement between women and men in three dimensions: reproductive health, empowerment and the labour market. See *Technical note 4* at http://hdr.undp.org/sites/default/files/hdr2018_technical_notes.pdf for details on how the Gender Inequality Index is calculated.

Maternal mortality ratio: Number of deaths due to pregnancy-related causes per 100,000 live births.

Adolescent birth rate: Number of births to women ages 15–19 per 1,000 women ages 15–19.

Share of seats in parliament: Proportion of seats held by women in the national parliament expressed as a percentage of total seats. For countries with a bicameral legislative system, the share of seats is calculated based on both houses.

Population with at least some secondary education: Percentage of the population ages 25 and older that has reached (but not necessarily completed) a secondary level of education.

Labour force participation rate: Proportion of the working-age population (ages 15 and older) that engages in the labour market, either by working or actively looking for work, expressed as a percentage of the working-age population.

MAIN DATA SOURCES

Column 1: HDRO calculations based on data in columns 3–9.
Column 2: Calculated based on data in column 1.
Column 3: UN Maternal Mortality Estimation Group (2017).
Column 4: UNDESA (2017a).
Column 5: IPU (2018).
Columns 6 and 7: UNESCO Institute for Statistics (2018) and Barro and Lee (2016).
Columns 8 and 9: ILO (2018a).

Human development indicators

TABLE 7

Population trends

		Population							Dependency ratio		Total fertility rate	
	Total		Average annual growth		Urban[a]	Under age 5	Ages 15–64	Ages 65 and older	Median age	(per 100 people ages 15–64)			
										Young age (0–14)	Old age (65 and older)		
	(millions)		(%)		(%)	(millions)			(years)			(births per woman)	
HDI rank	2017[b]	2030[b]	2005/2010	2015/2020[b]	2017	2017[b]	2017[b]	2017[b]	2015	2017[b]	2017[b]	2005/2010	2015/2020
VERY HIGH HUMAN DEVELOPMENT													
1 Norway[c]	5.3	6.0	1.1	0.9	81.9	0.3	3.5	0.9	39.2	27.2	25.7	1.9	1.8
2 Switzerland	8.5	9.2	1.1	0.8	73.8	0.4	5.7	1.6	42.2	22.3	27.6	1.5	1.6
3 Australia[d]	24.5	28.2	1.8	1.3	85.9	1.6	16.0	3.8	37.4	29.0	23.7	2.0	1.8
4 Ireland	4.8	5.2	1.9	0.8	62.9	0.3	3.1	0.7	36.9	33.6	21.6	2.0	2.0
5 Germany	82.1	82.2	−0.2	0.2	77.3	3.6	53.8	17.6	45.9	20.0	32.8	1.4	1.5
6 Iceland	0.3	0.4	1.6	0.8	93.8	0.0	0.2	0.0	36.0	30.7	22.0	2.1	1.9
7 Hong Kong, China (SAR)	7.4	8.0	0.6	0.8	100.0	0.3	5.3	1.2	43.2	15.9	22.6	1.0	1.3
7 Sweden	9.9	10.7	0.8	0.7	87.1	0.6	6.2	2.0	40.9	28.1	32.0	1.9	1.9
9 Singapore	5.7	6.3	2.4	1.4	100.0	0.3	4.1	0.7	40.0	20.8	17.9	1.3	1.3
10 Netherlands	17.0	17.6	0.4	0.3	91.1	0.9	11.0	3.2	42.1	25.3	29.0	1.8	1.8
11 Denmark	5.7	6.0	0.5	0.4	87.8	0.3	3.7	1.1	41.6	25.8	30.8	1.9	1.8
12 Canada	36.6	40.6	1.1	0.9	81.4	1.9	24.5	6.2	40.5	23.9	25.4	1.6	1.6
13 United States	324.5	354.7	0.9	0.7	82.1	19.7	213.1	50.0	37.6	28.8	23.5	2.1	1.9
14 United Kingdom	66.2	70.6	1.0	0.6	83.1	4.0	42.2	12.3	40.2	27.8	29.0	1.9	1.9
15 Finland[e]	5.5	5.7	0.4	0.4	85.3	0.3	3.4	1.2	42.5	26.3	34.0	1.8	1.8
16 New Zealand	4.7	5.2	1.1	0.9	86.5	0.3	3.1	0.7	37.3	30.5	23.6	2.1	2.0
17 Belgium	11.4	12.0	0.7	0.6	98.0	0.6	7.4	2.1	41.3	26.6	28.9	1.8	1.8
17 Liechtenstein	0.0	0.0	0.7	0.7	14.3	..	..	..	..	..	..	..	..
19 Japan	127.5	121.6	0.0	−0.2	91.5	5.3	76.6	34.5	46.3	21.5	45.0	1.3	1.5
20 Austria	8.7	8.9	0.4	0.2	58.1	0.4	5.8	1.7	43.2	21.1	28.8	1.4	1.5
21 Luxembourg	0.6	0.7	2.1	1.3	90.7	0.0	0.4	0.1	39.3	23.7	20.7	1.6	1.6
22 Israel	8.3	10.0	2.3	1.5	92.3	0.8	5.0	1.0	30.2	46.1	19.4	2.9	2.9
22 Korea (Republic of)	51.0	52.7	0.3	0.4	81.5	2.2	37.0	7.1	40.8	18.6	19.2	1.2	1.3
24 France	65.0	67.9	0.6	0.4	80.2	3.8	40.4	12.8	41.2	29.1	31.7	2.0	2.0
25 Slovenia	2.1	2.1	0.5	0.1	54.3	0.1	1.4	0.4	43.0	22.7	28.9	1.4	1.6
26 Spain[f]	46.4	46.1	1.2	0.0	80.1	2.0	30.5	9.0	43.2	22.3	29.5	1.4	1.4
27 Czechia	10.6	10.5	0.5	0.1	73.7	0.5	7.0	2.0	41.4	23.4	29.0	1.4	1.6
28 Italy	59.4	58.1	0.3	−0.1	70.1	2.4	37.7	13.7	45.9	21.3	36.3	1.4	1.5
29 Malta	0.4	0.4	0.5	0.3	94.5	0.0	0.3	0.1	40.9	21.8	29.4	1.4	1.5
30 Estonia	1.3	1.3	−0.4	−0.2	68.7	0.1	0.8	0.3	41.6	25.5	30.3	1.7	1.7
31 Greece	11.2	10.8	0.3	−0.2	78.7	0.5	7.3	2.3	43.3	21.7	31.2	1.5	1.3
32 Cyprus[g]	1.2	1.3	1.6	0.8	66.8	0.1	0.8	0.2	34.9	24.1	19.2	1.5	1.3
33 Poland	38.2	36.6	0.0	−0.2	60.1	1.8	26.1	6.4	39.7	21.7	24.5	1.4	1.3
34 United Arab Emirates	9.4	11.1	11.8	1.4	86.2	0.5	8.0	0.1	33.4	16.4	1.3	2.0	1.7
35 Andorra	0.1	0.1	1.4	−0.2	88.2	..	..	..	..	..	..	..	..
35 Lithuania	2.9	2.7	−1.4	−0.5	67.5	0.2	1.9	0.5	42.7	22.4	28.7	1.4	1.7
37 Qatar	2.6	3.2	14.4	2.4	99.1	0.1	2.2	0.0	31.3	16.4	1.5	2.2	1.9
38 Slovakia	5.4	5.4	0.0	0.0	53.8	0.3	3.8	0.8	39.2	22.1	21.7	1.3	1.5
39 Brunei Darussalam	0.4	0.5	1.2	1.3	77.3	0.0	0.3	0.0	30.0	31.8	6.3	1.8	1.9
39 Saudi Arabia	32.9	39.5	2.7	1.9	83.6	3.0	23.6	1.1	29.8	35.2	4.6	3.2	2.5
41 Latvia	1.9	1.7	−1.2	−1.0	68.1	0.1	1.3	0.4	42.5	23.8	30.5	1.5	1.6
41 Portugal	10.3	9.9	0.2	−0.4	64.7	0.4	6.7	2.2	43.9	21.0	33.2	1.4	1.2
43 Bahrain	1.5	2.0	6.7	4.3	89.2	0.1	1.2	0.0	31.2	25.3	3.0	2.3	2.0
44 Chile	18.1	19.6	1.0	0.8	87.5	1.2	12.4	2.0	33.7	29.6	16.2	1.9	1.8
45 Hungary	9.7	9.2	−0.3	−0.3	71.1	0.4	6.5	1.8	41.7	21.3	27.7	1.3	1.4
46 Croatia	4.2	3.9	−0.2	−0.6	56.7	0.2	2.7	0.8	42.6	22.4	30.1	1.5	1.5
47 Argentina	44.3	49.3	1.0	0.9	91.7	3.7	28.3	5.0	30.8	38.9	17.5	2.4	2.3
48 Oman	4.6	5.9	3.8	4.1	83.6	0.4	3.5	0.1	29.0	28.8	3.1	2.9	2.5
49 Russian Federation	144.0	140.5	−0.1	0.0	74.3	9.5	98.2	20.4	38.7	25.8	20.8	1.4	1.8
50 Montenegro	0.6	0.6	0.3	0.0	66.5	0.0	0.4	0.1	37.7	27.0	22.0	1.8	1.7
51 Bulgaria	7.1	6.4	−0.7	−0.7	74.7	0.3	4.6	1.5	43.5	21.9	32.0	1.5	1.6
52 Romania	19.7	18.5	−0.9	−0.5	53.9	0.9	13.2	3.5	41.3	22.8	26.7	1.5	1.5
53 Belarus	9.5	9.2	−0.3	−0.1	78.1	0.6	6.5	1.4	39.6	24.5	21.6	1.4	1.7
54 Bahamas	0.4	0.4	1.8	1.0	82.9	0.0	0.3	0.0	32.5	29.0	12.8	1.9	1.8
55 Uruguay	3.5	3.6	0.3	0.4	95.2	0.2	2.2	0.5	34.9	32.8	22.8	2.1	2.0
56 Kuwait	4.1	4.9	5.5	1.8	100.0	0.3	3.2	0.1	33.4	27.5	3.1	2.4	2.0
57 Malaysia[h]	31.6	36.8	1.8	1.4	75.4	2.6	21.9	2.0	27.7	35.0	9.1	2.2	2.0
58 Barbados	0.3	0.3	0.4	0.2	31.2	0.0	0.2	0.0	38.5	28.9	22.7	1.8	1.8
58 Kazakhstan	18.2	20.3	1.1	1.1	57.3	2.0	11.8	1.3	29.3	42.9	10.7	2.5	2.6

HUMAN DEVELOPMENT INDICES AND INDICATORS: 2018 STATISTICAL UPDATE

		Population							Dependency ratio			
	Total		Average annual growth		Urban[a]	Under age 5	Ages 15–64	Ages 65 and older	Median age	(per 100 people ages 15–64)		Total fertility rate	
	(millions)		(%)		(%)	(millions)			(years)	Young age (0–14)	Old age (65 and older)	(births per woman)	
HDI rank	2017[b]	2030[b]	2005/2010	2015/2020[b]	2017	2017[b]	2017[b]	2017[b]	2015	2017[b]	2017[b]	2005/2010	2015/2020
HIGH HUMAN DEVELOPMENT													
60 Iran (Islamic Republic of)	81.2	88.9	1.1	1.0	74.4	6.7	57.5	4.4	29.5	33.4	7.7	1.8	1.6
60 Palau	0.0	0.0	0.6	1.1	79.4	..	..	..	..	..	..	..	..
62 Seychelles	0.1	0.1	0.6	0.5	56.3	0.0	0.1	0.0	34.6	32.2	12.4	2.3	2.3
63 Costa Rica	4.9	5.4	1.4	1.0	78.6	0.3	3.4	0.5	31.4	31.4	13.7	2.0	1.8
64 Turkey	80.7	88.4	1.3	1.4	74.6	6.7	54.0	6.6	29.9	37.3	12.2	2.2	2.0
65 Mauritius[i]	1.3	1.3	0.4	0.2	40.8	0.1	0.9	0.1	35.6	26.0	15.5	1.7	1.4
66 Panama	4.1	4.9	1.8	1.6	67.4	0.4	2.7	0.3	28.4	42.3	12.2	2.6	2.5
67 Serbia[j]	8.8	8.4	−0.4	−0.3	55.9	0.5	5.8	1.5	40.0	24.9	26.2	1.6	1.6
68 Albania	2.9	2.9	−0.9	0.1	59.4	0.2	2.0	0.4	36.2	25.1	19.0	1.6	1.7
69 Trinidad and Tobago	1.4	1.4	0.5	0.3	53.2	0.1	0.9	0.1	33.9	29.8	14.4	1.8	1.7
70 Antigua and Barbuda	0.1	0.1	1.2	1.0	24.7	0.0	0.1	0.0	30.7	34.5	10.0	2.2	2.0
70 Georgia[k]	3.9	3.7	−1.2	−0.3	58.2	0.3	2.6	0.6	38.0	29.1	22.5	1.8	2.0
72 Saint Kitts and Nevis	0.1	0.1	1.1	0.9	30.8	..	..	..	..	..	..	..	..
73 Cuba	11.5	11.5	0.1	0.1	77.0	0.6	8.0	1.7	41.1	23.2	21.3	1.6	1.7
74 Mexico	129.2	147.5	1.6	1.2	79.9	11.5	85.9	8.9	27.5	40.1	10.3	2.4	2.1
75 Grenada	0.1	0.1	0.3	0.5	36.2	0.0	0.1	0.0	27.2	39.7	11.0	2.3	2.1
76 Sri Lanka	20.9	21.5	0.7	0.4	18.4	1.6	13.8	2.1	32.3	36.4	15.3	2.3	2.0
77 Bosnia and Herzegovina	3.5	3.4	−0.3	−0.2	47.9	0.2	2.4	0.6	41.0	20.4	23.9	1.3	1.4
78 Venezuela (Bolivarian Republic of)	32.0	36.7	1.6	1.3	88.2	3.0	21.0	2.1	27.4	41.9	10.1	2.6	2.3
79 Brazil	209.3	225.5	1.0	0.8	86.3	14.8	145.9	17.9	31.3	31.2	12.3	1.9	1.7
80 Azerbaijan[l]	9.8	10.7	1.1	1.0	55.3	0.9	6.9	0.6	30.3	32.9	8.5	1.8	2.0
80 Lebanon	6.1	5.4	1.7	0.6	88.4	0.5	4.2	0.5	28.5	33.8	12.4	1.6	1.7
80 The former Yugoslav Republic of Macedonia	2.1	2.1	0.1	0.1	57.7	0.1	1.5	0.3	37.4	23.8	18.9	1.5	1.6
83 Armenia	2.9	2.9	−0.7	0.1	63.1	0.2	2.0	0.3	33.9	29.1	16.3	1.7	1.6
83 Thailand	69.0	69.6	0.5	0.2	49.2	3.7	49.2	7.9	37.8	24.3	15.9	1.6	1.5
85 Algeria	41.3	48.8	1.6	1.7	72.1	4.7	26.7	2.6	27.5	45.4	9.6	2.7	2.7
86 China	1,409.5	1,441.2	0.6	0.4	58.0	85.1	1,010.4	150.0	37.0	24.7	14.8	1.6	1.6
86 Ecuador	16.6	19.6	1.7	1.4	63.7	1.6	10.7	1.2	26.6	44.1	11.0	2.7	2.4
88 Ukraine[m]	44.2	41.2	−0.5	−0.5	69.2	2.3	30.1	7.3	40.3	22.8	24.2	1.4	1.6
89 Peru	32.2	36.8	1.2	1.2	77.7	3.0	21.1	2.3	27.5	41.8	10.9	2.6	2.4
90 Colombia	49.1	53.1	1.2	0.8	80.4	3.7	33.8	3.8	30.1	34.1	11.1	2.1	1.8
90 Saint Lucia	0.2	0.2	1.1	0.4	18.6	0.0	0.1	0.0	32.6	26.4	13.6	1.6	1.4
92 Fiji	0.9	1.0	0.9	0.7	55.7	0.1	0.6	0.1	27.6	43.6	9.5	2.8	2.5
92 Mongolia	3.1	3.6	1.4	1.5	68.4	0.4	2.0	0.1	27.1	44.7	6.1	2.4	2.7
94 Dominican Republic	10.8	12.1	1.4	1.1	80.3	1.1	6.9	0.8	26.1	46.0	11.0	2.7	2.4
95 Jordan	9.7	11.1	4.6	2.2	90.7	1.2	5.9	0.4	22.1	58.5	6.3	3.7	3.3
95 Tunisia	11.5	12.8	1.0	1.1	68.6	1.1	7.8	0.9	31.1	35.3	11.8	2.0	2.2
97 Jamaica	2.9	2.9	0.5	0.3	55.4	0.2	2.0	0.3	29.4	33.6	14.3	2.3	2.0
98 Tonga	0.1	0.1	0.6	0.9	23.2	0.0	0.1	0.0	21.3	61.4	10.0	4.0	3.6
99 Saint Vincent and the Grenadines	0.1	0.1	0.1	0.2	51.8	0.0	0.1	0.0	29.8	34.7	11.3	2.1	1.9
100 Suriname	0.6	0.6	1.1	0.9	66.0	0.1	0.4	0.0	28.4	39.7	10.4	2.6	2.3
101 Botswana	2.3	2.8	1.6	1.8	68.7	0.3	1.5	0.1	24.4	48.6	6.1	2.9	2.7
101 Maldives	0.4	0.5	2.7	1.8	39.4	0.0	0.3	0.0	27.9	32.3	5.7	2.3	2.0
103 Dominica	0.1	0.1	0.2	0.5	70.2	..	..	..	..	..	..	..	..
104 Samoa	0.2	0.2	0.7	0.6	18.5	0.0	0.1	0.0	21.2	63.3	9.7	4.5	3.9
105 Uzbekistan	31.9	36.7	1.5	1.4	50.6	3.2	21.6	1.4	26.3	41.4	6.6	2.5	2.2
106 Belize	0.4	0.5	2.5	2.0	45.6	0.0	0.2	0.0	23.5	48.5	6.0	2.8	2.5
106 Marshall Islands	0.1	0.1	0.1	0.1	76.6	..	..	..	..	..	..	..	..
108 Libya	6.4	7.3	1.3	1.3	79.8	0.6	4.3	0.3	27.2	41.8	6.6	2.4	2.2
108 Turkmenistan	5.8	6.8	1.4	1.6	51.2	0.7	3.7	0.2	25.6	47.7	6.6	2.7	2.8
110 Gabon	2.0	2.6	3.1	2.2	89.0	0.3	1.2	0.1	22.6	60.2	7.5	4.2	3.7
110 Paraguay	6.8	7.8	1.4	1.2	61.3	0.7	4.4	0.4	24.9	45.8	9.9	2.9	2.5
112 Moldova (Republic of)[n]	4.1	3.8	−0.4	−0.2	42.6	0.2	3.0	0.4	35.6	21.4	14.8	1.3	1.2
MEDIUM HUMAN DEVELOPMENT													
113 Philippines	104.9	125.4	1.7	1.5	46.7	11.6	66.6	5.0	24.1	50.0	7.6	3.3	2.9
113 South Africa	56.7	64.5	1.1	1.2	65.8	5.7	37.2	3.0	26.1	44.1	8.1	2.6	2.4
115 Egypt	97.6	119.7	1.8	1.9	42.7	12.9	59.9	5.0	24.7	54.5	8.4	3.0	3.2
116 Indonesia	264.0	295.6	1.3	1.1	54.7	24.7	177.7	14.0	28.0	40.6	7.9	2.5	2.3
116 Viet Nam	95.5	106.3	1.0	1.0	35.2	7.7	66.7	6.8	30.4	33.0	10.2	1.9	2.0

TABLE 7 Population trends | 45

TABLE 7 POPULATION TRENDS

		Population							Dependency ratio			
	Total		Average annual growth		Urban[a]	Under age 5	Ages 15–64	Ages 65 and older	Median age	(per 100 people ages 15–64)		Total fertility rate
										Young age (0–14)	Old age (65 and older)	
	(millions)		(%)		(%)	(millions)			(years)			(births per woman)
HDI rank	2017[b]	2030[b]	2005/2010	2015/2020[b]	2017	2017[b]	2017[b]	2017[b]	2015	2017[b]	2017[b]	2005/2010	2015/2020
118 Bolivia (Plurinational State of)	11.1	13.2	1.7	1.5	69.1	1.2	6.8	0.7	24.1	51.3	10.9	3.4	2.8
119 Palestine, State of[o]	4.9	6.7	2.6	2.6	75.9	0.7	2.8	0.1	19.3	69.0	5.3	4.6	3.9
120 Iraq	38.3	53.3	2.6	2.8	70.3	5.8	21.6	1.2	19.4	71.6	5.6	4.6	4.3
121 El Salvador	6.4	6.8	0.4	0.5	71.3	0.6	4.1	0.5	25.8	42.5	12.9	2.4	2.1
122 Kyrgyzstan	6.0	7.0	1.3	1.4	36.1	0.9	3.8	0.3	25.3	50.0	7.1	2.8	2.9
123 Morocco	35.7	40.9	1.2	1.3	61.9	3.5	23.5	2.4	27.9	41.6	10.3	2.6	2.4
124 Nicaragua	6.2	7.0	1.3	1.1	58.3	0.6	4.1	0.3	25.2	44.3	8.3	2.6	2.2
125 Cabo Verde	0.5	0.6	1.1	1.3	65.3	0.1	0.4	0.0	23.8	46.2	6.8	2.9	2.3
125 Guyana	0.8	0.8	–0.1	0.6	26.5	0.1	0.5	0.0	24.6	44.1	8.1	2.7	2.5
127 Guatemala	16.9	21.2	2.2	1.9	50.7	2.0	10.2	0.8	21.3	58.2	7.8	3.6	2.9
127 Tajikistan	8.9	11.2	2.2	2.1	27.0	1.2	5.5	0.3	22.4	57.5	5.7	3.5	3.3
129 Namibia	2.5	3.2	1.3	2.1	49.0	0.3	1.5	0.1	21.0	61.4	5.9	3.6	3.3
130 India	1,339.2	1,513.0	1.5	1.1	33.6	119.8	886.9	80.2	26.7	42.0	9.0	2.8	2.3
131 Micronesia (Federated States of)	0.1	0.1	–0.5	0.6	22.6	0.0	0.1	0.0	21.5	53.4	7.7	3.6	3.1
132 Timor-Leste	1.3	1.7	1.6	2.1	30.2	0.2	0.7	0.0	17.4	82.5	6.7	6.5	5.3
133 Honduras	9.3	11.1	2.1	1.6	56.5	1.0	5.9	0.4	23.0	49.7	7.3	3.2	2.4
134 Bhutan	0.8	0.9	2.1	1.2	40.2	0.1	0.6	0.0	26.3	38.7	7.1	2.6	2.0
134 Kiribati	0.1	0.1	2.1	1.7	53.3	0.0	0.1	0.0	22.4	57.3	6.4	3.9	3.6
136 Bangladesh	164.7	185.6	1.2	1.0	35.9	15.2	109.6	8.4	25.6	42.6	7.7	2.5	2.1
137 Congo	5.3	7.3	3.3	2.6	66.5	0.8	2.9	0.2	18.9	77.8	6.3	5.0	4.6
138 Vanuatu	0.3	0.4	2.4	2.1	25.2	0.0	0.2	0.0	22.2	60.1	7.4	3.6	3.2
139 Lao People's Democratic Republic	6.9	8.0	1.6	1.4	34.4	0.8	4.3	0.3	22.7	52.1	6.4	3.4	2.6
140 Ghana	28.8	37.3	2.6	2.2	55.4	4.1	16.8	1.0	20.4	66.3	5.8	4.4	3.9
141 Equatorial Guinea	1.3	1.9	4.6	3.6	71.6	0.2	0.8	0.0	22.2	62.0	4.7	5.4	4.6
142 Kenya	49.7	67.0	2.7	2.5	26.6	7.1	28.3	1.3	19.0	71.2	4.7	4.7	3.8
143 Sao Tome and Principe	0.2	0.3	2.3	2.2	72.0	0.0	0.1	0.0	18.1	78.9	5.3	4.9	4.4
144 Eswatini (Kingdom of)	1.4	1.7	1.7	1.7	23.6	0.2	0.8	0.0	20.4	62.3	5.3	3.8	3.0
144 Zambia	17.1	24.9	2.8	3.0	43.0	2.9	9.0	0.4	17.1	84.9	4.7	5.6	4.9
146 Cambodia	16.0	18.8	1.5	1.5	23.0	1.8	10.3	0.7	24.0	48.6	6.9	3.1	2.5
147 Angola	29.8	44.7	3.6	3.3	64.8	5.4	15.1	0.7	16.4	92.2	4.7	6.4	5.6
148 Myanmar	53.4	58.9	0.7	0.9	30.3	4.5	36.0	3.1	27.7	39.8	8.5	2.6	2.2
149 Nepal	29.3	33.2	1.1	1.1	19.3	2.7	18.5	1.7	23.2	48.8	9.2	3.0	2.1
150 Pakistan	197.0	244.2	2.1	1.9	36.4	25.1	119.6	8.9	22.5	57.3	7.4	4.0	3.4
151 Cameroon	24.1	33.0	2.7	2.6	55.8	3.9	13.0	0.8	18.3	79.0	5.8	5.3	4.6
LOW HUMAN DEVELOPMENT													
152 Solomon Islands	0.6	0.8	2.3	1.9	23.3	0.1	0.4	0.0	19.9	67.4	6.1	4.4	3.8
153 Papua New Guinea	8.3	10.5	2.4	2.0	13.1	1.0	5.0	0.3	21.7	59.6	6.3	4.1	3.6
154 Tanzania (United Republic of)[p]	57.3	83.7	3.1	3.1	33.1	9.9	29.8	1.8	17.3	86.4	6.0	5.6	4.9
155 Syrian Arab Republic	18.3	26.6	2.8	0.2	53.5	2.0	10.8	0.8	20.2	61.9	7.4	3.4	2.8
156 Zimbabwe	16.5	21.5	1.7	2.3	32.2	2.5	9.3	0.5	19.0	73.6	5.0	4.0	3.6
157 Nigeria	190.9	264.1	2.6	2.6	49.5	32.4	101.7	5.3	17.9	82.6	5.2	5.9	5.4
158 Rwanda	12.2	16.0	2.6	2.4	17.1	1.7	6.9	0.4	19.4	70.6	5.2	4.9	3.8
159 Lesotho	2.2	2.6	0.9	1.3	27.7	0.3	1.3	0.1	21.3	58.9	7.5	3.4	3.0
159 Mauritania	4.4	6.1	2.8	2.7	52.8	0.7	2.5	0.1	19.7	70.1	5.5	5.1	4.6
161 Madagascar	25.6	35.6	2.9	2.7	36.5	3.8	14.3	0.7	18.7	73.0	5.2	4.8	4.1
162 Uganda	42.9	63.8	3.4	3.2	23.2	7.9	21.5	0.9	15.8	95.2	4.3	6.4	5.5
163 Benin	11.2	15.6	2.8	2.7	46.8	1.8	6.0	0.4	18.2	78.9	6.0	5.5	4.9
164 Senegal	15.9	22.1	2.8	2.8	46.7	2.6	8.6	0.5	18.3	79.2	5.6	5.1	4.7
165 Comoros	0.8	1.1	2.4	2.2	28.8	0.1	0.5	0.0	19.7	69.5	5.2	4.9	4.2
165 Togo	7.8	10.5	2.7	2.5	41.2	1.2	4.3	0.2	18.9	74.8	5.1	5.0	4.4
167 Sudan	40.5	54.8	2.1	2.4	34.4	6.0	22.5	1.4	18.9	73.4	6.4	5.0	4.4
168 Afghanistan	35.5	46.7	2.8	2.4	25.2	5.3	19.2	0.9	17.3	79.8	4.8	6.4	4.4
168 Haiti	11.0	12.5	1.5	1.2	54.3	1.2	6.8	0.5	23.0	53.0	7.7	3.6	2.9
170 Côte d'Ivoire	24.3	33.3	2.1	2.5	50.3	3.9	13.3	0.7	18.3	77.7	5.4	5.4	4.8
171 Malawi	18.6	26.6	3.0	2.9	16.7	3.0	9.9	0.6	17.4	82.9	5.6	5.7	4.5
172 Djibouti	1.0	1.1	1.7	1.5	77.6	0.1	0.6	0.0	23.7	48.0	6.5	3.6	2.8
173 Ethiopia	105.0	139.6	2.7	2.4	20.3	15.4	58.7	3.7	18.6	72.5	6.3	5.3	4.0
174 Gambia	2.1	3.0	3.2	3.0	60.6	0.4	1.1	0.0	17.0	86.6	4.5	5.8	5.3
175 Guinea	12.7	17.6	2.2	2.6	35.8	2.0	6.9	0.4	18.4	77.4	5.7	5.5	4.7
176 Congo (Democratic Republic of the)	81.3	120.4	3.3	3.2	43.9	14.8	41.2	2.5	16.8	91.3	6.0	6.6	6.0
177 Guinea-Bissau	1.9	2.5	2.4	2.4	42.9	0.3	1.0	0.1	18.9	74.8	5.4	5.2	4.5

HUMAN DEVELOPMENT INDICES AND INDICATORS: 2018 STATISTICAL UPDATE

		Population							Dependency ratio		Total fertility rate	
	Total	Average annual growth		Urban[a]	Under age 5	Ages 15–64	Ages 65 and older	Median age	(per 100 people ages 15–64)			
	(millions)	(%)		(%)	(millions)			(years)	Young age (0–14)	Old age (65 and older)	(births per woman)	
HDI rank	2017[b]	2030[b]	2005/2010	2015/2020[b]	2017	2017[b]	2017[b]	2017[b]	2015	2017[b]	2017[b]	2005/2010	2015/2020
178 Yemen	28.3	36.8	2.7	2.3	36.0	4.1	16.1	0.8	19.2	69.8	5.1	5.0	3.8
179 Eritrea	5.1	6.7	2.0	2.3	39.5	0.7	2.8	0.2	18.9	76.5	6.6	4.8	4.0
180 Mozambique	29.7	42.4	2.9	2.9	35.5	5.0	15.4	0.9	17.2	86.1	6.1	5.7	5.1
181 Liberia	4.7	6.5	3.8	2.5	50.7	0.7	2.6	0.1	18.6	75.8	5.5	5.2	4.5
182 Mali	18.5	27.1	3.3	3.0	41.6	3.4	9.2	0.5	16.0	95.8	5.1	6.7	5.9
183 Burkina Faso	19.2	27.4	3.0	2.9	28.7	3.3	10.1	0.5	17.0	86.2	4.6	6.1	5.2
184 Sierra Leone	7.6	9.7	2.6	2.1	41.6	1.1	4.2	0.2	18.3	76.0	4.6	5.6	4.3
185 Burundi	10.9	15.8	3.3	3.2	12.7	2.0	5.7	0.3	17.6	85.8	4.9	6.5	5.6
186 Chad	14.9	21.5	3.3	3.0	22.9	2.7	7.5	0.4	16.1	93.6	4.9	6.9	5.8
187 South Sudan	12.6	17.3[T]	4.3	2.7	19.3	2.0	6.9	0.4	18.6	75.9	6.3	5.6	4.7
188 Central African Republic	4.7	6.1	1.5	1.6	41.0	0.7	2.5	0.2	17.8	81.3	6.9	5.3	4.8
189 Niger	21.5	35.0	3.7	3.8	16.4	4.4	10.1	0.5	14.9	106.2	5.4	7.6	7.2
OTHER COUNTRIES OR TERRITORIES													
.. Korea (Democratic People's Rep. of)	25.5	26.7	0.6	0.5	61.7	1.7	17.8	2.4	34.0	29.5	13.6	2.0	1.9
.. Monaco	0.0	0.0	1.9	0.5	100.0	..	..	..	..	..	..	..	..
.. Nauru	0.0	0.0	−0.2	−0.1	100.0	..	..	..	..	..	..	..	..
.. San Marino	0.0	0.0	1.2	0.5	97.1	..	..	..	..	..	..	..	..
.. Somalia	14.7	21.5	2.9	2.9	44.4	2.7	7.5	0.4	16.5	91.3	5.4	7.1	6.1
.. Tuvalu	0.0	0.0	1.0	0.9	61.5	..	..	..	..	..	..	..	..
Human development groups													
Very high human development	1,439.3	1,503.3	0.7	0.4	80.1	82.9	948.3	242.5	39.7	26.2	25.6	1.7	1.8
High human development	2,378.9	2,497.0	0.8	0.6	64.3	162.9	1,669.6	230.1	34.4	28.7	13.8	1.8	1.8
Medium human development	2,732.9	3,177.5	1.5	1.3	39.5	275.4	1,772.4	149.1	25.7	45.8	8.4	3.0	2.6
Low human development	926.2	1,291.2	2.8	2.6	35.9	150.7	497.5	27.9	17.9	80.6	5.6	5.6	4.9
Developing countries	6,259.9	7,220.8	1.4	1.3	49.7	608.2	4,090.4	423.7	28.1	42.7	10.4	2.8	2.6
Regions													
Arab States	409.5	513.6	2.5	1.9	58.6	50.4	255.9	18.4	24.3	52.8	7.2	3.5	3.2
East Asia and the Pacific	2,091.4	2,205.9	0.8	0.6	54.7	146.2	1,470.1	192.8	34.3	29.1	13.1	1.8	1.9
Europe and Central Asia	243.9	259.3	0.7	0.8	63.0	19.9	163.7	23.6	32.2	34.6	14.4	2.0	2.0
Latin America and the Caribbean	640.2	713.1	1.3	1.0	80.3	53.1	429.2	51.2	29.2	37.2	11.9	2.3	2.0
South Asia	1,869.0	2,134.4	1.5	1.2	35.3	176.5	1,226.1	106.6	26.1	43.7	8.7	2.9	2.4
Sub-Saharan Africa	1,005.8	1,394.4	2.8	2.7	39.7	162.2	545.4	30.9	18.3	78.7	5.7	5.4	4.7
Least developed countries	1,002.5	1,334.2	2.4	2.3	33.0	145.1	569.4	36.1	19.9	69.7	6.3	4.7	4.1
Small island developing states	57.4	64.8	1.2	1.1	55.3	5.6	36.6	4.3	27.9	44.4	11.8	2.9	2.7
Organisation for Economic Co-operation and Development	1,292.6	1,363.4	0.7	0.5	80.4	75.7	843.4	217.2	39.0	27.5	25.8	1.8	1.8
World	7,550.3[T]	8,551.2[T]	1.2[T]	1.1[T]	54.8[T]	677.9[T]	4,936.6[T]	656.8[T]	29.6[T]	39.6[T]	13.3[T]	2.6[T]	2.5[T]

NOTES

a Because data are based on national definitions of what constitutes a city or metropolitan area, cross-country comparison should be made with caution.
b Projections based on medium-fertility variant.
c Includes Svalbard and Jan Mayen Islands.
d Includes Christmas Island, Cocos (Keeling) Islands and Norfolk Island.
e Includes Åland Islands.
f Includes Canary Islands, Ceuta and Melilla.
g Includes Northern Cyprus.
h Includes Sabah and Sarawak.
i Includes Agalega, Rodrigues and Saint Brandon.
j Includes Kosovo.
k Includes Abkhazia and South Ossetia.
l Includes Nagorno-Karabakh.
m Includes Crimea.
n Includes Transnistria.
o Includes East Jerusalem.
p Includes Zanzibar.
T From original data source.

DEFINITIONS

Total population: De facto population in a country, area or region as of 1 July.

Population average annual growth: Average annual exponential growth rate for the period specified.

Urban population: De facto population living in areas classified as urban according to the criteria used by each country or area as of 1 July.

Population under age 5: De facto population in a country, area or region under age 5 as of 1 July.

Population ages 15–64: De facto population in a country, area or region ages 15–64 as of 1 July.

Population ages 65 and older: De facto population in a country, area or region ages 65 and older as of 1 July.

Median age: Age that divides the population distribution into two equal parts—that is, 50 percent of the population is above that age and 50 percent is below it.

Young age dependency ratio: Ratio of the population ages 0–14 to the population ages 15–64, expressed as the number of dependants per 100 people of working age (ages 15–64).

Old-age dependency ratio: Ratio of the population ages 65 and older to the population ages 15–64, expressed as the number of dependants per 100 people of working age (ages 15–64).

Total fertility rate: Number of children who would be born to a woman if she were to live to the end of her child-bearing years and bear children at each age in accordance with prevailing age-specific fertility rates.

MAIN DATA SOURCES

Columns 1–4 and 6–13: UNDESA (2017a).

Column 5: UNDESA (2018a).

TABLE 8

Health outcomes

		Infants exclusively breastfed	Infants lacking immunization		Child malnutrition	Mortality rate				Incidence		HIV prevalence, adult	Healthy life expectancy at birth	Current health expenditure
			SDG 3.b	SDG 3.b	SDG 2.2	SDG 3.2	SDG 3.2	SDG 3	SDG 3	SDG 3.3	SDG 3.3	SDG 3.3		SDG 3.c
			DPT	Measles	Stunting (moderate or severe)	Infant	Under-five	Female	Male	Malaria	Tuberculosis			
								Adult						
		(% ages 0–5 months)	(% of one-year-olds)		(% under age 5)	(per 1,000 live births)		(per 1,000 people)		(per 1,000 people at risk)	(per 100,000 people)	(% ages 15–49)	(years)	(% of GDP)
HDI rank		2011–2016[a]	2017	2017	2010–2016[a]	2016	2016	2016	2016	2016	2016	2016	2016	2015
VERY HIGH HUMAN DEVELOPMENT														
1	Norway	..	1	4	..	2.1	2.6	44[b]	69[b]	..	6.1	..	73.0	10.0
2	Switzerland	..	2	5	..	3.6	4.1	37[b]	63[b]	..	7.8	..	73.5	12.1
3	Australia	..	2	5	2.0[c]	3.1	3.7	45[b]	76[b]	..	6.1	0.1[d]	73.0	9.4
4	Ireland	..	2	8	..	3.0	3.6	47[b]	81[b]	..	7.1	0.2	72.1	7.8
5	Germany	..	1	3	..	3.2	3.8	50[e]	92[e]	..	8.1	..	71.6	11.2
6	Iceland	..	3	8	..	1.6	2.1	..	..	..	2.1	..	73.0	8.6
7	Hong Kong, China (SAR)	..	..	..	..	..	..	36	67	..	69.0	..	..	..
7	Sweden	..	1	3	..	2.4	2.9	40	64	..	8.2	0.2	72.4	11.0
9	Singapore	..	2	5	..	2.2	2.8	39	63	..	51.0	..	76.2	4.3
10	Netherlands	..	2	7	..	3.2	3.8	50[b]	67[b]	..	5.9	0.2	72.1	10.7
11	Denmark	..	1	3	..	3.7	4.4	52[b]	87[b]	..	6.1	..	71.8	10.3
12	Canada	..	4	11	..	4.3	4.9	..	..	..	5.2	..	73.2	10.4
13	United States	24.4	3	8	2.1	5.6	6.5	80[b]	134[e]	..	3.1	0.5[b]	68.5	16.8
14	United Kingdom	..	2	8	..	3.7	4.3	54[b]	84[b]	..	9.9	..	71.9	9.9
15	Finland	..	2	6	..	1.9	2.3	43[e]	94[e]	..	4.7	..	71.7	9.4
16	New Zealand	..	5	7	..	4.5	5.4	..	..	..	7.3	..	72.8	9.3
17	Belgium	..	1	4	..	3.1	3.9	54[e]	89[e]	..	10.0	..	71.6	10.5
17	Liechtenstein	..	..	..	..	..	..	..	..	..	..	..	..	..
19	Japan	..	1	4	7.1	2.0	2.7	39[b]	73[b]	..	16.0	..	74.8	10.9
20	Austria	..	6	4	..	2.9	3.5	46[b]	86[b]	..	8.2	..	72.4	10.3
21	Luxembourg	..	1	1	..	2.0	2.4	38[b]	79[b]	..	5.8	..	72.6	6.0
22	Israel	..	1	2	..	2.9	3.6	41[b]	72[b]	..	3.5	..	72.9	7.4
22	Korea (Republic of)	..	2	2	2.5	2.9	3.4	37	86	0.3	77.0	..	73.0	7.4
24	France	..	1	10	..	3.2	3.9	49[e]	101[e]	..	7.7	0.4	73.4	11.1
25	Slovenia	..	2	7	..	1.8	2.3	44[b]	95[b]	..	6.5	0.1[d]	70.5	8.5
26	Spain	..	2	4	..	2.7	3.3	38[b]	77[b]	..	10.0	0.4	73.8	9.2
27	Czechia	..	2	3	..	2.5	3.2	53[b]	115[b]	..	5.0	0.1[d]	69.3	7.3
28	Italy	..	2	8	..	2.8	3.3	37[b]	65[b]	..	6.1	0.3	73.2	9.0
29	Malta	..	2	9	..	5.9	6.8	40	67	..	13.0	0.1[d]	72.2	9.6
30	Estonia	..	6	7	..	2.3	2.9	65[b]	181[b]	..	16.0	..	68.2	6.5
31	Greece	..	1	3	..	3.1	3.8	41	89	..	4.4	..	72.0	8.4
32	Cyprus	..	2	10	..	2.1	2.6	34	67	..	5.6	..	73.3	6.8
33	Poland	..	1	4	..	4.0	4.7	64[b]	163[b]	..	18.0	..	68.5	6.3
34	United Arab Emirates	..	3	1	..	6.6	7.7	56	79	..	0.8	..	66.7	3.5
35	Andorra	..	1	1	..	2.4	2.7	..	..	..	6.0	..	..	12.0
35	Lithuania	..	3	6	..	4.3	5.3	85[b]	250[b]	..	53.0	0.2	66.1	6.5
37	Qatar	29.3	2	1	..	7.3	8.5	46	65	..	23.0	0.1[d]	68.6	3.1
38	Slovakia	..	1	4	..	4.9	5.9	63[b]	154[b]	..	5.9	0.1[d]	68.3	6.9
39	Brunei Darussalam	..	1	3	19.7[c]	8.5	9.9	72	102	..	66.0	..	67.9	2.6
39	Saudi Arabia	..	1	4	..	11.1	12.9	77	96	0.2	10.0	0.1[d]	65.7	5.8
41	Latvia	..	2	4	..	3.9	4.6	89[b]	242[b]	..	37.0	0.7	66.2	5.8
41	Portugal	..	1	2	..	2.9	3.5	42[e]	104[e]	..	20.0	..	72.0	9.0
43	Bahrain	..	2	1	..	6.5	7.6	58	73	..	12.0	0.1[d]	68.1	5.2
44	Chile	..	2	7	1.8	7.2	8.3	66	108	..	16.0	0.5	69.7	8.1
45	Hungary	..	1	1	..	4.4	5.2	84[b]	180[b]	..	8.8	..	66.8	7.2
46	Croatia	..	2	11	..	4.0	4.7	55	130	..	12.0	0.1[d]	69.0	7.4
47	Argentina	32.7	9	11	..	9.9	11.1	74	151	0.0	24.0	0.4	68.4	6.8
48	Oman	32.8	1	1	14.1	9.2	10.7	68	107	..	9.0	..	65.6	3.8
49	Russian Federation	..	3	2	..	6.6	7.7	120[b]	322[b]	..	66.0	..	63.5	5.6
50	Montenegro	16.8	5	42	9.4	3.5	3.8	65	123	..	16.0	0.1[d]	68.1	6.0
51	Bulgaria	..	4	6	..	6.5	7.6	..	..	..	27.0	0.1[d]	66.4	8.2
52	Romania	15.8[f]	7	14	..	7.7	9.0	79	184	..	74.0	0.1[d]	66.6	5.0
53	Belarus	19.0	3	3	..	2.9	3.9	90[b]	261[b]	..	52.0	0.4	65.5	6.1
54	Bahamas	..	2	10	..	8.6	10.6	118	197	..	26.0	3.3	66.8	7.4
55	Uruguay	..	3	5	10.7	7.9	9.2	76	133	..	29.0	0.6	68.8	9.2
56	Kuwait	..	1	1	4.9	7.2	8.4	57	93	..	24.0	0.1[d]	66.3	4.0
57	Malaysia	..	1	7	20.7	7.1	8.3	84	157	0.2	92.0	0.4	66.6	4.0
58	Barbados	19.7[g]	10	8	7.7	11.4	12.3	73	123	..	1.2	1.3	67.0	7.5
58	Kazakhstan	37.8	1	1	8.0	10.1	11.4	117	295	..	67.0	0.2	63.4	3.9

HUMAN DEVELOPMENT INDICES AND INDICATORS: **2018 STATISTICAL UPDATE**

		Infants exclusively breastfed	SDG 3.b Infants lacking immunization		SDG 2.2 Child malnutrition	SDG 3.2 Mortality rate	SDG 3.2	SDG 3	SDG 3	SDG 3.3 Incidence	SDG 3.3	SDG 3.3 HIV prevalence, adult	Healthy life expectancy at birth	SDG 3.c Current health expenditure
			DPT	Measles	Stunting (moderate or severe)	Infant	Under-five	Female	Male	Malaria	Tuberculosis			
		(% ages 0–5 months)	(% of one-year-olds)		(% under age 5)	(per 1,000 live births)		Adult (per 1,000 people)		(per 1,000 people at risk)	(per 100,000 people)	(% ages 15–49)	(years)	(% of GDP)
HDI rank		2011–2016a	2017	2017	2010–2016a	2016	2016	2016	2016	2016	2016	2016	2016	2015
HIGH HUMAN DEVELOPMENT														
60	Iran (Islamic Republic of)	53.1	1	1	6.8	13.0	15.1	61	100	0.2	14.0	0.1 d	65.4	7.6
60	Palau	..	1	4	..	13.7	15.9	..	..	..	123.0	..	..	10.6
62	Seychelles	..	2	1	7.9	12.3	14.3	89	232	..	15.0	..	65.7	3.4
63	Costa Rica	32.5	1	4	5.6 c	7.7	8.8	59	109	0.0	9.5	0.4	70.9	8.1
64	Turkey	30.1	2	4	9.5	10.9	12.7	70	138	0.0	18.0	..	66.0	4.1
65	Mauritius	21.0 f	4	11	..	12.2	13.7	93	190	..	22.0	..	65.8	5.5
66	Panama	21.5	4	2	19.1 c	14.1	16.4	79	148	0.4	55.0	0.8	69.4	7.0
67	Serbia	12.8	2	14	6.0	5.1	5.8	77	149	..	19.0	0.1 d	67.4	9.4
68	Albania	38.6 f	1	4	23.2 c	12.0	13.5	50	79	..	16.0	0.1 d	68.1	6.8
69	Trinidad and Tobago	12.8 f	4	7	11.0	16.5	18.5	121	214	..	18.0	1.2	63.3	6.0
70	Antigua and Barbuda	..	4	12	..	5.1	8.5	106	151	..	3.4	..	67.0	4.8
70	Georgia	54.8 f	2	5	11.3 c	9.5	10.7	78	224	0.0	92.0	0.5	64.9	7.9
72	Saint Kitts and Nevis	..	1	7	..	7.6	9.3	..	..	..	0.0	..	..	5.6
73	Cuba	33.2	1	1	..	4.2	5.5	70	106	..	6.9	0.4	69.9	..
74	Mexico	30.8	1	4	12.4	12.6	14.6	79	140	0.4	22.0	0.3	67.7	5.9
75	Grenada	..	2	15	..	14.4	16.0	96	184	..	6.4	..	64.7	5.0
76	Sri Lanka	75.8 f	1	1	17.3	8.0	9.4	73	196	0.0	65.0	0.1 d	66.8	3.0
77	Bosnia and Herzegovina	18.5	8	31	8.9	5.2	6.0	64	125	..	32.0	..	67.2	9.4
78	Venezuela (Bolivarian Republic of)	..	5	4	13.4 c	14.0	16.3	89	191	44.7	32.0	0.6	66.1	3.2
79	Brazil	38.6 f	1	3	7.1 c	13.5	15.1	94	191	6.7	42.0	0.6	66.0	8.9
80	Azerbaijan	12.1	3	2	18.0	27.2	30.9	85	173	0.0	66.0	0.1 d	64.9	6.7
80	Lebanon	26.6 f	18	21	..	6.9	8.1	49	69	..	12.0	0.1 d	66.1	7.4
80	The former Yugoslav Republic of Macedonia	23.0	3	17	4.9	10.7	12.2	67	125	..	16.0	0.1 d	67.1	6.1
83	Armenia	44.5	3	4	9.4	11.9	13.4	74	174	..	44.0	0.2	66.3	10.1
83	Thailand	23.1	1	1	10.5	10.5	12.2	92	202	1.6	172.0	1.1	66.8	3.8
85	Algeria	25.7	5	12	11.7	21.6	25.2	83	106	0.0	70.0	0.1 d	65.5	7.1
86	China	20.8	1	1	8.1	8.5	9.9	67	92	0.0	64.0	..	68.7	5.3
86	Ecuador	40.0 f	5	19	23.9	17.8	20.9	85	159	3.8	50.0	0.3	67.9	8.5
88	Ukraine	19.7	35	14	..	7.8	9.1	..	..	..	87.0	0.9	64.0	6.1
89	Peru	68.4	10	17	13.1	11.9	15.3	93	152	17.8	117.0	0.3	67.5	5.3
90	Colombia	42.8 f	6	7	12.6	13.1	15.3	88	189	17.2	32.0	0.4	67.1	6.2
90	Saint Lucia	..	11	13	2.5	11.8	13.3	106	163	..	1.9	..	66.4	6.0
92	Fiji	39.8 f	1	6	..	18.7	22.0	135	233	..	59.0	0.1 d	61.3	3.6
92	Mongolia	47.1	1	1	10.8	15.4	17.9	127	294	..	183.0	0.1 d	61.9	3.9
94	Dominican Republic	4.7	1	14	7.1	25.5	30.7	118	202	0.3	60.0	1.0	65.2	6.2
95	Jordan	22.7	1	7	7.8	15.1	17.6	91	126	..	5.6	0.1 d	66.4	6.3
95	Tunisia	8.5	1	2	10.1	11.7	13.6	70	110	..	38.0	0.1 d	66.3	6.7
97	Jamaica	23.8	5	5	6.2	13.2	15.3	99	163	..	4.5	1.7	66.9	5.9
98	Tonga	52.2	14	15	8.1	14.1	16.4	100	165	..	8.6	..	64.3	5.9
99	Saint Vincent and the Grenadines	..	1	1	..	15.2	16.6	127	180	..	6.3	..	63.4	4.2
100	Suriname	2.8 f	10	3	8.8	17.8	20.0	118	220	1.4	26.0	1.4	63.2	6.5
101	Botswana	20.3 f	2	3	31.4 c	32.6	40.6	179	277	2.4	326.0	21.9	57.5	6.0
101	Maldives	47.8 f	1	1	18.6 c	7.3	8.5	55	78	..	49.0	..	69.8	11.5
103	Dominica	..	2	23	..	31.2	34.0	..	..	..	7.8	..	..	5.4
104	Samoa	51.3 f	16	42	4.9	14.8	17.3	81	138	..	7.7	..	66.0	5.6
105	Uzbekistan	26.4 f	1	1	19.6 c	21.4	24.1	101	180	0.0	76.0	..	64.5	6.2
106	Belize	33.2	11	10	15.0	12.8	14.9	126	218	0.0	38.0	1.8	62.5	6.2
106	Marshall Islands	31.3 f	3	17	..	29.1	35.4	..	..	..	422.0	..	..	22.1
108	Libya	..	1	6	21.0 c	11.0	12.9	96	171	..	40.0	..	62.3	..
108	Turkmenistan	58.9	1	1	11.5	43.4	51.0	131	246	..	60.0	..	61.4	6.3
110	Gabon	6.0	19	37	17.0	34.3	47.4	212	253	206.2	485.0	3.6	58.7	2.7
110	Paraguay	24.4 f	5	8	5.6	17.0	19.9	125	165	0.0	42.0	0.5	65.3	7.8
112	Moldova (Republic of)	36.4	9	7	6.4	13.7	15.9	98	241	..	101.0	0.6	63.6	10.2
MEDIUM HUMAN DEVELOPMENT														
113	Philippines	34.0 f	11	11	33.4	21.5	27.1	136	261	0.5	554.0	0.1 d	61.7	4.4
113	South Africa	31.6	26	40	27.4	34.2	43.3	274	396	1.1	781.0	18.9	55.7	8.2
115	Egypt	39.7	5	6	22.3	19.4	22.8	109	186	..	14.0	0.1 d	61.1	4.2
116	Indonesia	41.5	4	25	36.4	22.2	26.4	143	204	9.2	391.0	0.4	61.7	3.3
116	Viet Nam	24.3	2	3	24.6	17.3	21.6	66	181	0.1	133.0	0.4	67.5	5.7

TABLE 8 Health outcomes | 49

TABLE 8 HEALTH OUTCOMES

	Infants exclusively breastfed	Infants lacking immunization (SDG 3.b)		Child malnutrition (SDG 2.2)	Mortality rate				Incidence		HIV prevalence, adult (SDG 3.3)	Healthy life expectancy at birth	Current health expenditure (SDG 3.c)
		DPT	Measles	Stunting (moderate or severe)	Infant (SDG 3.2)	Under-five (SDG 3.2)	Female (SDG 3)	Male (SDG 3)	Malaria (SDG 3.3)	Tuberculosis (SDG 3.3)			
	(% ages 0–5 months)	(% of one-year-olds)		(% under age 5)	(per 1,000 live births)		Adult (per 1,000 people)		(per 1,000 people at risk)	(per 100,000 people)	(% ages 15–49)	(years)	(% of GDP)
HDI rank	2011–2016a	2017	2017	2010–2016a	2016	2016	2016	2016	2016	2016	2016	2016	2015
118 Bolivia (Plurinational State of)	64.3	9	17	16.1	29.5	36.9	149	214	2.7	114.0	0.3	63.0	6.4
119 Palestine, State of	38.6	1	1	7.4	16.6	19.4	94	135	..	1.0	..	..	..
120 Iraq	19.6	27	29	22.1	25.9	31.2	128	195	0.0	43.0	..	59.0	3.4
121 El Salvador	47.0	5	15	13.6	12.9	15.0	101	258	0.0	60.0	0.6	65.5	6.9
122 Kyrgyzstan	41.1	6	5	12.9	18.8	21.1	108	247	0.0	145.0	0.2	63.5	8.2
123 Morocco	27.8	1	1	14.9	23.3	27.1	65	75	..	103.0	0.1 d	65.3	5.5
124 Nicaragua	31.7	1	1	17.3	16.8	19.7	103	190	7.8	48.0	0.2	66.9	7.8
125 Cabo Verde	59.6 f	3	4	..	18.2	21.4	100	146	0.7	137.0	0.8	64.5	4.8
125 Guyana	23.3	3	1	11.3	26.9	32.4	169	247	77.7	93.0	1.6	58.3	4.5
127 Guatemala	53.2	12	14	46.7	23.9	28.5	112	212	0.8	24.0	0.5	64.2	5.7
127 Tajikistan	34.3	2	2	26.8	37.1	43.1	103	164	0.0	85.0	0.3	63.5	6.9
129 Namibia	48.5	6	20	22.7	32.3	45.2	256	349	29.3	446.0	13.8	55.9	8.9
130 India	54.9	9	12	37.9	34.6	43.0	139	212	18.8	211.0	0.3	59.3	3.9
131 Micronesia (Federated States of)	..	3	24	..	27.5	33.3	147	180	..	177.0	..	61.1	13.1
132 Timor-Leste	62.3	20	30	50.2	42.4	49.7	122	172	0.9	498.0	..	59.2	3.1
133 Honduras	31.2	1	3	22.6	16.0	18.7	119	172	1.7	40.0	0.4	66.8	7.6
134 Bhutan	51.4	1	3	33.5	26.8	32.4	204	204	0.0	178.0	..	60.7	3.5
134 Kiribati	69.0 f	4	19	..	42.4	54.3	155	238	..	566.0	..	57.8	7.6
136 Bangladesh	55.3	1	6	36.2	28.2	34.2	107	148	0.6	221.0	0.1 d	63.3	2.6
137 Congo	32.9	25	30	21.2	38.5	54.1	237	273	204.7	378.0	3.1	56.7	3.4
138 Vanuatu	72.6	9	20	28.5	23.1	27.6	103	154	14.7	56.0	..	62.7	3.5
139 Lao People's Democratic Republic	40.4	11	18	44.2	48.9	63.9	170	214	7.8	175.0	0.3	57.9	2.8
140 Ghana	52.3	1	5	18.8	41.2	58.8	221	261	285.6	156.0	1.6	56.4	5.9
141 Equatorial Guinea	7.4	56	70	26.2	66.2	90.9	311	349	238.8	181.0	6.2	53.8	2.7
142 Kenya	61.4	7	11	26.2	35.6	49.2	179	258	85.3	348.0	5.4	58.9	5.2
143 Sao Tome and Principe	73.8	4	10	17.2	26.2	33.8	162	218	11.2	99.0	..	60.7	9.8
144 Eswatini (Kingdom of)	63.8	4	11	25.5	52.4	70.4	356	497	1.9	398.0	27.2	50.2	7.0
144 Zambia	72.5	5	4	40.0	43.8	63.4	246	346	189.8	376.0	12.4	54.3	5.4
146 Cambodia	65.2	6	16	32.4	26.3	30.6	139	205	8.9	345.0	0.6	60.8	6.0
147 Angola	37.5	39	58	37.6	54.6	82.5	203	277	120.3	370.0	1.9	55.8	2.9
148 Myanmar	51.2	6	17	29.4	40.1	50.8	163	225	7.2	361.0	0.8	58.4	4.9
149 Nepal	66.1	5	10	36.0	28.4	34.5	130	171	0.9	154.0	0.2	61.3	6.1
150 Pakistan	37.7	17	24	45.0	64.2	78.8	140	178	10.6	268.0	0.1 d	57.7	2.7
151 Cameroon	28.2	7	23	31.7	52.8	79.7	321	348	271.3	203.0	3.8	51.1	5.1
LOW HUMAN DEVELOPMENT													
152 Solomon Islands	73.7 f	1	16	31.6	21.8	25.8	125	164	144.8	84.0	..	61.9	8.0
153 Papua New Guinea	56.1 f	31	38	49.5	42.4	54.3	191	256	179.4	432.0	0.9	58.0	3.8
154 Tanzania (United Republic of)	59.2	1	1	34.5	40.3	56.7	199	249	144.2	287.0	4.7	56.5	6.1
155 Syrian Arab Republic	42.6 f	37	33	27.5 c	14.2	17.5	79	270	..	21.0	..	55.8	..
156 Zimbabwe	47.8	6	10	27.1	40.0	56.4	320	380	77.9	208.0	13.5	54.4	10.3
157 Nigeria	17.4	51	58	43.6	66.9	104.3	333	371	349.6	219.0	2.9	48.9	3.6
158 Rwanda	87.3	1	5	36.7	29.2	38.5	171	225	392.7	50.0	3.1	59.9	7.9
159 Lesotho	66.9	2	10	33.4	72.4	93.3	463	555	..	724.0	25.0	46.6	8.4
159 Mauritania	41.4	11	22	27.9	54.4	81.4	179	225	88.5	102.0	0.5	56.4	4.6
161 Madagascar	41.9	20	42	49.2 c	34.0	46.4	189	239	64.4	237.0	0.2	58.3	5.2
162 Uganda	65.5	5	20	28.9	37.7	53.0	268	346	187.2	201.0	6.5	54.9	7.3
163 Benin	41.4	14	26	34.0	63.1	97.6	217	264	297.3	59.0	1.0	53.5	4.0
164 Senegal	33.3	3	10	17.1	33.6	47.1	151	222	49.0	140.0	0.4	58.8	4.0
165 Comoros	12.1	4	10	31.1	55.0	73.3	199	250	1.8	35.0	0.1 d	56.6	8.0
165 Togo	57.5	8	9	27.6	50.7	75.7	252	285	360.4	46.0	2.1	53.9	6.6
167 Sudan	55.4	2	10	38.2	44.8	65.1	192	249	35.3	82.0	0.2	55.7	6.3
168 Afghanistan	43.3	27	38	40.9	53.2	70.4	202	245	30.8	189.0	0.1 d	53.0	10.3
168 Haiti	39.7	21	47	22.0	50.9	67.0	210	272	13.9	188.0	2.1	55.3	6.9
170 Côte d'Ivoire	12.1	1	22	21.6	66.0	91.8	371	411	223.2	153.0	2.7	48.3	5.4
171 Malawi	61.2	7	17	37.4	38.9	55.1	228	341	249.1	159.0	9.2	56.2	9.3
172 Djibouti	1.3 f	26	25	33.5	53.5	64.2	226	273	9.6	335.0	1.3	56.6	4.4
173 Ethiopia	57.5	15	35	38.4	41.0	58.4	194	245	53.1	177.0	1.1	57.5	4.0
174 Gambia	46.8	7	10	24.6	42.2	65.3	231	287	129.6	174.0	1.7	54.4	6.7
175 Guinea	20.5	37	52	32.4	58.3	89.0	243	270	386.5	176.0	1.5	52.2	4.5

HUMAN DEVELOPMENT INDICES AND INDICATORS: 2018 STATISTICAL UPDATE

		SDG 3.b	SDG 3.b	SDG 2.2	SDG 3.2	SDG 3.2	SDG 3	SDG 3	SDG 3.3	SDG 3.3	SDG 3.3		SDG 3.c
	Infants exclusively breastfed	Infants lacking immunization		Child malnutrition	Mortality rate				Incidence		HIV prevalence, adult	Healthy life expectancy at birth	Current health expenditure
		DPT	Measles	Stunting (moderate or severe)	Infant	Under-five	Female	Male	Malaria	Tuberculosis			
							Adult						
	(% ages 0–5 months)	(% of one-year-olds)		(% under age 5)	(per 1,000 live births)		(per 1,000 people)		(per 1,000 people at risk)	(per 100,000 people)	(% ages 15–49)	(years)	(% of GDP)
HDI rank	2011–2016a	2017	2017	2010–2016a	2016	2016	2016	2016	2016	2016	2016	2016	2015
176 Congo (Democratic Republic of the)	47.6	18	20	42.7	72.0	94.3	232	280	291.9	323.0	0.7	52.5	4.3
177 Guinea-Bissau	52.5	5	19	27.6	57.8	88.1	241	292	73.0	374.0	3.1	51.7	6.9
178 Yemen	10.3	24	35	46.4	43.2	55.3	195	243	30.5	48.0	0.1 d	55.1	6.0
179 Eritrea	68.7 f	3	1	50.3	32.9	44.5	213	287	17.2	74.0	0.6	57.4	3.3
180 Mozambique	41.0	10	15	42.9	53.1	71.3	285	356	307.8	551.0	12.3	52.2	5.4
181 Liberia	55.2	1	13	32.1	51.2	67.4	216	255	237.0	308.0	1.6	54.5	15.2
182 Mali	32.6	27	39	30.4	68.0	110.6	253	272	459.7	56.0	1.0	50.7	5.8
183 Burkina Faso	50.1	5	12	27.3	52.7	84.6	238	269	423.3	51.0	0.8	52.9	5.4
184 Sierra Leone	32.0	2	20	37.8	83.3	113.5	388	399	303.5	304.0	1.7	47.6	18.3
185 Burundi	83.1	6	10	55.9	48.4	71.7	261	319	156.2	118.0	1.1	52.6	8.2
186 Chad	0.3	45	63	39.8	75.2	127.3	338	382	167.6	153.0	1.3	47.2	4.6
187 South Sudan	45.1 f	65	80	31.3	59.2	90.7	309	335	159.0	146.0	2.7	50.6	2.5
188 Central African Republic	34.3 f	31	51	40.7	88.5	123.6	380	414	311.6	407.0	4.0	44.9	4.8
189 Niger	23.3	7	22	42.2	50.9	91.3	231	259	378.9	93.0	0.4	52.5	7.2
OTHER COUNTRIES OR TERRITORIES													
.. Korea (Democratic People's Rep. of)	68.9	2	1	27.9	15.1	20.0	99	166	0.5	513.0	..	64.6	..
.. Monaco	..	1	13	..	2.8	3.4	..	..	..	0.0	..	..	2.0
.. Nauru	67.2 f	1	5	24.0 c	28.5	34.6	..	..	..	112.0	..	..	4.8
.. San Marino	..	12	18	..	2.5	2.8	..	..	..	0.0	..	..	6.8
.. Somalia	5.3 f	48	54	25.3 c	82.6	132.5	276	332	60.2	270.0	0.4	50.0	..
.. Tuvalu	34.7 f	1	5	10.0 c	21.4	25.3	..	..	..	207.0	..	..	15.0
Human development groups													
Very high human development	..	3	6	..	5.2	6.1	67	133	..	21.3	0.4	69.9	12.1
High human development	27.6	2	3	9.5	11.2	12.9	74	118	..	59.3	0.5	67.7	5.8
Medium human development	47.2	9	15	34.9	34.3	43.1	139	210	22.3	249.1	0.9	60.0	4.2
Low human development	40.1	22	32	38.2	53.9	78.4	248	301	212.8	201.4	2.7	53.3	4.8
Developing countries	39.9	11	16	28.6	32.7	43.1	125	181	43.0	164.5	1.1	62.2	5.4
Regions													
Arab States	31.0	12	15	24.2	27.5	35.9	113	160	..	49.6	0.1	61.2	4.9
East Asia and the Pacific	28.3	3	7	17.8	14.2	17.0	85	128	..	154.0	0.5	66.8	5.1
Europe and Central Asia	29.9	6	5	13.1	15.7	17.8	86	178	..	54.8	0.5	65.0	4.9
Latin America and the Caribbean	38.3	4	8	12.8	14.8	17.4	91	172	7.8	41.4	0.5	66.7	7.4
South Asia	52.4	10	13	37.4	37.8	46.6	132	198	15.3	206.3	0.2	59.7	4.2
Sub-Saharan Africa	41.1	21	31	36.4	52.9	77.3	256	313	214.9	262.0	4.5	53.7	5.3
Least developed countries	48.4	14	23	36.9	47.9	67.4	193	244	125.6	222.5	1.9	56.5	4.8
Small island developing states	35.7	13	24	25.3	33.3	42.9	138	200	..	142.9	1.2	62.4	5.9
Organisation for Economic Co-operation and Development	..	2	6	..	6.0	7.0	60	110	..	12.7	0.4	70.7	12.4
World	39.4	10	15	27.4	29.9	39.3	115	173	..	140.0	1.1	63.5	9.9

NOTES

a Data refer to the most recent year available during the period specified.
b Refers to 2014.
c Refers to a year between 2006 and 2009.
d 0.1 or less.
e Refers to 2015.
f Refers to a year earlier than that specified.
g Based on small denominators (typically 25–50 unweighted cases).

DEFINITIONS

Infants exclusively breastfed: Percentage of children ages 0–5 months who are fed exclusively with breast milk in the 24 hours prior to the survey.

Infants lacking immunization against DPT: Percentage of surviving infants who have not received their first dose of diphtheria, pertussis and tetanus vaccine.

Infants lacking immunization against measles: Percentage of surviving infants who have not received the first dose of measles vaccine.

Child malnutrition (stunting moderate or severe): Percentage of children under age 5 who are more than two standard deviations below the median height-for-age of the reference population, according to the 2006 World Health Organization Child Growth Standards.

Infant mortality rate: Probability of dying between birth and exactly age 1, expressed per 1,000 live births.

Under-five mortality rate: Probability of dying between birth and exactly age 5, expressed per 1,000 live births.

Adult mortality rate: Probability that a 15-year-old will die before reaching age 60, expressed per 1,000 people.

Malaria incidence: Number of malaria cases, expressed per 1,000 people at risk. People at risk are those who live in an area where malaria transmission occurs.

Tuberculosis incidence: The estimated number of new and relapse tuberculosis cases of all forms, including cases in people living with HIV, expressed per 100,000 people.

HIV prevalence, adult: Percentage of the population ages 15–49 that is living with HIV.

Healthy life expectancy at birth: Average number of years that a person can expect to live in full health by taking into account years lived in less than full health because of disease and injury.

Current health expenditure: Spending on healthcare goods and services, expressed as a percentage of GDP. It excludes capital health expenditures such as buildings, machinery, information technology and stocks of vaccines for emergency or outbreaks.

MAIN DATA SOURCES

Column 1: UNICEF (2017).

Columns 2 and 3: WHO and UNICEF (2018).

Column 4: UNICEF, WHO and World Bank (2018).

Columns 5 and 6: UN Inter-agency Group for Child Mortality Estimation (2017).

Columns 7, 8 and 11: World Bank (2018a).

Columns 9 and 10: United Nations Statistics Division (2018a).

Columns 12 and 13: WHO (2018).

TABLE 9

Education achievements

	Literacy rate (SDG 4.6)		Population with at least some secondary education (SDG 4.6)	Gross enrolment ratio				Primary school dropout rate	Survival rate to the last grade of lower secondary general education	Government expenditure on education (SDG 1.a)
	Adult (% ages 15 and older)	Youth (% ages 15–24)		Pre-primary (SDG 4.2)	Primary (SDG 4.1)	Secondary (SDG 4.1)	Tertiary (SDG 4.3)			
		Female / Male	(% ages 25 and older)	(% of preschool-age children)	(% of primary school-age population)	(% of secondary school-age population)	(% of tertiary school-age population)	(% of primary school cohort)	(%)	(% of GDP)
HDI rank	2006–2016a	2006–2016a / 2006–2016a	2006–2017a	2012–2017a	2012–2017a	2012–2017a	2012–2017a	2007–2016a	2006–2016a	2012–2017a

VERY HIGH HUMAN DEVELOPMENT

HDI rank	Country	Adult	Female	Male	Pop. sec. ed.	Pre-primary	Primary	Secondary	Tertiary	Dropout	Survival	Gov. exp.
1	Norway	..	..	..	95.7	96	100	114	81	0.4	100	7.7
2	Switzerland	..	..	..	96.8	105	104	102	58	0.6	99	5.1
3	Australia	..	..	..	90.0	169	101	154	122	..	..	5.2
4	Ireland	..	..	..	88.3	113	101	126	84	..	99	4.9
5	Germany	..	..	..	96.5	107	102	101	66	3.5	54	4.9
6	Iceland	..	..	..	100.0	97	99	119	76	2.1	99	7.8
7	Hong Kong, China (SAR)	..	..	..	78.4	108	107	103	72	1.8	98	3.3
7	Sweden	..	..	..	88.5	94	123	140	62	0.4	99	7.7
9	Singapore	97.0	99.9	99.9	79.4	..	101	108	..	1.3	100	2.9
10	Netherlands	..	..	..	88.3	95	103	133	80	..	..	5.5
11	Denmark	..	..	..	90.7	96	102	129	81	0.2	100	7.6
12	Canada	..	..	..	100.0	..	101	113	..	..	..	..
13	United States	..	..	..	95.3	69	99	97	..	..	..	5.0
14	United Kingdom	..	..	..	82.9	96	102	125	57	..	..	5.6
15	Finland	..	..	..	100.0	83	100	152	87	0.2	100	7.2
16	New Zealand	..	..	..	98.9	92	99	114	82	..	..	6.3
17	Belgium	..	..	..	84.4	117	103	164	75	..	96	6.6
17	Liechtenstein	..	..	..	..	103	105	116	35	2.7	85	..
19	Japan	..	..	..	93.3	86	99	102	63	0.2	..	3.6
20	Austria	..	..	..	100.0	104	102	101	83	0.4	100	5.4
21	Luxembourg	..	..	..	100.0	93	99	102	20	17.1	99	4.0
22	Israel	..	..	..	89.1	111	104	104	64	0.8	98	5.7
22	Korea (Republic of)	..	..	..	95.6	95	98	100	93	0.5	99	5.1
24	France	..	..	..	83.2	109	107	111	65	..	99	5.5
25	Slovenia	..	..	..	98.1	92	99	110	80	1.4	99	5.3
26	Spain	98.3	99.6	99.6	74.8	95	104	128	91	0.7	92	4.3
27	Czechia	..	..	..	99.8	105	99	105	64	0.5	92	4.0
28	Italy	98.8	99.9	99.9	79.6	99	101	103	63	0.8	99	4.1
29	Malta	93.3	99.4	98.4	77.6	112	105	96	49	3.4	99	7.2
30	Estonia	99.9	100.0	99.9	100.0	88	97	111	72	2.0	100	5.5
31	Greece	97.1	98.8	98.6	69.2	47	95	99	117	8.3	99	..
32	Cyprus	98.7	99.8	99.8	78.6	80	99	100	60	2.4	100	6.1
33	Poland	..	..	..	86.2	70	110	107	67	2.0	98	4.9
34	United Arab Emirates	..	..	..	69.0 b	82	111	96	37	8.0	97	..
35	Andorra	100.0	100.0	100.0	72.5	..	..	..	..	28.8	93	3.3
35	Lithuania	99.8	99.9	99.8	93.8	90	101	103	66	1.8	97	4.5
37	Qatar	97.7	99.6	98.4	68.4	60	104	93	15	1.5	98	3.6
38	Slovakia	..	..	..	99.3	93	99	91	53	1.0	88	4.6
39	Brunei Darussalam	96.1	99.5	99.2	69.7 b	70	107	93	31	3.6	100	4.4
39	Saudi Arabia	94.4	99.1	99.3	72.8	25	116	117	67	25.8	86	..
41	Latvia	99.9	99.9	99.8	99.3	87	98	112	68	4.8	96	5.3
41	Portugal	94.5	99.5	99.4	52.7	93	105	118	63	..	..	5.1
43	Bahrain	94.6	97.6	98.6	59.2	55	101	104	47	1.4	99	2.7
44	Chile	96.3	99.1	99.0	80.6	85	100	100	90	0.6	99	4.9
45	Hungary	..	..	..	96.8	82	102	102	48	1.6	96	4.6
46	Croatia	99.1	99.7	99.7	95.7	63	95	98	67	2.6	99	4.6
47	Argentina	98.1	99.5	99.1	64.8 b	74	110	107	86	4.7	85	5.9
48	Oman	93.0	99.0	98.5	66.4	57	109	107	45	0.9	99	6.2
49	Russian Federation	99.7	99.8	99.7	95.6	89	102	105	82	0.7	98	3.8
50	Montenegro	98.4	99.1	99.4	89.4	56	96	91	57	6.8	95	..
51	Bulgaria	98.4	97.7	98.1	94.8	81	95	100	71	6.5	46	4.1
52	Romania	98.6	99.0	99.0	89.5	87	89	89	48	6.0	93	3.1
53	Belarus	99.6	99.8	99.8	91.9	99	102	104	87	1.2	99	5.0
54	Bahamas	..	..	..	87.5	32	95	90	..	10.5	97	..
55	Uruguay	98.5	99.2	98.6	54.1	90	107	112	56	1.2	84	..
56	Kuwait	95.7	99.4	99.2	51.2	68	101	98	33	3.9	97	..
57	Malaysia	93.1	98.5	98.4	80.0	94	103	85	44	8.0	93	4.8
58	Barbados	..	..	..	92.9 b	80	93	107	..	6.6	96	5.1
58	Kazakhstan	99.8	99.9	99.9	98.8	54	108	113	50	1.7	99	3.0

HUMAN DEVELOPMENT INDICES AND INDICATORS: **2018 STATISTICAL UPDATE**

TABLE 9 Education achievements

		SDG 4.6	SDG 4.6	SDG 4.6	SDG 4.2	SDG 4.1	SDG 4.1	SDG 4.3			SDG 1.a
		Literacy rate		Population with at least some secondary education	Gross enrolment ratio				Primary school dropout rate	Survival rate to the last grade of lower secondary general education	Government expenditure on education
		Adult (% ages 15 and older)	Youth (% ages 15–24)		Pre-primary	Primary	Secondary	Tertiary			
			Female / Male	(% ages 25 and older)	(% of preschool-age children)	(% of primary school-age population)	(% of secondary school-age population)	(% of tertiary school-age population)	(% of primary school cohort)	(%)	(% of GDP)
HDI rank		2006–2016[a]	2006–2016[a] / 2006–2016[a]	2006–2017[a]	2012–2017[a]	2012–2017[a]	2012–2017[a]	2012–2017[a]	2007–2016[a]	2006–2016[a]	2012–2017[a]

HIGH HUMAN DEVELOPMENT

HDI rank	Country	Adult	Female	Male	Pop. secondary	Pre-primary	Primary	Secondary	Tertiary	Dropout	Survival	Gov. exp.
60	Iran (Islamic Republic of)	84.7	97.7	98.2	68.5	51	109	89	69	2.5	97	3.4
60	Palau	96.6	99.2	98.2	97.1	75	115	115	64	..	..	..
62	Seychelles	94.0	99.4	98.6	..	103	113	93	21	3.2	99	..
63	Costa Rica	97.4	99.3	99.0	52.9	78	110	126	54	5.6	67	7.1
64	Turkey	95.6	99.2	99.8	52.2	29	103	103	95	12.0	90	4.4
65	Mauritius	92.7	98.6	97.7	65.8	105	102	93	39	3.5	97	5.1
66	Panama	94.1	97.3	97.9	71.2	50	96	76	47	14.0	77	..
67	Serbia	98.8	99.7	99.7	88.6	59	101	96	62	1.9	96	4.0
68	Albania	97.2	99.0	99.4	92.9	88	110	95	61	11.2	93	3.5
69	Trinidad and Tobago	..	..	..	73.4	..	..	..	..	10.6	86	..
70	Antigua and Barbuda	..	..	..	..	86	88	94	22	8.7	84	..
70	Georgia	99.6	99.7	99.7	95.5	..	103	104	52	0.8	99	3.8
72	Saint Kitts and Nevis	..	..	..	..	..	..	..	..	4.6	93	2.8
73	Cuba	99.8	99.9	99.9	86.9	102	101	100	34	5.4	96	..
74	Mexico	94.5	99.0	98.9	59.3[b]	71	104	97	37	7.8	90	5.3
75	Grenada	..	..	..	..	89	101	101	91	..	90	10.3
76	Sri Lanka	91.2	98.6	97.7	82.8	94	102	98	19	1.6	96	3.5
77	Bosnia and Herzegovina	97.0	99.7	99.7	79.9	..	..	..	..	4.4	96	..
78	Venezuela (Bolivarian Republic of)	97.1	99.1	98.4	69.2	69	97	86	..	17.5	76	..
79	Brazil	91.7	99.3	98.4	60.0	92	115	100	51	..	74	5.9
80	Azerbaijan	99.8	99.9	100.0	95.6	23	106	..	27	1.1	96	3.0
80	Lebanon	91.2	99.3	99.2	54.3	86	89	60	38	15.9	88	2.5
80	The former Yugoslav Republic of Macedonia	..	..	..	47.8	36	94	82	41	2.6	96	..
83	Armenia	99.7	99.9	99.8	97.2	52	94	86	51	5.3	97	2.8
83	Thailand	92.9	98.3	98.0	44.8	68	101	121	46	15.0	91	4.1
85	Algeria	75.1	91.7	95.7	37.7[b]	..	114	..	43	6.4	75	..
86	China	95.1	99.6	99.7	77.4	84	101	95	48	..	92	..
86	Ecuador	94.4	99.1	99.0	52.2	72	104	107	46	9.3	91	5.0
88	Ukraine	100.0	100.0	100.0	95.1[b]	84	100	97	83	4.5	95	5.9
89	Peru	94.2	98.7	99.1	62.2	89	103	98	..	9.5	96	3.8
90	Colombia	94.2	98.9	98.2	50.2	..	114	98	59	10.0	71	4.5
90	Saint Lucia	..	..	..	45.9	82	..	88	19	9.9	97	5.7
92	Fiji	..	..	..	76.0[b]	..	106	89	..	2.8	87	3.9
92	Mongolia	98.3	98.9	98.0	88.8	176	104	100	65	2.1	96	5.2
94	Dominican Republic	92.0	98.0	97.2	56.6	44	102	77	53	16.2	86	..
95	Jordan	97.9	99.2	99.0	83.5	..	..	70	36	2.1	96	3.9
95	Tunisia	79.0	95.8	96.6	51.8	44	115	93	33	6.8	78	6.6
97	Jamaica	..	..	..	66.3	76	..	84	27	5.1	97	5.4
98	Tonga	99.4	99.5	99.4	92.6	39	108	90	..	..	..	..
99	Saint Vincent and the Grenadines	..	..	..	..	99	103	107	..	8.7	92	5.8
100	Suriname	92.9	97.3	98.1	58.2	94	121	79	..	8.7	75	..
101	Botswana	..	..	..	89.2[b]	20	105	..	23	6.0	99	..
101	Maldives	98.6	99.4	99.1	47.1[b]	99	102	..	14	17.8	91	4.3
103	Dominica	..	..	..	..	84	112	100	..	20.5	88	3.4
104	Samoa	99.0	99.5	99.0	74.5	41	108	84	..	6.7	98	4.1
105	Uzbekistan	100.0	100.0	100.0	99.9	27	103	93	9	0.8	98	..
106	Belize	..	..	..	78.6	50	115	87	24	1.2	69	7.4
106	Marshall Islands	98.3	98.8	98.2	92.1	40	89	73	43	16.5	97	..
108	Libya	..	..	..	57.4[b]	..	..	..	..	..	..	..
108	Turkmenistan	..	..	..	..	58	88	86	8	..	..	3.0
110	Gabon	82.3	89.4	87.4	57.6[b]	..	..	..	..	..	..	2.7
110	Paraguay	95.1	98.6	98.0	48.0	38	106	77	..	15.9	84	5.0
112	Moldova (Republic of)	99.1	99.6	99.3	96.4	84	92	86	41	5.2	93	6.7

MEDIUM HUMAN DEVELOPMENT

HDI rank	Country	Adult	Female	Male	Pop. secondary	Pre-primary	Primary	Secondary	Tertiary	Dropout	Survival	Gov. exp.
113	Philippines	96.4	98.8	97.4	73.2	100	113	88	35	24.2	86	..
113	South Africa	94.4	99.2	98.7	75.7	79	103	103	20	..	..	5.9
115	Egypt	75.1	90.3	93.6	64.5[b]	30	104	86	34	3.9	92	..
116	Indonesia	95.4	99.7	99.7	48.8	60	103	86	28	18.1	97	3.6
116	Viet Nam	93.5	96.8	97.4	69.4	87	110	..	28	4.0	91	5.7

TABLE 9 EDUCATION ACHIEVEMENTS

		SDG 4.6 Literacy rate		SDG 4.6 Population with at least some secondary education	SDG 4.2 Gross enrolment ratio	SDG 4.1	SDG 4.1	SDG 4.3	Primary school dropout rate	Survival rate to the last grade of lower secondary general education	SDG 1.a Government expenditure on education
		Adult (% ages 15 and older)	Youth (% ages 15–24)		Pre-primary	Primary	Secondary	Tertiary			
			Female	Male	(% ages 25 and older)	(% of preschool-age children)	(% of primary school–age population)	(% of secondary school–age population)	(% of tertiary school–age population)	(% of primary school cohort)	(%)	(% of GDP)
HDI rank		2006–2016[a]	2006–2016[a]	2006–2016[a]	2006–2017[a]	2012–2017[a]	2012–2017[a]	2012–2017[a]	2012–2017[a]	2007–2016[a]	2006–2016[a]	2012–2017[a]
118	Bolivia (Plurinational State of)	92.5	99.4	99.4	58.2	74	98	86	..	4.1	96	7.3
119	Palestine, State of	96.9	99.3	99.5	60.4	54	94	84	43	1.7	85	5.7
120	Iraq	43.7	48.6	57.0	47.7	..	..	..	..	..	..	..
121	El Salvador	88.0	98.4	97.5	43.3	66	100	74	28	22.0	77	3.5
122	Kyrgyzstan	99.2	99.8	99.7	98.4	31	106	98	46	1.7	97	6.0
123	Morocco	69.4	87.8	94.6	31.3[b]	50	110	70	32	7.4	84	..
124	Nicaragua	..	..	..	47.5[b]	..	..	..	..	51.6	64	..
125	Cabo Verde	86.8	98.7	97.6	29.4	72	97	85	22	9.9	80	5.4
125	Guyana	85.6	97.0	96.3	63.3[b]	92	96	99	12	7.8	88	3.2
127	Guatemala	81.3	93.3	95.5	37.8	45	101	64	21	25.2	95	2.8
127	Tajikistan	..	..	..	93.1[b]	10	99	87	31	1.0	97	5.2
129	Namibia	88.3	95.3	93.5	40.4[b]	22	111	..	..	9.4	78	..
130	India	69.3	81.8	90.0	51.6	13	115	75	27	9.8	97	3.8
131	Micronesia (Federated States of)	..	..	..	..	33	96	..	..	..	..	12.5
132	Timor-Leste	58.3	78.6	80.5	..	16	109	74	..	19.5	96	..
133	Honduras	89.0	97.2	94.9	35.5	41	96	65	20	17.4	85	5.9
134	Bhutan	57.0	84.5	90.4	9.6	25	95	84	11	21.1	83	7.4
134	Kiribati	..	..	..	..	..	105	..	..	..	94	..
136	Bangladesh	72.8	93.5	90.9	45.5[b]	34	119	69	17	33.8	87	2.5
137	Congo	79.3	76.9	85.7	48.4[b]	13	104	52	9	29.7	81	..
138	Vanuatu	..	..	..	..	102	120	55	..	28.5	71	5.5
139	Lao People's Democratic Republic	58.3	67.1	77.3	39.2[b]	40	110	67	17	20.4	77	2.9
140	Ghana	71.5	83.2	88.3	62.1	117	105	60	16	15.0	79	6.2
141	Equatorial Guinea	..	..	..	..	43	62	..	..	27.9	84	..
142	Kenya	78.7	86.1	86.9	34.6	77	105	..	..	7.0	81	5.3
143	Sao Tome and Principe	90.1	96.4	97.1	38.9	51	110	90	13	7.3	81	3.7
144	Eswatini (Kingdom of)	83.1	94.7	92.2	31.3[b]	..	108	67	5	20.9	64	7.1
144	Zambia	83.0	86.5	91.2	44.3[b]	..	102	..	4	44.5	89	..
146	Cambodia	73.9	85.9	88.4	21.3	19	110	..	13	26.5	67	1.9
147	Angola	66.0	70.6	84.9	..	..	..	..	9	68.1	..	..
148	Myanmar	75.6	84.4	85.1	25.8[b]	24	112	61	16	25.2	69	2.2
149	Nepal	59.6	80.2	89.9	34.6	86	134	71	12	26.5	95	3.7
150	Pakistan	57.0	65.5	79.8	37.3	72	98	46	10	22.7	94	2.8
151	Cameroon	71.3	76.4	85.4	36.2	40	119	62	17	42.9	89	2.8
LOW HUMAN DEVELOPMENT												
152	Solomon Islands	..	..	..	..	99	115	48	..	36.6	85	..
153	Papua New Guinea	..	..	..	12.2[b]	..	112	40	..	..	..	..
154	Tanzania (United Republic of)	77.9	84.6	87.0	14.3	32	81	32	4	33.3	58	3.5
155	Syrian Arab Republic	..	..	..	41.0	6	76	49	39	6.8	10	..
156	Zimbabwe	88.7	93.2	87.6	58.7	42	99	47	8	23.1	94	7.5
157	Nigeria	51.1	58.0	75.6	..	..	94	56	..	35.6	..	..
158	Rwanda	68.3	83.5	81.1	15.8	18	137	37	8	41.9	78	3.5
159	Lesotho	76.6	94.0	79.6	29.0[b]	33	104	52	9	30.7	67	..
159	Mauritania	45.5	47.7	66.4	18.4[b]	10	94	32	5	62.9	71	2.6
161	Madagascar	71.6	75.3	78.4	..	29	144	38	5	64.9	68	2.1
162	Uganda	70.2	81.7	85.8	31.7	13	100	..	5	65.0	82	2.3
163	Benin	32.9	40.9	63.9	25.4[b]	24	132	59	13	42.7	76	4.4
164	Senegal	42.8	50.1	61.1	17.1	16	83	48	11	37.6	68	7.1
165	Comoros	49.2	69.6	73.8	..	21	105	61	9	29.1	67	4.3
165	Togo	63.7	78.4	89.7	39.1	17	124	..	12	45.9	13	5.1
167	Sudan	53.5	62.7	68.7	17.0[b]	48	74	46	17	20.6	97	..
168	Afghanistan	31.7	32.1	61.9	25.1[b]	..	105	55	8	..	..	3.2
168	Haiti	48.7	70.5	74.4	33.2[b]	..	..	..	..	..	..	..
170	Côte d'Ivoire	43.9	47.0	59.1	26.1	8	97	46	9	18.0	85	4.8
171	Malawi	62.1	73.4	72.5	21.1[b]	81	139	37	..	45.9	31	4.7
172	Djibouti	..	..	..	..	7	64	44	..	15.6	93	..
173	Ethiopia	39.0	47.0	63.0	15.8	30	102	35	8	61.8	68	4.5
174	Gambia	42.0	56.1	66.0	35.3[b]	39	97	..	3	24.9	96	2.8
175	Guinea	32.0	37.2	57.0	11.7	..	94	40	11	34.1	76	2.4
176	Congo (Democratic Republic of the)	77.0	79.7	91.0	50.7	4	108	46	7	54.7	90	2.3

HUMAN DEVELOPMENT INDICES AND INDICATORS: 2018 STATISTICAL UPDATE

		SDG 4.6 Literacy rate		SDG 4.6 Population with at least some secondary education	SDG 4.2	SDG 4.1 Gross enrolment ratio	SDG 4.1	SDG 4.3		Primary school dropout rate	Survival rate to the last grade of lower secondary general education	SDG 1.a Government expenditure on education
		Adult (% ages 15 and older)	Youth (% ages 15–24)		Pre-primary	Primary	Secondary	Tertiary				
			Female	Male	(% ages 25 and older)	(% of preschool-age children)	(% of primary school-age population)	(% of secondary school-age population)	(% of tertiary school-age population)	(% of primary school cohort)	(%)	(% of GDP)
HDI rank		2006–2016[a]	2006–2016[a]	2006–2016[a]	2006–2017[a]	2012–2017[a]	2012–2017[a]	2012–2017[a]	2012–2017[a]	2007–2016[a]	2006–2016[a]	2012–2017[a]
177	Guinea-Bissau	45.6	49.8	71.3	..	..	..	..	..	..	..	2.1
178	Yemen	..	..	..	27.1[b]	2	92	51	..	30.5	85	..
179	Eritrea	64.7	82.6	91.3	..	14	54	33	2	26.9	80	..
180	Mozambique	50.6	56.5	79.8	19.3	..	106	33	7	66.8	75	6.5
181	Liberia	42.9	37.2	63.5	29.0[b]	156	94	37	12	32.2	92	2.8
182	Mali	33.1	39.2	60.5	13.1	4	77	43	5	38.4	66	3.8
183	Burkina Faso	34.6	44.0	57.0	8.5	3	91	36	6	31.2	72	4.2
184	Sierra Leone	32.4	50.9	64.5	25.6[b]	12	115	40	..	48.9	80	2.9
185	Burundi	61.6	75.0	85.3	9.3	14	131	48	5	55.7	72	5.4
186	Chad	22.3	22.4	40.7	..	1	88	23	3	49.0	84	2.9
187	South Sudan	26.8	29.6	44.1	33.2	10	67	10	..	..	..	1.8
188	Central African Republic	36.8	27.0	48.9	21.8[b]	..	106	15	3	53.4	40	..
189	Niger	15.5	15.1	34.5	6.6[b]	8	74	24	2	35.6	57	6.0
OTHER COUNTRIES OR TERRITORIES												
..	Korea (Democratic People's Rep. of)	100.0	100.0	100.0	..	50	..	93	28	..	..	..
..	Monaco	..	..	..	..	..	..	..	..	..	97	1.4
..	Nauru	..	..	..	..	69	107	78	..	..	..	..
..	San Marino	..	..	..	..	107	93	95	60	3.8	98	..
..	Somalia	..	..	..	..	..	..	..	..	..	..	..
..	Tuvalu	..	..	..	..	117	119	96	..	9.0	..	..
Human development groups												
Very high human development		..	..	..	89.3	83	102	106	71	..	..	4.9
High human development		94.2	99.1	99.2	72.1	76	103	96	50	..	88	..
Medium human development		74.3	84.7	90.4	51.1	33	110	73	24	16.3	93	3.9
Low human development		52.5	59.1	72.1	24.8	20	98	43	9	43.1	69	..
Developing countries		81.1	85.1	90.4	59.8	45	105	75	32	22.8	89	..
Regions												
Arab States		73.4	82.4	86.7	50.4	30	98	74	36	12.3	82	..
East Asia and the Pacific		94.4	98.4	98.6	71.0	78	103	92	41	..	91	..
Europe and Central Asia		98.2	99.6	99.9	81.2	41	102	99	62	5.9	94	4.3
Latin America and the Caribbean		92.8	98.3	98.0	59.6	75	107	96	49	..	81	5.5
South Asia		68.7	80.7	88.7	50.4	23	112	71	25	13.5	96	3.6
Sub-Saharan Africa		59.9	65.6	76.5	34.0	29	100	46	9	43.0	74	4.9
Least developed countries		59.6	68.0	76.9	29.6	24	103	48	10	45.2	77	3.1
Small island developing states		..	..	..	57.3	..	106	73	..	..	..	..
Organisation for Economic Co-operation and Development		..	..	..	86.0	79	102	105	68	..	..	5.0
World		82.1	85.5	90.7	66.5	50	105	79	36	21.4	89	4.8

NOTES

a Data refer to the most recent year available during the period specified.
b Based on Barro and Lee (2016).

DEFINITIONS

Adult literacy rate: Percentage of the population ages 15 and older that can, with understanding, both read and write a short simple statement on everyday life.

Youth literacy rate: Percentage of the population ages 15–24 that can, with understanding, both read and write a short simple statement on everyday life.

Population with at least some secondary education: Percentage of the population ages 25 and older that has reached (but not necessarily completed) a secondary level of education.

Gross enrolment ratio: Total enrolment in a given level of education (pre-primary, primary, secondary or tertiary), regardless of age, expressed as a percentage of the official school-age population for the same level of education.

Primary school dropout rate: Percentage of students from a given cohort who have enrolled in primary school but who drop out before reaching the last grade of primary education. It is calculated as 100 minus the survival rate to the last grade of primary education and assumes that observed flow rates remain unchanged throughout the cohort life and that dropouts do not re-enter school.

Survival rate to the last grade of lower secondary general education: Percentage of a cohort of students enrolled in the first grade of a lower secondary general education in a given school year who are expected to reach the last grade, regardless of repetition.

Government expenditure on education: Current, capital and transfer spending on education, expressed as a percentage of GDP.

MAIN DATA SOURCES

Columns 1–3 and 5–10: UNESCO Institute for Statistics (2018).

Column 4: UNESCO Institute for Statistics (2018) and Barro and Lee (2016).

Column 11: World Bank (2018a).

TABLE 10

National income and composition of resources

		Gross domestic product (GDP) SDG 8.1		Gross fixed capital formation	General government final consumption expenditure		Total tax revenue	Taxes on income, profits and capital gains	Debts Domestic credit provided by financial sector	Total debt service	Prices SDG 17.4 Consumer price index
		Total	Per capita								
		(2011 PPP $ billions)	(2011 PPP $)	Annual growth (%)	(% of GDP)	Total (% of GDP)	Average annual growth (%)	(% of GDP)	(% of total tax revenue)	(% of GDP)	(% of GNI)	(2010=100)
HDI rank		2017	2017	2017	2012–2017[a]	2012–2017[a]	2012–2017[a]	2007–2017[a]	2007–2017[a]	2012–2017[a]	2016	2017
VERY HIGH HUMAN DEVELOPMENT												
1	Norway	342.3	64,800	1.0	24.1	24.0	2.2	22.0	21.1	150.3	..	115
2	Switzerland	486.0	57,410	0.0	24.5	12.0	1.0	9.8	22.8	179.7	..	98
3	Australia	1,098.3	44,649	0.3	24.0	18.5	4.1	22.3	64.2	177.1	..	116
4	Ireland	324.1	67,335	6.5	23.4	12.0	1.8	18.8	40.4	84.2	..	105
5	Germany	3,740.2	45,229	1.8	20.3	19.5	1.5	11.2	17.4	127.3	..	109
6	Iceland	15.9	46,483	1.9	22.1	23.3	2.6	38.5	21.0	100.2	..	122
7	Hong Kong, China (SAR)	414.3	56,055	3.0	21.8	9.9	3.4	..	..	210.6	..	126[b]
7	Sweden	472.7	46,949	0.8	24.9	26.0	0.4	27.7	16.0	165.1	..	106
9	Singapore	480.0	85,535	3.5	24.8	10.9	4.1	13.7	32.4	140.8	..	113
10	Netherlands	830.5	48,473	2.5	20.3	24.3	1.2	22.2	26.9	191.9	..	111
11	Denmark	269.3	46,683	1.5	20.4	25.0	1.2	33.7	44.4	200.7	..	109
12	Canada	1,615.8	44,018	1.8	23.0	20.8	2.3	12.2	54.2	..	..	112
13	United States	17,662.3	54,225	1.5	19.5	14.3	1.0	10.9	53.7	241.9	..	112
14	United Kingdom	2,624.6	39,753	1.1	16.9	18.4	0.1	25.6	33.7	167.5	..	116
15	Finland	223.7	40,586	2.3	22.6	23.1	1.3	21.0	15.4	120.8	..	110
16	New Zealand	173.0	36,086	0.9	24.0	18.0	2.0	27.2	51.8	..	..	111
17	Belgium	485.1	42,659	1.4	23.3	23.4	1.3	23.1	32.7	135.7	..	113
17	Liechtenstein	..	..	..	..	..	..	..	..	..	..	..
19	Japan	4,944.9	39,002	1.9	23.5	19.8	1.3	11.1	46.5	345.1	..	104
20	Austria	400.3	45,437	2.2	23.5	19.5	0.9	25.7	26.4	126.7	..	114
21	Luxembourg	56.5	94,278	−0.7	17.0	16.4	1.8	25.7	30.5	193.5	..	111
22	Israel	288.7	33,132	1.4	20.3	22.3	3.9	23.4	30.1	81.1	..	106
22	Korea (Republic of)	1,849.6	35,938	2.6	31.1	15.3	3.4	14.8	27.2	170.1	..	113
24	France	2,591.2	38,606	1.4	22.5	23.6	1.5	23.1	25.4	157.7	..	107
25	Slovenia	64.9	31,401	4.9	18.5	18.3	2.3	18.6	10.9	68.1	..	107
26	Spain	1,596.1	34,272	2.9	20.6	18.5	1.6	13.8	33.6	178.6	..	108
27	Czechia	345.3	32,606	4.0	25.2	19.1	1.6	14.7	14.8	62.1	..	111
28	Italy	2,132.6	35,220	1.6	17.5	18.6	0.1	23.7	31.2	166.2	..	109
29	Malta	17.0	36,513	4.1	23.2	16.5	−1.8	26.2	34.5	117.3	..	110
30	Estonia	38.8	29,481	4.9	23.7	20.3	0.8	1.4	20.4	4.8	..	115
31	Greece	264.4	24,574	1.5	12.6	20.0	−1.1	26.7	18.7	116.7	..	101
32	Cyprus	27.8	32,415	2.6[b]	21.1	14.9	2.7	24.3	23.8	241.3	..	101
33	Poland	1,033.6	27,216	4.5	18.0	17.5	2.7	16.2	12.3	73.7	..	110
34	United Arab Emirates	632.6	67,293	−0.6	23.0	12.3	3.4	0.0	..	100.8	..	113
35	Andorra	..	..	2.3	..	..	..	..	..	..	..	..
35	Lithuania	83.5	29,524	5.3	18.8	16.5	1.2	4.9	17.0	13.4	..	113
37	Qatar	308.6	116,936	−1.1	..	23.1	1.1	14.7	40.2	147.2	..	115[b]
38	Slovakia	164.0	30,155	3.2	21.2	19.2	0.2	17.4	18.8	79.2	..	110
39	Brunei Darussalam	30.8	71,809	0.0	34.6	26.5	7.4	..	..	28.6	..	99
39	Saudi Arabia	1,615.5	49,045	−2.7	22.7	24.9	0.8	..	..	39.1	..	122
41	Latvia	48.6	25,064	5.6	19.9	18.1	4.1	23.9	10.3	76.3	..	111
41	Portugal	287.6	27,937	3.0	16.2	17.6	−0.2	22.5	24.1	154.1	..	109
43	Bahrain	64.6	43,291	−0.8	25.9	17.1	0.3	1.1	0.5	90.9	..	115
44	Chile	411.1	22,767	0.7	21.6	14.0	4.0	17.4	33.9	128.0	..	125
45	Hungary	261.9	26,778	4.3	21.5	20.1	0.3	23.4	17.3	58.4	..	114
46	Croatia	93.5	22,670	4.0	19.9	19.7	2.0	19.1	6.0	77.0	..	107
47	Argentina	838.2	18,934	1.9	14.8	18.1	2.0	12.2	12.4	39.2	4.8	..
48	Oman	176.0	37,961	−4.8	34.3	27.8	0.8	2.5	2.6	69.5	..	112
49	Russian Federation	3,636.7	24,766	−0.4[b]	21.7	18.0	0.4	9.1	−1.3	52.8	5.7	168
50	Montenegro	10.2	16,409	4.3	25.2	18.7	1.3	..	..	60.4	11.2	113
51	Bulgaria	131.4	18,563	4.3	19.2	16.0	3.2	20.0	16.1	55.3	15.3	108
52	Romania	456.6	23,313	7.6	22.6	15.1	0.7	16.8	20.9	32.9	10.3	114
53	Belarus	163.2	17,168	2.4	25.0	14.6	−1.3	13.8	2.4	41.9	13.0	..
54	Bahamas	11.0	27,718	0.4	26.3	13.0	9.6	14.2	..	72.4	..	111
55	Uruguay	71.0	20,551	2.3	16.7	14.3	−1.3	23.7	31.0	35.3	..	175
56	Kuwait	271.1	65,531	−4.8	..	25.9	2.9	1.4	0.6	92.2	..	125
57	Malaysia	847.8	26,808	4.4	25.3	12.2	5.4	13.8	46.9	145.3	3.6	120
58	Barbados	4.9	16,978	1.4	17.6	13.1	..	26.1	29.7	..	..	124
58	Kazakhstan	433.9	24,056	2.6	22.7	11.6	2.3	9.9	29.1	41.9	16.3	169

HUMAN DEVELOPMENT INDICES AND INDICATORS: **2018 STATISTICAL UPDATE**

TABLE 10 National income and composition of resources

		Gross domestic product (GDP) SDG 8.1		Gross fixed capital formation	General government final consumption expenditure		Total tax revenue	Taxes on income, profits and capital gains	Debts SDG 17.4		Prices
		Total	Per capita		Total	Average annual growth (%)			Domestic credit provided by financial sector	Total debt service	Consumer price index
		(2011 PPP $ billions)	(2011 PPP $)	Annual growth (%)	(% of GDP)	(% of GDP)		(% of GDP)	(% of total tax revenue)	(% of GDP)	(% of GNI)	(2010=100)
HDI rank		2017	2017	2017	2012–2017a	2012–2017a	2012–2017a	2007–2017a	2007–2017a	2012–2017a	2016	2017
HIGH HUMAN DEVELOPMENT												
60	Iran (Islamic Republic of)	1,548.8	19,083	3.2	20.5	13.2	3.7	7.4	19.3	77.6	0.5	340
60	Palau	0.3	13,240	−4.7	23.3	27.9	0.8	19.7	8.0	..	..	118
62	Seychelles	2.5	26,382	2.9	35.3	27.5	..	31.7	29.4	44.5	..	123
63	Costa Rica	76.2	15,525	2.2	17.2	17.3	2.9	14.0	15.8	82.8	5.2	123
64	Turkey	2,029.1	25,129	5.8	29.8	14.5	5.0	18.3	16.3	77.9	8.9	175
65	Mauritius	25.7	20,293	3.7	17.3	15.1	2.4	18.1	19.2	124.9	17.3	125
66	Panama	91.3	22,267	3.7	40.6	10.6	8.4	..	..	83.3	12.6	122
67	Serbia	98.7	14,049	2.4	18.5	15.9	1.0	19.7	7.6	54.2	16.5	139
68	Albania	33.9	11,803	3.9	25.2	11.5	2.5	17.6	11.5	63.3	4.6	115
69	Trinidad and Tobago	39.4	28,763	−2.6	..	..	..	27.1	48.5	47.7	..	140
70	Antigua and Barbuda	2.2	21,491	2.3	..	..	..	16.5	10.7	59.4	..	112
70	Georgia	36.2	9,745	5.0	29.5	17.1	−2.1	23.5	35.4	61.6	19.7	124
72	Saint Kitts and Nevis	1.4	24,654	0.8	..	..	..	20.4	24.9	76.3	..	106
73	Cuba	..	..	4.2 c	8.6	32.2	0.0	..	..	..	..	..
74	Mexico	2,239.2	17,336	0.8	22.3	11.8	0.1	13.6	35.7	55.2	7.6	130
75	Grenada	1.5	13,594	3.2	..	..	..	19.4	14.9	49.2	3.4	107
76	Sri Lanka	250.2	11,669	2.0	26.4	8.5	−5.2	12.3	15.3	71.9	4.0	147
77	Bosnia and Herzegovina	41.1	11,714	3.3	16.8	19.8	1.6	20.0	7.5	56.8	15.8	104
78	Venezuela (Bolivarian Republic of)	514.7 d	16,745 d	−5.2 d	21.6	14.6	0.2	..	..	61.9	5.0 d	2,740 b
79	Brazil	2,951.7	14,103	0.2	15.6	20.0	−0.6	12.9	21.8	111.3	6.7	156
80	Azerbaijan	156.3	15,847	−1.0	23.6	11.5	2.2	15.6	17.3	29.5	4.2	149
80	Lebanon	81.3	13,368	0.8	21.8	13.3	−4.8	13.9	21.3	209.6	9.0	119
80	The former Yugoslav Republic of Macedonia	27.3	13,111	−0.1	23.3	15.6	−1.5	16.8	15.6	59.8	8.4	111
83	Armenia	25.8	8,788	7.3	17.3	14.2	13.1	21.3	39.8	58.2	13.8	124
83	Thailand	1,123.8	16,278	3.6	24.0	16.9	1.7	15.5	30.7	164.7	3.6	111
85	Algeria	574.9	13,914	−0.1	29.9	17.3	1.3	37.2	60.2	66.8	0.2	142
86	China	21,223.9	15,309	6.3	41.9	14.3	..	9.4	20.6	215.2	1.1	119
86	Ecuador	175.9	10,582	1.5	24.3	14.4	3.8	..	..	38.1	5.5	124
88	Ukraine	335.4	7,894	2.7 b	16.0	20.4	3.3	19.6	15.2	58.7	16.0	235
89	Peru	393.6	12,237	1.3	20.6	13.4	4.4	13.8	31.5	..	3.6	125
90	Colombia	650.4	13,255	0.9	22.9	19.1	4.0	13.3	17.5	53.7	4.8	132
90	Saint Lucia	2.3	12,952	2.2	..	..	..	20.4	22.8	74.0	2.7	108
92	Fiji	7.9	8,703	3.0	16.4	24.1	..	25.5	22.5	120.9	2.9	125
92	Mongolia	36.4	11,841	4.2	23.8	12.3	−3.2	11.3	9.6	65.3	15.5	172
94	Dominican Republic	157.2	14,601	3.4	21.9	12.2	6.5	13.5	25.3	57.8	5.7	129
95	Jordan	80.9	8,337	−0.6	20.0	19.8	2.4	15.3	10.8	108.3	6.4	119
95	Tunisia	125.1	10,849	0.8	19.6	20.0	10.3	21.1	26.7	96.9	4.6	138
97	Jamaica	23.7	8,194	0.2	21.7	13.7	0.7	26.1	31.9	53.7	14.2	151
98	Tonga	0.6	5,426	1.8	33.0	18.9	..	..	..	32.6	3.7	113 b
99	Saint Vincent and the Grenadines	1.2	10,727	1.4	..	..	..	23.9	24.9	56.1	4.2	107
100	Suriname	7.8	13,767	−0.8	56.5	11.7	..	19.5	31.9	48.2	..	264
101	Botswana	36.2	15,807	0.5	31.1	18.1	0.5	20.8	29.3	17.1	1.1	141
101	Maldives	6.6	15,184	6.7	..	..	..	19.5	20.4	68.5	3.2	136
103	Dominica	0.7	9,673	−4.7	..	..	..	22.1	13.7	32.4	4.7	103
104	Samoa	1.2	6,022	1.8	..	..	..	24.3	19.0	78.7	3.0	112
105	Uzbekistan	202.5	6,253	3.5	24.9	15.1	..	17.3	19.9	..	2.0	..
106	Belize	2.9	7,824	−1.2	18.6	16.7	2.0	23.4	28.9	71.9	5.8	106
106	Marshall Islands	0.2	3,819	2.4	16.2	53.9	3.5	17.8	11.3	..	..	..
108	Libya	114.0	17,882	25.1	..	..	..	..	..	40.3	..	126 e
108	Turkmenistan	94.4	16,389	4.7	47.2	8.9	..	..	..	..	0.1	..
110	Gabon	33.5	16,562	−1.2	27.9	14.6	−4.3	..	..	18.7	2.6	111 b
110	Paraguay	60.1	8,827	−0.5	19.1	11.8	1.5	13.2	12.8	44.0	5.1	135
112	Moldova (Republic of)	18.4	5,190	4.6	21.9	19.0	0.0	19.3	11.1	24.3	6.0	154
MEDIUM HUMAN DEVELOPMENT												
113	Philippines	797.3	7,599	5.1	25.2	11.3	7.3	13.7	42.0	66.3	2.9	120
113	South Africa	697.3	12,295	0.1	18.7	20.9	0.6	27.1	49.3	78.7	4.4	146
115	Egypt	1,029.2	10,550	2.2	14.8	10.1	2.5	12.5	24.1	99.0	2.0	231
116	Indonesia	2,953.7	11,189	3.9	32.2	9.1	2.1	10.3	42.8	47.0	7.5	142
116	Viet Nam	589.7	6,172	5.7	23.1	6.5	7.3	19.1	35.5	141.8	3.7	156

TABLE 10 NATIONAL INCOME AND COMPOSITION OF RESOURCES

		Gross domestic product (GDP) SDG 8.1			Gross fixed capital formation	General government final consumption expenditure		Total tax revenue	Taxes on income, profits and capital gains	Debts SDG 17.4 Domestic credit provided by financial sector	Total debt service	Prices Consumer price index
		Total	Per capita			Total	Average annual growth (%)					
		(2011 PPP $ billions)	(2011 PPP $)	Annual growth (%)	(% of GDP)	(% of GDP)		(% of GDP)	(% of total tax revenue)	(% of GDP)	(% of GNI)	(2010=100)
HDI rank		2017	2017	2017	2012–2017[a]	2012–2017[a]	2012–2017[a]	2007–2017[a]	2007–2017[a]	2012–2017[a]	2016	2017
118	Bolivia (Plurinational State of)	76.1	6,886	2.7	21.3	17.0	4.9	17.0	9.6	68.3	2.3	142
119	Palestine, State of	20.8	4,450	–6.1	22.4	26.3	0.9	5.6	3.3	..	..	111[b]
120	Iraq	599.5	15,664	–3.6	17.4	20.7	..	2.0	4.8	8.7	..	119
121	El Salvador	46.5	7,292	1.8	15.5	15.8	0.8	17.6	28.3	89.3	5.3	110
122	Kyrgyzstan	21.0	3,393	2.5	30.3	17.4	1.5	16.9	10.8	20.5	6.9	152
123	Morocco	271.6	7,485	–0.2[b]	30.5	19.3	0.8	23.3	25.4	109.4	3.7	109
124	Nicaragua	33.1	5,321	3.7	28.1	15.3	3.5	16.3	34.6	51.4	6.3	147
125	Cabo Verde	3.4	6,223	2.6	34.5	19.1	2.0	17.9	24.1	86.7	2.8	108
125	Guyana	5.8	7,435	2.3	30.1	19.0	..	..	..	60.2	2.3	110[b]
127	Guatemala	125.6	7,424	0.7	12.3	9.7	1.5	10.4	35.8	40.5	4.6	133
127	Tajikistan	25.8	2,897	4.9	30.7	14.1	1.1	..	..	15.8	7.8	149[b]
129	Namibia	24.2	9,542	–2.9	16.0	24.5	1.9	28.5	40.4	78.9	..	146
130	India	8,606.5	6,427	5.4	28.5	11.4	10.9	11.0	46.6	75.0	3.4	160
131	Micronesia (Federated States of)	0.3	3,299	1.4	..	..	..	6.0	8.0	–41.2	..	113[c]
132	Timor-Leste	8.5	6,570	–10.0	25.2	36.3	–0.2	9.8	17.0	–7.2	..	142
133	Honduras	42.1	4,542	3.1	23.1	13.8	1.9	17.3	23.4	58.4	5.1	138
134	Bhutan	7.0	8,709	5.5	47.2	16.8	6.0	13.2	24.4	53.5	3.8	158
134	Kiribati	0.2	1,981	1.3	..	..	..	24.5	7.5	..	..	100[c]
136	Bangladesh	580.3	3,524	6.2	30.5	6.0	7.8	8.8	25.2	63.7	0.8	161
137	Congo	25.7	4,881	–7.0	26.3	11.6	46.3	9.4	8.1	38.9	2.0	119[c]
138	Vanuatu	0.8	2,922	2.3	25.9	14.9	–1.1	16.6	0.0	58.0	0.9	108[b]
139	Lao People's Democratic Republic	43.9	6,397	5.3	29.0	12.9	–1.3	12.9	16.0	..	3.7	129
140	Ghana	121.9	4,228	6.1	15.3	9.8	81.4	13.7	23.8	30.6	4.4	232
141	Equatorial Guinea	28.7	22,605	–6.7	12.0	23.5	1.5	11.5	36.9	21.1	..	121
142	Kenya	148.8	2,993	2.3	18.9	14.3	8.4	15.8	37.4	42.6	1.6	172
143	Sao Tome and Principe	0.6	3,053	1.6	..	..	..	14.6	12.8	23.1	0.8	172
144	Eswatini (Kingdom of)	10.6	7,739	0.2	12.4	22.3	7.0	28.6	18.6	24.1	1.0	155
144	Zambia	63.1	3,689	1.0	36.4	16.1	..	14.9	36.9	21.8	3.1	181
146	Cambodia	58.3	3,645	5.2	21.9	5.1	6.5	15.3	18.3	74.4	4.2	125
147	Angola	173.3	5,819	–2.6	7.8	13.4	20.0	10.3	42.4	29.5	8.4	281
148	Myanmar	298.4	5,592	5.4	34.7	19.0	..	5.8	12.9	41.1	0.2	145
149	Nepal	71.6	2,443	6.3	33.8	11.7	12.2	21.3	22.5	87.1	1.1	171
150	Pakistan	991.9	5,035	3.7	14.5	11.3	5.3	9.2	27.4	53.9	1.4	157
151	Cameroon	80.9	3,365	0.5	21.6	11.5	–0.9	..	..	16.6	2.6	115
LOW HUMAN DEVELOPMENT												
152	Solomon Islands	1.3	2,206	1.2	..	..	..	26.7	23.1	28.5	2.0	127
153	Papua New Guinea	31.5	3,823	0.1	..	..	..	13.5	50.4	44.3	20.0	136[b]
154	Tanzania (United Republic of)	149.3	2,683	3.7[b]	33.7	14.0	12.3	11.9	..	20.2	1.1	175
155	Syrian Arab Republic	..	..	..	..	..	..	14.2	30.2	..	0.0[f]	143[g]
156	Zimbabwe	31.4	1,900	1.1	16.8	27.5	28.2	21.4	32.1	..	7.5	106
157	Nigeria	1,019.0	5,338	–1.8	14.7	5.4	–15.1	1.5	26.9	23.3	0.6	214
158	Rwanda	22.6	1,854	3.6	22.9	15.2	10.7	14.8	22.4	19.0	1.6	147
159	Lesotho	6.4	2,851	4.2	24.0	34.9	2.9	36.4	22.8	15.5	2.2	143
159	Mauritania	15.9	3,598	0.7	58.5	21.7	8.7	..	..	29.6	4.9	128
161	Madagascar	36.2	1,416	1.4	15.2	10.7	2.4	11.4	9.0	19.0	1.3	161
162	Uganda	72.8	1,698	0.6	23.5	8.0	–10.9	13.5	30.0	23.2	3.6	166
163	Benin	23.1	2,064	2.7	28.6	15.1	2.0	15.4	16.7	25.9	1.1	109
164	Senegal	39.2	2,471	3.8	25.1	15.2	3.5	20.5	22.0	43.9	2.9	107
165	Comoros	1.2	1,414	0.2	212.0	16.1	1.4	..	..	30.2	1.0	104[e]
165	Togo	11.1	1,430	3.0	26.6	14.0	2.0	21.9	11.4	43.8	2.0	110
167	Sudan	181.0	4,467	2.2[b]	18.3	5.8	15.5	..	..	22.5	0.3	350[c]
168	Afghanistan	64.1	1,804	0.1	17.7	12.3	0.3	7.6	6.0	–2.4	0.2	138[b]
168	Haiti	18.2	1,653	–0.1	43.4	3.6	3.6	..	..	31.6	1.1	181
170	Côte d'Ivoire	87.5	3,601	5.1	20.9	12.0	10.9	15.2	10.8	33.8	4.4	112
171	Malawi	20.4	1,095	1.0	13.4	80.1	8.3	17.3	38.6	19.6	1.4	342
172	Djibouti	..	..	2.5	24.9	32.4	4.9	..	..	35.0	3.4	116
173	Ethiopia	181.6	1,730	7.6	39.0	12.3	13.8	8.8	17.5	..	1.7	249
174	Gambia	3.3	1,562	0.4	19.2	12.0	3.4	15.1	18.0	55.9	4.0	140[b]
175	Guinea	26.5	2,081	9.9	75.1	14.3	8.8	..	..	22.9	0.7	219
176	Congo (Democratic Republic of the)	65.7	808	0.4	20.6	5.5	–32.8	8.4	11.9	11.6	1.3	134[b]

HUMAN DEVELOPMENT INDICES AND INDICATORS: 2018 STATISTICAL UPDATE

		SDG 8.1 Gross domestic product (GDP)			Gross fixed capital formation	General government final consumption expenditure		Total tax revenue	Taxes on income, profits and capital gains	SDG 17.4 Debts Domestic credit provided by financial sector	Total debt service	Prices Consumer price index
		Total	Per capita									
		(2011 PPP $ billions)	(2011 PPP $)	Annual growth (%)	(% of GDP)	Total (% of GDP)	Average annual growth (%)	(% of GDP)	(% of total tax revenue)	(% of GDP)	(% of GNI)	(2010=100)
HDI rank		2017	2017	2017	2012–2017ª	2012–2017ª	2012–2017ª	2007–2017ª	2007–2017ª	2012–2017ª	2016	2017
177	Guinea-Bissau	2.9	1,549	3.3	10.4	9.3	4.9	..	..	14.1	0.4	112
178	Yemen	40.8 ᵇ	1,479 ᵇ	−35.9 ᵇ	1.7	16.8	−23.0	..	..	30.1	0.5	158 ᵈ
179	Eritrea	..	..	..	..	..	..	..	..	..	0.9 ʰ	..
180	Mozambique	33.7	1,136	0.8	21.7	27.2	4.8	20.1	35.2	32.6	4.5	171
181	Liberia	3.6	753	−0.1	20.1	15.9	−10.2	20.3	31.2	36.6	0.6	181
182	Mali	37.3	2,014	2.2	19.3	17.4	17.3	15.4	22.4	27.3	0.9	110
183	Burkina Faso	32.7	1,703	3.7	24.6	23.9	10.4	15.8	20.3	31.6	1.1	108
184	Sierra Leone	10.5	1,390	1.9	18.9	12.4	17.9	8.6	28.1	21.9	1.1	176
185	Burundi	7.6	702	−2.6	16.9	21.5	2.0	12.2	14.5	32.8	2.0	189
186	Chad	26.3	1,768	−5.9	20.6	4.3	8.3	..	..	25.2	0.4	116 ᶜ
187	South Sudan	19.2 ᵇ	1,570 ᵇ	−16.3 ᵇ	17.3	19.0	..	..	..	13.4	..	4,584
188	Central African Republic	3.1	661	2.9	17.7	8.0	0.0	9.3	7.8	30.5	1.4	187 ᶜ
189	Niger	19.9	926	1.0	33.7	15.0	2.7	..	..	19.1	1.3	109
OTHER COUNTRIES OR TERRITORIES												
..	Korea (Democratic People's Rep. of)	..	..	..	..	..	..	..	..	..	..	..
..	Monaco	..	..	..	..	..	..	..	..	..	..	..
..	Nauru	0.2	12,896	−0.4	..	..	..	..	..	..	..	..
..	San Marino	1.9	56,861	0.6	..	..	..	15.4	15.4	..	..	111
..	Somalia	..	..	..	9.5	5.4	..	..	..	..	0.0	..
..	Tuvalu	—	3,575	2.4	..	..	..	..	..	..	..	..
Human development groups												
	Very high human development	57,964.1	40,078	—	21.0	17.4	1.3	14.6	37.9	196.4	..	—
	High human development	35,766.3	15,280	—	34.3	15.0	..	11.2	23.4	168.6	3.0	—
	Medium human development	18,684.2	6,836	—	25.8	11.9	7.9	12.2	39.8	67.2	3.9	—
	Low human development	2,346.9	2,609	—	21.2	9.9	−2.1	7.5	24.2	23.9	1.7	—
Developing countries		62,657.3	10,199	—	30.9	14.5	3.7	11.3	27.4	133.2	3.3	—
Regions												
	Arab States	6,187.6	16,472	—	22.2	18.9	2.2	10.6	38.7	72.9	2.4	—
	East Asia and the Pacific	28,026.4	13,737	—	39.6	13.8	..	10.0	24.6	194.7	1.8	—
	Europe and Central Asia	3,753.3	15,563	—	27.2	14.6	3.9	17.3	16.7	66.5	10.1	—
	Latin America and the Caribbean	9,076.7	14,469	—	18.8	16.7	1.0	13.6	25.8	78.4	6.2	—
	South Asia	12,127.1	6,485	—	26.5	11.2	9.0	10.4	39.2	72.4	2.7	—
	Sub-Saharan Africa	3,486.3	3,489	—	19.9	13.8	2.8	13.8	38.4	40.3	3.0	—
Least developed countries		2,483.6	2,536	—	25.9	11.4	7.9	10.9	25.1	38.4	2.0	—
Small island developing states		371.1	8,078	—	18.9	20.5	..	..	..	59.5	8.6	—
Organisation for Economic Co-operation and Development		51,412.2	39,590	—	21.1	17.3	1.3	15.0	38.5	204.3	..	—
World		**114,763.7**	**15,439**	—	**24.6**	**16.3**	**1.9**	**13.5**	**35.1**	**177.1**	**3.5**	—

NOTES

a Data refer to the most recent year available during the period specified.
b Refers to 2016.
c Refers to 2015.
d Refers to 2014.
e Refers to 2013.
f Refers to 2007.
g Refers to 2012.
h Refers to 2011.

DEFINITIONS

Gross domestic product (GDP): Sum of gross value added by all resident producers in the economy plus any product taxes and minus any subsidies not included in the value of the products, expressed in 2011 international dollars using purchasing power parity (PPP) rates.

GDP per capita: GDP in a particular period divided by the total population in the same period.

GDP per capita, annual growth: Annual percentage growth rate of GDP per capita based on constant local currency.

Gross fixed capital formation: Value of acquisitions of new or existing fixed assets by the business sector, governments and households (excluding their unincorporated enterprises) less disposals of fixed assets, expressed as a percentage of GDP. No adjustment is made for depreciation of fixed assets.

General government final consumption expenditure: All government current expenditures for purchases of goods and services (including compensation of employees and most expenditures on national defence and security but excluding government military expenditures that are part of government capital formation), expressed as a percentage of GDP.

Total tax revenue: Compulsory transfers to the central government for public purposes, expressed as a percentage of GDP.

Taxes on income, profits and capital gains: Taxes levied on the actual or presumptive net income of individuals, on the profits of corporations and enterprises and on capital gains, whether realized or not, on land, securities and other assets.

Domestic credit provided by financial sector: Credit to various sectors on a gross basis (except credit to the central government, which is net), expressed as a percentage of GDP.

Total debt service: Sum of principal repayments and interest actually paid in foreign currency, goods or services on long-term debt; interest paid on short-term debt; and repayments (repurchases and charges) to the International Monetary Fund, expressed as a percentage of gross national income (GNI).

Consumer price index: Index that reflects changes in the cost to the average consumer of acquiring a basket of goods and services that may be fixed or changed at specified intervals, such as yearly.

MAIN DATA SOURCES

Columns 1–11: World Bank (2018a).

TABLE 11

Work and employment

			Employment				Unemployment		Work that is a risk to human development		Employment-related social security
		SDG 9.2	SDG 9.2			SDG 8.5	SDG 8.5	SDG 8.6	SDG 8.7		SDG 1.3
		Employment to population ratio[a]	Labour force participation rate[a]	Employment in agriculture[a]	Employment in services[a]	Total[a]	Youth[a]	Youth not in school or employment	Child labour	Working poor at PPP$3.10 a day[a]	Old-age pension recipients[b]
		(% ages 15 and older)		(% of total employment)		(% of labour force)	(% ages 15–24)		(% ages 5–17)	(% of total employment)	(% of statutory pension age population)
HDI rank		2017	2017	2017	2017	2017	2017	2012–2017[c]	2010–2016[c]	2017	2006–2016[c]
VERY HIGH HUMAN DEVELOPMENT											
1	Norway	61.5	64.2	2.1	78.5	4.2	10.0	5.4	..	..	100.0
2	Switzerland	65.2	68.4	3.5	75.8	4.8	8.4	7.0	..	..	100.0
3	Australia	61.1	64.8	2.6	78.3	5.7	12.6	8.7	..	..	74.3
4	Ireland	56.2	60.0	5.4	75.5	6.4	13.6	12.5	..	..	95.8
5	Germany	58.2	60.5	1.3	71.5	3.7	6.4	6.7	..	..	100.0
6	Iceland	75.1	77.3	3.6	79.8	2.9	6.2	4.1	..	..	85.6
7	Hong Kong, China (SAR)	58.5	60.4	0.2	86.7	3.2	9.2	6.1	..	1.2	72.9
7	Sweden	59.7	64.0	1.9	80.0	6.8	18.3	6.5	..	..	100.0
9	Singapore	67.1	68.5	0.1	83.6	2.0	4.6	4.0	..	0.3	0.0
10	Netherlands	60.4	63.5	2.2	81.3	4.9	8.8	4.6	..	..	100.0
11	Denmark	59.4	63.1	2.6	78.6	5.9	11.4	5.8	..	..	100.0
12	Canada	61.0	65.2	2.0	78.4	6.4	12.3	10.2	..	..	100.0
13	United States	59.1	61.9	1.7	79.5	4.4	9.5	16.5	..	..	100.0
14	United Kingdom	59.7	62.3	1.1	80.5	4.3	11.7	10.9	..	..	100.0
15	Finland	53.2	58.3	3.9	73.8	8.7	19.9	9.9	..	..	100.0
16	New Zealand	65.8	69.2	6.6	73.1	4.9	12.8	11.8	..	..	100.0
17	Belgium	49.3	53.2	1.3	77.4	7.4	19.0	9.9	..	..	100.0
17	Liechtenstein	..	..	..	..	..	..	..	..	..	..
19	Japan	58.5	60.2	3.5	70.9	2.8	4.6	3.5	..	..	100.0
20	Austria	57.0	60.3	4.3	70.1	5.5	10.4	7.7	..	..	100.0
21	Luxembourg	54.6	57.9	1.0	87.1	5.7	17.0	5.4	..	..	100.0
22	Israel	61.4	64.2	1.1	81.6	4.3	7.7	14.9	..	..	99.1
22	Korea (Republic of)	60.3	62.6	4.9	70.3	3.8	10.7	..	..	0.2	77.6
24	France	49.9	55.2	2.9	76.8	9.7	23.6	11.8	..	..	100.0
25	Slovenia	52.4	56.3	4.9	62.5	6.9	13.3	8.0	..	..	100.0
26	Spain	47.8	57.8	4.1	76.4	17.4	39.4	14.6	..	..	100.0
27	Czechia	58.1	59.9	2.9	59.3	3.1	8.3	7.0	..	..	100.0
28	Italy	43.1	48.6	3.9	69.8	11.3	36.9	19.8	..	..	100.0
29	Malta	52.1	54.5	1.3	79.3	4.3	10.0	8.5	..	..	100.0
30	Estonia	58.5	62.8	3.9	66.2	6.8	13.9	9.1	..	..	100.0
31	Greece	41.6	52.9	12.1	72.6	21.4	42.8	15.8	..	..	77.4
32	Cyprus	56.0	62.8	3.5	79.4	10.8	23.1	16.0	..	..	100.0
33	Poland	53.8	56.6	10.6	58.1	5.0	14.7	10.5	..	..	100.0
34	United Arab Emirates	78.3	79.7	0.4	60.7	1.7	5.1	..	..	0.5	..
35	Andorra	..	..	..	..	..	..	..	..	..	..
35	Lithuania	56.3	60.6	7.8	67.2	7.1	13.5	9.4	..	..	100.0
37	Qatar	86.8	86.9	1.3	43.6	0.2	0.5	0.0	..	0.0	18.0
38	Slovakia	55.1	59.8	2.9	60.8	7.9	18.2	12.3	..	..	100.0
39	Brunei Darussalam	62.3	67.1	0.5	81.8	7.1	28.2	17.2	..	0.3	81.7
39	Saudi Arabia	52.9	56.1	6.3	71.2	5.7	34.7	16.1	..	0.2	..
41	Latvia	55.1	60.6	7.5	68.5	9.1	17.0	11.2	..	..	100.0
41	Portugal	52.9	58.2	6.8	68.3	9.0	23.0	10.6	..	..	100.0
43	Bahrain	71.3	72.2	1.0	63.9	1.3	5.8	..	..	..	40.1
44	Chile	58.0	62.3	9.6	67.6	7.0	16.8	12.3	5.9	1.9	78.6
45	Hungary	53.2	55.6	5.0	64.8	4.3	11.3	11.1	..	..	100.0
46	Croatia	45.8	51.3	7.5	65.4	10.8	25.9	16.9	..	..	57.6
47	Argentina	54.6	59.9	0.5	76.1	8.7	24.7	19.7	..	2.8	89.3
48	Oman	59.0	70.2	6.5	55.3	16.0	48.2	..	..	0.5	24.7
49	Russian Federation	60.3	63.5	6.7	66.4	5.2	16.3	12.4	..	0.1	91.2
50	Montenegro	40.7	48.4	7.6	74.3	16.0	33.1	0.0	9.4	0.4	52.3
51	Bulgaria	50.1	53.4	6.3	64.5	6.3	14.4	18.2	..	..	100.0
52	Romania	50.5	53.2	22.9	48.0	5.2	18.4	17.4	..	..	100.0
53	Belarus	63.7	64.0	9.9	59.0	0.5	1.1	..	1.0	0.3	100.0
54	Bahamas	66.3	75.8	4.0	84.3	12.6	25.7	..	..	0.2	84.2
55	Uruguay	59.6	64.8	8.2	71.9	8.1	24.5	18.7	..	0.8	76.5
56	Kuwait	67.6	69.0	3.5	69.8	2.1	15.5	..	..	0.1	27.3
57	Malaysia	62.3	64.5	11.0	61.6	3.4	10.9	11.7	..	1.1	19.8
58	Barbados	59.5	65.9	2.9	77.9	9.7	29.0	..	..	1.4	0.4	68.3
58	Kazakhstan	67.6	71.0	18.1	61.2	4.9	4.7	9.5	..	0.2	82.6

HUMAN DEVELOPMENT INDICES AND INDICATORS: **2018 STATISTICAL UPDATE**

TABLE 11 Work and employment

		Employment				Unemployment		Work that is a risk to human development		Employment-related social security
			SDG 9.2	SDG 9.2	SDG 8.5	SDG 8.5	SDG 8.6	SDG 8.7		SDG 1.3
		Employment to population ratio[a]	Labour force participation rate[a]	Employment in agriculture[a]	Employment in services[a]	Total[a]	Youth[a]	Youth not in school or employment	Child labour	Working poor at PPP$3.10 a day[a]	Old-age pension recipients[b]
		(% ages 15 and older)		(% of total employment)		(% of labour force)	(% ages 15–24)	(% ages 5–17)[c]	(% of total employment)	(% of statutory pension age population)
HDI rank		2017	2017	2017	2017	2017	2017	2012–2017[c]	2010–2016[c]	2017	2006–2016[c]
HIGH HUMAN DEVELOPMENT											
60	Iran (Islamic Republic of)	38.4	44.2	17.1	50.5	13.1	30.3	..	..	1.1	26.4
60	Palau	..	..	..	..	..	..	..	..	..	48.0
62	Seychelles	..	..	..	..	..	..	..	..	..	100.0
63	Costa Rica	54.5	59.5	12.0	69.5	8.5	22.7	20.1	5.3	1.5	68.8
64	Turkey	45.8	51.6	19.4	53.8	11.3	20.3	24.0	..	1.1	20.0
65	Mauritius	54.5	58.7	7.3	66.7	7.2	23.3	..	..	1.9	100.0
66	Panama	63.2	66.9	15.1	66.7	5.6	14.2	26.3	2.6	4.3	37.3
67	Serbia	46.0	53.5	19.0	56.6	14.1	32.8	17.6	7.0	0.5	46.1
68	Albania	48.3	56.1	40.3	41.1	13.9	30.0	32.8	3.3	1.5	77.0
69	Trinidad and Tobago	59.1	62.1	3.7	69.7	4.8	11.4	52.1	..	0.9	98.4
70	Antigua and Barbuda	..	..	..	..	..	..	..	..	..	83.5
70	Georgia	59.8	67.6	40.9	46.6	11.6	29.3	..	1.6	16.8	91.9
72	Saint Kitts and Nevis	..	..	..	..	..	..	..	..	..	44.7
73	Cuba	53.0	54.3	18.6	64.9	2.6	5.5	..	..	2.7	..
74	Mexico	59.2	61.3	13.1	61.1	3.5	6.9	18.7	4.9	11.3	25.2
75	Grenada	..	..	..	..	..	..	..	..	..	34.0
76	Sri Lanka	51.4	53.5	26.7	47.7	4.1	20.7	27.7	..	10.1	25.2
77	Bosnia and Herzegovina	34.7	46.6	19.1	48.7	25.6	55.4	26.4	..	0.2	29.6
78	Venezuela (Bolivarian Republic of)	58.5	63.6	10.2	66.5	8.1	17.6	..	..	15.9	59.4
79	Brazil	55.5	63.7	10.3	68.8	12.9	30.5	24.8	5.4	6.4	78.3
80	Azerbaijan	62.8	66.1	37.4	48.5	5.0	13.7	..	..	1.5	81.1
80	Lebanon	44.2	47.2	3.2	76.5	6.3	16.5	..	..	0.4	0.0
80	The former Yugoslav Republic of Macedonia	42.4	55.0	16.4	53.8	23.0	46.9	24.3	7.6	4.9	71.4
83	Armenia	49.2	60.1	34.4	49.7	18.2	39.0	36.6	4.1	10.1	68.5
83	Thailand	67.8	68.6	32.8	44.7	1.1	5.9	15.0	..	0.6	83.0
85	Algeria	37.3	41.4	12.8	40.2	10.0	23.9	21.2	4.3	9.7	63.6
86	China	65.7	68.9	17.5	55.9	4.7	10.8	..	..	9.7	100.0
86	Ecuador	64.9	68.3	26.9	54.5	4.9	10.9	17.6	..	10.8	52.0
88	Ukraine	49.1	54.2	14.9	59.8	9.5	23.3	18.3	3.2	0.3	91.9
89	Peru	73.8	76.7	28.4	55.7	3.7	9.0	16.9	14.5	8.8	19.3
90	Colombia	64.1	70.4	16.1	64.5	9.0	18.4	21.9	3.6	8.4	51.7
90	Saint Lucia	54.0	68.3	15.3	67.4	21.0	45.0	..	3.3	..	26.5
92	Fiji	54.6	58.3	39.5	47.2	6.3	18.8	20.1	..	11.2	10.6
92	Mongolia	55.2	59.3	30.4	50.6	7.0	18.9	20.5	16.6	2.1	100.0
94	Dominican Republic	63.1	66.8	12.4	70.2	5.5	12.4	25.4	7.0	3.8	11.1
95	Jordan	33.3	39.1	3.7	69.5	14.9	39.8	..	1.7	12.0	42.2
95	Tunisia	39.8	46.9	13.7	43.7	15.2	35.8	..	2.3	5.3	33.8
97	Jamaica	58.9	67.2	18.6	66.0	12.5	29.7	..	2.9	5.8	30.3
98	Tonga	58.8	59.5	31.7	36.8	1.2	2.8	..	..	..	1.0
99	Saint Vincent and the Grenadines	56.8	69.6	6.2	81.0	18.3	39.6	..	..	..	76.6
100	Suriname	49.1	53.4	2.7	73.2	8.1	15.9	..	3.8	12.7	..
101	Botswana	58.9	71.9	26.2	60.3	18.1	35.7	..	..	21.2	100.0
101	Maldives	62.6	65.8	7.5	67.7	5.0	13.8	20.5	..	9.6	99.7
103	Dominica	..	..	..	..	..	..	..	..	..	38.5
104	Samoa	28.9	31.5	5.8	79.3	8.2	18.0	37.9	..	..	49.5
105	Uzbekistan	60.9	65.7	21.9	40.4	7.2	14.6	..	..	14.9	98.1
106	Belize	62.0	67.1	15.4	69.5	7.6	16.6	22.4	3.3	10.4	64.6
106	Marshall Islands	..	..	..	..	..	..	..	..	..	64.2
108	Libya	43.2	52.5	12.4	60.9	17.7	46.0	..	..	10.4	43.3
108	Turkmenistan	63.2	65.5	8.2	46.8	3.4	6.5	..	0.3	2.5	..
110	Gabon	41.3	51.4	41.9	45.6	19.6	36.5	..	19.6	15.2	38.8
110	Paraguay	66.3	70.4	21.2	59.3	5.8	12.8	37.7	17.9	4.4	22.2
112	Moldova (Republic of)	40.6	42.5	33.3	49.6	4.5	12.8	27.8	..	0.9	75.2
MEDIUM HUMAN DEVELOPMENT											
113	Philippines	60.6	62.3	26.0	56.3	2.8	7.9	22.2	..	18.2	39.8
113	South Africa	39.6	54.7	5.6	71.1	27.7	57.4	31.2	..	16.4	92.6
115	Egypt	42.2	48.0	24.8	49.6	12.1	34.4	27.6	4.8	42.7	37.5
116	Indonesia	63.4	66.3	31.2	47.1	4.3	15.6	21.5	..	27.6	14.0
116	Viet Nam	76.6	78.2	40.9	34.1	2.1	7.0	0.6	13.1	7.8	39.9

TABLE 11 Work and employment | 61

TABLE 11 WORK AND EMPLOYMENT

		Employment				Unemployment			Work that is a risk to human development		Employment-related social security
		SDG 9.2	SDG 9.2	SDG 8.5	SDG 8.5	SDG 8.5	SDG 8.6	SDG 8.7		SDG 1.3	
	Employment to population ratio[a]	Labour force participation rate[a]	Employment in agriculture[a]	Employment in services[a]	Total[a]	Youth[a]	Youth not in school or employment	Child labour	Working poor at PPP$3.10 a day[a]	Old-age pension recipients[b]	
	(% ages 15 and older)		(% of total employment)		(% of labour force)	(% ages 15–24)		(% ages 5–17)	(% of total employment)	(% of statutory pension age population)	
HDI rank	2017	2017	2017	2017	2017	2017	2012–2017[c]	2010–2016[c]	2017	2006–2016[c]	
118 Bolivia (Plurinational State of)	65.3	67.4	27.0	50.6	3.1	6.6	10.9	..	9.7	100.0
119 Palestine, State of	33.1	45.9	9.6	61.1	27.9	44.5	32.3	9.4	2.9	8.0
120 Iraq	42.7	46.5	18.7	61.6	8.2	18.0	40.6	5.6	31.6	56.0
121 El Salvador	58.6	61.4	18.8	60.0	4.5	9.9	29.9	10.0	6.3	18.1
122 Kyrgyzstan	57.2	61.6	26.7	51.1	7.3	15.7	20.4	16.2	16.7	100.0
123 Morocco	44.4	49.0	37.5	43.0	9.3	18.0	..	..	8.2	39.8
124 Nicaragua	63.7	66.6	29.4	53.0	4.4	8.5	1.4	..	8.8	23.7
125 Cabo Verde	54.2	60.4	67.7	25.4	10.3	17.8	..	..	37.2	85.8
125 Guyana	50.9	57.7	13.4	60.1	11.8	26.3	35.2	10.8	6.4	100.0
127 Guatemala	60.3	62.0	29.4	49.6	2.7	5.8	27.3	..	13.4	8.3
127 Tajikistan	53.2	59.3	51.6	32.0	10.3	18.9	..	..	16.9	92.8
129 Namibia	47.3	61.7	20.2	60.2	23.3	45.5	33.4	..	26.4	98.4
130 India	51.9	53.8	42.7	33.5	3.5	10.5	27.5	..	42.9	24.1
131 Micronesia (Federated States of)	..	..	..	..	..	..	..	..	..	..
132 Timor-Leste	37.5	38.8	25.0	59.8	3.4	11.6	24.3	..	23.1	89.7
133 Honduras	65.1	68.1	28.5	50.3	4.5	8.2	27.8	..	21.9	56.9
134 Bhutan	65.2	66.8	56.8	33.5	2.4	10.2	..	3.5	9.6	3.2
134 Kiribati	..	..	..	..	..	..	..	..	..	..
136 Bangladesh	54.0	56.5	39.1	39.9	4.4	11.4	28.9	..	67.3	33.4
137 Congo	62.1	69.7	37.2	36.9	11.0	22.5	..	23.3	52.5	22.1
138 Vanuatu	66.8	70.5	64.9	29.2	5.2	10.6	..	..	..	3.5
139 Lao People's Democratic Republic	77.8	78.3	61.3	29.0	0.7	1.7	..	12.3	77.2	5.6
140 Ghana	75.1	76.9	40.7	45.2	2.4	4.9	25.5	19.9	25.7	33.3
141 Equatorial Guinea	55.1	59.2	59.5	34.1	6.9	14.2	..	..	13.0	..
142 Kenya	57.9	65.4	38.0	47.8	11.5	26.2	..	..	26.8	24.8
143 Sao Tome and Principe	50.3	58.1	17.1	68.8	13.4	27.1	..	18.2	..	52.5
144 Eswatini (Kingdom of)	40.0	54.3	69.1	18.5	26.4	54.8	..	7.8	34.4	86.0
144 Zambia	69.0	74.8	53.3	34.8	7.8	15.4	..	..	67.0	8.8
146 Cambodia	84.5	84.6	26.7	46.3	0.2	0.4	12.7	12.6	46.4	3.2
147 Angola	71.3	77.6	50.6	40.8	8.2	19.1	..	18.7	59.0	14.5
148 Myanmar	64.6	65.1	49.9	33.5	0.8	1.7	18.6	..	41.9	..
149 Nepal	81.9	84.2	71.7	20.2	2.7	4.3	..	21.7	32.6	62.5
150 Pakistan	52.2	54.4	42.0	34.3	4.0	7.7	30.4	..	31.2	2.3
151 Cameroon	73.0	76.2	62.0	28.7	4.3	8.9	..	38.9	38.3	13.0
LOW HUMAN DEVELOPMENT										
152 Solomon Islands	70.0	71.5	69.6	20.6	2.1	4.4	..	17.9	43.5	13.1
153 Papua New Guinea	68.1	69.9	20.6	71.8	2.7	5.0	..	..	46.8	0.9
154 Tanzania (United Republic of)	81.5	83.3	66.7	27.3	2.2	3.9	14.9	24.3	68.3	3.2
155 Syrian Arab Republic	34.8	41.1	22.9	44.4	15.2	34.9	..	..	62.5	16.7
156 Zimbabwe	79.3	83.6	68.5	24.1	5.2	11.4	..	..	74.8	6.2
157 Nigeria	51.3	55.2	36.6	51.8	7.0	13.4	20.4	31.5	71.7	7.8
158 Rwanda	85.0	86.2	66.5	25.4	1.3	2.1	4.7	19.0	70.8	4.7[d]
159 Lesotho	48.4	66.5	10.4	49.1	27.3	38.5	..	..	55.3	94.0
159 Mauritania	44.4	49.4	75.9	16.9	10.2	18.6	39.5	17.4	15.9	9.3[e]
161 Madagascar	84.9	86.5	74.4	16.4	1.8	3.0	3.8	..	86.4	4.6
162 Uganda	69.2	70.7	69.0	24.1	2.1	2.9	5.9	20.6	52.4	6.6
163 Benin	69.1	70.9	43.2	38.3	2.5	5.2	20.0	41.3	73.5	9.7
164 Senegal	54.4	57.2	53.4	26.5	4.9	5.5	36.2	22.8	63.2	23.5
165 Comoros	41.2	43.1	54.9	29.8	4.3	10.0	..	28.5	28.1	..
165 Togo	76.1	77.6	37.8	44.9	1.8	2.8	..	22.6	61.4	10.9
167 Sudan	40.5	46.5	53.3	27.5	12.8	28.4	..	18.1	23.2	4.6
168 Afghanistan	49.5	54.2	62.2	31.1	8.8	17.7	..	21.4	98.2	10.7
168 Haiti	58.6	68.1	41.3	46.5	14.0	36.0	..	35.5	50.7	1.0[f]
170 Côte d'Ivoire	55.8	57.3	48.3	45.3	2.6	3.7	36.0	29.1	48.5	7.7
171 Malawi	72.3	77.0	84.7	6.9	6.0	8.0	..	19.4	82.6	2.3
172 Djibouti	55.6	59.0	29.8	40.5	5.8	11.7	..	..	..	12.0[e]
173 Ethiopia	78.2	82.5	68.2	22.4	5.2	7.4	10.5	48.6	51.5	15.3
174 Gambia	53.7	59.3	27.1	57.6	9.5	12.9	34.0	..	62.3	17.0
175 Guinea	61.3	64.2	68.2	25.9	4.5	5.5	..	32.8	69.4	8.8
176 Congo (Democratic Republic of the)	69.8	72.4	81.9	7.0	3.7	7.3	21.4	26.7	90.5	15.0

TABLE 11 Work and employment

		Employment				Unemployment			Work that is a risk to human development		Employment-related social security
		SDG 9.2	SDG 9.2	SDG 8.5	SDG 8.5		SDG 8.6	SDG 8.7		SDG 1.3
		Employment to population ratio[a]	Labour force participation rate[a]	Employment in agriculture[a]	Employment in services[a]	Total[a]	Youth[a]	Youth not in school or employment	Child labour	Working poor at PPP$3.10 a day[a]	Old-age pension recipients[b]
		(% ages 15 and older)		(% of total employment)		(% of labour force)	(% ages 15–24)		(% ages 5–17)	(% of total employment)	(% of statutory pension age population)
HDI rank		2017	2017	2017	2017	2017	2017	2012–2017[c]	2010–2016[c]	2017	2006–2016[c]
177	Guinea-Bissau	67.3	71.6	83.5	9.6	6.1	11.6	..	36.2	78.2	6.2
178	Yemen	32.7	37.9	44.5	42.6	13.8	25.5	44.8	..	81.2	8.5
179	Eritrea	76.2	81.4	83.9	9.1	6.4	11.3	..	..	75.2	..
180	Mozambique	59.0	78.8	73.3	22.4	25.0	42.7	10.1	..	76.8	17.3
181	Liberia	54.3	55.7	43.0	45.1	2.4	3.3	..	14.0	68.7	..
182	Mali	65.9	71.5	57.6	33.9	7.9	18.0	24.9	37.1	75.9	2.7
183	Burkina Faso	62.3	66.5	28.3	39.8	6.3	8.6	..	42.0	66.8	2.7
184	Sierra Leone	55.3	57.9	60.6	33.3	4.5	9.0	10.1	38.8	74.8	0.9
185	Burundi	77.7	78.9	91.5	6.1	1.6	2.9	6.2	31.6	89.5	4.0
186	Chad	67.0	71.1	87.2	7.9	5.9	10.1	..	39.0	65.5	1.6
187	South Sudan	64.0	72.3	64.9	16.1	11.5	17.6	..	..	..	..
188	Central African Republic	67.2	71.5	85.6	6.4	6.0	10.6	..	30.5	91.2	..
189	Niger	78.6	78.9	75.6	16.8	0.3	0.5	..	34.4	73.9	5.8
OTHER COUNTRIES OR TERRITORIES											
..	Korea (Democratic People's Rep. of)	76.6	80.5	67.1	15.4	4.8	11.7	..	..	77.0	..
..	Monaco	..	..	..	..	..	..	..	..	..	..
..	Nauru	..	..	..	..	..	..	..	..	..	56.5
..	San Marino	..	..	..	..	..	..	..	..	..	..
..	Somalia	43.4	46.1	86.2	6.2	6.0	11.0	..	..	71.3	..
..	Tuvalu	..	..	..	..	..	..	..	..	..	19.5[g]
Human development groups											
	Very high human development	57.3	60.7	4.1	72.7	5.8	14.5	12.6	..	..	95.7
	High human development	61.3	65.2	17.5	56.7	6.3	15.3	..	..	8.6	85.5
	Medium human development	55.4	58.1	39.5	38.6	4.7	12.7	26.0	..	37.1	27.0
	Low human development	62.7	66.9	60.7	28.8	6.7	12.2	..	30.8	68.4	9.4
Developing countries		59.0	62.4	31.7	46.0	5.7	13.6	..	..	27.6	59.1
Regions											
	Arab States	43.7	48.6	23.4	49.9	10.6	27.5	..	..	24.7	36.2
	East Asia and the Pacific	66.0	68.8	22.7	52.3	4.2	10.5	..	..	13.8	87.0
	Europe and Central Asia	52.1	57.4	21.1	52.4	9.5	18.7	21.5	..	4.1	66.2
	Latin America and the Caribbean	59.0	64.3	14.3	64.3	8.2	18.5	21.6	6.9	8.8	58.6
	South Asia	51.9	54.1	42.2	34.6	4.1	11.1	28.0	..	42.7	23.6
	Sub-Saharan Africa	64.5	69.5	57.2	31.8	7.7	13.6	..	31.2	61.6	21.1
Least developed countries		64.8	68.4	60.2	27.2	5.5	10.9	..	..	64.2	18.6
Small island developing states		58.7	63.0	24.5	60.8	6.7	17.1	..	..	22.6	25.9
Organisation for Economic Co-operation and Development		56.2	59.7	4.7	72.6	6.0	13.0	14.2	..	..	92.3
World		**58.6**	**62.0**	**26.5**	**51.1**	**5.7**	**13.6**	**21.7**	..	**26.5**	**71.5**

NOTES

a Estimates modelled by the International Labour Organization.
b Because statutory pension ages differ by country, cross-country comparisons should be made with caution.
c Data refer to the most recent year available during the period specified.
d Refers to 2004.
e Refers to 2002.
f Refers to 2001.
g Refers to 2005.

DEFINITIONS

Employment to population ratio: Percentage of the population ages 15 years and older that is employed.

Labour force participation rate: Percentage of a country's working-age population that engages actively in the labour market, either by working or looking for work. It provides an indication of the relative size of the supply of labour available to engage in the production of goods and services.

Employment in agriculture: Share of total employment that is employed in agriculture.

Employment in services: Share of total employment that is employed in services.

Total unemployment rate: Percentage of the labour force population ages 15 and older that is not in paid employment or self-employed but is available for work and has taken steps to seek paid employment or self-employment.

Youth unemployment rate: Percentage of the labour force population ages 15–24 that is not in paid employment or self-employed but is available for work and has taken steps to seek paid employment or self-employment.

Youth not in school or employment: Percentage of people ages 15–24 who are not in employment or in education or training.

Child labour: Percentage of children ages 5–11 who, during the reference week, engaged in at least one hour of economic activity or at least 28 hours of household chores; children ages 12–14 who, during the reference week, engaged in at least 14 hours of economic activity or at least 28 hours of household chores; children ages 15–17 who, during the reference week, engaged in at least 43 hours of economic activity or household chores; or children ages 5–17 who, during the reference week, engaged in hazardous working conditions.

Working poor at PPP$3.10 a day: Proportion of employed people who live on less than $3.10 (in purchasing power parity terms) a day, expressed as a percentage of the total employed population ages 15 and older.

Old-age pension recipients: Proportion of people older than the statutory pensionable age receiving an old-age pension (contributory, noncontributory or both), expressed as a percentage of the eligible population.

MAIN DATA SOURCES

Columns 1–7 and 9: ILO (2018a).

Column 8: United Nations Statistics Division (2018a).

Column 10: ILO (2018b).

TABLE 12

Human security

		SDG 16.9	SDG 1.5, 11.5	SDG 1.5, 11.5	SDG 1.5, 11.5, 13.1		SDG 16.3	SDG 16.1	SDG 3.4		SDG 2.1		
		Birth registration	Refugees by country of origin	Internally displaced persons	Homeless people due to natural disaster	Orphaned children	Prison population	Homicide rate	Suicide rate (per 100,000 people)		Justification of wife beating (% ages 15–49)		Depth of food deficit
		(% under age 5)	(thousands)	(thousands)	(average annual per million people)	(thousands)	(per 100,000 people)	(per 100,000 people)	Female	Male	Female	Male	(kilocalories per person per day)
HDI rank		2016–2017[a]	2017[b]	2017	2007/2017	2016	2004–2015[a]	2011–2016[a]	2015	2015	2010–2016[a]	2010–2016[a]	2014/2016
VERY HIGH HUMAN DEVELOPMENT													
1	Norway	100[c]	0.0	..	0	..	71	0.5	5.7	12.9	..	..	3
2	Switzerland	100[c]	0.0	..	0	..	84	0.5	6.0	15.5	..	..	5
3	Australia	100[c]	0.0	..	30	150	151	0.9	5.6	15.3	..	..	8
4	Ireland	100[c]	0.0	..	0	35	80	0.8	4.2	18.0	..	..	1
5	Germany	100[c]	0.1	..	0	..	78	1.2	4.5	13.9	..	..	3
6	Iceland	100[c]	0.0	..	0	..	45	0.3	6.3	17.2	..	..	4
7	Hong Kong, China (SAR)	..	0.0	..	0	..	114	0.4	..	..	..	..	8
7	Sweden	100[c]	0.0	..	0	55	55	1.1	7.6	17.8	..	..	10
9	Singapore	..	0.0	..	0	..	227	0.3	5.5	11.9	..	..	..
10	Netherlands	100[c]	0.0	..	0	100	69	0.6	6.0	12.9	..	..	10
11	Denmark	100[c]	0.0	..	0	..	61	1.0	4.7	13.5	..	..	5
12	Canada	100[c]	0.1	..	18	..	106	1.7	5.6	15.3	..	..	2
13	United States	100[c]	0.3	..	51	..	698	5.4	5.8	19.5	..	..	0
14	United Kingdom	100[c]	0.1	..	43	..	146[d]	1.2	3.2	11.7	..	..	3
15	Finland	100[c]	0.0	..	0	..	57	1.4	7.2	21.4	..	..	4
16	New Zealand	100[c]	0.0	..	6	..	194	1.0	6.3	18.7	..	..	15
17	Belgium	100[c]	0.1	..	0	..	105	1.9[e]	9.1	23.4	..	..	1
17	Liechtenstein	100[c]	..	..	..	..	21[f]	2.7	..	..	..	..	..
19	Japan	100[c]	0.1	..	46	..	48	0.3	9.2	21.7	..	..	12
20	Austria	100[c]	0.0	..	0	..	95	0.7	5.3	18.5	..	..	1
21	Luxembourg	100[c]	0.0	..	0	..	112	0.7	5.2	11.6	..	..	2
22	Israel	100[c]	0.5	..	0	..	256	1.4	2.3	8.7	..	..	0
22	Korea (Republic of)	..	0.2	..	5	..	101	0.7	13.4	36.1	..	..	6
24	France	100[c]	0.1	..	1	540	95[f]	1.4	5.9	19.0	..	..	2
25	Slovenia	100[c]	0.0	..	46	..	73	0.5	6.0	24.5	..	..	8
26	Spain	100[c]	0.0	..	29	250	136	0.6	2.9	9.4	..	..	9
27	Czechia	100[c]	1.3	..	0	..	195	0.6	3.9	17.7	..	..	5
28	Italy	100[c]	0.1	..	116	300	86	0.7	2.2	8.7	..	..	2
29	Malta	100[c]	..	..	..	..	135	0.9	2.0	8.2	..	..	4
30	Estonia	100[c]	0.3	..	0	..	216	3.2	4.8	26.4	..	..	20
31	Greece	100[c]	0.1	..	33	..	109	0.8	1.2	5.4	..	..	5
32	Cyprus	100[c]	0.0	217.0	0	..	94[f]	1.1	1.0	6.7	..	..	34
33	Poland	100	1.1	..	0	..	191	0.7	4.9	32.7	..	..	3
34	United Arab Emirates	100	0.1	..	0	..	229	0.9	0.9	3.6	..	..	30
35	Andorra	100[c]	0.0	..	..	..	72	1.2	..	..	..	..	..
35	Lithuania	100[c]	0.1	..	0	..	268	5.2	8.1	47.1	..	..	14
37	Qatar	..	0.0	..	0	..	53	0.4	1.2	7.3	7	16	..
38	Slovakia	100[c]	0.9	..	0	..	184	1.0	2.5	18.1	..	..	22
39	Brunei Darussalam	..	0.0	..	0	..	132	0.5	1.3	1.4	..	..	17
39	Saudi Arabia	..	1.2	..	31	230	161	1.5	2.2	5.5	..	..	32
41	Latvia	100[c]	0.2	..	0	30	239	3.4	4.8	31.9	..	..	9
41	Portugal	100[c]	0.0	..	28	..	138	0.6	3.7	14.3	..	..	3
43	Bahrain	..	0.5	..	0	..	301	0.5	2.9	9.5	..	..	..
44	Chile	99	0.5	..	4,515	140	247	3.5	3.3	15.3	..	..	26
45	Hungary	100[c]	3.3	..	0	..	187	2.1	6.9	25.8	..	..	14
46	Croatia	..	24.9	..	0	..	89	1.0	5.7	19.2	..	..	11
47	Argentina	100	0.1	..	15	630	160	5.9	4.8	23.7	2	..	26
48	Oman	..	0.0	..	0	..	36	0.7	1.3	6.4	8	..	47
49	Russian Federation	100[c]	61.6	19.0	9	..	445	10.8[g]	5.6	32.2	..	..	6
50	Montenegro	99	0.7	..	0	..	174	4.5	5.3	12.4	3	5	2
51	Bulgaria	100	0.7	..	16	..	125	1.1	4.8	18.3	..	..	24
52	Romania	..	1.2	..	0	230	143	1.2[e]	2.5	16.4	..	..	5
53	Belarus	100	3.7	..	0	140	306	3.6	5.4	35.0	4	4	8
54	Bahamas	..	0.4	..	0	..	363	28.4	0.4	2.9	..	..	72
55	Uruguay	100	0.0	..	268	45	291	7.7	6.3	25.2	2	..	9
56	Kuwait	..	1.1	..	0	..	92	1.8	2.1	5.7	..	..	15
57	Malaysia	..	0.5	..	90	470	171	2.1	3.4	9.5	..	..	15
58	Barbados	99	0.2	..	0	..	322	10.9	0.1	0.5	3	..	31
58	Kazakhstan	100	2.4	..	47	470	234	4.8[h]	9.6	48.1	14	17	17

HUMAN DEVELOPMENT INDICES AND INDICATORS: 2018 STATISTICAL UPDATE

		SDG 16.9	SDG 1.5, 11.5	SDG 1.5, 11.5	SDG 1.5, 11.5, 13.1		SDG 16.3	SDG 16.1	SDG 3.4		SDG 5.1		SDG 2.1
		Birth registration	Refugees by country of origin	Internally displaced persons	Homeless people due to natural disaster	Orphaned children	Prison population	Homicide rate	Suicide rate (per 100,000 people)		Justification of wife beating (% ages 15–49)		Depth of food deficit
		(% under age 5)	(thousands)	(thousands)	(average annual per million people)	(thousands)	(per 100,000 people)	(per 100,000 people)	Female	Male	Female	Male	(kilocalories per person per day)
HDI rank		2016–2017[a]	2017[b]	2017	2007/2017	2016	2004–2015[a]	2011–2016[a]	2015	2015	2010–2016[a]	2010–2016[a]	2014/2016
HIGH HUMAN DEVELOPMENT													
60	Iran (Islamic Republic of)	99	118.3	..	27	740	287	2.5	2.9	4.2	..	..	39
60	Palau	..	0.0	..	5,457	..	343	3.1	..	..	..	..	..
62	Seychelles	..	0.0	..	0	..	799	12.7	1.9	15.7	..	..	..
63	Costa Rica	100	0.2	..	0	44	352	11.9	2.0	12.6	4	..	39
64	Turkey	99	61.4	1,113.0	41	..	220	4.3	4.7	12.6	13	..	1
65	Mauritius	..	0.1	..	0	..	155	1.8	3.7	14.0	..	..	38
66	Panama	96	0.0	..	0	..	392	9.7	1.1	10.1	6	..	64
67	Serbia	99	35.0	..	15	..	148	1.4	5.5	19.5	4	7[i]	40
68	Albania	99	12.2	..	7	..	189	2.7	2.4	5.3	30[j]	36[j]	38
69	Trinidad and Tobago	94	0.3	..	0	25	258	30.9	4.5	22.4	8[j]	..	35
70	Antigua and Barbuda	..	0.1	..	1,316	..	373	10.3	0.0	0.0	..	..	209
70	Georgia	100	6.5	289.0	132	52	274[f]	1.0	1.5	9.7	7[j]	..	52
72	Saint Kitts and Nevis	..	0.1	..	0	..	607	34.2	..	..	..	..	..
73	Cuba	100	5.3	..	1,299	87	510	5.0	4.2	17.0	4[j]	7[j]	5
74	Mexico	95	11.7	345.0	60	1,600	212	19.3	2.1	8.1	5	..	29
75	Grenada	..	0.1	..	0	..	398	10.2	0.5	0.0	..	..	204
76	Sri Lanka	97	115.6	42.0	5,321	..	92	2.5[h]	13.3	58.8	53[i,j]	..	195
77	Bosnia and Herzegovina	100	17.7	99.0	0	..	73[d]	1.3	1.9	7.1	5	6	14
78	Venezuela (Bolivarian Republic of)	81	9.3	..	6	520	178	56.3	1.1	5.4	..	..	88
79	Brazil	96	0.9	..	76	3,200	301	29.5	2.7	9.6	..	..	14
80	Azerbaijan	94	10.3	393.0	68	140	236	2.1	1.1	5.3	28	58[j]	8
80	Lebanon	100	5.3	11.0	0	..	120	4.0	2.0	4.0	10[i,j]	..	39
80	The former Yugoslav Republic of Macedonia	100	1.7	0.1	0	..	147	1.6	3.1	9.9	15	..	28
83	Armenia	99	10.8	8.4[k]	0	..	130	3.0	1.8	8.0	10	23	31
83	Thailand	100	0.2	41.0	24	830	461	3.2	7.7	18.2	9	9	69
85	Algeria	100	4.0	2.5[k]	6	470	162	1.4	1.3	5.0	59[j]	..	32
86	China	..	207.7	..	150	..	119[f]	0.6	9.5	7.7	..	..	76
86	Ecuador	94	1.3	..	86	260	162	5.9	3.7	11.5	..	..	80
88	Ukraine	100	139.3	800.0	7	820	195[f]	6.3	6.2	28.7	3	9	18
89	Peru	98	2.6	59.0	187	490	242	7.7	2.9	9.2	..	..	52
90	Colombia	97	76.7	6,509.0	31	760	244	25.5	2.1	10.1	..	..	50
90	Saint Lucia	92	1.0	..	0	..	349	19.3	1.6	12.0	7	..	131
92	Fiji	..	0.7	..	0	..	174	2.3	4.3	13.5	..	..	31
92	Mongolia	99	2.2	..	0	..	266	5.7	9.2	48.2	10	9[j]	141
94	Dominican Republic	88	0.4	..	125	250	233	15.2	2.6	12.2	2	8[j]	96
95	Jordan	99	2.1	..	0	..	150	1.5	2.4	5.3	70[j]	..	28
95	Tunisia	99	1.8	..	0	..	212	3.0	4.1	6.7	30	..	37
97	Jamaica	100	2.2	..	38	45	145	47.0	0.3	2.6	5	..	61
98	Tonga	93	0.0	..	0	..	166	1.0	3.3	5.1	29	21	..
99	Saint Vincent and the Grenadines	..	1.3	..	499	..	378	36.5	0.4	4.9	..	..	43
100	Suriname	99	0.0	..	0	13	183	..	12.6	41.6	13	..	55
101	Botswana	83	0.3	..	0	110	188	..	6.2	19.5	..	..	192
101	Maldives	93	0.1	..	0	..	341	0.8	8.9	13.1	31[i,j]	14[i,j]	58
103	Dominica	..	0.0	..	844	..	300	8.4	..	..	..	..	42
104	Samoa	59	0.0	..	0	..	250	3.1	2.8	11.4	37	30	20
105	Uzbekistan	100	3.4	..	0	..	150	..	5.2	13.6	70[j]	61[j]	43
106	Belize	96	0.1	..	0	7	449	37.6	2.0	14.7	5	5	40
106	Marshall Islands	96	0.0	..	0	..	66	..	..	..	56[j]	58[j]	..
108	Libya	..	11.2	197.0	0	..	99	2.5	2.8	9.2	..	..	..
108	Turkmenistan	100	0.4	..	0	..	583	..	5.2	15.8	26	..	37
110	Gabon	90	0.2	..	41	74	210	8.0	7.0	18.1	50	40	47
110	Paraguay	93	0.1	..	28	120	158	9.3	6.1	13.7	..	..	85
112	Moldova (Republic of)	100	2.3	..	0	68	215[f]	3.2	3.9	22.3	11	13	62
MEDIUM HUMAN DEVELOPMENT													
113	Philippines	90	0.4	445.0	138	2,900	121	11.0[h]	1.9	5.8	13	..	96
113	South Africa	85	0.5	..	25	3,000	292	34.0	5.1	20.7	..	..	32
115	Egypt	99	22.1	82.0	1	1,700	76	2.5	1.8	4.5	36[j]	..	32
116	Indonesia	73	7.0	13.0	32	5,300	64	0.5	1.6	4.5	35	18[j]	53
116	Viet Nam	96	334.1	..	480	1,300	154	1.5	3.4	11.3	28	..	80

TABLE 12 HUMAN SECURITY

		SDG 16.9	SDG 1.5, 11.5	SDG 1.5, 11.5	SDG 1.5, 11.5, 13.1		SDG 16.3	SDG 16.1	SDG 3.4		SDG 2.1			
		Birth registration	Refugees by country of origin	Internally displaced persons	Homeless people due to natural disaster	Orphaned children	Prison population	Homicide rate	Suicide rate (per 100,000 people)		Justification of wife beating (% ages 15–49)		Depth of food deficit	
		(% under age 5)	(thousands)	(thousands)	(average annual per million people)	(thousands)	(per 100,000 people)	(per 100,000 people)	Female	Male	Female	Male	(kilocalories per person per day)	
HDI rank		2016–2017[a]	2017[b]	2017	2007/2017	2016	2004–2015[a]	2011–2016[a]	2015	2015	2010–2016[a]	2010–2016[a]	2014/2016	
118	Bolivia (Plurinational State of)	76	0.5	..	45	280	122	6.3	14.4	26.7	16[j]	..	136	
119	Palestine, State of	99	99.6[l]	231.0	11	..	..	0.7	..	..	..	..	..	
120	Iraq	99	360.6	2,648.0	7	..	123	9.9	3.5	4.8	51	..	235	
121	El Salvador	99	25.9	..	261	150	492	82.8	4.4	19.2	8	..	85	
122	Kyrgyzstan	98	2.8	..	104	130	166	4.5	3.4	13.4	33	50	43	
123	Morocco	94	3.1	..	0	400	222	1.2	3.5	7.0	64[j]	..	25	
124	Nicaragua	85	1.5	..	2	110	171	7.4	4.2	15.9	14[i,j]	..	128	
125	Cabo Verde	91	0.0	..	0	8	286	11.5	7.0	18.5	17[i,j]	16[i,j]	100	
125	Guyana	89	0.3	..	0	21	259	18.4	15.5	46.0	10	10	60	
127	Guatemala	96	16.3	242.0	368	460	121	27.3	1.5	4.2	11	7	104	
127	Tajikistan	88	1.4	..	19	180	121	1.6	2.5	7.2	60	..	227	
129	Namibia	87	1.4	..	0	110	144	17.1	5.5	16.4	28	22	207	
130	India	80	7.9	806.0	461	..	33	3.2	14.2	17.9	47[j]	42[j]	105	
131	Micronesia (Federated States of)	..	..	..	0	..	127	4.7	6.7	15.7	..	..	..	
132	Timor-Leste	55	0.0	..	156	..	50	3.9	5.6	13.2	86	81	180	
133	Honduras	94	14.4	190.0	106	170	196	56.5	2.6	5.8	12	10	109	
134	Bhutan	100	8.0	..	0	..	145	1.1	9.9	13.9	68	..	..	
134	Kiribati	94	0.0	..	73	..	136	7.5	6.6	23.6	76[j]	60[j]	20	
136	Bangladesh	20	16.8	432.0	131	2,300	43	2.5	6.6	5.3	28[i]	36[i,j]	107	
137	Congo	96	13.3	108.0	246	210	27	9.3	6.1	17.9	54	40	189	
138	Vanuatu	43	0.0	..	0	..	87	2.1	3.3	10.8	60	60	44	
139	Lao People's Democratic Republic	75	7.1	..	1	170	71	7.0	9.9	18.5	58	49	124	
140	Ghana	71	17.0	..	18	1,100	53	1.7	3.9	17.8	28	13	50	
141	Equatorial Guinea	54	0.1	..	0	45	129	2.3	13.2	39.1	53	52	..	
142	Kenya	67	7.6	159.0	12	2,300	118	4.9	4.5	17.1	42	36	120	
143	Sao Tome and Principe	95	0.0	..	0	..	101	3.4	1.7	3.6	19	14	84	
144	Eswatini (Kingdom of)	54	0.2	..	0	100	289	..	9.6	27.3	20	17	136	
144	Zambia	11	0.3	..	124	1,000	125	5.3	5.0	18.2	47	32	378	
146	Cambodia	73	12.2	..	356	420	105	1.8	8.5	17.9	50[i]	27[i]	108	
147	Angola	25	8.3	..	364	1,500	106	4.8	14.3	38.1	25	20	89	
148	Myanmar	81	1,106.6	635.0	37	1,300	113	2.3	3.3	5.9	51	49	121	
149	Nepal	56	8.4	0.0	14	660	59	2.2	6.2	8.2	43	22[j]	54	
150	Pakistan	34	128.9	249.0	72	3,900	43	4.4	2.4	2.5	42[i]	32[i]	151	
151	Cameroon	66	11.0	239.0	199	1,300	115	4.2	8.5	27.1	36	39	50	
LOW HUMAN DEVELOPMENT															
152	Solomon Islands	88	0.1	..	163	..	56	..	5.0	13.7	77	57	88	
153	Papua New Guinea	..	0.4	12.0	0	300	61	..	5.9	18.1	..	..	..	
154	Tanzania (United Republic of)	26	0.7	..	51	2,300	69	7.0	5.8	16.5	58	40	237	
155	Syrian Arab Republic	96	6,290.9	6,784.0	0	..	60	..	1.2	5.2	..	..	..	
156	Zimbabwe	44	17.4	..	82	..	145	6.7	10.3	26.9	39	33	356	
157	Nigeria	47	216.0	1,707.0	7	11,600	31	9.8	9.9	20.3	35	25	48	
158	Rwanda	56	259.0	..	83	450	434[f]	2.5	3.5	24.3	41	18	321	
159	Lesotho	43	0.0	..	113	..	92	41.2	8.2	19.9	37[j]	40	101	
159	Mauritania	66	36.5	..	54	130	44	9.9	5.7	14.5	27[i]	21[i]	35	
161	Madagascar	83	0.3	..	1,819	870	83	7.7	3.9	12.5	45	46[i]	306	
162	Uganda	30	6.4	24.0	718	2,300	115	11.5	7.6	18.3	58	44	284	
163	Benin	85	0.6	..	1,431	470	77	6.2	8.4	22.7	36	17	67	
164	Senegal	68	26.6	22.0	0	480	62	7.4	5.2	20.2	57	25	71	
165	Comoros	87	0.6	..	0	..	31	7.7	8.0	17.2	39	17	..	
165	Togo	78	8.1	1.5[k]	177	330	64	9.0	8.7	23.1	29	18	77	
167	Sudan	67	691.4[m]	2,072.0	869	1,500	50	..	6.3	16.6	34	..	184	
168	Afghanistan	42	2,621.1	1,286.0	227	1,400	74	6.3	3.1	10.9	80[i]	72[i]	145	
168	Haiti	80	28.4	..	869	420	97	10.0	6.0	17.7	17	15	468	
170	Côte d'Ivoire	72	40.0	16.0	42	1,400	52	11.6	14.4	38.8	48	42	113	
171	Malawi	67	0.4	..	148	960	73	1.7	4.8	18.0	16	13	179	
172	Djibouti	92	1.8	..	0	33	68	6.5	6.5	15.4	..	..	96	
173	Ethiopia	3	87.5	1,078.0	2	3,500	128	7.6	5.6	20.7	63	28	201	
174	Gambia	72	14.6	..	20	92	58	9.1	7.7	15.5	58	33	69	
175	Guinea	75	20.3	..	32	490	26	8.8	7.5	15.5	92	66	122	
176	Congo (Democratic Republic of the)	25	611.9	4,480.0	31	3,900	32	13.5	7.3	17.3	75	61	..	
177	Guinea-Bissau	24	1.9	..	41	110	..	9.5	5.8	13.6	42	29	204	

HUMAN DEVELOPMENT INDICES AND INDICATORS: 2018 STATISTICAL UPDATE

		SDG 16.9	SDG 1.5, 11.5	SDG 1.5, 11.5	SDG 1.5, 11.5, 13.1		SDG 16.3	SDG 16.1	SDG 3.4		SDG 2.1
		Birth registration	Refugees by country of origin	Internally displaced persons	Homeless people due to natural disaster	Orphaned children	Prison population	Homicide rate	Suicide rate (per 100,000 people)	Justification of wife beating (% ages 15–49)	Depth of food deficit
		(% under age 5)	(thousands)	(thousands)	(average annual per million people)	(thousands)	(per 100,000 people)	(per 100,000 people)	Female / Male	Female / Male	(kilocalories per person per day)
HDI rank		2016–2017ᵃ	2017ᵇ	2017	2007/2017	2016	2004–2015ᵃ	2011–2016ᵃ	2015 / 2015	2010–2016ᵃ / 2010–2016ᵃ	2014/2016
178	Yemen	31	23.6	2,014.0	4	880	53	6.7	6.2 / 12.6	49 / ..	201
179	Eritrea	..	464.1	..	0	150	..	8.0	5.4 / 23.4	51 / 45	..
180	Mozambique	48	0.1	10.0	245	2,400	61	3.4	6.7 / 20.5	23 / 20	192
181	Liberia	25	6.0	..	84	210	39	3.2	4.9 / 16.1	43 / 24	366
182	Mali	87	150.3	38.0	276	700	33	10.9	6.7 / 14.5	73 / 51	24
183	Burkina Faso	77	2.7	4.9	330	660	34	0.4	10.1 / 25.1	44 / 34	159
184	Sierra Leone	77	4.5	..	30	310	55	1.7	14.7 / 29.7	63 / 34	228
185	Burundi	75	439.3	57.0	396	610	93	6.0	6.3 / 20.3	73 / 44	..
186	Chad	12	16.3	158.0	87	810	39	9.0	7.9 / 20.9	74 / 51	246
187	South Sudan	35	2,439.8ⁿ	1,899.0	0	660	65	13.9	5.4 / 14.3	79 / ..	..
188	Central African Republic	61	545.5	689.0	433	320	16	19.8	9.3 / 30.3	80 / 75	490
189	Niger	64	1.4	144.0	192	910	39	4.4	5.5 / 11.5	60 / 27	67
OTHER COUNTRIES OR TERRITORIES											
..	Korea (Democratic People's Rep. of)	100	1.2	..	929	..	..	4.4ᵒ	14.3 / 17.3	.. / ..	336
..	Monaco	100ᶜ	0.0	..	..	..	74ᶠ	..	.. / ..	.. / ..	..
..	Nauru	83	..	..	..	..	140	..	.. / ..	.. / ..	..
..	San Marino	100ᶜ	0.0	..	..	..	..	..	.. / ..	.. / ..	..
..	Somalia	3	986.4	825.0	158	640	..	4.3	4.8 / 12.7	76 ⁱʲ / ..	..
..	Tuvalu	50	0.0	..	0	..	110	18.6	.. / ..	70ʲ / 73ʲ	..
Human development groups											
Very high human development		100	109.0ᵖ	236.0ᵖ	87	..	284	3.2	5.6 / 19.5	.. / ..	7
High human development		..	884.7ᵖ	9,909.0ᵖ	160	..	174	6.4	7.1 / 9.3	.. / ..	61
Medium human development		72	2,245.6ᵖ	6,479.0ᵖ	279	..	66	4.5	8.8 / 13.2	41 / 37	100
Low human development		45	15,076.7ᵖ	22,496.4ᵖ	208	3,987	68	8.5	7.2 / 18.8	51 / 36	163
Developing countries		68	19,206.1ᵖ	39,709.4ᵖ	232	..	111	5.7	7.8 / 12.6	40 / ..	92
Regions											
Arab States		83	8,507.1ᵖ	14,866.5ᵖ	97	..	116	3.3	3.1 / 7.1	46 / ..	83
East Asia and the Pacific		..	1,680.4ᵖ	1,146.0ᵖ	151	..	125	1.4	7.6 / 8.0	.. / ..	78
Europe and Central Asia		98	311.9ᵖ	2,702.5ᵖ	27	..	209	4.2	5.1 / 18.8	22 / ..	26
Latin America and the Caribbean		94	202.1ᵖ	7,345.0ᵖ	237	1,497	244	23.1	3.0 / 11.1	.. / ..	47
South Asia		67	3,025.1ᵖ	2,815.0ᵖ	415	..	48	3.3	11.4 / 14.8	45 / 41	108
Sub-Saharan Africa		46	5,479.4ᵖ	10,834.4ᵖ	161	3,877	88	9.5	7.4 / 20.4	49 / 34	142
Least developed countries		40	10,665.9ᵖ	15,869.4ᵖ	234	1,835	75	6.3	6.4 / 15.3	49 / 38	169
Small island developing states		82	44.0ᵖ	12.0ᵖ	465	..	226	12.6	4.6 / 15.7	13 / 14	157
Organisation for Economic Co-operation and Development		99	82.5ᵖ	1,458.0ᵖ	99	..	273	4.1	5.4 / 17.0	.. / ..	7
World		71	19,303.6ᵖ	39,945.4ᵖ	198	..	143	5.3	7.4 / 13.8	.. / ..	77

NOTES

a Data refer to the most recent year available during the period specified.

b Data refer to people recognized as refugees under the 1951 UN Convention, the 1967 UN Protocol and the 1969 Organization of African Unity Convention. In the absence of government figures, the Office of the UN High Commissioner for Refugees (UNHCR) has estimated the refugee population in many industrialized countries based on 10 years of individual asylum-seeker recognition.

c Estimates of 100 percent are assumed given the completeness of the civil registration system, which registers all vital events (including births).

d HDRO calculations based on data from ICPR (2016).

e Refers to offences of intentional homicide.

f For more detailed country notes, see www.prisonstudies.org.

g Data are from the Prosecutor-General of the Russian Federation and include victims of attempted homicide.

h Changes in definitions and/or counting rules are reported by the Member State to indicate a break in the time series.

i Differs from standard definition or refers to only part of the country.

j Refers to years or periods other than those specified.

k Refers to 2016.

l Refers to Palestinian refugees under the UNHCR mandate only. Another 5,340,443 Palestinian refugees are under the responsibility of United Nations Relief and Works Agency for Palestinian Refugees in the Near East (UNRWA 2017).

m May include citizens of South Sudan.

n An unknown number of refugees and asylum-seekers from South Sudan may be included under data for Sudan.

o WHO estimate used because other data were unavailable. The Government of the Democratic People's Republic of Korea does not agree with this estimate.

p Unweighted sum of national estimates.

DEFINITIONS

Birth registration: Percentage of children under age 5 who were registered at the moment of the survey. It includes children whose birth certificate was seen by the interviewer and children whose mother or caretaker says the birth has been registered.

Refugees by country of origin: Number of people who have fled their country of origin because of a well founded fear of persecution due to their race, religion, nationality, political opinion or membership in a particular social group and who cannot or do not want to return to their country of origin.

Internally displaced persons: Number of people who have been forced to leave their homes or places of habitual residence—in particular, as a result of or to avoid the effects of armed conflict, situations of generalized violence, violations of human rights or natural or human-made disasters—and who have not crossed an internationally recognized state border.

Homeless people due to natural disaster: Average annual number of people who lack a shelter for living quarters as a result of natural disasters, who carry their few possessions with them and who sleep in the streets, in doorways or on piers, or in any other space, on a more or less random basis, expressed per million people.

Orphaned children: Number of children (ages 0–17) who have lost one or both parents due to any cause.

Prison population: Number of adult and juvenile prisoners—including pretrial detainees, unless otherwise noted—expressed per 100,000 people.

Homicide rate: Number of unlawful deaths purposefully inflicted on a person by another person, expressed per 100,000 people.

Suicide rate: Number of deaths from purposely self-inflicted injuries, expressed per 100,000 people in the reference population.

Justification of wife beating: Percentage of women and men ages 15–49 who consider a husband to be justified in hitting or beating his wife for at least one of the following reasons: if his wife burns the food, argues with him, goes out without telling him, neglects the children or refuses sexual relations.

Depth of the food deficit: Number of kilocalories needed to lift the undernourished from their status, holding all other factors constant.

MAIN DATA SOURCES

Column 1: United Nations Statistics Division (2018a).

Column 2: UNHCR (2018).

Column 3: IDMC (2018).

Column 4: CRED EM-DAT (2018) and UNDESA (2017a).

Columns 5, 10 and 11: UNICEF (2018).

Column 6: ICPR (2016).

Column 7: UNODC (2018).

Columns 8 and 9: WHO (2018).

Column 12: FAO (2018a).

TABLE 13

Human and capital mobility

		Trade	Financial flows SDG 17.3			SDG 17.3	Human mobility			Communication SDG 17.8, 17.8		SDG 9.c	
		Exports and imports	Foreign direct investment, net inflows	Private capital flows	Net official development assistance received[a]	Remittances, inflows	Net migration rate	Stock of immigrants	International student mobility	International inbound tourists	Internet users Total	Female	Mobile phone subscriptions
		(% of GDP)	(% of GDP)	(% of GDP)	(% of GNI)	(% of GDP)	(per 1,000 people)	(% of population)	(% of total tertiary enrolment)	(thousands)	(% of population)	(% of female population)	(per 100 people) / (% change)
HDI rank		2017[b]	2017[b]	2017[b]	2016[c]	2017[b]	2010/2015[d]	2017	2017[b]	2016[e]	2016	2017[b]	2016 / 2010–2016
VERY HIGH HUMAN DEVELOPMENT														
1	Norway	68.5	−1.2	6.5	..	0.15	8.8[e]	15.1[e]	−2.9	5,960	97.3	97.4	109.0	−4.9
2	Switzerland	118.9	5.6	−4.8	..	0.37	9.8	29.6	13.2	9,205	89.1	86.1	133.8	8.7
3	Australia	41.9	3.7	−3.6	..	0.15	8.0[f]	28.8[f]	16.8	8,263	88.2	84.9	110.1	8.2
4	Ireland	207.9	15.4	−30.5	..	0.19	−6.0	16.9	1.2	10,100	85.0	86.0	103.2	1.5
5	Germany	86.9	2.1	7.5	..	0.46	4.4	14.8	3.8	35,555	89.6	81.2	126.3	15.6
6	Iceland	89.8	−29.4	10.8	..	0.88	−1.3	12.5	−6.3	1,792	98.2	98.0	120.8	13.4
7	Hong Kong, China (SAR)	375.1	35.8	−17.8	..	0.13	2.1	39.1	−1.7	26,553	87.5	86.3	240.8	22.6
7	Sweden	86.4	5.4	0.4	..	0.55	5.3	17.6	2.2	6,782	89.7	89.0	127.5	8.9
9	Singapore	322.4	19.6	−1.4	..	..	12.7	46.0	10.2	12,914	81.0	83.6	150.5	3.4
10	Netherlands	161.2	38.1	5.7	..	0.18	0.7	12.1	8.9	15,828	90.4	89.2	123.0	7.0
11	Denmark	103.4	−0.7	4.3	..	0.42	3.8	11.5	9.2	10,781	97.0	97.5	122.3	5.8
12	Canada	64.1	1.7	−1.7	..	0.08	6.5	21.5	..	19,824	89.8	..	84.7	12.1
13	United States	26.6	1.8	−0.9	..	0.03	2.9	15.3	4.3	75,608	76.2	74.9	122.9	33.0
14	United Kingdom	62.5	1.8	−0.3	..	0.17	3.1	13.4	17.1	35,814	94.8	94.8	120.0	−1.0
15	Finland	76.7	4.3	1.1	..	0.35	3.0[g]	6.2[g]	4.6	2,789	87.7	86.6	133.9	−14.4
16	New Zealand	51.3	1.6	0.0	..	0.23	4.0	22.7	17.9	3,370	88.5	..	124.4	15.5
17	Belgium	169.4	−6.3	7.5	..	2.13	4.7	11.1	8.5	7,481	86.5	85.4	110.5	−0.6
17	Liechtenstein	..	..	..	..	..	..	65.1	−42.5	60	98.1	..	117.6	19.3
19	Japan	31.3	0.4	2.0	..	0.09	0.6	1.8	2.6	24,040	93.2	91.8	130.6	36.2
20	Austria	104.7	3.3	5.6	..	0.72	6.3	19.0	12.3	28,121	84.3	80.7	163.8	12.5
21	Luxembourg	424.0	45.8	−23.8	..	2.78	18.1	45.3	−99.9	1,054	98.1	97.3	132.7	−7.3
22	Israel	58.4	5.4	−3.1	..	0.28	0.5	23.6	−0.9	2,900	79.7	78.7	129.0	5.2
22	Korea (Republic of)	80.8	1.1	4.7	..	0.41	0.7	2.3	−1.6	17,242	92.8	90.9	120.7	17.8
24	France	62.9	2.0	0.4	..	0.97	1.1	12.2	6.3	82,570	85.6	85.5	104.4	13.9
25	Slovenia	154.8	2.1	5.8	..	0.82	1.6	11.8	−0.4	3,032	75.5	74.1	114.8	10.7
26	Spain	65.5	0.3	3.5	..	0.23	−2.4[h]	12.8[h]	0.9	75,315	80.6	78.6	111.2	1.2
27	Czechia	151.7	4.3	−7.2	..	1.66	1.1	4.1	7.4	9,321	76.5	74.8	117.7	−4.2
28	Italy	59.5	1.0	5.0	..	0.51	0.9	10.0	1.7	52,372	61.3	57.2	153.0	−2.4
29	Malta	261.5	27.8	−22.3	..	1.88	4.5	10.6	−0.3	1,966	77.3	77.2	123.9	13.2
30	Estonia	151.6	3.3	8.0	..	1.93	−1.6	14.7	−2.7	3,147	87.2	87.4	144.6	16.6
31	Greece	67.5	2.0	−13.7	..	0.15	−2.9	10.9	−0.9	24,799	69.1	67.1	112.1	4.4
32	Cyprus	131.6	48.6	−23.0	..	1.67	4.0[i]	16.0[i]	−50.2	3,187	75.9	74.4	133.4	6.8
33	Poland	102.8	1.2	−1.3	..	1.31	−0.4	1.7	1.9	17,471	73.3	72.8	138.7	13.2
34	United Arab Emirates	172.8	2.5	..	..	..	11.0	88.4	41.5	..	90.6	88.9	214.7	62.5
35	Andorra	..	..	..	..	..	..	53.3	−198.2	2,831	97.9	..	92.0	18.7
35	Lithuania	160.6	2.3	2.2	..	2.76	−9.7	4.3	−4.2	2,296	74.4	74.7	144.6	−7.7
37	Qatar	89.1	0.6	−5.1	..	0.40	56.5	65.2	18.1	2,938	94.3	91.7	142.1	15.7
38	Slovakia	189.2	6.2	−2.9	..	2.26	0.4	3.4	−10.6	2,027	80.5	79.3	128.4	17.1
39	Brunei Darussalam	85.2	−1.3	6.4	..	..	1.0	25.3	−30.9	219	90.0	90.0	123.7	10.5
39	Saudi Arabia	61.7	1.2	−1.5	..	0.04	10.8	37.0	−0.3	18,049	73.8	92.9	148.5	−21.0
41	Latvia	122.3	3.8	6.5	..	4.18	−8.1	13.2	−0.6	1,793	79.8	78.9	134.5	23.6
41	Portugal	85.2	4.6	0.5	..	0.21	−2.7	8.5	1.3	11,223	70.4	69.0	111.6	−2.7
43	Bahrain	139.6	1.5	9.9	..	..	6.4	48.4	−1.6	10,158	98.0	99.0	210.1	66.4
44	Chile	55.7	2.3	1.0	0.1	0.02	0.9	2.7	−0.4	5,641	66.0	..	130.1	11.4
45	Hungary	172.4	−10.7	1.2	..	3.33	0.6	5.2	5.1	5,302	79.3	78.4	120.8	−0.2
46	Croatia	100.4	3.8	−2.1	0.2	4.53	−1.5	13.4	−5.1	13,809	72.7	68.7	104.8	−8.0
47	Argentina	25.0	1.9	−7.1	0.0	0.09	0.1	4.9	..	5,559	71.0	70.1	145.3	5.0
48	Oman	76.8	2.5	−9.0	0.0	0.06	45.2	44.7	−8.8	2,292	69.9	67.4	155.2	2.5
49	Russian Federation	46.7	1.8	0.2	..	0.51	1.4	8.1	3.0	24,571	73.1	72.6	159.2	−4.1
50	Montenegro	106.2	11.5	−11.9	1.9	9.09	−1.0	11.3	..	1,662	69.9	65.9	165.6	−11.7
51	Bulgaria	131.1	2.9	4.0	..	3.88	−0.7	2.2	−4.7	8,252	59.8	59.1	125.8	−8.7
52	Romania	85.0	2.3	−3.9	..	2.03	−3.0	1.9	−1.4	10,223	59.5	56.9	115.8	−2.8
53	Belarus	133.6	2.3	−4.6	0.0	2.20	1.6	11.4	−2.1	9,424	71.1	70.9	120.7	10.6
54	Bahamas	75.5	0.6	−0.4	..	..	5.2	15.6	..	1,482	80.0	..	92.1	−22.4
55	Uruguay	40.0	0.0	−3.3	0.0	0.18	−1.8	2.3	..	3,037	66.4	64.2	148.6	13.0
56	Kuwait	94.7	0.1	26.9	..	0.02	38.7	75.5	..	307	78.4	..	133.1	0.3
57	Malaysia	135.9	3.0	−0.4	0.0	0.52	5.3[j]	8.5[j]	4.5	26,757	78.8	76.7	140.8	16.9
58	Barbados	80.7	5.0	0.9	0.4	2.33	1.5	12.1	3.9	632	79.5	..	116.6	−6.9
58	Kazakhstan	60.3	2.8	−5.8	0.0	0.22	1.9	20.0	−12.1	6,509	74.6	73.3	142.0	20.0

HUMAN DEVELOPMENT INDICES AND INDICATORS: **2018 STATISTICAL UPDATE**

TABLE 13 Human and capital mobility

	Trade	SDG 17.3	Financial flows	SDG 17.3		Human mobility		SDG 8.9	SDG 17.6, 17.8	Communication	SDG 9.c		
	Exports and imports	Foreign direct investment, net inflows	Private capital flows	Net official development assistance received[a]	Remittances, inflows	Net migration rate	Stock of immigrants	International student mobility	International inbound tourists	Internet users Total	Internet users Female	Mobile phone subscriptions	
	(% of GDP)	(% of GDP)	(% of GDP)	(% of GNI)	(% of GDP)	(per 1,000 people)	(% of population)	(% of total tertiary enrolment)	(thousands)	(% of population)	(% of female population)	(per 100 people)	(% change)
HDI rank	2017[b]	2017[b]	2017[b]	2016[c]	2017[b]	2010/2015[d]	2017	2017[b]	2016[c]	2016	2017[b]	2016	2010–2016
HIGH HUMAN DEVELOPMENT													
60 Iran (Islamic Republic of)	46.1	0.8	..	0.0	0.31	−1.0	3.3	−0.7	4,942	53.2	52.1	100.3	38.4
60 Palau	126.7	11.6	−10.0	6.1	0.83	..	23.0	18.9	138	..	..	..	..
62 Seychelles	192.0	8.4	−9.1	0.4	1.46	−4.8	13.6	−38.6	303	56.5	..	161.2	25.3
63 Costa Rica	67.6	5.3	−5.5	0.2	0.98	0.8	8.4	..	2,925	66.0	66.3	171.5	149.2
64 Turkey	54.2	1.3	−3.8	0.4	0.12	4.3	6.0	0.4	30,289	58.3	56.6	94.4	10.5
65 Mauritius	97.1	2.9	−19.9	0.3	0.01	−1.9[k]	2.3[k]	−12.8	1,275	52.2	49.5	143.7	50.6
66 Panama	87.3	9.8	−10.1	0.0	0.86	1.5	4.7	..	2,007	54.0	52.5	127.5	−30.1
67 Serbia	113.7	6.9	−4.3	1.8	8.66	−2.2[l]	9.1[l]	−1.6	1,281	67.1	65.0	130.2	−4.2
68 Albania	78.1	7.9	−9.2	1.4	10.05	−6.4	1.8	−14.9	4,070	66.4	..	115.2	25.8
69 Trinidad and Tobago	..	−1.7	4.0	0.0	0.61	..	3.7	..	410	73.3	..	158.7	11.3
70 Antigua and Barbuda	88.7	3.4	−2.0	0.0	2.02	−0.1	28.1	−19.3	265	73.0	..	178.3	0.5
70 Georgia	112.6	11.9	−10.0	3.4	11.83	−14.9[m]	2.0[m]	−1.7	6,361	58.0	56.7	140.9	49.9
72 Saint Kitts and Nevis	113.5	9.3	−6.1	3.9	1.12	..	13.7	61.6	122	76.8	..	139.7	−10.2
73 Cuba	31.6	..	..	0.1	..	−1.3	0.1	4.1	3,968	38.8	39.7	34.7	292.6
74 Mexico	77.6	2.8	−2.9	0.1	2.66	−0.5	0.9	−0.4	35,079	59.5	58.1	87.6	12.5
75 Grenada	108.5	8.6	−2.2	0.8	0.11	−8.1	6.6	64.1	156	55.9	..	110.9	−4.8
76 Sri Lanka	51.1	1.6	−3.5	0.5	8.25	−4.7	0.2	−5.9	2,051	32.1	..	124.0	44.3
77 Bosnia and Herzegovina	86.9	2.4	−1.6	2.6	10.99	−8.9	1.1	−3.9	777	54.7	..	96.8	15.8
78 Venezuela (Bolivarian Republic of)	48.1	0.2	0.2	0.0	0.03	−0.5	4.5	−0.6	601	60.0	..	87.4	−9.0
79 Brazil	24.1	3.4	−2.5	0.0	0.13	0.0	0.4	−0.3	6,578	60.9	61.1	117.5	17.5
80 Azerbaijan	90.7	7.0	−7.3	0.2	2.78	0.0[n]	2.6[n]	−18.3	2,044	78.2	74.7	104.8	4.0
80 Lebanon	70.0	5.3	−17.5	2.3	15.34	49.1	31.9	1.9	1,688	76.1	..	81.4	23.3
80 The former Yugoslav Republic of Macedonia	124.0	3.8	−2.0	1.6	2.77	−0.9	6.3	−4.1	510	72.2	70.6	98.5	−5.3
83 Armenia	88.5	2.1	−1.2	3.0	13.34	−2.1	6.5	−3.1	1,260	67.0	63.4	117.4	−12.6
83 Thailand	121.7	2.0	3.1	0.1	1.48	0.5	5.2	−0.6	32,530	47.5	47.0	173.8	62.8
85 Algeria	60.4	1.0	−0.9	0.1	1.23	−0.8	0.6	−0.9	2,039	42.9	..	115.8	27.6
86 China	37.8	1.4	−0.6	0.0	0.23	−0.2	0.1	−1.6	59,270	53.2	..	97.3	53.9
86 Ecuador	42.0	0.6	−6.9	0.3	2.76	−0.5	2.4	−1.5	1,418	54.1	53.5	84.7	−14.4
88 Ukraine	102.2	2.2	−3.6	1.6	10.85	−0.9[o]	11.2[o]	−1.3	13,333	52.5	46.5	135.2	14.8
89 Peru	46.9	3.2	−6.3	0.2	1.44	−1.6	0.3	..	3,744	45.5	42.6	116.2	17.3
90 Colombia	34.9	4.7	−4.0	0.4	1.81	−0.6	0.3	−1.0	3,317	58.1	58.2	120.6	24.5
90 Saint Lucia	..	5.8	−5.4	1.0	1.88	0.0	7.2	−7.9	348	46.7	..	99.2	−13.6
92 Fiji	78.0	5.9	−5.1	2.4	5.41	−6.6	1.5	..	792	46.5	..	116.2	43.2
92 Mongolia	116.6	13.0	−16.9	3.1	2.38	−1.1	0.6	−5.2	404	22.3	..	111.2	20.2
94 Dominican Republic	52.9	4.7	−7.2	0.3	8.14	−3.0	3.9	1.2	5,959	61.3	..	81.8	−9.0
95 Jordan	92.6	4.2	−6.5	7.1	11.06	23.9	33.3	7.2	3,858	62.3	..	103.8	12.7
95 Tunisia	99.9	1.7	−1.6	1.6	4.73	−1.2	0.5	−4.5	5,724	49.6	..	125.2	19.9
97 Jamaica	77.1	5.6	0.7	0.2	17.08	−6.5	0.8	..	2,182	45.0	44.9	113.4	0.2
98 Tonga	89.4	2.2	..	19.7	34.24	−15.4	4.6	..	59	40.0	..	74.7	43.2
99 Saint Vincent and the Grenadines	83.6	11.9	−12.2	1.2	5.28	−9.1	4.2	..	79	55.6	..	102.7	−14.8
100 Suriname	129.6	4.8	−4.0	0.5	0.02	−1.9	8.5	..	256	45.4	..	144.5	45.9
101 Botswana	97.1	2.3	2.8	0.6	0.21	1.4	7.3	−3.7	1,528	39.4	33.8	146.2	24.6
101 Maldives	150.4	11.3	−17.3	0.7	0.09	11.2	15.4	..	1,286	59.1	..	189.9	40.0
103 Dominica	100.4	5.4	−5.0	1.5	10.43	..	9.2	..	78	67.0	..	106.7	−27.8
104 Samoa	79.2	0.3	1.4	11.4	16.68	−13.4	2.5	..	134	29.4	..	77.4	60.1
105 Uzbekistan	58.1	0.1	..	0.7	3.70	−0.4	3.6	−11.2	1,969	46.8	..	74.0	1.0
106 Belize	112.8	1.4	−1.4	2.0	4.91	4.5	16.0	..	386	44.6	..	61.9	2.4
106 Marshall Islands	111.5	−1.6	0.0	4.8	14.76	..	6.2	−18.0	10	29.8	..	29.2[p]	..
108 Libya	108.7	1.5	−2.0	0.5	..	−14.0	12.4	..	..	20.3	..	121.7	−31.1
108 Turkmenistan	117.7	12.5	..	0.1	0.02	−1.9	3.4	−106.8	..	18.0	..	151.4	140.9
110 Gabon	71.2	5.0	1.6	0.3	..	9.6	13.8	..	..	48.1	..	149.6	52.4
110 Paraguay	84.6	1.5	−2.9	0.3	2.37	−2.7	2.4	..	1,308	51.3	48.8	111.4	16.8
112 Moldova (Republic of)	113.2	2.6	−2.5	4.5	20.17	−0.5[q]	3.5[q]	−16.1	121	71.0	66.9	93.3	49.4
MEDIUM HUMAN DEVELOPMENT													
113 Philippines	70.7	3.2	−1.3	0.1	10.46	−1.3	0.2	−0.2	5,967	55.5	..	109.4	23.3
113 South Africa	58.2	0.4	−3.0	0.4	0.25	3.0	7.1	3.4	10,044	54.0	..	147.1	50.7
115 Egypt	44.8	3.1	−13.2	0.6	9.57	−0.6	0.5	0.8	5,258	41.2	38.2	102.2	21.6
116 Indonesia	39.5	2.2	−4.0	0.0	0.89	−0.7	0.1	−0.5	11,519	25.4	23.5	147.7	69.5
116 Viet Nam	200.3	6.3	−6.9	1.5	6.16	−0.4	0.1	−2.8	10,013	46.5	..	127.5	1.1

TABLE 13 HUMAN AND CAPITAL MOBILITY

			Trade	SDG 17.3	Financial flows		SDG 17.3		Human mobility		SDG 8.9	SDG 17.6, 17.8	Communication		SDG 9.c	
			Exports and imports	Foreign direct investment, net inflows	Private capital flows	Net official development assistance received[a]	Remittances, inflows	Net migration rate	Stock of immigrants	International student mobility	International inbound tourists	Internet users		Mobile phone subscriptions	
												Total	Female		
			(% of GDP)	(% of GDP)	(% of GDP)	(% of GNI)	(% of GDP)	(per 1,000 people)	(% of population)	(% of total tertiary enrolment)	(thousands)	(% of population)	(% of female population)	(per 100 people)	(% change)
HDI rank			2017[b]	2017[b]	2017[b]	2016[c]	2017[b]	2010/2015[d]	2017	2017[b]	2016[c]	2016	2017[b]	2016	2010–2016
118	Bolivia (Plurinational State of)		56.7	1.9	−5.4	2.1	3.48	−1.2	1.3	..	959	39.7	32.2	92.8	28.2
119	Palestine, State of		74.2	1.4	−2.0	15.7	14.78	−2.0[r]	5.2[s]	−12.7	400	61.2	47.5	77.5	21.1
120	Iraq		73.9	0.1	0.5	1.3	0.52	2.8	1.0	..	892	21.2	..	81.2	7.4
121	El Salvador		72.5	1.3	−4.4	0.5	20.37	−7.7	0.7	−1.8	1,434	29.0	25.6	151.9	21.6
122	Kyrgyzstan		102.2	1.2	−1.3	8.0	32.86	−4.9	3.3	1.5	2,930	34.5	..	127.8	31.4
123	Morocco		83.5	2.4	−1.4	2.0	6.27	−1.8	0.3	−3.0	10,332	58.3	53.5	117.7	19.3
124	Nicaragua		96.7	6.5	−5.9	3.3	10.10	−4.6	0.7	..	1,504	24.6	..	125.9	82.4
125	Cabo Verde		103.1	6.2	−3.1	7.2	11.99	−4.3	2.8	−25.8	598	50.3	49.8	111.6	50.7
125	Guyana		100.8	0.9	1.2	2.0	7.49	−7.2	2.0	−16.6	235	35.7	..	75.6	0.7
127	Guatemala		45.7	1.4	−2.4	0.4	11.18	−0.6	0.5	..	1,906	34.5	..	110.1	−10.8
127	Tajikistan		56.6	2.8	−9.8	4.1	31.56	−2.5	3.1	−6.9	414	20.5	..	107.6	38.4
129	Namibia		84.2	3.2	−1.8	1.5	0.31	−0.1	3.8	−33.7	1,469	31.0	..	107.3	19.5
130	India		40.6	1.5	−2.3	0.1	2.66	−0.4	0.4	−0.7	14,569	29.5	..	85.2	39.4
131	Micronesia (Federated States of)		99.0	0.3	−4.3	13.2	7.13	−15.8	2.6	..	30	..	..	..	..
132	Timor-Leste		39.3	0.2	−11.7	10.0	2.95	−8.5	0.9	..	66	25.2	..	117.6	175.9
133	Honduras		102.4	5.5	−7.8	2.0	18.81	−0.4	0.4	−1.4	880	30.0	..	86.0	−25.9
134	Bhutan		74.0	−0.4	0.4	2.5	1.72	2.6	6.5	−31.0	210	41.8	..	87.5	61.5
134	Kiribati		105.3	1.1	1.3	19.5	9.36	−4.0	2.6	..	6	13.7	..	45.5	340.4
136	Bangladesh		35.3	0.9	−0.7	1.1	5.41	−3.2	0.9	−2.9	125	18.2	5.1	83.4	86.9
137	Congo		138.6	25.6	−42.5	1.2	0.35	−2.6	7.6	−22.8	224	8.1	..	105.8	24.8
138	Vanuatu		97.9	4.2	−2.3	16.5	2.25	0.5	1.2	..	95	24.0	..	80.8	12.4
139	Lao People's Democratic Republic		75.8	6.3	−9.0	2.6	0.74	−5.5	0.7	−4.6	3,315	21.9	..	58.6	−8.6
140	Ghana		90.6	6.9	−12.2	3.2	7.47	−0.4	1.4	0.9	897	34.7	..	135.8	90.9
141	Equatorial Guinea		94.4	0.5	..	0.1	..	16.9	17.5	..	..	23.8	..	47.1	12.3
142	Kenya		39.4	0.9	0.5	3.1	2.62	−0.2	2.2	..	1,268	26.0	..	80.4	33.2
143	Sao Tome and Principe		..	10.5	−10.3	13.2	4.65	−6.0	1.1	..	29	28.0	..	89.1	51.5
144	Eswatini (Kingdom of)		102.2	0.7	−1.2	4.0	2.58	−1.0	2.4	−34.4	947	28.6	..	74.1	22.8
144	Zambia		71.6	3.4	−4.9	4.7	0.36	−0.5	0.9	..	956	25.5	..	72.4	84.2
146	Cambodia		124.9	11.4	−9.8	3.9	1.74	−2.0	0.5	−2.9	5,012	32.4	32.4	126.3	121.8
147	Angola		57.6	4.3	−1.1	0.2	0.00	0.7	2.1	..	397	13.0	..	45.1	12.1
148	Myanmar		39.1	6.8	−6.7	2.5	3.70	−1.9	0.1	−1.1	2,907	25.1	..	95.7	7,976.7
149	Nepal		51.8	0.8	..	5.0	28.31	−2.7	1.7	−7.7	753	19.7	..	110.8	225.7
150	Pakistan		25.8	0.9	−1.3	1.0	6.46	−1.3	1.7	..	966	15.5	9.5	70.6	21.5
151	Cameroon		36.9	2.1	−1.8	2.4	0.80	−0.3	2.2	−7.3	822	25.0	..	79.9	84.6
LOW HUMAN DEVELOPMENT																
152	Solomon Islands		98.4	2.8	−2.2	15.6	1.23	−4.3	0.4	..	23	11.0	..	69.5	217.6
153	Papua New Guinea		..	−0.2	0.5	2.8	0.01	0.0	0.4	..	184	9.6	..	46.8	74.2
154	Tanzania (United Republic of)		42.3	2.9	−2.6	4.9	0.84	−0.8[t]	0.9[t]	..	1,233	13.0	..	72.1	58.3
155	Syrian Arab Republic		..	..	..	..	..	−41.8	5.5	..	5,070	31.9	..	72.4	30.2
156	Zimbabwe		61.5	2.1	−1.5	4.4	11.17	−3.3	2.4	−12.0	2,168	23.1	14.6	79.7	45.9
157	Nigeria		20.7	0.9	−2.9	0.6	5.85	−0.4	0.6	..	1,889	25.7	..	83.0	50.7
158	Rwanda		51.0	3.2	−1.9	13.9	2.36	−1.4	3.6	−6.1	932	20.0	..	74.9	116.2
159	Lesotho		125.4	1.6	−1.6	4.4	15.19	−2.4	0.3	−12.5	1,196	27.4	..	103.6	114.1
159	Mauritania		109.3	11.7	−11.7	6.3	1.54	2.1	3.8	−19.8	..	18.0	..	84.0	9.3
161	Madagascar		74.5	5.4	−3.9	6.5	2.28	−0.1	0.1	−1.9	293	4.7	..	32.1	−11.9
162	Uganda		44.4	2.7	−0.9	7.4	4.79	−0.8	3.9	7.4	1,323	21.9	..	55.0	45.5
163	Benin		79.4	1.5	−1.2	5.7	2.87	−0.9	2.3	4.0	267	12.0	..	81.8	6.3
164	Senegal		69.8	2.7	−4.2	5.2	13.67	−1.4	1.7	−0.1	1,007	25.7	..	98.5	52.5
165	Comoros		619.0	1.3	−1.6	8.8	21.33	−2.7	1.5	−78.8	27	7.9	..	57.1	138.3
165	Togo		100.0	5.8	1.5	3.6	8.36	−0.3	3.6	−13.4	338	11.3	..	72.4	80.9
167	Sudan		21.5	0.9	−0.9	0.9	0.18	−3.2	1.8	..	741	28.0	11.0	70.3	33.5
168	Afghanistan		55.9	0.3	−0.4	20.6	1.82	2.9	0.4	−7.4	..	10.6	..	62.3	75.8
168	Haiti		75.3	1.3	−1.2	13.3	29.25	−2.9	0.4	..	516	12.2	..	60.0	49.9
170	Côte d'Ivoire		48.6	1.6	−2.8	1.9	0.94	0.6	9.0	−3.7	1,583	26.5	..	115.8	51.5
171	Malawi		65.3	4.4	−4.6	23.5	0.65	−0.4	1.3	−20.3	849	9.6	..	39.7	93.0
172	Djibouti		108.5	9.1	..	10.4	3.37	1.4	12.1	−40.2	63	13.1	..	36.6	88.3
173	Ethiopia		31.5	5.5	−5.0	5.6	1.01	−0.1	1.2	..	871	15.4	..	50.0	540.1
174	Gambia		60.8	−0.2	..	9.8	21.25	−1.5	9.8	..	161	18.5	..	139.2	59.4
175	Guinea		140.1	16.3	−14.4	6.4	0.53	−4.4	1.0	−6.1	35	9.8	..	87.1	135.1

HUMAN DEVELOPMENT INDICES AND INDICATORS: 2018 STATISTICAL UPDATE

TABLE 13 Human and capital mobility

		Trade	Financial flows (SDG 17.3 / SDG 17.2 / SDG 17.3)				Human mobility				Communication (SDG 17.6, 17.8 / SDG 9.c)			
		Exports and imports	Foreign direct investment, net inflows	Private capital flows	Net official development assistance received[a]	Remittances, inflows	Net migration rate	Stock of immigrants	International student mobility	International inbound tourists	Internet users Total	Internet users Female	Mobile phone subscriptions	Mobile phone subscriptions
		(% of GDP)	(% of GDP)	(% of GDP)	(% of GNI)	(% of GDP)	(per 1,000 people)	(% of population)	(% of total tertiary enrolment)	(thousands)	(% of population)	(% of female population)	(per 100 people)	(% change)
HDI rank		2017[b]	2017[b]	2017[b]	2016[c]	2017[b]	2010/2015[d]	2017	2017[b]	2016[c]	2016	2017[b]	2016	2010–2016
176	Congo (Democratic Republic of the)	75.0	3.4	−2.5	6.2	0.05	0.0	1.1	−0.2	191	6.2	..	36.7	100.3
177	Guinea-Bissau	59.0	1.2	0.3	16.5	7.69	−1.2	1.3	..	44	3.8	..	70.8	62.7
178	Yemen	33.5	−3.1	−0.1	7.1	18.40	−0.6	1.4	−1.1	367	24.6	..	59.6	26.9
179	Eritrea	37.5	1.5	..	5.2		−6.9	0.3	..	142	1.2	..	10.2	142.0
180	Mozambique	108.9	18.8	−18.7	14.2	1.39	−0.2	0.8	−0.9	1,639	17.5	..	52.1	74.7
181	Liberia	121.7	21.6	−33.4	44.8	26.89	−0.9	2.1	..	..	7.3	..	67.6	69.7
182	Mali	63.1	0.9	−1.0	8.9	6.80	−3.7	2.1	−9.1	173	11.1	..	112.4	127.6
183	Burkina Faso	62.8	3.4	0.5	9.2	3.45	−1.5	3.7	−2.9	152	14.0	..	82.6	125.9
184	Sierra Leone	79.4	3.9	−3.7	21.9	1.30	−0.6	1.3	..	55	11.8	..	84.9	174.2
185	Burundi	38.2	0.0	−1.6	24.7	0.96	−1.5	2.8	−1.2	187	5.2	0.7	50.9	166.0
186	Chad	73.5	5.9	..	6.8		1.5	3.3	−15.5	120	5.0	..	43.1	78.2
187	South Sudan	116.7	−0.6	..	64.5	24.07	7.7	6.7	..	..	..	..	22.1	48.2
188	Central African Republic	44.3	1.8	..	28.4		−17.6	1.9	4.0	121	4.0	..	27.2	23.4
189	Niger	49.6	4.0	−4.7	12.8	2.44	−0.3	1.4	−8.5	152	4.3	0.7	42.2	88.9
OTHER COUNTRIES OR TERRITORIES														
..	Korea (Democratic People's Rep. of)	..	..	..	..	..	−0.2	0.2	−0.3	..	..	..	14.2	709.3
..	Monaco	..	..	..	..	..	54.9	..	..	336	95.2	..	86.5	37.0
..	Nauru	150.6	0.0	..	18.3	..	..	32.7	..	..	..	..	87.2	41.1
..	San Marino	..	..	..	..	..	..	15.7	..	60	..	..	110.1	12.0
..	Somalia	77.7	5.0	..	17.4	..	−3.5	0.3	..	..	1.9	..	46.5	764.0
..	Tuvalu	..	0.6	1.9	60.7	10.83	..	1.3	..	3	46.0	..	68.5	350.8
Human development groups														
	Very high human development	59.8	2.7	0.3	..	0.29	2.6	12.9	3.8	812,209	80.3	78.8	130.0	9.7
	High human development	44.4	1.9	−1.4	0.1	0.75	−0.1	1.4	−1.3	251,232	53.9	..	102.9	26.1
	Medium human development	52.1	2.1	−3.2	0.6	3.71	−0.7	0.8	−0.9	100,347	29.8	..	95.9	257.2
	Low human development	39.1	2.3	−2.9	4.3	4.28	−1.5	1.8	−3.5	24,111	17.1	..	65.1	88.7
Developing countries		49.5	1.9	−1.8	0.4	1.46	−0.4	1.7	−1.1	470,139	38.5	..	95.0	98.6
Regions														
	Arab States	84.0	1.6	−1.7	1.6	2.62	0.8	9.3	0.2	70,176	42.9	..	101.6	37.7
	East Asia and the Pacific	46.1	1.7	−0.9	0.1	0.66	−0.3	0.4	−1.3	159,233	48.4	..	107.7	462.1
	Europe and Central Asia	69.1	2.4	−4.3	0.7	2.42	0.6	7.4	−2.4	82,954	56.2	58.3	109.6	24.2
	Latin America and the Caribbean	43.8	2.8	−3.2	0.1	1.39	−0.6	1.4	−0.4	94,971	56.7	..	108.4	15.5
	South Asia	40.3	1.4	−2.1	0.4	3.16	−0.8	0.7	−1.0	24,902	27.6	..	84.6	70.2
	Sub-Saharan Africa	51.3	2.5	−3.4	2.7	2.81	−0.3	2.2	−1.8	37,904	20.0	..	73.4	70.5
Least developed countries		50.0	3.3	−2.8	4.5	3.87	−1.3	1.4	−3.0	27,090	15.7	..	66.5	348.0
Small island developing states		59.9	3.2	−4.6	1.5	6.76	−2.4	1.8	0.7	21,543	33.9	..	70.4	47.1
Organisation for Economic Co-operation and Development		54.9	2.4	0.5	..	0.32	2.0	10.5	3.6	681,890	78.7	76.6	117.6	8.6
World		**55.2**	**2.5**	**−0.4**	**0.4**	**0.73**	**0.0**	**3.4**	**0.0**	**1,188,297**	**45.7**	**..**	**100.5**	**72.9**

NOTES

a A negative value refers to net official development assistance disbursed by donor countries.
b Data refer to 2017 or the most recent year available.
c Data refer to 2016 or the most recent year available.
d Data are average annual estimates for 2010–2015.
e Includes Svalbard and Jan Mayen Islands.
f Includes Christmas Island, Cocos (Keeling) Islands and Norfolk Island.
g Includes Åland Islands.
h Includes Canary Islands, Ceuta and Melilla.
i Includes Northern Cyprus.
j Includes Sabah and Sarawak.
k Includes Agalega, Rodrigues and Saint Brandon.
l Includes Kosovo.
m Includes Abkhazia and South Ossetia.
n Includes Nagorno-Karabakh.
o Includes Crimea.
p Refers to 2015.
q Includes Transnistria.
r Includes East Jerusalem.
s Includes East Jerusalem. Refugees are not part of the foreign-born migrant stock in the State of Palestine.
t Includes Zanzibar.

DEFINITIONS

Exports and imports: Sum of exports and imports of goods and services, expressed as a percentage of gross domestic product (GDP). It is a basic indicator of openness to foreign trade and economic integration and indicates the dependence of domestic producers on foreign demand (exports) and of domestic consumers and producers on foreign supply (imports), relative to the country's economic size (GDP).

Foreign direct investment, net inflows: Sum of equity capital, reinvestment of earnings, other long-term capital and short-term capital, expressed as a percentage of GDP.

Private capital flows: Net foreign direct investment and portfolio investment, expressed as a percentage of GDP.

Net official development assistance received: Disbursements of loans made on concessional terms (net of repayments of principal) and grants by official agencies to promote economic development and welfare in countries and territories on the Development Assistance Committee list of aid recipients, expressed as a percentage of the recipient country's gross national income (GNI).

Remittances, inflows: Earnings and material resources transferred by international migrants or refugees to recipients in their country of origin or countries in which the migrant formerly resided.

Net migration rate: Ratio of the difference between the number of in-migrants and out-migrants from a country to the average population, expressed per 1,000 people.

Stock of immigrants: Ratio of the stock of immigrants into a country, expressed as a percentage of the country's population. The definition of immigrant varies across countries but generally includes the stock of foreign-born people, the stock of foreign people (according to citizenship) or a combination of the two.

International student mobility: Total number of tertiary students from abroad (inbound students) studying in a given country minus the number of students at the same level of education from that country studying abroad (outbound students), expressed as a percentage of total tertiary enrolment in the country.

International inbound tourists: Arrivals of nonresident visitors (overnight visitors, tourists, same-day visitors and excursionists) at national borders.

Internet users: People with access to the worldwide network.

Mobile phone subscriptions: Number of subscriptions for the mobile phone service, expressed per 100 people.

MAIN DATA SOURCES

Columns 1, 2, 4, 5 and 9: World Bank (2018a).
Column 3: HDRO calculations based on data from World Bank (2018a).
Column 6: UNDESA (2017a).
Column 7: UNDESA (2017b).
Column 8: UNESCO Institute for Statistics (2018).
Columns 10–12: ITU (2018).
Column 13: HDRO calculations based on data from ITU (2018).

TABLE 14

Supplementary indicators: perceptions of well-being

		Perceptions of individual well-being (SDG 16.1)							Perceptions about community			Perceptions about government		
	Education quality	Health care quality	Standard of living	Feeling safe		Freedom of choice		Overall life satisfaction, index	Local labour market	Volunteered time	Community	Confidence in judicial system	Actions to preserve the environment	Trust in national government
				(% answering yes)		(% satisfied)		(0, least satisfied, to 10, most satisfied)						
	(% satisfied)	(% satisfied)	(% satisfied)	Female	Male	Female	Male		(% answering good)	(% answering yes)	(% answering yes)	(% answering yes)	(% satisfied)	(% answering yes)
HDI rank	2012–2017[a]	2012–2017[a]	2012–2017[a]	2012–2017[a]	2012–2017[a]	2012–2017[a]	2012–2017[a]	2012–2017[a]	2012–2017[a]	2012–2017[a]	2012–2017[a]	2012–2017[a]	2012–2017[a]	2012–2017[a]
VERY HIGH HUMAN DEVELOPMENT														
1 Norway	90	88	95	89	98	96	94	7.6	52	32	95	88	70	72
2 Switzerland	83	90	92	84	86	92	89	7.5	35	37	93	78	77	82
3 Australia	68	84	88	45	81	90	90	7.3	32	40	89	55	52	45
4 Ireland	84	63	81	71	81	89	91	7.1	49	40	91	74	69	60
5 Germany	68	85	83	67	72	83	82	7.1	59	26	92	68	61	62
6 Iceland	80	78	87	74	94	94	93	7.5	79	27	83	55	46	37
7 Hong Kong, China (SAR)	46	58	82	85	93	84	82	5.4	53	19	90	75	44	55
7 Sweden	68	77	92	62	87	95	92	7.3	63	13	93	69	68	56
9 Singapore	86	93	88	94	96	92	91	6.4	37	39	95	89	87	93
10 Netherlands	81	89	92	73	94	92	92	7.5	63	37	94	71	64	67
11 Denmark	78	90	95	74	90	96	95	7.6	62	23	94	85	70	57
12 Canada	77	77	87	75	93	96	93	7.4	58	33	92	67	65	65
13 United States	67	77	84	60	85	88	86	7.0	65	39	82	61	47	39
14 United Kingdom	70	75	80	78	82	87	75	7.1	47	33	87	68	63	44
15 Finland	86	79	83	78	98	95	96	7.8	49	26	96	83	76	60
16 New Zealand	72	82	88	53	83	94	94	7.3	52	40	89	63	61	61
17 Belgium	79	90	82	57	84	86	85	6.9	41	27	87	60	56	45
17 Liechtenstein	..	..	..	..	..	..	..	..	..	..	..	..	..	..
19 Japan	60	71	70	67	82	75	80	5.9	47	23	81	67	54	41
20 Austria	69	87	87	80	82	87	88	7.3	34	26	83	73	69	44
21 Luxembourg	74	87	88	76	83	90	89	7.1	29	33	90	76	78	74
22 Israel	65	77	73	67	85	75	76	7.3	42	23	82	55	47	39
22 Korea (Republic of)	55	70	67	63	74	54	51	5.9	22	15	78	26	26	36
24 France	69	77	78	68	77	83	82	6.6	17	31	88	59	54	37
25 Slovenia	81	79	77	82	93	93	90	6.2	40	35	91	29	72	24
26 Spain	56	66	71	80	84	76	73	6.2	24	17	80	42	40	27
27 Czechia	71	73	79	61	85	78	79	6.8	57	19	91	50	66	34
28 Italy	57	53	67	55	61	62	63	6.2	10	17	65	30	22	23
29 Malta	81	87	88	67	88	93	91	6.7	80	25	87	51	58	75
30 Estonia	63	58	61	59	83	78	84	5.9	32	16	88	55	58	41
31 Greece	42	35	39	49	65	43	41	5.1	9	7	76	42	23	14
32 Cyprus	56	54	73	66	90	76	80	6.1	44	26	89	42	53	31
33 Poland	77	55	67	60	73	82	80	6.2	46	15	83	52	54	50
34 United Arab Emirates	73	92	91	..	..	95	96	7.0	50	23	94	..	96	..
35 Andorra	..	..	..	..	..	..	..	..	..	..	..	..	..	..
35 Lithuania	54	52	36	56	67	68	67	6.3	35	18	84	46	61	32
37 Qatar	72	..	86	87	96	89	91	6.4	66	19	92	..	91	..
38 Slovakia	62	62	69	59	75	67	67	6.4	24	22	91	39	50	34
39 Brunei Darussalam	..	..	..	..	..	..	..	..	..	..	..	..	..	..
39 Saudi Arabia	72	80	85	..	..	78	82	6.3	54	12	90	..	71	..
41 Latvia	54	45	45	53	73	66	62	6.0	21	9	84	30	54	26
41 Portugal	69	65	70	65	87	90	91	5.7	47	15	89	45	48	50
43 Bahrain	73	80	82	..	..	87	90	6.2	40	33	90	..	73	..
44 Chile	49	33	77	40	52	73	83	6.3	30	15	78	21	33	27
45 Hungary	58	56	68	57	72	63	65	6.1	44	12	81	50	46	38
46 Croatia	64	60	55	63	76	71	70	5.3	28	11	75	48	51	21
47 Argentina	55	51	63	34	47	81	83	6.0	17	15	75	25	42	31
48 Oman	..	..	..	..	..	..	..	..	..	..	..	..	..	..
49 Russian Federation	52	35	47	41	67	70	67	5.6	20	11	71	36	35	56
50 Montenegro	54	41	48	67	75	57	65	5.6	22	9	65	35	28	35
51 Bulgaria	45	45	48	54	64	66	66	5.1	26	5	80	22	32	33
52 Romania	65	68	58	61	76	80	81	6.1	33	6	84	41	29	30
53 Belarus	54	42	44	54	70	60	55	5.6	10	19	77	46	51	45
54 Bahamas	..	..	..	..	..	..	..	..	..	..	..	..	..	..
55 Uruguay	57	67	71	40	59	89	88	6.3	19	15	78	41	58	41
56 Kuwait	55	79	90	..	..	88	88	6.1	46	11	86	..	75	..
57 Malaysia	75	78	75	35	54	62	71	6.3	54	33	78	55	62	44
58 Barbados	..	..	..	..	..	..	..	..	..	..	..	..	..	..
58 Kazakhstan	64	56	73	62	72	71	70	5.9	35	16	84	55	51	76

TABLE 14 Supplementary indicators: perceptions of well-being

		Perceptions of individual well-being							Perceptions about community			Perceptions about government		
	Education quality	Health care quality	Standard of living	Feeling safe		Freedom of choice		Overall life satisfaction, index	Local labour market	Volunteered time	Community	Confidence in judicial system	Actions to preserve the environment	Trust in national government
				(% answering yes)		(% satisfied)		(0, least satisfied, to 10, most satisfied)	(% answering good)	(% answering yes)	(% answering yes)	(% answering yes)		(% answering yes)
	(% satisfied)	(% satisfied)	(% satisfied)	Female	Male	Female	Male						(% satisfied)	
HDI rank	2012–2017ᵃ	2012–2017ᵃ	2012–2017ᵃ	2012–2017ᵃ	2012–2017ᵃ	2012–2017ᵃ	2012–2017ᵃ	2012–2017ᵃ	2012–2017ᵃ	2012–2017ᵃ	2012–2017ᵃ	2012–2017ᵃ	2012–2017ᵃ	2012–2017ᵃ
HIGH HUMAN DEVELOPMENT														
60 Iran (Islamic Republic of)	50	57	63	67	81	70	64	4.7	23	20	71	57	48	71
60 Palau	..	..	..	..	..	..	..	..	..	..	..	..	..	..
62 Seychelles	..	..	..	..	..	..	..	..	..	..	..	..	..	..
63 Costa Rica	81	63	79	43	53	91	94	7.2	31	17	83	45	61	41
64 Turkey	50	62	68	53	63	65	61	5.6	40	9	74	53	46	59
65 Mauritius	76	78	81	58	75	91	91	6.2	43	38	90	67	76	61
66 Panama	69	55	76	47	57	86	89	6.6	46	21	84	42	51	39
67 Serbia	65	53	45	64	84	63	66	5.1	22	6	72	45	33	51
68 Albania	61	50	43	52	69	71	77	4.6	20	7	67	29	43	46
69 Trinidad and Tobago	62	52	51	43	61	85	83	6.2	32	31	80	29	24	27
70 Antigua and Barbuda	..	..	..	..	..	..	..	..	..	..	..	..	..	..
70 Georgia	55	53	31	74	83	73	78	4.5	9	17	72	33	30	30
72 Saint Kitts and Nevis	..	..	..	..	..	..	..	..	..	..	..	..	..	..
73 Cuba	..	..	..	..	..	..	..	..	..	..	..	..	..	..
74 Mexico	61	55	76	33	47	86	84	6.4	45	14	73	32	43	26
75 Grenada	..	..	..	..	..	..	..	..	..	..	..	..	..	..
76 Sri Lanka	74	73	65	56	69	78	80	4.3	45	45	82	68	58	52
77 Bosnia and Herzegovina	56	54	49	65	71	51	55	5.1	16	7	66	24	22	13
78 Venezuela (Bolivarian Republic of)	48	26	33	15	19	63	63	5.1	19	15	66	22	34	24
79 Brazil	51	36	66	23	40	76	76	6.3	18	13	65	38	33	17
80 Azerbaijan	57	38	57	63	87	69	67	5.2	26	12	78	36	59	77
80 Lebanon	66	49	59	46	58	61	60	5.2	21	12	78	30	15	22
80 The former Yugoslav Republic of Macedonia	59	53	49	65	78	75	72	5.2	28	5	72	31	33	44
83 Armenia	53	42	35	76	79	63	56	4.3	17	9	60	29	39	25
83 Thailand	86	84	69	60	73	89	89	5.9	38	12	90	65	78	61
85 Algeria	49	38	67	49	67	40	43	5.2	16	17	58	28	23	..
86 China	66	65	78	73	87	84	85	5.1	36	7	80	..	68	..
86 Ecuador	78	59	75	47	61	87	88	5.8	32	18	82	49	72	64
88 Ukraine	46	24	31	47	62	57	51	4.3	18	15	79	11	17	11
89 Peru	54	38	70	40	51	80	80	5.7	42	20	71	21	47	25
90 Colombia	51	40	75	36	48	82	85	6.2	33	17	81	25	44	22
90 Saint Lucia	..	..	..	..	..	..	..	..	..	..	..	..	..	..
92 Fiji	..	..	..	..	..	..	..	..	..	..	..	..	..	..
92 Mongolia	44	36	66	43	56	64	66	5.3	5	36	74	36	27	28
94 Dominican Republic	78	52	67	28	41	85	84	5.6	34	32	74	30	55	46
95 Jordan	55	67	62	71	86	75	76	4.8	28	9	69	..	53	..
95 Tunisia	36	26	46	55	70	46	46	4.1	18	8	55	46	20	25
97 Jamaica	73	56	44	54	71	83	85	5.9	30	29	67	29	30	35
98 Tonga	..	..	..	..	..	..	..	..	..	..	..	..	..	..
99 Saint Vincent and the Grenadines	..	..	..	..	..	..	..	..	..	..	..	..	..	..
100 Suriname	82	78	64	57	63	85	88	6.3	34	22	90	71	65	72
101 Botswana	54	64	29	30	38	83	78	3.5	31	16	59	78	82	77
101 Maldives	..	..	..	..	..	..	..	..	..	..	..	..	..	..
103 Dominica	..	..	..	..	..	..	..	..	..	..	..	..	..	..
104 Samoa	..	..	..	..	..	..	..	..	..	..	..	..	..	..
105 Uzbekistan	81	83	81	79	91	96	99	6.4	69	20	95	82	89	96
106 Belize	62	50	66	44	57	88	84	6.0	40	26	74	37	62	38
106 Marshall Islands	..	..	..	..	..	..	..	..	..	..	..	..	..	..
108 Libya	51	42	70	42	58	75	79	5.6	44	24	75	..	55	..
108 Turkmenistan	..	..	83	75	80	69	68	5.2	39	35	88	..	61	..
110 Gabon	21	21	42	23	27	62	65	4.8	27	10	47	32	36	29
110 Paraguay	69	52	81	47	52	87	89	5.9	42	22	89	29	39	31
112 Moldova (Republic of)	56	36	56	35	50	55	50	5.3	6	13	71	20	18	13
MEDIUM HUMAN DEVELOPMENT														
113 Philippines	86	82	75	56	65	93	92	5.6	69	28	89	72	83	84
113 South Africa	67	57	42	23	41	80	76	4.5	28	34	53	52	42	42
115 Egypt	34	36	62	71	81	57	55	3.9	15	6	78	65	31	62
116 Indonesia	82	78	73	73	91	86	84	5.1	56	53	86	72	71	83
116 Viet Nam	77	62	74	54	67	83	88	5.2	40	14	81	66	53	81

TABLE 14 SUPPLEMENTARY INDICATORS: PERCEPTIONS OF WELL-BEING

		Perceptions of individual well-being (SDG 16.1)							Perceptions about community			Perceptions about government		
		Education quality	Health care quality	Standard of living	Feeling safe		Freedom of choice		Overall life satisfaction, index	Local labour market	Volunteered time	Community	Confidence in judicial system	Actions to preserve the environment	Trust in national government
					(% answering yes)		(% satisfied)		(0, least satisfied, to 10, most satisfied)						
		(% satisfied)	(% satisfied)	(% satisfied)	Female	Male	Female	Male		(% answering good)	(% answering yes)	(% answering yes)	(% answering yes)	(% satisfied)	(% answering yes)
HDI rank		2012–2017a	2012–2017a	2012–2017a	2012–2017a	2012–2017a	2012–2017a	2012–2017a	2012–2017a	2012–2017a	2012–2017a	2012–2017a	2012–2017a	2012–2017a	2012–2017a
118	Bolivia (Plurinational State of)	67	44	74	38	50	86	86	5.7	36	21	78	22	61	43
119	Palestine, State of	64	61	60	49	64	65	61	4.6	13	9	77	36	39	41
120	Iraq	39	37	65	58	62	60	61	4.5	25	19	63	49	36	42
121	El Salvador	66	47	75	43	49	73	77	6.3	33	15	83	27	40	27
122	Kyrgyzstan	72	66	81	48	56	82	87	5.6	49	18	91	37	52	56
123	Morocco	34	27	79	67	82	78	80	5.3	36	9	75	28	51	38
124	Nicaragua	81	63	75	62	63	92	90	6.5	49	22	85	45	73	59
125	Cabo Verde	..	..	..	..	..	..	..	..	..	..	..	..	..	..
125	Guyana	..	..	..	..	..	..	..	..	..	..	..	..	..	..
127	Guatemala	73	47	84	44	60	88	93	6.3	40	28	87	49	57	46
127	Tajikistan	82	80	71	87	89	80	76	5.8	51	36	81	74	71	93
129	Namibia	62	57	41	36	49	77	84	4.4	35	21	57	59	61	75
130	India	79	65	76	69	77	83	89	4.0	44	15	85	83	77	84
131	Micronesia (Federated States of)	..	..	..	..	..	..	..	..	..	..	..	..	..	..
132	Timor-Leste	..	..	..	..	..	..	..	..	..	..	..	..	..	..
133	Honduras	76	61	74	55	61	88	89	6.0	42	32	87	44	59	50
134	Bhutan	93	86	89	59	67	83	79	5.1	51	39	93	97	99	95
134	Kiribati	..	..	..	..	..	..	..	..	..	..	..	..	..	..
136	Bangladesh	80	63	79	70	84	82	90	4.3	31	13	84	80	76	88
137	Congo	55	37	54	44	51	66	74	4.9	29	14	64	39	48	47
138	Vanuatu	..	..	..	..	..	..	..	..	..	..	..	..	..	..
139	Lao People's Democratic Republic	81	71	79	63	75	77	84	4.6	57	4	92	72	80	84
140	Ghana	55	52	52	63	70	78	76	5.5	32	36	60	59	51	67
141	Equatorial Guinea	..	..	..	..	..	..	..	..	..	..	..	..	..	..
142	Kenya	64	51	54	54	64	88	82	4.5	47	45	70	57	56	64
143	Sao Tome and Principe	..	..	..	..	..	..	..	..	..	..	..	..	..	..
144	Eswatini (Kingdom of)	..	..	..	..	..	..	..	..	..	..	..	..	..	..
144	Zambia	66	58	43	43	53	82	79	3.9	48	34	62	63	63	72
146	Cambodia	90	82	80	50	60	96	95	4.6	65	6	91	59	90	75
147	Angola	46	29	35	39	53	30	37	3.8	43	17	50	44	37	57
148	Myanmar	79	75	69	71	79	88	87	4.2	54	34	88	65	73	82
149	Nepal	78	63	72	51	70	81	84	4.7	63	27	85	65	66	56
150	Pakistan	63	46	70	56	62	70	70	5.8	33	13	78	57	49	56
151	Cameroon	51	43	53	40	49	77	73	5.1	45	16	68	47	53	58
LOW HUMAN DEVELOPMENT															
152	Solomon Islands	..	..	..	..	..	..	..	..	..	..	..	..	..	..
153	Papua New Guinea	..	..	..	..	..	..	..	..	..	..	..	..	..	..
154	Tanzania (United Republic of)	58	43	35	60	71	81	78	3.3	50	8	71	77	66	91
155	Syrian Arab Republic	24	38	20	17	47	32	45	3.5	17	20	36	27	38	..
156	Zimbabwe	66	63	46	42	63	80	69	3.6	33	18	67	66	51	68
157	Nigeria	60	57	53	52	65	81	83	5.3	39	37	67	53	56	56
158	Rwanda	81	77	35	83	93	89	91	3.1	32	18	70	91	93	98
159	Lesotho	48	36	34	37	49	74	73	3.8	44	20	55	71	45	70
159	Mauritania	27	27	50	40	52	50	49	4.7	33	14	53	27	24	29
161	Madagascar	56	39	30	38	47	56	57	4.1	40	31	77	46	40	54
162	Uganda	45	39	45	54	65	74	77	4.0	43	26	64	51	55	66
163	Benin	51	40	38	52	54	73	65	4.9	41	17	55	60	51	62
164	Senegal	51	38	53	40	53	69	66	4.7	32	15	62	60	49	61
165	Comoros	49	24	38	67	77	50	57	4.0	30	18	75	34	39	46
165	Togo	48	37	42	49	58	68	70	4.4	43	14	52	43	55	48
167	Sudan	28	22	52	64	78	25	29	4.1	18	23	50	..	11	..
168	Afghanistan	51	32	19	15	24	37	44	2.7	11	11	63	24	39	26
168	Haiti	25	15	22	48	46	52	44	3.8	23	31	45	37	32	44
170	Côte d'Ivoire	45	35	36	49	50	71	71	5.0	51	7	59	42	44	52
171	Malawi	58	57	38	42	47	85	84	3.4	63	26	73	59	82	62
172	Djibouti	..	..	..	..	..	..	..	..	..	..	..	..	..	..
173	Ethiopia	72	45	42	62	70	69	73	4.2	48	23	63	60	70	77
174	Gambia	73	49	57	47	63	75	80	4.1	45	30	77	68	62	80
175	Guinea	45	42	58	51	56	71	73	4.9	54	24	74	54	58	64

HUMAN DEVELOPMENT INDICES AND INDICATORS: 2018 STATISTICAL UPDATE

				SDG 16.1 Perceptions of individual well-being					Perceptions about community			Perceptions about government		
	Education quality	Health care quality	Standard of living	Feeling safe		Freedom of choice		Overall life satisfaction, index	Local labour market	Volunteered time	Community	Confidence in judicial system	Actions to preserve the environment	Trust in national government
				(% answering yes)		(% satisfied)		(0, least satisfied, to 10, most satisfied)						
	(% satisfied)	(% satisfied)	(% satisfied)	Female	Male	Female	Male		(% answering good)	(% answering yes)	(% answering yes)	(% answering yes)	(% satisfied)	(% answering yes)
HDI rank	2012–2017[a]	2012–2017[a]	2012–2017[a]	2012–2017[a]	2012–2017[a]	2012–2017[a]	2012–2017[a]	2012–2017[a]	2012–2017[a]	2012–2017[a]	2012–2017[a]	2012–2017[a]	2012–2017[a]	2012–2017[a]
176 Congo (Democratic Republic of the)	48	42	51	36	54	69	67	4.3	37	29	57	43	50	48
177 Guinea-Bissau	..	..	..	..	..	..	..	..	..	..	..	..	..	..
178 Yemen	43	22	38	37	70	52	60	3.3	6	6	74	24	10	25
179 Eritrea	..	..	..	..	..	..	..	..	..	..	..	..	..	..
180 Mozambique	70	56	59	49	54	79	82	4.3	54	27	78	67	66	76
181 Liberia	42	37	41	34	47	69	76	4.4	48	47	57	53	48	55
182 Mali	35	44	50	58	59	71	72	4.7	63	20	65	39	48	50
183 Burkina Faso	51	40	38	51	60	59	56	4.6	50	19	63	48	44	54
184 Sierra Leone	45	45	43	54	55	70	70	4.1	45	37	65	49	44	74
185 Burundi	54	37	26	43	42	47	39	2.9	10	10	47	..	41	..
186 Chad	53	44	58	50	50	61	58	4.6	34	16	71	44	55	47
187 South Sudan	34	24	22	43	41	41	47	2.8	37	29	42	41	29	46
188 Central African Republic	37	28	30	50	54	64	63	3.5	54	27	62	60	49	65
189 Niger	44	43	52	64	69	67	62	4.6	36	20	68	65	57	60
OTHER COUNTRIES OR TERRITORIES														
.. Korea (Democratic People's Rep. of)	..	..	..	..	..	..	..	..	..	..	..	..	..	..
.. Monaco	..	..	..	..	..	..	..	..	..	..	..	..	..	..
.. Nauru	..	..	..	..	..	..	..	..	..	..	..	..	..	..
.. San Marino	..	..	..	..	..	..	..	..	..	..	..	..	..	..
.. Somalia	67	55	75	86	85	91	91	4.7	41	24	92	62	86	70
.. Tuvalu	..	..	..	..	..	..	..	..	..	..	..	..	..	..
Human development groups														
Very high human development	64	68	74	60	77	79	79	6.5	43	25	82	54	49	44
High human development	63	59	73	61	75	80	81	5.3	34	10	77	..	58	..
Medium human development	74	62	72	64	75	81	84	4.5	43	21	82	73	69	77
Low human development	53	44	44	49	60	68	69	4.3	39	24	64	52	52	60
Developing countries	66	58	68	60	72	78	80	4.8	39	17	78	62	62	65
Regions														
Arab States	43	40	63	59	74	57	61	4.6	24	13	70	45	37	..
East Asia and the Pacific	..	..	..	..	..	..	..	..	..	..	..	..	..	..
Europe and Central Asia	58	55	60	59	71	69	67	5.4	36	14	79	46	47	55
Latin America and the Caribbean	56	43	68	32	45	80	80	6.1	29	16	72	33	41	27
South Asia	76	62	74	66	75	80	85	4.2	40	15	83	77	72	79
Sub-Saharan Africa	57	47	46	49	60	73	73	4.4	42	27	64	55	55	62
Least developed countries	60	48	52	54	65	69	71	4.1	40	21	70	59	58	67
Small island developing states	..	..	..	..	..	..	..	..	..	..	..	..	..	..
Organisation for Economic Co-operation and Development	64	71	77	61	76	81	79	6.6	46	26	82	55	49	42
World	66	60	69	61	74	79	80	5.1	40	19	78	60	60	61

TABLE 14

NOTES

a Data refer to the most recent year available during the period specified.

DEFINITIONS

Satisfaction with education quality: Percentage of respondents answering "satisfied" to the Gallup World Poll question, "Are you satisfied or dissatisfied with the education system or the schools?"

Satisfaction with health care quality: Percentage of respondents answering "satisfied" to the Gallup World Poll question, "Are you satisfied or dissatisfied with the availability of quality healthcare?"

Satisfaction with standard of living: Percentage of respondents answering "satisfied" to the Gallup World Poll question, "Are you satisfied or dissatisfied with your standard of living, all the things you can buy and do?"

Feeling safe: Percentage of respondents answering "yes" to the Gallup World Poll question, "Do you feel safe walking alone at night in the city or area where you live?"

Satisfaction with freedom of choice: Percentage of respondents answering "satisfied" to the Gallup World Poll question, "In this country, are you satisfied or dissatisfied with your freedom to choose what you do with your life?"

Overall life satisfaction, index: Average response to the Gallup World Poll question, "Please imagine a ladder, with steps numbered from zero at the bottom to ten at the top. Suppose we say that the top of the ladder represents the best possible life for you, and the bottom of the ladder represents the worst possible life for you. On which step of the ladder would you say you personally feel you stand at this time, assuming that the higher the step the better you feel about your life, and the lower the step the worse you feel about it? Which step comes closest to the way you feel?"

Perception of local labour market: Percentage of respondents answering "good" to the Gallup World Poll question, "Thinking about the job situation in the city or area where you live today, would you say that it is now a good time or a bad time to find a job?"

Volunteered time: Percentage of respondents answering "yes" to the Gallup World Poll question, "In the past month have you volunteered your time to an organization?"

Satisfaction with community: Percentage of respondents answering "yes" to the Gallup World Poll question, "Are you satisfied or dissatisfied with the city or area where you live?"

Confidence in judicial system: Percentage of respondents answering "yes" to the Gallup World Poll question, "In this country, do you have confidence in the judicial system and courts?"

Satisfaction with actions to preserve the environment: Percentage of respondents answering "satisfied" to Gallup World Poll question, "In this country, are you satisfied or dissatisfied with the efforts to preserve the environment?"

Trust in national government: Percentage of respondents answering "yes" to the Gallup World Poll question, "In this country, do you have confidence in the national government?"

MAIN DATA SOURCES

Columns 1–14: Gallup (2018).

TABLE 14 Supplementary indicators: perceptions of well-being

TABLE 15

Status of fundamental human rights treaties

Country	ICERD: International Convention on the Elimination of All Forms of Racial Discrimination, 1965 — Entry into force: 4 January 1969 — Year of ratification	ICCPR: International Covenant on Civil and Political Rights, 1966 — Entry into force: 23 March 1969 — Year of ratification	ICESCR: International Covenant on Economic, Social and Cultural Rights, 1966 — Entry into force: 3 January 1976 — Year of ratification	CEDAW: Convention on the Elimination of All Forms of Discrimination against Women, 1979 — Entry into force: 3 September 1981 — Year of ratification	CAT: Convention against Torture and Other Cruel, Inhuman or Degrading Treatment or Punishment, 1984 — Entry into force: 26 June 1987 — Year of ratification	CRC: Convention on the Rights of the Child, 1989 — Entry into force: 2 September 1990 — Year of ratification	ICMW: International Convention on the Protection of the Rights of All Migrant Workers and Members of Their Families, 1990 — Entry into force: 1 July 2003 — Year of ratification	CRC-AC: Optional Protocol to the Convention on the Rights of the Child on the involvement of children in armed conflict, 2000 — Entry into force: 12 February 2002 — Year of ratification	CRC-SC: Optional Protocol to the Convention on the Rights of the Child on the sale of children, child prostitution and child pornography, 2000 — Entry into force: 18 January 2002 — Year of ratification	ICPED: International Convention for the Protection of All Persons from Enforced Disappearance, 2006 — Entry into force: 23 December 2010 — Year of ratification	CRPD: Convention on the Rights of Persons with Disabilities, 2006 — Entry into force: 3 May 2008 — Year of ratification
Afghanistan	1983	1983	1983	2003	1987	1994		2003	2002		2012
Albania	1994	1991	1991	1994	1994	1992	2007	2008	2008	2007	2013
Algeria	1972	1989	1989	1996	1989	1993	2005	2009	2006		2009
Andorra	2006	2006		1997	2006	1996		2001	2001		2014
Angola		1992	1992	1986		1990		2007	2005		2014
Antigua and Barbuda	1988			1989	1993	1993			2002		2016
Argentina	1968	1986	1986	1985	1986	1990	2007	2002	2003	2007	2008
Armenia	1993	1993	1993	1993	1993	1993		2005	2005	2011	2010
Australia	1975	1980	1975	1983	1989	1990		2006	2007		2008
Austria	1972	1978	1978	1982	1987	1992		2002	2004	2012	2008
Azerbaijan	1996	1992	1992	1995	1996	1992	1999	2002	2002		2009
Bahamas	1975	2008	2008	1993	2018	1991		2015	2015		2015
Bahrain	1990	2006	2007	2002	1998	1992		2004	2004		2011
Bangladesh	1979	2000	1998	1984	1998	1990	2011	2000	2000		2007
Barbados	1972	1973	1973	1980		1990					2013
Belarus	1969	1973	1973	1981	1987	1990		2006	2002		2016
Belgium	1975	1983	1983	1985	1999	1991		2002	2006	2011	2009
Belize	2001	1996	2015	1990	1986	1990	2001	2003	2003	2015	2011
Benin	2001	1992	1992	1992	1992	1990		2005	2005	2017	2012
Bhutan				1981		1990		2009	2009		
Bolivia (Plurinational State of)	1970	1982	1982	1990	1999	1990	2000	2004	2003	2008	2009
Bosnia and Herzegovina	1993	1993	1993	1993	1993	1993	1996	2003	2002	2012	2010
Botswana	1974	2000		1996	2000	1995		2004	2003		
Brazil	1968	1992	1992	1984	1989	1990		2004	2004	2010	2008
Brunei Darussalam				2006		1995		2016	2006		2016
Bulgaria	1966	1970	1970	1982	1986	1991		2002	2002		2012
Burkina Faso	1974	1999	1999	1987	1999	1990	2003	2007	2006	2009	2009
Burundi	1977	1990	1990	1992	1993	1990		2008	2007		2014
Cabo Verde	1979	1993	1993	1980	1992	1992	1997	2002	2002		2011
Cambodia	1983	1992	1992	1992	1992	1992		2004	2002	2013	2012
Cameroon	1971	1984	1984	1994	1986	1993		2013			
Canada	1970	1976	1976	1981	1987	1991		2000	2005		2010
Central African Republic	1971	1981	1981	1991	2016	1992		2017	2012	2016	2016
Chad	1977	1995	1995	1995	1995	1990		2002	2002		
Chile	1971	1972	1972	1989	1988	1990	2005	2003	2003	2009	2008
China	1981		2001	1980	1988	1992		2008	2002		2008
Colombia	1981	1969	1969	1982	1987	1991	1995	2005	2003	2012	2011
Comoros	2004			1994	2017	1993			2007		2016
Congo	1988	1983	1983	1982	2003	1993	2017	2010	2009		2014
Congo (Democratic Republic of the)	1976	1976	1976	1986	1996	1990		2001	2001		2015
Costa Rica	1967	1968	1968	1986	1993	1990		2003	2002	2012	2008
Côte d'Ivoire	1973	1992	1992	1995	1995	1991		2012	2011		2014
Croatia	1992	1992	1992	1992	1992	1992		2002	2002		2007
Cuba	1972			1980	1995	1991		2007	2001	2009	2007
Cyprus	1967	1969	1969	1985	1991	1991		2010	2006		2011
Czechia	1993	1993	1993	1993	1993	1993		2001	2013	2017	2009
Denmark	1971	1972	1972	1983	1987	1991		2002	2003		2009
Djibouti	2011	2002	2002	1998	2002	1990		2011	2011		2012
Dominica		1993	1993	1980		1991		2002	2002		2012
Dominican Republic	1983	1978	1978	1982	2012	1991		2014	2006		2009
Ecuador	1966	1969	1969	1981	1988	1990	2002	2004	2004	2009	2008
Egypt	1967	1982	1982	1981	1986	1990	1993	2007	2002		2008
El Salvador	1979	1979	1979	1981	1996	1990	2003	2002	2004		2007
Equatorial Guinea	2002	1987	1987	1984	2002	1992			2003		
Eritrea	2001	2002	2001	1995	2014	1994		2005	2005		
Estonia	1991	1991	1991	1991	1991	1991		2014	2004		2012

HUMAN DEVELOPMENT INDICES AND INDICATORS: 2018 STATISTICAL UPDATE

Country	ICERD: International Convention on the Elimination of All Forms of Racial Discrimination, 1965 — Entry into force: 4 January 1969 — Year of ratification	ICCPR: International Covenant on Civil and Political Rights, 1966 — Entry into force: 23 March 1976 — Year of ratification	ICESCR: International Covenant on Economic, Social and Cultural Rights, 1966 — Entry into force: 3 January 1976 — Year of ratification	CEDAW: Convention on the Elimination of All Forms of Discrimination against Women, 1979 — Entry into force: 3 September 1981 — Year of ratification	CAT: Convention against Torture and Other Cruel, Inhuman or Degrading Treatment or Punishment, 1984 — Entry into force: 26 June 1987 — Year of ratification	CRC: Convention on the Rights of the Child, 1989 — Entry into force: 2 September 1990 — Year of ratification	ICMW: International Convention on the Protection of the Rights of All Migrant Workers and Members of Their Families, 1990 — Entry into force: 1 July 2003 — Year of ratification	CRC-AC: Optional Protocol to the Convention on the Rights of the Child on the involvement of children in armed conflict, 2000 — Entry into force: 12 February 2002 — Year of ratification	CRC-SC: Optional Protocol to the Convention on the Rights of the Child on the sale of children, child prostitution and child pornography, 2000 — Entry into force: 18 January 2002 — Year of ratification	ICPED: International Convention for the Protection of All Persons from Enforced Disappearance, 2006 — Entry into force: 23 December 2010 — Year of ratification	CRPD: Convention on the Rights of Persons with Disabilities, 2006 — Entry into force: 3 May 2008 — Year of ratification
Eswatini	1969	2004	2004	2004	2004	1995		2012	2012		2012
Ethiopia	1976	1993	1993	1981	1994	1991		2014	2014		2010
Fiji	1973			1995	2016	1993					2017
Finland	1970	1975	1975	1986	1989	1991		2002	2012		2016
France	1971	1980	1980	1983	1986	1990		2003	2003	2008	2010
Gabon	1980	1983	1983	1983	2000	1994		2010	2007	2011	2007
Gambia	1978	1979	1978	1993		1990			2010		2015
Georgia	1999	1994	1994	1994	1994	1994		2010	2005		2014
Germany	1969	1973	1973	1985	1990	1992		2004	2009	2009	2009
Ghana	1966	2000	2000	1986	2000	1990	2000	2014			2012
Greece	1970	1997	1985	1983	1988	1993		2003	2008	2015	2012
Grenada	2013	1991	1991	1990		1990		2012	2012		2014
Guatemala	1983	1992	1988	1982	1990	1990	2003	2002	2002		2009
Guinea	1977	1978	1978	1982	1989	1990	2000	2016	2011		2008
Guinea-Bissau	2010	2010	1992	1985	2013	1990		2014	2010		2014
Guyana	1977	1977	1977	1980	1988	1991	2010	2010	2010		2014
Haiti	1972	1991	2013	1981		1995			2014		2009
Holy See	1969				2002	1990		2001	2001		
Honduras	2002	1997	1981	1983	1996	1990	2005	2002	2002	2008	2008
Hungary	1967	1974	1974	1980	1987	1991		2010	2010		2007
Iceland	1967	1979	1979	1985	1996	1992		2001	2001		2016
India	1968	1979	1979	1993		1992		2005	2005		2007
Indonesia	1999	2006	2006	1984	1998	1990	2012	2012	2012		2011
Iran (Islamic Republic of)	1968	1975	1975			1994			2007		2009
Iraq	1970	1971	1971	1986	2011	1994		2008	2008	2010	2013
Ireland	2000	1989	1989	1985	2002	1992		2002			2018
Israel	1979	1991	1991	1991	1991	1991		2005	2008		2012
Italy	1976	1978	1978	1985	1989	1991		2002	2002	2015	2009
Jamaica	1971	1975	1975	1984		1991	2008	2002	2011		2007
Japan	1995	1979	1979	1985	1999	1994		2004	2005	2009	2014
Jordan	1974	1975	1975	1992	1991	1991		2007	2006		2008
Kazakhstan	1998	2006	2006	1998	1998	1994		2003	2001	2009	2015
Kenya	2001	1972	1972	1984	1997	1990		2002			2008
Kiribati				2004		1995		2015	2015		2013
Korea (Democratic People's Rep. of)		1981	1981	2001		1990			2014		2016
Korea (Republic of)	1978	1990	1990	1984	1995	1991		2004	2004		2008
Kuwait	1968	1996	1996	1994	1996	1991		2004	2004		2013
Kyrgyzstan	1997	1994	1994	1997	1997	1994	2003	2003	2003		
Lao People's Democratic Republic	1974	2009	2007	1981	2012	1991		2006	2006		2009
Latvia	1992	1992	1992	1992	1992	1992		2005	2006		2010
Lebanon	1971	1972	1972	1997	2000	1991			2004		
Lesotho	1971	1992	1992	1995	2001	1992	2005	2003	2003	2013	2008
Liberia	1976	2004	2004	1984	2004	1993					2012
Libya	1968	1970	1970	1989	1989	1993	2004	2004	2004		2018
Liechtenstein	2000	1998	1998	1995	1990	1995		2005	2013		
Lithuania	1998	1991	1991	1994	1996	1992		2003	2004	2013	2010
Luxembourg	1978	1983	1983	1989	1987	1994		2004	2011		2011
Madagascar	1969	1971	1971	1989	2005	1991	2015	2004	2004		2015
Malawi	1996	1993	1993	1987	1996	1991		2010	2009	2017	2009
Malaysia				1995		1995		2012	2012		2010
Maldives	1984	2006	2006	1993	2004	1991		2004	2002		2010
Mali	1974	1974	1974	1985	1999	1990	2003	2002	2002	2009	2008
Malta	1971	1990	1990	1991	1990	1990		2002	2010	2015	2012
Marshall Islands		2018	2018	2006	2018	1993					2015
Mauritania	1988	2004	2004	2001	2004	1991	2007		2007	2012	2012
Mauritius	1972	1973	1973	1984	1992	1990		2009	2011		2010

TABLE 15 Status of fundamental human rights treaties

TABLE 15 STATUS OF FUNDAMENTAL HUMAN RIGHTS TREATIES

Country	ICERD: International Convention on the Elimination of All Forms of Racial Discrimination, 1965 Entry into force: 4 January 1969 Year of ratification	ICCPR: International Covenant on Civil and Political Rights, 1966 Entry into force: 23 March 1969 Year of ratification	ICESCR: International Covenant on Economic, Social and Cultural Rights, 1966 Entry into force: 3 January 1976 Year of ratification	CEDAW: Convention on the Elimination of All Forms of Discrimination against Women, 1979 Entry into force: 3 September 1981 Year of ratification	CAT: Convention against Torture and Other Cruel, Inhuman or Degrading Treatment or Punishment, 1984 Entry into force: 26 June 1987 Year of ratification	CRC: Convention on the Rights of the Child, 1989 Entry into force: 2 September 1990 Year of ratification	ICMW: International Convention on the Protection of the Rights of All Migrant Workers and Members of Their Families, 1990 Entry into force: 1 July 2003 Year of ratification	CRC-AC: Optional Protocol to the Convention on the Rights of the Child on the involvement of children in armed conflict, 2000 Entry into force: 12 February 2002 Year of ratification	CRC-SC: Optional Protocol to the Convention on the Rights of the Child on the sale of children, child prostitution and child, pornography, 2000 Entry into force: 18 January 2002 Year of ratification	ICPED: International Convention for the Protection of All Persons from Enforced Disappearance, 2006 Entry into force: 23 December 2010 Year of ratification	CRPD: Convention on the Rights of Persons with Disabilities, 2006 Entry into force: 3 May 2008 Year of ratification
Mexico	1975	1981	1981	1981	1986	1990	1999	2002	2002	2008	2007
Micronesia (Federated States of)				2004		1993			2015	2012	2016
Moldova (Republic of)	1993	1993	1993	1994	1995	1993		2004	2007		2010
Monaco	1995	1997	1997	2005	1991	1993		2001	2008		2017
Mongolia	1969	1974	1974	1981	2002	1990		2004	2003	2015	2009
Montenegro	2006	2006	2006	2006	2006	2006		2007	2006	2011	2009
Morocco	1970	1979	1979	1993	1993	1993	1993	2002	2001	2013	2009
Mozambique	1983	1993		1997	1999	1994	2013	2004	2003		2012
Myanmar			2017	1997		1991			2012		2011
Namibia	1982	1994	1994	1992	1994	1990		2002	2002		2007
Nauru				2011	2012	1994					2012
Nepal	1971	1991	1991	1991	1991	1990		2007	2006		2010
Netherlands	1971	1978	1978	1991	1988	1995		2009	2005	2011	2016
New Zealand	1972	1978	1978	1985	1989	1993		2001	2011		2008
Nicaragua	1978	1980	1980	1981	2005	1990	2005	2005	2004		2007
Niger	1967	1986	1986	1999	1998	1990	2009	2012	2004	2015	2008
Nigeria	1967	1993	1993	1985	2001	1991	2009	2012	2010	2009	2010
Norway	1970	1972	1972	1981	1986	1991		2003	2001		2013
Oman	2003			2006		1996		2004	2004		2009
Pakistan	1966	2010	2008	1996	2010	1990		2016	2011		2011
Palau						1995					2013
Palestine, State of	2014	2014	2014	2014	2014	2014		2014	2017		2014
Panama	1967	1977	1977	1981	1987	1990		2001	2001	2011	2007
Papua New Guinea	1982	2008	2008	1995		1993					2013
Paraguay	2003	1992	1992	1987	1990	1990	2008	2002	2003	2010	2008
Peru	1971	1978	1978	1982	1988	1990	2005	2002	2002	2012	2008
Philippines	1967	1986	1974	1981	1986	1990	1995	2003	2002		2008
Poland	1968	1977	1977	1980	1989	1991		2005	2005		2012
Portugal	1982	1978	1978	1980	1989	1990		2003	2003	2014	2009
Qatar	1976	2018	2018	2009	2000	1995		2002	2001		2008
Romania	1970	1974	1974	1982	1990	1990		2001	2001		2011
Russian Federation	1969	1973	1973	1981	1987	1990		2008	2013		2012
Rwanda	1975	1975	1975	1981	2008	1991	2008	2002	2002		2008
Saint Kitts and Nevis	2006			1985		1990					
Saint Lucia	1990			1982		1993		2014	2013		
Saint Vincent and the Grenadines	1981	1981	1981	1981	2001	1993	2005	2011	2005		2010
Samoa		2008		1992		1994		2016	2016	2012	2016
San Marino	2002	1985	1985	2003	2006	1991		2011	2011		2008
Sao Tome and Principe	2017	2017	2017	2003	2017	1991	2017				2015
Saudi Arabia	1997			2000	1997	1996		2011	2010		2008
Senegal	1972	1978	1978	1985	1986	1990	1999	2004	2003	2008	2010
Serbia	2001	2001	2001	2001	2001	2001		2003	2002	2011	2009
Seychelles	1978	1992	1992	1992	1992	1990	1994	2010	2012	2017	2009
Sierra Leone	1967	1996	1996	1988	2001	1990		2002	2001		2010
Singapore	2017			1995		1995		2008			2013
Slovakia	1993	1993	1993	1993	1993	1993		2006	2004	2014	2010
Slovenia	1992	1992	1992	1992	1993	1992		2004	2004		2008
Solomon Islands	1982		1982	2002		1995					
Somalia	1975	1990	1990		1990	2015					
South Africa	1998	1998	2015	1995	1998	1995		2009	2003		2007
South Sudan				2015	2015	2015					
Spain	1968	1977	1977	1984	1987	1990		2002	2001	2009	2007
Sri Lanka	1982	1980	1980	1981	1994	1991	1996	2000	2006	2016	2016
Sudan	1977	1986	1986			1990		2005	2004		2009
Suriname	1984	1976	1976	1993		1993			2012		2017
Sweden	1971	1971	1971	1980	1986	1990		2003	2007		2008

HUMAN DEVELOPMENT INDICES AND INDICATORS: 2018 STATISTICAL UPDATE

Country	ICERD: International Convention on the Elimination of All Forms of Racial Discrimination, 1965 — Entry into force: 4 January 1969 — Year of ratification	ICCPR: International Covenant on Civil and Political Rights, 1966 — Entry into force: 23 March 1969 — Year of ratification	ICESCR: International Covenant on Economic, Social and Cultural Rights, 1966 — Entry into force: 3 January 1976 — Year of ratification	CEDAW: Convention on the Elimination of All Forms of Discrimination against Women, 1979 — Entry into force: 3 September 1981 — Year of ratification	CAT: Convention against Torture and Other Cruel, Inhuman or Degrading Treatment or Punishment, 1984 — Entry into force: 26 June 1987 — Year of ratification	CRC: Convention on the Rights of the Child, 1989 — Entry into force: 2 September 1990 — Year of ratification	ICMW: International Convention on the Protection of the Rights of All Migrant Workers and Members of Their Families, 1990 — Entry into force: 1 July 2003 — Year of ratification	CRC-AC: Optional Protocol to the Convention on the Rights of the Child on the involvement of children in armed conflict, 2000 — Entry into force: 12 February 2002 — Year of ratification	CRC-SC: Optional Protocol to the Convention on the Rights of the Child on the sale of children, child prostitution and child pornography, 2000 — Entry into force: 18 January 2002 — Year of ratification	ICPED: International Convention for the Protection of All Persons from Enforced Disappearance, 2006 — Entry into force: 23 December 2010 — Year of ratification	CRPD: Convention on the Rights of Persons with Disabilities, 2006 — Entry into force: 3 May 2008 — Year of ratification
Switzerland	1994	1992	1992	1997	1986	1997		2002	2006	2016	2014
Syrian Arab Republic	1969	1969	1969	2003	2004	1993	2005	2003	2003		2009
Tajikistan	1995	1999	1999	1993	1995	1993	2002	2002	2002		
Tanzania (United Republic of)	1972	1976	1976	1985		1991		2004	2003		2009
Thailand	2003	1996	1999	1985	2007	1992		2006	2006		2008
The former Yugoslav Republic of Macedonia	1994	1994	1994	1994	1994	1993		2004	2003		2011
Timor-Leste	2003	2003	2003	2003	2003	2003	2004	2004	2003		
Togo	1972	1984	1984	1983	1987	1990		2005	2004	2014	2011
Tonga	1972					1995					
Trinidad and Tobago	1973	1978	1978	1990		1991					2015
Tunisia	1967	1969	1969	1985	1988	1992		2003	2002	2011	2008
Turkey	2002	2003	2003	1985	1988	1995	2004	2004	2002		2009
Turkmenistan	1994	1997	1997	1997	1999	1993		2005	2005		2008
Tuvalu				1999		1995					2013
Uganda	1980	1995	1987	1985	1986	1990	1995	2002	2001		2008
Ukraine	1969	1973	1973	1981	1987	1991		2005	2003	2015	2010
United Arab Emirates	1974			2004	2012	1997			2016		2010
United Kingdom	1969	1976	1976	1986	1988	1991		2003	2009		2009
United States	1994	1992			1994			2002	2002		
Uruguay	1968	1970	1970	1981	1986	1990	2001	2003	2003	2009	2009
Uzbekistan	1995	1995	1995	1995	1995	1994		2008	2008		
Vanuatu		2008		1995	2011	1993		2007	2007		2008
Venezuela (Bolivarian Republic of)	1967	1978	1978	1983	1991	1990	2016	2003	2002		2013
Viet Nam	1982	1982	1982	1982	2015	1990		2001	2001		2015
Yemen	1972	1987	1987	1984	1991	1991		2007	2004		2009
Zambia	1972	1984	1984	1985	1998	1991				2011	2010
Zimbabwe	1991	1991	1991	1991		1990		2013	2012		2013

DEFINITIONS

ICERD: International Convention on the Elimination of All Forms of Racial Discrimination, 1965: Prohibits all forms of racial discrimination—defined as any distinction, exclusion, restriction or preference based on race, colour, descent, or national or ethnic origin which has the purpose or effect of nullifying or impairing the equal recognition, enjoyment or exercise of human rights and fundamental freedoms and sets out the obligations of the state to combat this phenomenon. The Convention also requires a state to take appropriate measures against racial discrimination, including the propagation of racist ideas advocated by groups and organizations.

ICCPR: International Covenant on Civil and Political Rights, 1966: Says that all individuals possess civil and political rights, starting with the right to self-determination and including the right to life, the right to liberty and freedom of movement, the freedom of religion, of speech and of assembly, the right to equality between men and women, the right to equality before the law and the right to effective legal recourse. Some of these rights, such as the right not to be arbitrarily deprived of one's life, freedom from torture and other forms of cruel, inhuman and degrading treatment, may not be suspended or derogated even in a state of emergency. The ICCPR, its optional protocols, the ICESCR and the Universal Declaration of Human Rights together form the International Bill of Human Rights.

ICESCR: International Covenant on Economic, Social and Cultural Rights, 1966: Establishes economic, social and cultural rights, including the right to work in just and favourable conditions, to social protection, to an adequate standard of living, to the highest attainable standards of physical and mental health, to education, to participate in cultural life, and to enjoy the benefits of scientific progress. The ICESCR is part of the International Bill of Human Rights.

CEDAW: Convention on the Elimination of All Forms of Discrimination against Women, 1979: Is the first global and comprehensive legally binding international treaty aimed at the elimination of all forms of sex-based discrimination against women. It requires states to incorporate the principle of gender equality in their national constitutions or other appropriate legislation and to ensure the practical realisation of that principle. Discrimination against women is defined as any distinction, exclusion or restriction made on the basis of sex which has the effect or purpose of impairing or nullifying the recognition, enjoyment or exercise by women, irrespective of their marital status, on a basis of equality of men and women, of human rights and fundamental freedoms in the political, economic, social, cultural, civil or any other field.

CAT: Convention against Torture and Other Cruel, Inhuman or Degrading Treatment or Punishment, 1984: Defines and outlaws torture and other forms of ill-treatment under all circumstances, requires states to criminalize it under domestic law, to prevent its occurrence, to properly educate their law enforcement and other personnel about the prohibition of torture, to impartially investigate allegations of torture and to offer fair and adequate compensation to any victim. The Convention clearly states that no circumstances of any kind, including orders from a superior, a state of war or a state of emergency, can justify an act of torture — the ban is absolute. States commit to not extradite, deport or refoule a person if they are at risk of being tortured in the territory to which they would return, and to the universal obligation to prosecute or extradite any individual accused of having committed torture.

CRC: Convention on the Rights of the Child, 1989: Defines a child as a person under the age of 18, unless national law sets a lower age of majority, and sets standards for health, education, legal, civil, and social services for children in accordance with four general principles: non-discrimination between children; the best interest of the child; the right to life, survival and development of the child; and respect for the views of the child.

ICMW: International Convention on the Protection of the Rights of All Migrant Workers and Members of Their Families, 1990: Establishes minimum standards that states should apply to migrant workers and members of their families, regardless of their migratory status. Such standards apply to the entire migration process, from preparation for migration, departure and transit to the total period of stay and remunerated activity in the state of employment and the return to the state of origin or of habitual residence.

CRC-AC: Optional Protocol to the Convention on the Rights of the Child on the involvement of children in armed conflict, 2000: Requires states to take all feasible measures to ensure that members of their armed forces under the age of 18 do not take a direct part in hostilities, to ban compulsory recruitment below the age of 18, to ensure any voluntary member of the armed forces under the age of 18 does not take direct part in hostilities and to take legal measures to prohibit independent armed groups from recruiting and using children under the age of 18 in conflicts.

CRC-SC: Optional Protocol to the Convention on the Rights of the Child on the sale of children, child prostitution and child pornography, 2000: Prohibits the sale of children for sexual and non-sexual purposes, child prostitution and child pornography and provides states with detailed requirements to end the exploitation and abuse of children. It requires ratifying states to provide legal and other support to child victims and to criminalise and punish the activities related to these offences not only for those offering or delivering children for any of the purposes, but also for anyone accepting the child for these activities.

ICPED: International Convention for the Protection of All Persons from Enforced Disappearance, 2006: Prohibits enforced disappearance, defined as the abduction or deprivation of liberty of a person by state authorities, followed by the denial of those authorities to disclose the whereabouts or fate of the person, and establishes minimum legal standards on its prevention, combating impunity, effective law enforcement and upholding the rights of victims. The convention also enshrines the right of victims to the truth and to reparations.

CRPD: Convention on the Rights of Persons with Disabilities, 2006: Guarantees the full and equal enjoyment of all human rights and fundamental freedoms to persons with disabilities and promotes respect for their inherent dignity. It considers disability as the result of an interaction between an individual's condition and an inaccessible society. The barriers that can make society inaccessible are manifold and the Convention identifies these barriers as discriminatory and requires their removal. In adopting a rights-based approach to disability, the Convention moves away from viewing disability as a sickness inherent in the individual requiring either a medical intervention (medical approach) to fix the person, or a charitable intervention (charity approach) based on voluntary assistance rather than individual right.

MAIN DATA SOURCE

Columns 1–11: UNOHCHR (2018).

TABLE 15 Status of fundamental human rights treaties

Human development dashboards

DASHBOARD 1

Quality of human development

Country groupings (terciles)

Top third | Middle third | Bottom third

Three-colour coding is used to visualize partial grouping of countries by indicator. For each indicator countries are divided into three groups of approximately equal size (terciles): the top third, the middle third and the bottom third. Aggregates are colour coded using the same tercile cutoffs. See Notes after the table.

	Quality of health			SDG 4.c	SDG 4.a Quality of education		SDG 4.1			SDG 7.1	SDG 6.1 Quality of standard of living	SDG 6.2
	Lost health expectancy	Physicians	Hospital beds	Pupil–teacher ratio, primary school	Primary school teachers trained to teach	Proportion of schools with access to the Internet	Programme for International Student Assessment (PISA) score			Vulnerable employment[a]	Rural population with access to electricity	Population using improved drinking-water sources	Population using improved sanitation facilities
	(%)	(per 10,000 people)		(pupils per teacher)	(%)		Mathematics[b]	Reading[c]	Science[c]	(% of total employment)		(%)	
HDI rank	2016	2007–2017[d]	2007–2014[d]	2012–2017[d]	2009–2017[d]	2008–2013[d]	2015	2015	2015	2017	2016	2015	2015
VERY HIGH HUMAN DEVELOPMENT													
1 Norway	11.5	43.9	33	9	..	100	502	513	498	5.2	100.0	100.0	98.1
2 Switzerland	11.8	42.5	50	10	..	..	521	492	506	9.5	100.0	100.0	99.9
3 Australia	11.9	35.0	39	..	..	..	494	503	510	10.8	100.0	100.0	100.0
4 Ireland	11.5	29.6	29	16	..	..	504	521	503	11.9	100.0	98.9	92.2
5 Germany	11.7	41.9	82	12	..	..	506	509	509	6.0	100.0	100.0	99.2
6 Iceland	11.4	37.9	32	10	..	..	488	482	473	7.8	100.0	100.0	98.8
7 Hong Kong, China (SAR)	..	..	..	14	97	100	548	527	523	6.0	..	100.0	96.3
7 Sweden	12.1	41.9	27	12	..	100	494	500	493	6.4	100.0	100.0	99.3
9 Singapore	8.1	22.8	20	..	..	100[e]	564	535	556	8.3	..	100.0	100.0
10 Netherlands	11.7	34.8	47	12	..	..	512	503	509	12.7	100.0	100.0	97.7
11 Denmark	11.6	36.6	35	11	..	100	511	500	502	5.8	100.0	100.0	99.6
12 Canada	11.6	25.4	27	..	..	..	516	527	528	11.0	100.0	98.9	98.5
13 United States	12.7	25.7	29	14	..	..	470	497	496	6.3	100.0	99.2	100.0
14 United Kingdom	11.6	28.3	29	17	..	100	492	498	509	13.1	100.0	100.0	99.1
15 Finland	12.0	32.0	55	13	..	100	511	526	531	10.1	100.0	100.0	99.4
16 New Zealand	11.4	30.6	23	14	..	..	495	509	513	12.2	100.0	100.0	100.0
17 Belgium	11.8	30.1	65	11	..	100	507	499	502	10.8	100.0	100.0	99.5
17 Liechtenstein	..	..	..	8	..	..	..	..	..	..	100.0	100.0	100.0
19 Japan	11.2	23.7	137	16	..	99[e]	532	516	538	8.8	100.0	98.9	100.0
20 Austria	11.6	52.3	76	10	..	100	497	485	495	8.1	100.0	100.0	100.0
21 Luxembourg	11.9	29.2	54	8	..	..	486	481	483	6.1	100.0	100.0	97.6
22 Israel	11.4	35.8	33	12	..	..	470	479	467	12.2	100.0	100.0	100.0
22 Korea (Republic of)	11.7	23.3	103	17	..	100	524	517	516	24.1	100.0	99.6	99.9
24 France	11.5	32.4	64	18	..	..	493	499	495	7.6	100.0	100.0	98.7
25 Slovenia	12.8	28.2	46	17	..	..	510	505	513	10.6	100.0	99.5	99.1
26 Spain	11.2	38.7	31	13	..	100	486	496	493	11.9	100.0	99.9	99.9
27 Czechia	12.5	36.8	68	19	..	100	492	487	493	14.2	100.0	99.9	99.1
28 Italy	11.6	40.2	34	12	..	..	490	485	481	17.7	100.0	100.0	99.3
29 Malta	11.4	39.1	48	13	..	100	479	447	465	8.8	100.0	100.0	100.0
30 Estonia	12.4	34.3	53	11	..	99	520	519	534	5.7	100.0	99.6	99.6
31 Greece	11.3	62.6	48	10	..	..	454	467	455	26.5	100.0	100.0	99.0
32 Cyprus	9.1	25.0	35	12	..	100	437	443	433	12.6	100.0	100.0	99.4
33 Poland	11.9	22.9	65	10	..	81	504	506	501	17.0	100.0	97.9	98.1
34 United Arab Emirates	13.6	15.6	11	25	100	..	427	434	437	0.4	100.0	99.6	100.0
35 Andorra	..	36.9	25	10	100	100	..	..	..	..	100.0	100.0	100.0
35 Lithuania	11.9	43.8	70	13	..	100	478	472	475	10.2	100.0	97.4	93.6
37 Qatar	12.1	19.6	12	12	49	53	402	402	418	0.2	100.0	100.0	100.0
38 Slovakia	11.8	34.5	60	15	..	..	475	453	461	12.2	100.0	97.9	98.9
39 Brunei Darussalam	11.1	17.5	28	10	85	100	..	..	..	5.1	100.0	99.5	96.3
39 Saudi Arabia	12.2	25.7	21	12	100	..	..	..	..	3.0	100.0	100.0	100.0
41 Latvia	11.8	32.1	59	11	..	100	482	488	490	8.9	100.0	98.6	92.9
41 Portugal	11.7	44.3	34	13	..	..	492	498	501	13.1	100.0	99.9	99.4
43 Bahrain	13.9	9.2	21	12	84	100	..	..	..	1.8	100.0	100.0	100.0
44 Chile	12.3	10.3	21	18	..	78[e]	423	459	447	23.9	100.0	100.0	99.9
45 Hungary	12.0	30.9	72	11	..	99	477	470	477	5.9	100.0	100.0	98.0
46 Croatia	11.9	31.3	59	14	..	100	464	487	475	8.7	100.0	99.6	97.5
47 Argentina	11.1	39.1	47	..	..	36	456[f]	475[f]	475[f]	21.4	100.0	99.6	94.8
48 Oman	14.8	19.2	17	..	..	90	..	..	..	9.1	100.0	90.9	99.3
49 Russian Federation	11.7	39.8	97	20	..	80[e]	494	495	487	6.3	100.0	96.4	88.8
50 Montenegro	11.3	23.4	40	..	..	..	418	427	411	11.7	100.0	97.6	95.9
51 Bulgaria	11.3	40.0	64	18	..	..	441	432	446	8.2	100.0	99.3	86.0
52 Romania	11.4	26.7	61	19	..	..	444	434	435	25.7	100.0	100.0	81.8

DASHBOARD 1 QUALITY OF HUMAN DEVELOPMENT

		Quality of health			Quality of education SDG 4.c / SDG 4.a / SDG 4.1			Programme for International Student Assessment (PISA) score			Quality of standard of living SDG 7.1 / SDG 6.1 / SDG 6.2			
		Lost health expectancy	Physicians	Hospital beds	Pupil–teacher ratio, primary school	Primary school teachers trained to teach	Proportion of schools with access to the Internet	Mathematics[b]	Reading[c]	Science[c]	Vulnerable employment[a]	Rural population with access to electricity	Population using improved drinking-water sources	Population using improved sanitation facilities
		(%)	(per 10,000 people)		(pupils per teacher)	(%)					(% of total employment)	(%)		
HDI rank		2016	2007–2017[d]	2007–2014[d]	2012–2017[d]	2009–2017[d]	2008–2013[d]	2015	2015	2015	2017	2016	2015	2015
53	Belarus	11.8	40.7	113	18	99	61[e]	..	..	..	2.7	100.0	98.0	94.3
54	Bahamas	11.7	22.6	29	19	90	..	..	..	..	14.6	100.0	97.8	92.0
55	Uruguay	10.7	37.4	25	12	100	96	418	437	435	23.9	100.0	99.2	95.7
56	Kuwait	11.3	26.1	22	9	79	..	..	..	..	1.9	100.0	100.0	100.0
57	Malaysia	11.5	15.3	19	12	100	91	..	..	..	22.2	100.0	96.4	99.6
58	Barbados	11.4	18.1	62	13	69	100[e]	..	..	..	15.9	100.0	98.1	96.5
58	Kazakhstan	10.9	32.7	72	21	100	97	..	..	..	25.6	100.0	91.1	97.8
HIGH HUMAN DEVELOPMENT														
60	Iran (Islamic Republic of)	13.6	14.9	1	27	100	87	..	..	..	41.4	100.0	94.9	88.3
60	Palau	..	11.9	48	..	..	..	..	..	..	..	97.2	99.6	100.0
62	Seychelles	10.4	9.8	36	14	83	..	..	..	..	..	100.0	96.3	100.0
63	Costa Rica	11.0	11.5	12	12	94	39	400	427	420	14.0	100.0	99.7	97.1
64	Turkey	13.6	17.5	25	18	..	86	420	428	425	28.5	100.0	98.9	96.4
65	Mauritius	12.0	20.0	34	18	100	85	..	..	..	16.2	100.0	99.9	93.1
66	Panama	11.0	15.9	22	22	99	22	..	..	..	32.2	81.3	95.0	76.9
67	Serbia	11.7	24.6	54	15	56	..	..	..	..	28.1	100.0	91.2	94.6
68	Albania	10.8	12.9	26	18	..	96	413	405	427	57.2	100.0	91.4	97.7
69	Trinidad and Tobago	11.9	18.2	27	..	88	56[e]	417	427	425	16.5	100.0	96.9	92.1
70	Antigua and Barbuda	10.7	..	21	14	65	88	..	..	..	..	96.5	96.7	87.5
70	Georgia	10.6	47.8	26	9	95	100	404	401	411	57.0	100.0	93.3	84.9
72	Saint Kitts and Nevis	..	..	23	14	72	100	..	..	..	..	100.0	..	..
73	Cuba	11.6	75.2	53	9	100	..	..	..	..	10.3	100.0	95.2	90.8
74	Mexico	11.6	22.3	15	27	97	12[e,g]	408	423	416	27.2	100.0	98.3	89.2
75	Grenada	11.8	..	35	15	63	61	..	..	..	..	92.3	95.6	78.3
76	Sri Lanka	11.2	8.8	36	23	70	18	..	..	..	40.1	94.6	92.3	94.2
77	Bosnia and Herzegovina	13.1	18.9	35	17	..	100	..	..	..	20.9	100.0	97.7	94.8
78	Venezuela (Bolivarian Republic of)	10.8	..	9	..	..	..	..	..	..	31.9	96.4	97.4	94.9
79	Brazil	12.1	18.5	23	22	..	46	377	407	401	27.9	100.0	97.5	86.1
80	Azerbaijan	11.2	34.0	47	15	90	27[e]	..	..	..	56.1	100.0	84.4	89.3
80	Lebanon	13.4	23.8	35	12	..	..	396	347	386	25.6	100.0	92.3	95.4
80	The former Yugoslav Republic of Macedonia	11.5	28.8	45	14	..	..	371	352	384	22.8	100.0	96.8	90.9
83	Armenia	11.4	28.0	39	..	..	100	..	..	..	41.6	100.0	98.9	91.6
83	Thailand	11.5	4.7	21	17	100	98	415	409	421	50.2	100.0	98.2	95.0
85	Algeria	14.2	12.1	17	24	100	53	360	350	376	27.9	99.0	93.5	87.5
86	China	10.1	36.3	38	17	..	..	531[h]	494[h]	518[h]	33.0	100.0	95.8	75.0
86	Ecuador	11.3	16.7	16	25	82	22	..	..	..	45.6	99.8	92.6	86.1
88	Ukraine	11.7	30.0	90	13	86	..	..	..	..	15.6	100.0	97.7	95.9
89	Peru	11.1	11.2	15	18	..	..	387	398	397	50.3	75.6	89.9	76.8
90	Colombia	10.7	18.2	15	24	95	71[e]	390	425	416	47.1	95.7	96.5	84.4
90	Saint Lucia	12.1	1.0	16	15	79	100	..	..	..	29.1	98.4	98.2	90.9
92	Fiji	12.3	8.4	21	28	100	..	..	..	..	38.4	98.0	93.7	95.7
92	Mongolia	11.3	32.6	68	30	100	91	..	..	..	46.9	44.2	83.2	59.2
94	Dominican Republic	11.2	14.9	17	19	85	5[e]	328	358	332	40.9	100.0	94.5	82.7
95	Jordan	10.6	34.3	18	18	100	85	380	408	409	9.5	100.0	98.6	96.7
95	Tunisia	12.8	12.9	21	16	100	81	367	361	386	20.8	100.0	94.2	93.1
97	Jamaica	12.0	4.7	17	26	100	93[e,i]	..	..	..	37.9	96.0	92.9	85.4
98	Tonga	12.5	5.6	26	22	97	..	..	..	..	54.5	96.6	99.9	93.5
99	Saint Vincent and the Grenadines	11.9	..	52	15	84	68	..	..	..	9.1	100.0	95.1	87.2
100	Suriname	12.0	..	31	14	100	6[i,j]	..	..	..	13.6	69.3	94.7	79.2
101	Botswana	13.1	3.8	18	23	99	23	..	..	..	15.0	37.5	79.2	60.0
101	Maldives	11.0	36.1	43	10	83	100[e]	..	..	..	20.7	100.0	97.9	95.9
103	Dominica	..	..	38	13	66	71	..	..	..	..	100.0	96.5	77.9
104	Samoa	12.2	3.4	10	..	..	..	..	..	..	32.0	100.0	95.5	96.6
105	Uzbekistan	10.7	24.5	44	21	99	..	..	..	..	24.7	100.0	..	100.0
106	Belize	11.3	8.3	11	20	73	..	..	..	..	26.8	88.4	97.1	87.2
106	Marshall Islands	..	4.6	27	..	..	..	..	..	..	..	89.1	78.2	86.9
108	Libya	13.4	20.9	37	..	..	..	..	..	..	36.0	96.4	96.8	99.7
108	Turkmenistan	10.0	22.9	40	..	..	..	..	..	..	21.1	100.0	94.5	96.6
110	Gabon	11.5	4.1	63	..	..	..	..	..	..	32.2	55.0	87.5	40.9

HUMAN DEVELOPMENT INDICES AND INDICATORS: 2018 STATISTICAL UPDATE

		Quality of health			Quality of education SDG 4.c / SDG 4.a			SDG 4.1 Programme for International Student Assessment (PISA) score			Quality of standard of living SDG 7.1 / SDG 6.1 / SDG 6.2			
		Lost health expectancy	Physicians	Hospital beds	Pupil–teacher ratio, primary school	Primary school teachers trained to teach	Proportion of schools with access to the Internet	Mathematics[b]	Reading[c]	Science[c]	Vulnerable employment[a]	Rural population with access to electricity	Population using improved drinking-water sources	Population using improved sanitation facilities
		(%)	(per 10,000 people)		(pupils per teacher)	(%)					(% of total employment)	(%)		
HDI rank		2016	2007–2017[d]	2007–2014[d]	2012–2017[d]	2009–2017[d]	2008–2013[d]	2015	2015	2015	2017	2016	2015	2015
110	Paraguay	12.0	12.9	13	24	92	9	..	..	..	39.1	96.1	98.9	91.2
112	Moldova (Republic of)	11.1	32.0	62	17	99	..	420	416	428	28.7	100.0	86.7	78.4
MEDIUM HUMAN DEVELOPMENT														
113	Philippines	11.0	..	10	30	100	12 [e,k]	..	..	..	35.4	86.3	90.5	75.0
113	South Africa	12.4	8.2	28	30	..	..	..	..	..	9.6	67.9	84.7	73.1
115	Egypt	13.3	8.1	5	23	74	49	..	..	..	20.1	100.0	98.4	93.2
116	Indonesia	11.0	2.0	9	14	..	42 [k]	386	397	403	47.5	94.8	89.5	67.9
116	Viet Nam	11.5	8.2	20	20	100	..	495	487	525	55.9	100.0	91.2	78.2
118	Bolivia (Plurinational State of)	11.9	4.7	11	18	58	..	..	..	..	31.3	79.1	92.9	52.6
119	Palestine, State of	..	..	..	24	100	30 [l]	..	..	..	39.9	100.0	87.6	96.0
120	Iraq	15.5	8.5	13	..	..	..	..	..	..	35.2	100.0	86.1	85.7
121	El Salvador	11.1	16.0	11	28	96	24	..	..	..	35.7	98.8	93.0	91.1
122	Kyrgyzstan	11.0	18.5	48	25	21	6	..	..	..	36.5	100.0	87.3	96.6
123	Morocco	14.1	6.2	9	27	100	3	..	..	..	50.7	100.0	83.0	83.5
124	Nicaragua	11.4	9.1	9	..	75	6 [k]	..	..	..	39.4	56.6	82.3	76.3
125	Cabo Verde	11.8	7.9	21	21	93	..	..	..	..	37.5	91.8	86.5	65.2
125	Guyana	11.9	2.1	20	23	70	4 [e,k]	..	..	..	29.7	81.9	95.1	86.2
127	Guatemala	12.3	9.0	6	22	..	..	..	..	..	34.7	86.4	93.6	67.4
127	Tajikistan	10.4	17.1	55	22	100	..	..	..	..	47.5	100.0	74.1	95.5
129	Namibia	12.2	3.7	27	..	96	..	..	..	..	25.3	28.7	78.8	33.8
130	India	13.9	7.6	7	35	70	..	..	..	..	77.5	77.6	87.6	44.2
131	Micronesia (Federated States of)	12.3	1.8	32	20	..	..	..	..	..	..	70.7	88.4	..
132	Timor-Leste	13.8	0.8	59	..	..	..	..	..	..	49.4	49.2	70.2	44.0
133	Honduras	11.2	..	7	28	..	..	..	..	..	36.1	72.2	92.2	79.8
134	Bhutan	14.1	3.8	18	38	100	43 [e]	..	..	..	71.5	100.0	97.6	62.9
134	Kiribati	12.6	2.0	13	26	73	..	..	..	..	..	82.2	64.4	39.8
136	Bangladesh	12.9	4.7	6	34	50	5 [e]	..	..	..	57.5	68.9	97.3	46.9
137	Congo	11.8	1.0	16	44	80	..	..	..	..	74.9	22.6	68.3	15.0
138	Vanuatu	12.9	1.9	17	27	28	..	..	..	..	73.5	46.4	90.5	53.5
139	Lao People's Democratic Republic	12.1	4.9	15	23	97	..	..	..	..	82.9	80.3	80.4	72.6
140	Ghana	11.1	1.0	9	27	55	..	..	..	..	66.1	66.6	77.8	14.3
141	Equatorial Guinea	9.7	..	21	23	37	..	..	..	..	35.7	52.6	49.6	74.5
142	Kenya	11.7	2.0	14	31	97	..	..	..	..	54.3	39.3	58.5	29.8
143	Sao Tome and Principe	11.7	..	29	31	27	..	..	..	..	34.1	51.1	79.7	40.1
144	Eswatini (Kingdom of)	13.1	1.5	21	28	82	..	..	..	..	19.1	61.2	67.6	58.0
144	Zambia	12.8	0.9	20	48	93	..	..	..	..	77.6	2.7	61.2	31.1
146	Cambodia	12.4	1.4	7	43	100	7 [e]	..	..	..	51.0	36.5	75.0	48.8
147	Angola	10.9	1.4	8	..	47	..	..	..	..	66.7	16.0	41.0	39.4
148	Myanmar	12.6	5.7	6	22	98	..	..	..	..	58.2	39.8	67.5	64.7
149	Nepal	12.7	6.0	50	21	97	5	..	..	..	78.9	85.2	87.7	46.1
150	Pakistan	13.2	9.8	6	48	75	..	..	..	..	59.7	98.8	88.5	58.3
151	Cameroon	12.1	0.8	13	43	59	..	..	..	..	71.7	21.3	65.3	38.8
LOW HUMAN DEVELOPMENT														
152	Solomon Islands	12.9	1.9	13	25	66	..	..	..	..	62.7	41.5	64.0	31.3
153	Papua New Guinea	11.9	0.6	..	45	100	..	..	..	..	74.7	15.5	36.6	18.6
154	Tanzania (United Republic of)	11.6	0.2	7	43	99	..	..	..	..	83.5	16.9	50.1	23.5
155	Syrian Arab Republic	12.6	15.5	15	..	..	..	..	..	..	35.6	100.0	96.7	92.9
156	Zimbabwe	11.4	0.8	17	36	86	..	..	..	..	65.7	15.6	66.6	38.6
157	Nigeria	11.3	4.0	5	..	66	..	..	..	..	80.4	41.1	67.3	32.6
158	Rwanda	11.9	0.6	16	58	90	..	..	..	..	80.0	17.8	56.7	62.3
159	Lesotho	11.9	..	13	34	83	10	..	..	..	59.0	15.7	71.6	43.8
159	Mauritania	11.8	0.7	4	36	85	..	..	..	..	45.0	2.3 [m]	69.6	44.6
161	Madagascar	11.8	1.4	2	41	15	..	..	..	..	85.4	17.3	50.6	9.7
162	Uganda	12.2	0.9	5	43	..	..	..	..	..	74.5	18.0	38.9	19.2
163	Benin	12.5	1.5	5	45	69	..	..	..	..	88.0	18.0	67.0	13.9
164	Senegal	12.0	0.7	3	32	70	5	..	..	..	44.3	38.3	75.2	48.4
165	Comoros	11.5	..	22	28	75	..	..	..	..	63.9	72.2	83.3	34.2
165	Togo	11.0	0.5	7	41	73	..	..	..	..	80.3	19.4	62.8	13.9
167	Sudan	14.4	30.6	8	..	60	4	..	..	..	40.5	22.2	58.9	34.6

DASHBOARD 1 Quality of human development

DASHBOARD 1 QUALITY OF HUMAN DEVELOPMENT

		Quality of health			SDG 4.c	SDG 4.a Quality of education	SDG 4.1					SDG 7.1	SDG 6.1 Quality of standard of living	SDG 6.2
		Lost health expectancy	Physicians	Hospital beds	Pupil–teacher ratio, primary school	Primary school teachers trained to teach	Proportion of schools with access to the Internet	Programme for International Student Assessment (PISA) score			Vulnerable employment[e]	Rural population with access to electricity	Population using improved drinking-water sources	Population using improved sanitation facilities
		(%)	(per 10,000 people)		(pupils per teacher)	(%)		Mathematics[b]	Reading[c]	Science[c]	(% of total employment)	(%)		
HDI rank		2016	2007–2017[d]	2007–2014[d]	2012–2017[d]	2009–2017[d]	2008–2013[d]	2015	2015	2015	2017	2016	2015	2015
168	Afghanistan	15.5	3.0	5	44	..	..	..	..	..	66.1	79.0	63.0	39.2
168	Haiti	12.9	..	13	..	..	..	..	..	..	87.5	0.5[n]	64.2	30.5
170	Côte d'Ivoire	11.6	1.4	4	43	100	..	..	..	..	73.3	38.1	73.1	29.9
171	Malawi	12.5	0.2	13	70	91	..	..	..	..	59.9	4.0	67.2	43.5
172	Djibouti	11.3	2.3	14	30	100	..	..	..	..	39.1	2.0[o]	76.9	51.4
173	Ethiopia	12.2	0.2	63	..	85	2	..	..	..	88.2	26.5	39.1	7.1
174	Gambia	12.1	1.1	11	39	88	..	..	..	..	71.2	15.5	80.1	41.7
175	Guinea	12.8	0.8	3	46	75	..	..	..	..	90.1	6.9	67.4	22.0
176	Congo (Democratic Republic of the)	13.2	0.9	8	33	95	..	..	..	..	53.5	0.4[m]	41.8	19.7
177	Guinea-Bissau	13.5	0.5	10	..	39	..	..	..	..	65.3	4.0[m]	69.2	21.5
178	Yemen	15.7	3.1	7	27	..	..	..	..	..	43.6	57.7	70.4	59.7
179	Eritrea	11.6	..	7	43	61	..	..	..	..	46.3	39.3	19.3	11.3
180	Mozambique	13.2	0.6	7	55	93	..	..	..	..	84.6	5.0	47.3	23.6
181	Liberia	13.3	0.2	8	30	47	..	..	..	..	77.7	1.3	69.9	16.9
182	Mali	12.6	0.9	1	39	52	..	..	..	..	87.9	1.8	74.3	31.3
183	Burkina Faso	12.2	0.5	4	42	73	..	..	..	..	87.2	0.8	53.9	22.5
184	Sierra Leone	10.3	0.2	4	37	54	..	..	..	..	87.7	2.5	58.1	14.5
185	Burundi	12.5	..	19	50	100	..	..	..	..	92.4	1.7	55.9	50.5
186	Chad	13.0	0.4	4	57	65	..	..	..	..	91.5	2.2	42.5	9.5
187	South Sudan	13.6	..	..	47	44	..	..	..	..	49.7	5.9	50.4	10.4
188	Central African Republic	15.3	0.5	10	83	58	..	..	..	..	67.5	0.4	54.1	25.1
189	Niger	12.1	0.2	3	36	56	..	..	..	..	88.5	4.7	45.8	12.9
OTHER COUNTRIES OR TERRITORIES														
..	Korea (Democratic People's Rep. of)	10.2	35.1	132	21	..	..	..	..	..	66.0	39.2	99.6	77.1
..	Monaco	..	66.5	138	14	..	..	..	..	..	..	..	100.0	100.0
..	Nauru	..	13.9	50	40	100	..	..	..	..	..	..	100.0	65.6
..	San Marino	..	63.6	38	6	..	..	..	..	..	..	100.0	100.0	100.0
..	Somalia	9.7	0.3	..	..	..	..	..	..	..	72.3	11.6	40.0	16.2
..	Tuvalu	..	10.9	..	13	..	..	..	..	..	..	98.5	99.3	91.4
Human development groups														
	Very high human development	11.8	30.8	58	14	..	—	—	—	—	10.4	100.0	99.0	97.9
	High human development	10.9	29.2	32	18	..	—	—	—	—	33.1	99.4	96.0	81.0
	Medium human development	13.0	6.7	9	29	75	—	—	—	—	63.2	78.9	86.9	54.1
	Low human development	12.5	3.2	13	41	80	—	—	—	—	75.1	24.4	56.6	27.6
Developing countries		12.0	15.6	20	25	..	—	—	—	—	50.0	74.4	86.1	61.7
Regions														
	Arab States	13.6	13.5	12	20	89	—	—	—	—	26.3	78.9	87.1	81.2
	East Asia and the Pacific	10.5	27.5	31	17	..	—	—	—	—	37.9	94.0	93.5	74.6
	Europe and Central Asia	12.0	24.7	51	18	..	—	—	—	—	26.8	100.0	95.0	95.8
	Latin America and the Caribbean	11.6	20.4	20	22	..	—	—	—	—	32.3	90.5	96.2	85.6
	South Asia	13.7	7.8	8	35	71	—	—	—	—	72.1	79.8	88.4	48.3
	Sub-Saharan Africa	12.0	1.9	15	39	79	—	—	—	—	72.2	23.2	57.7	28.1
Least developed countries		12.7	3.2	14	37	76	—	—	—	—	70.5	31.2	61.5	32.0
Small island developing states		12.0	25.7	27	19	92	—	—	—	—	46.9	47.9	78.6	61.6
Organisation for Economic Co-operation and Development		12.0	28.5	50	16	..	—	—	—	—	12.7	100.0	99.3	98.2
World		12.0	18.3	27	23	..	—	—	—	—	42.6	76.3	88.3	67.7

NOTES

Three-colour coding is used to visualize partial grouping of countries and aggregates by indicator. For each indicator countries are divided into three groups of approximately equal size (terciles): the top third, the middle third and the bottom third. Aggregates are colour coded using the same tercile cutoffs. See *Technical note 6* at http://hdr.undp.org/sites/default/files/hdr2018_technical_notes.pdf for details about partial grouping in this table.

a Estimates modelled by the International Labour Organization.
b Average score for Organisation for Economic Co-operation and Development (OECD) countries is 490.
c Average score for OECD countries is 493.
d Data refer to the most recent year available during the period specified.
e Public institutions only.
f Refers to the adjudicated region of Ciudad Autónoma de Buenos Aires.
g Refers only to International Standard Classification of Education (ISCED) level 2.
h Refers to the provinces of Beijing, Guangdong, Jiangsu and Shanghai.
i Refers only to ISCED level 3.
j There are no private institutions at ISCED level 3.
k Refers only to ISCED levels 1 and 2.
l Refers to West Bank schools only.
m Refers to 2014.
n Refers to 2013.
o Refers to 2015.

DEFINITIONS

Lost health expectancy: Relative difference between life expectancy and healthy life expectancy, expressed as a percentage of life expectancy at birth.

Physicians: Number of medical doctors (physicians), both generalists and specialists, expressed per 10,000 people.

Hospital beds: Number of hospital beds available, expressed per 10,000 people.

Pupil–teacher ratio, primary school: Average number of pupils per teacher in primary education.

Primary school teachers trained to teach: Percentage of primary school teachers who have received the minimum organized teacher training (preservice or in-service) required for teaching at the primary level.

Proportion of schools with access to the Internet: Proportion of primary and secondary schools with access to the Internet for educational purposes.

Programme for International Student Assessment (PISA) score: Score obtained in testing of skills and knowledge of 15-year-old students in mathematics, reading and science.

Vulnerable employment: Percentage of employed people engaged as unpaid family workers and own-account workers.

Rural population with access to electricity: People living in rural areas with access to electricity, expressed as a percentage of the total rural population. It includes electricity sold commercially (both on grid and off grid) and self-generated electricity but excludes unauthorized connections.

Population using improved drinking-water sources: Percentage of the population using improved drinking-water sources, which by nature of their construction and design are likely to protect the source from outside contamination, in particular from faecal matter. Improved drinking water sources include piped water into a dwelling, plot or yard; a public tap or standpipe, a tube well or borehole, a protected dug well, a protected spring and rainwater collection.

Population using improved sanitation facilities: Percentage of the population using improved sanitation facilities, which hygienically separate human excreta from human contact. Improved sanitation facilities include flush or pour-flush toilets to a piped sewer system, a septic tank or pit latrine, a ventilated improved pit latrine, a pit latrine with slab and a composting toilet. Sanitation facilities that are shared with other households or open to public use are not considered improved.

MAIN DATA SOURCES

Column 1: HDRO calculations based on data on healthy life expectancy at birth and life expectancy at birth from WHO (2018).

Columns 2, 3, 12 and 13: WHO (2018).

Columns 4 and 5: UNESCO Institute for Statistics (2018).

Column 6: WSIS (2014).

Columns 7–9: OECD (2017b).

Column 10: ILO (2018a).

Column 11: World Bank (2018a).

DASHBOARD 2

Life-course gender gap

Country groupings (terciles)

Top third | Middle third | Bottom third

Three-colour coding is used to visualize partial grouping of countries by indicator. For each indicator countries are divided into three groups of approximately equal size (terciles): the top third, the middle third and the bottom third. Aggregates are colour coded using the same tercile cutoffs. See *Notes* after the table.

		SDG 4.2	SDG 4.1	SDG 4.1	SDG 8.5	SDG 4.6	SDG 8.5	SDG 8.3	SDG 5.5	SDG 5.4		SDG 1.3
		Childhood and youth						**Adulthood**				**Older age**
		Sex ratio at birth[a]	Gross enrolment ratio (female to male ratio)			Youth unemployment rate	Population with at least some secondary education	Total unemployment rate	Share of employment in nonagriculture, female	Share of seats in parliament	Time spent on unpaid domestic chores and care work		Old-age pension recipients
											Women ages 15 and older		
		(male to female births)	Pre-primary	Primary	Secondary	(female to male ratio)	(female to male ratio)	(female to male ratio)	(% of total employment in nonagriculture)	(% held by women)	(% of 24-hour day)	(female to male ratio)	(female to male ratio)
HDI rank		2015–2020[b]	2012–2017[c]	2012–2017[c]	2012–2017[c]	2017	2010–2017[c]	2017	2017	2017	2007–2017[c]	2007–2017[c]	2008–2015[c]
VERY HIGH HUMAN DEVELOPMENT													
1	Norway	1.06	1.00	1.00	0.97	0.86	1.01	0.73	48.0	41.4	15.3	1.2	1.00
2	Switzerland	1.05	0.99	0.99	0.96	0.98	0.99	1.04	46.8	29.3	16.8	1.6	1.00
3	Australia	1.06	0.96	1.00	0.87	0.91	1.00	1.04	46.6	32.7	..	..	..
4	Ireland	1.06	1.00	1.00	1.02	0.87	1.05	0.73	47.4	24.3	..	..	..
5	Germany	1.06	0.99	0.99	0.95	0.90	0.99	0.85	46.8	31.5	15.9[d]	1.6[d]	1.00
6	Iceland	1.05	1.01	1.00	1.01	0.95	1.00	1.04	47.9	38.1	..	..	..
7	Hong Kong, China (SAR)	1.07	0.99	0.98	0.97	0.88	0.92	0.83	49.2	..	10.8	3.3	..
7	Sweden	1.06	1.00	1.04	1.14	0.92	1.00	0.90	48.3	43.6	16.0	1.3	1.00
9	Singapore	1.07	..	1.00	0.99	1.35	0.92	1.05	45.0	23.0	..	..	..
10	Netherlands	1.05	1.00	1.00	1.02	0.96	0.96	1.18	46.3	35.6	14.7[e]	1.6[e]	1.00
11	Denmark	1.06	0.99	0.99	1.03	0.92	0.99	1.15	47.9	37.4	15.6[e]	1.4[e]	1.00
12	Canada	1.06	..	1.00	1.01	0.89	1.00	0.80	48.0	30.1	14.6	1.5	1.00
13	United States	1.05	0.98	1.00	1.01	0.91	1.00	0.98	46.2	19.7	15.9	1.6	1.00
14	United Kingdom	1.05	0.96	1.00	1.03	0.88	0.97	0.95	46.8	28.5	12.7	1.8	1.00
15	Finland	1.05	1.00	1.00	1.10	0.93	1.00	0.96	49.0	42.0	14.5[d]	1.5[d]	1.00
16	New Zealand	1.06	1.01	1.01	1.06	1.02	1.00	1.18	48.3	38.3	18.1[f]	1.7[f]	1.00
17	Belgium	1.05	0.99	1.00	1.14	0.93	0.95	0.93	46.3	41.4	15.9[f]	1.6[f]	1.00
17	Liechtenstein	..	1.06	0.96	0.78	..	..	..	..	12.0	..	..	..
19	Japan	1.06	..	1.00	1.01	0.90	1.03	0.87	43.5	13.7	14.4[d]	4.7[d]	..
20	Austria	1.06	1.00	0.99	0.96	0.94	1.00	0.86	47.2	33.6	18.3[d]	1.9[d]	1.00
21	Luxembourg	1.05	0.97	1.00	1.04	0.96	1.00	1.09	45.3	28.3	14.4[d]	2.0[d]	1.00
22	Israel	1.05	1.00	1.01	1.02	1.05	0.97	1.05	47.3	27.5	..	..	..
22	Korea (Republic of)	1.07	1.00	1.00	1.00	0.97	0.94	0.92	42.0	17.0	14.0[d]	4.2[d]	..
24	France	1.05	1.01	1.00	1.01	0.99	0.94	0.96	47.7	35.4	15.8	1.7	1.00
25	Slovenia	1.05	0.98	1.00	1.00	0.98	0.98	1.16	46.8	28.7	..	..	1.00
26	Spain	1.06	1.00	1.01	1.01	1.01	0.93	1.18	46.5	38.6	19.0[e]	2.2[e]	1.00
27	Czechia	1.06	0.97	1.01	1.01	1.06	1.00	1.38	44.7	21.1	..	..	1.00
28	Italy	1.06	0.98	0.99	0.98	1.04	0.91	1.19	42.1	30.1	20.4	2.4	1.00
29	Malta	1.06	1.03	1.04	1.04	0.98	0.89	1.18	39.0	11.9	..	..	..
30	Estonia	1.06	0.97	1.00	1.00	0.85	1.00	0.82	49.8	26.7	17.2[d]	1.6[d]	..
31	Greece	1.07	1.01	0.99	0.93	1.08	0.89	1.43	41.9	18.3	17.5[d]	2.6[d]	0.55
32	Cyprus	1.07	0.99	1.00	0.99	1.11	0.95	1.06	47.3	17.9	..	..	..
33	Poland	1.06	0.97	1.01	0.97	1.02	0.93	1.02	45.6	25.5	17.6[d]	1.8[d]	1.00
34	United Arab Emirates	1.05	1.08	0.97	0.94	1.21	1.20	3.38	12.1	22.5	..	..	..
35	Andorra	..	..	..	..	..	0.98	..	..	32.1	..	..	..
35	Lithuania	1.05	0.99	1.00	0.95	0.91	0.95	0.73	52.6	21.3	..	..	1.00
37	Qatar	1.05	1.03	0.99	1.17	2.50	1.04	7.00	14.2	9.8	8.2	3.7	0.36
38	Slovakia	1.05	0.98	0.99	1.01	1.12	0.99	1.22	45.8	20.0	..	..	1.00
39	Brunei Darussalam	1.06	1.02	0.99	1.01	1.09	0.98	1.30	42.4	9.1	..	..	..
39	Saudi Arabia	1.03	0.99	0.98	0.77	1.29	0.90	5.29	14.9	19.9	..	..	..
41	Latvia	1.06	0.98	0.99	0.99	0.81	1.00	0.77	52.2	16.0	..	..	1.00
41	Portugal	1.06	0.98	0.96	0.97	1.04	0.97	1.03	49.9	34.8	17.8	1.7	1.00
43	Bahrain	1.04	0.99	1.02	1.01	2.00	1.12	8.60	20.6	15.0	..	..	..
44	Chile	1.04	0.98	0.97	1.01	1.09	0.98	1.15	43.1	15.8[g]	22.1[f]	2.2[f]	..
45	Hungary	1.06	0.96	1.00	0.98	1.00	0.98	1.00	46.8	10.1	16.6[d]	2.2[d]	1.00
46	Croatia	1.06	0.96	1.01	1.05	1.00	0.98	1.10	47.1	18.5	..	..	0.52
47	Argentina	1.04	1.01	1.00	1.06	1.17	1.05	1.49	40.1	38.9	23.4	2.5	..
48	Oman	1.05	1.05	1.03	0.94	1.22	1.15	2.30	11.2	8.8	18.9	2.5	..
49	Russian Federation	1.05	0.98	1.01	0.99	0.99	1.01	0.91	49.7	16.1	18.4	2.3	..

HUMAN DEVELOPMENT INDICES AND INDICATORS: 2018 STATISTICAL UPDATE

		SDG 4.2	SDG 4.1	SDG 4.1	SDG 8.5	SDG 4.6	SDG 8.5	SDG 8.3	SDG 5.5	SDG 5.4		SDG 1.3
			Childhood and youth					Adulthood				Older age
			Gross enrolment ratio			Youth unemployment rate	Population with at least some secondary education	Total unemployment rate	Share of employment in nonagriculture, female	Share of seats in parliament	Time spent on unpaid domestic chores and care work		Old-age pension recipients
		Sex ratio at birth[a]	(female to male ratio)								Women ages 15 and older		
		(male to female births)	Pre-primary	Primary	Secondary	(female to male ratio)	(female to male ratio)	(female to male ratio)	(% of total employment in nonagriculture)	(% held by women)	(% of 24-hour day)	(female to male ratio)	(female to male ratio)
HDI rank		2015–2020[b]	2012–2017[c]	2012–2017[c]	2012–2017[c]	2017	2010–2017[c]	2017	2017	2017	2007–2017[c]	2007–2017[c]	2008–2015[c]
50	Montenegro	1.06	0.92	0.97	1.00	0.98	0.90	0.92	44.6	23.5	..	..	..
51	Bulgaria	1.06	0.99	0.99	0.97	0.99	0.98	0.87	47.8	23.8	18.5[e]	2.0[e]	1.00
52	Romania	1.06	1.00	0.99	0.99	1.04	0.93	0.76	43.9	18.7	19.0[d]	2.0[d]	1.00
53	Belarus	1.06	0.96	1.00	0.98	1.10	0.94	1.00	51.5	33.1	19.2[d]	2.0[d]	..
54	Bahamas	1.06	1.07	1.05	1.06	1.18	1.00	1.20	48.0	21.8	..	..	..
55	Uruguay	1.05	1.01	0.98	..	1.18	1.07	1.52	46.6	22.3	19.9	2.4	1.04
56	Kuwait	1.05	1.03	1.04	1.08	1.31	1.11	1.56	29.0	3.1	..	..	..
57	Malaysia	1.06	1.06	1.01	1.06	1.07	0.97	1.26	39.8	13.1	..	..	..
58	Barbados	1.04	0.96	1.01	1.05	1.07	1.03	1.09	50.0	19.6	..	..	..
58	Kazakhstan	1.06	1.01	1.02	1.01	1.04	0.99	1.33	48.7	22.1	17.1[d]	2.2[d]	..
HIGH HUMAN DEVELOPMENT													
60	Iran (Islamic Republic of)	1.05	0.97	1.05	1.00	1.14	0.93	1.95	16.3	5.9	21.0	4.0	..
60	Palau	..	1.09	0.96	1.05	..	1.00	..	..	13.8	..	..	..
62	Seychelles	1.06	1.04	0.99	1.07	..	..	..	..	21.2	..	..	1.00
63	Costa Rica	1.05	1.00	1.01	1.05	1.25	1.04	1.59	40.6	35.1	21.3[f]	2.6[f]	0.75
64	Turkey	1.05	0.94	0.99	0.97	1.16	0.68	1.47	27.5	14.6	19.2	5.2	..
65	Mauritius	1.04	1.02	1.02	1.06	1.30	0.96	2.34	37.9	11.6	..	..	1.00
66	Panama	1.05	1.02	0.97	1.05	1.22	1.06	1.47	42.0	18.3	17.7	2.4	0.59
67	Serbia	1.05	1.00	1.00	1.01	1.09	0.91	1.12	45.1	34.4	19.2	2.2	0.93
68	Albania	1.08	0.99	0.97	0.93	0.96	1.00	0.93	37.5	27.9	21.7[d]	6.3[d]	0.61
69	Trinidad and Tobago	1.04	..	..	..	1.18	1.08	1.56	42.2	30.1	..	..	..
70	Antigua and Barbuda	1.03	0.98	0.94	1.02	..	..	..	..	20.0	..	..	0.95
70	Georgia	1.08	..	1.00	1.02	0.98	0.99	0.64	46.4	16.0	..	..	0.92
72	Saint Kitts and Nevis	..	..	..	..	..	..	..	..	13.3	..	..	0.77
73	Cuba	1.06	1.01	0.94	1.04	1.00	0.98	1.30	43.2	48.9	..	..	..
74	Mexico	1.05	1.02	1.01	1.09	1.08	0.95	1.03	40.5	41.4	28.1[f]	3.0[f]	0.50
75	Grenada	1.05	0.95	0.97	1.04	..	..	..	..	25.0	..	..	..
76	Sri Lanka	1.04	0.99	0.98	1.03	1.24	0.99	2.36	32.2	5.8	..	..	..
77	Bosnia and Herzegovina	1.06	..	..	..	1.23	0.81	2.09	32.7	19.3	..	..	..
78	Venezuela (Bolivarian Republic of)	1.05	1.01	0.97	1.08	1.16	1.08	1.22	42.4	22.2	..	..	0.72
79	Brazil	1.05	0.99	0.97	1.05	1.14	1.06	1.35	44.4	11.3	13.3	4.3	..
80	Azerbaijan	1.13	1.01	0.99	..	1.01	0.96	1.30	43.8	16.8	25.4	2.9	1.51
80	Lebanon	1.05	0.95	0.91	1.00	0.96	0.96	1.27	24.9	3.1	..	..	..
80	The former Yugoslav Republic of Macedonia	1.05	0.99	1.00	0.98	1.01	0.72	0.93	39.7	37.5	16.7[d]	3.0[d]	..
83	Armenia	1.13	1.10	1.01	1.05	1.18	0.99	1.23	42.4	18.1	21.7	5.0	1.17
83	Thailand	1.06	0.87	0.94	0.96	1.31	0.89	1.10	47.4	4.8	11.8[h]	3.2[h]	..
85	Algeria	1.05	..	0.95	..	1.14	0.99	2.07	17.5	21.3	21.7[f]	5.8[f]	..
86	China	1.15	1.01	1.01	1.02	0.92	0.90	0.84	42.3	24.2	16.2	2.6	..
86	Ecuador	1.05	1.05	1.01	1.03	1.28	1.00	1.59	42.7	38.0	19.8	4.4	..
88	Ukraine	1.06	0.97	1.02	0.98	0.94	0.99	0.74	49.2	12.3	..	..	..
89	Peru	1.05	1.01	1.00	1.00	1.01	0.85	1.03	46.7	27.7	22.7[f]	2.6[f]	..
90	Colombia	1.05	..	0.97	1.06	1.23	1.04	1.58	46.4	19.8	16.3[d]	3.7[d]	0.99
90	Saint Lucia	1.03	1.02	..	1.01	1.08	1.15	1.18	47.0	20.7	..	..	..
92	Fiji	1.06	..	0.99	1.11	1.30	1.13	1.71	34.3	16.0	15.2	2.9	..
92	Mongolia	1.03	1.00	0.98	1.01	1.04	1.06	0.75	47.4	17.1	19.9[f]	2.2[f]	1.00
94	Dominican Republic	1.05	1.04	0.92	1.10	1.49	1.08	2.16	45.0	24.3	..	..	0.38
95	Jordan	1.05	..	..	1.04	1.16	0.95	1.95	16.0	15.4	..	..	0.14
95	Tunisia	1.05	1.00	0.97	1.11	1.01	0.78	1.65	25.0	31.3	..	..	..
97	Jamaica	1.05	0.98	..	1.05	1.13	1.12	1.66	46.6	19.0	..	..	..
98	Tonga	1.05	0.98	0.99	1.09	1.04	1.00	1.00	53.6	7.7	..	..	..
99	Saint Vincent and the Grenadines	1.03	1.00	0.98	0.99	1.12	..	1.14	44.4	13.0	..	..	..
100	Suriname	1.07	1.04	1.00	1.32	1.41	1.02	2.36	37.9	25.5	..	..	..
101	Botswana	1.03	1.04	0.97	..	1.20	0.99	1.46	47.6	9.5	..	..	1.00
101	Maldives	1.07	0.99	1.00	..	0.99	0.91	1.30	28.5	5.9	..	..	..
103	Dominica	..	1.03	0.97	0.99	..	..	..	..	25.0	..	..	..
104	Samoa	1.08	1.09	1.01	1.10	1.22	1.11	1.34	38.2	10.0	..	..	..
105	Uzbekistan	1.08	0.96	0.98	0.99	1.04	1.00	0.97	39.4	16.4	..	..	..

DASHBOARD 2 Life-course gender gap | 87

DASHBOARD 2 LIFE-COURSE GENDER GAP

		SDG 4.2	SDG 4.1	SDG 4.1	SDG 8.5	SDG 4.6	SDG 8.5	SDG 8.3	SDG 5.5	SDG 5.4		SDG 1.3
		\multicolumn{4}{c}{Childhood and youth}		\multicolumn{4}{c}{Adulthood}			Older age
		\multicolumn{3}{c}{Gross enrolment ratio}	Youth unemployment rate	Population with at least some secondary education	Total unemployment rate	Share of employment in nonagriculture, female	Share of seats in parliament	Time spent on unpaid domestic chores and care work		Old-age pension recipients
	Sex ratio at birth[a]	\multicolumn{3}{c}{(female to male ratio)}						Women ages 15 and older		
	(male to female births)	Pre-primary	Primary	Secondary	(female to male ratio)	(female to male ratio)	(female to male ratio)	(% of total employment in nonagriculture)	(% held by women)	(% of 24-hour day)	(female to male ratio)	(female to male ratio)
HDI rank	2015–2020[b]	2012–2017[c]	2012–2017[c]	2012–2017[c]	2017	2010–2017[c]	2017	2017	2017	2007–2017[c]	2007–2017[c]	2008–2015[c]
106 Belize	1.03	1.00	0.95	1.01	1.60	1.01	3.25	43.3	11.1	..	..	..
106 Marshall Islands	..	0.93	1.02	1.10	..	0.99	..	..	9.1	..	..	..
108 Libya	1.06	..	..	..	1.21	1.54	1.86	22.5	16.0	..	..	..
108 Turkmenistan	1.05	0.97	0.98	0.96	1.16	..	1.16	40.6	25.8	..	..	..
110 Gabon	1.03	..	..	..	1.15	1.32	1.90	24.0	17.4	..	..	..
110 Paraguay	1.05	1.00	0.97	1.07	1.27	0.96	1.60	42.3	16.0	14.5	3.4	0.80
112 Moldova (Republic of)	1.06	0.99	0.99	1.01	0.97	0.98	0.52	52.2	22.8	19.0[d]	1.9[d]	..
MEDIUM HUMAN DEVELOPMENT												
113 Philippines	1.06	0.99	0.97	1.09	1.13	1.06	1.11	44.9	29.1	..	..	0.55
113 South Africa	1.03	1.00	0.93	0.99	1.11	0.96	1.20	44.1	41.0[i]	15.6[d]	2.4[d]	..
115 Egypt	1.06	0.98	1.00	0.98	1.16	0.82	2.98	16.4	14.9	22.4[d]	9.2[d]	..
116 Indonesia	1.05	0.89	0.96	1.04	1.01	0.84	0.87	39.4	19.8	..	..	..
116 Viet Nam	1.10	0.96	1.00	..	1.01	0.85	0.86	46.9	26.7	..	..	..
118 Bolivia (Plurinational State of)	1.05	0.99	0.98	0.98	1.16	0.85	1.46	41.0	51.8	..	..	1.00
119 Palestine, State of	1.05	1.00	1.00	1.10	1.07	0.94	1.15	19.1	..	17.8[d]	6.0[d]	..
120 Iraq	1.07	..	..	..	1.20	0.68	1.93	13.1	25.3	24.1[d]	5.8[d]	..
121 El Salvador	1.05	1.02	0.96	1.00	1.02	0.88	0.78	49.7	32.1	22.7	2.9	0.33
122 Kyrgyzstan	1.06	1.02	0.99	1.00	1.21	1.00	1.40	38.7	19.2	16.8[f]	1.8[f]	1.00
123 Morocco	1.06	0.84	0.95	0.85	0.98	0.80	1.11	17.8	18.4	20.8	7.0	..
124 Nicaragua	1.05	..	..	..	1.27	1.04	1.33	50.1	45.7	..	..	0.38
125 Cabo Verde	1.03	1.03	0.93	1.10	1.11	..	1.15	31.3	20.8[i]	..	..	..
125 Guyana	1.05	1.02	1.02	1.04	1.24	1.28	1.77	37.0	31.9	..	..	1.00
127 Guatemala	1.05	1.02	0.97	0.95	1.32	1.03	1.73	43.1	12.7	17.8	7.5	..
127 Tajikistan	1.07	0.86	0.99	0.90	1.10	1.14	1.11	24.4	20.0	..	..	..
129 Namibia	1.03	1.03	0.96	..	1.18	0.97	1.14	49.8	36.3	..	..	..
130 India	1.11	0.94	1.17	1.02	1.02	0.61	1.27	18.6	11.6	..	..	..
131 Micronesia (Federated States of)	1.06	0.92	1.00	..	..	..	..	..	0.0	..	..	..
132 Timor-Leste	1.05	1.01	0.98	1.07	1.40	..	1.55	30.1	32.3	..	..	1.13
133 Honduras	1.05	1.03	0.99	1.16	1.39	1.10	1.38	48.1	25.8[g]	17.3	4.0	..
134 Bhutan	1.04	1.07	1.01	1.10	1.23	0.43	1.74	32.1	8.3	15.0	2.5	..
134 Kiribati	1.06	..	1.03	..	..	..	..	..	6.5	..	..	..
136 Bangladesh	1.05	1.04	1.06	1.10	1.11	0.91	2.12	18.4	20.3	..	..	..
137 Congo	1.03	0.99	1.07	0.87	0.98	0.92	1.14	47.3	14.0	..	..	0.11
138 Vanuatu	1.07	0.97	0.98	1.06	1.05	..	1.30	41.5	0.0	..	..	..
139 Lao People's Democratic Republic	1.05	1.04	0.96	0.93	0.94	0.74	0.86	47.3	27.5	10.4[d]	4.2[d]	..
140 Ghana	1.05	1.02	1.01	0.97	1.09	0.78	1.18	52.7	12.7	14.4[d]	4.1[d]	..
141 Equatorial Guinea	1.03	1.02	0.99	..	1.01	..	1.09	30.3	19.7[g]	..	..	..
142 Kenya	1.03	0.98	1.00	..	1.30	0.80	1.94	39.5	23.3	..	..	..
143 Sao Tome and Principe	1.03	1.09	0.96	1.15	1.06	0.69	1.25	38.8	18.2	..	..	..
144 Eswatini (Kingdom of)	1.03	..	0.91	0.99	0.99	0.92	1.04	29.3	14.7	..	..	..
144 Zambia	1.03	..	1.01	..	1.03	0.75	1.15	37.8	18.0	..	..	..
146 Cambodia	1.05	1.06	0.97	..	0.80	0.54	1.00	50.3	18.5	..	..	..
147 Angola	1.03	..	..	..	1.02	..	1.13	42.8	30.5	..	..	..
148 Myanmar	1.03	1.04	0.97	1.10	1.13	1.29	1.29	42.0	10.2	..	..	..
149 Nepal	1.07	0.94	1.06	1.11	0.74	0.63	0.72	31.6	29.6	..	..	..
150 Pakistan	1.09	0.86	0.85	0.81	1.15	0.57	2.19	10.2	20.0	19.9[d]	11.0[d]	..
151 Cameroon	1.03	1.02	0.90	0.86	1.19	0.83	1.49	42.5	27.1	14.6[d]	3.1[d]	0.29
LOW HUMAN DEVELOPMENT												
152 Solomon Islands	1.07	1.00	0.99	0.95	1.07	..	1.10	40.0	2.0	..	..	..
153 Papua New Guinea	1.08	..	0.90	0.75	0.83	0.64	0.47	52.7	0.0	..	..	..
154 Tanzania (United Republic of)	1.03	1.02	1.03	0.92	1.22	0.70	1.65	44.1	37.2	16.5[k]	3.9[k]	..
155 Syrian Arab Republic	1.05	0.96	0.97	1.00	1.29	0.87	3.82	10.1	13.2	..	..	..
156 Zimbabwe	1.02	1.02	0.98	0.98	0.84	0.84	0.61	42.8	36.2	..	..	..
157 Nigeria	1.06	..	0.97	0.91	1.13	..	0.82	53.2	5.8	..	..	..
158 Rwanda	1.02	1.03	1.00	1.10	1.40	0.74	1.17	35.8	55.7	..	..	..
159 Lesotho	1.03	1.05	0.97	1.35	1.12	1.31	1.21	47.8	22.7	..	..	..
159 Mauritania	1.05	1.26	1.06	0.97	1.08	0.50	1.23	20.4	25.2	..	..	..

HUMAN DEVELOPMENT INDICES AND INDICATORS: **2018 STATISTICAL UPDATE**

HUMAN DEVELOPMENT INDICES AND INDICATORS: 2018 STATISTICAL UPDATE

		SDG 4.2	SDG 4.1	SDG 4.1	SDG 8.5	SDG 4.6	SDG 8.5	SDG 8.3	SDG 5.5	SDG 5.4		SDG 1.3
			Childhood and youth					Adulthood				Older age
			Gross enrolment ratio		Youth unemployment rate	Population with at least some secondary education	Total unemployment rate	Share of employment in nonagriculture, female	Share of seats in parliament	Time spent on unpaid domestic chores and care work		Old-age pension recipients
		Sex ratio at birth[a]	(female to male ratio)							Women ages 15 and older		
		(male to female births)	Pre-primary	Primary	Secondary	(female to male ratio)	(female to male ratio)	(female to male ratio)	(% of total employment in nonagriculture)	(% held by women)	(% of 24-hour day)	(female to male ratio)	(female to male ratio)
HDI rank		2015–2020[b]	2012–2017[c]	2012–2017[c]	2012–2017[c]	2017	2010–2017[c]	2017	2017	2017	2007–2017[c]	2007–2017[c]	2008–2015[c]
161	Madagascar	1.03	1.09	1.00	0.99	1.00	..	1.12	53.4	19.6	..	..	..
162	Uganda	1.03	1.04	1.03	..	1.32	0.82	1.87	39.3	34.3	..	..	..
163	Benin	1.04	1.03	0.93	0.71	1.11	0.56	1.17	55.7	7.2	..	..	..
164	Senegal	1.04	1.13	1.12	1.01	1.06	0.55	1.06	36.0	41.8	..	..	..
165	Comoros	1.05	1.07	0.93	1.07	0.88	..	1.15	35.2	6.1	..	..	..
165	Togo	1.02	1.03	0.95	..	0.82	0.50	0.76	52.9	17.6	..	..	..
167	Sudan	1.04	0.94	0.92	0.99	1.12	0.76	1.71	27.7	31.0	..	..	..
168	Afghanistan	1.06	..	0.68	0.57	1.05	0.31	1.59	11.6	27.4	..	..	..
168	Haiti	1.05	..	..	..	1.18	0.67	1.29	58.5	2.7	..	..	..
170	Côte d'Ivoire	1.03	1.01	0.89	0.73	1.32	0.52	1.57	46.9	9.2[l]	..	..	..
171	Malawi	1.03	1.01	1.03	0.89	1.08	0.66	1.37	32.2	16.7	..	..	..
172	Djibouti	1.04	0.99	0.89	0.83	1.06	..	1.29	43.2	10.8	..	..	..
173	Ethiopia	1.04	0.95	0.91	0.96	1.45	0.52	2.42	59.0	37.3	19.3[d]	2.9[d]	..
174	Gambia	1.03	1.07	1.08	..	1.40	0.69	1.84	39.0	10.3	..	..	..
175	Guinea	1.02	..	0.85	0.66	0.82	..	0.64	43.8	21.9	..	..	..
176	Congo (Democratic Republic of the)	1.03	1.07	0.99	0.64	1.11	0.56	1.39	35.8	8.2	..	..	..
177	Guinea-Bissau	1.03	..	..	..	1.06	..	1.20	29.8	13.7	..	..	..
178	Yemen	1.05	0.90	0.87	0.73	1.05	0.54	2.16	4.2	0.5	..	..	..
179	Eritrea	1.05	0.98	0.86	0.85	1.06	..	1.17	28.9	22.0	..	..	..
180	Mozambique	1.03	..	0.92	0.92	0.98	0.59	1.18	30.5	39.6	..	..	0.80
181	Liberia	1.05	0.97	0.90	0.78	1.27	0.47	1.00	49.0	9.9	6.3	2.4	..
182	Mali	1.05	1.05	0.88	0.74	1.07	0.45	1.19	43.6	8.8	..	..	0.11
183	Burkina Faso	1.05	1.00	0.98	0.95	1.56	0.52	2.22	48.3	11.0	..	..	0.13
184	Sierra Leone	1.02	1.12	1.01	0.91	0.65	0.59	0.70	51.9	12.4	..	..	..
185	Burundi	1.03	1.02	1.01	0.97	0.69	0.72	0.55	21.7	37.8	..	..	0.29
186	Chad	1.03	0.94	0.78	0.46	1.10	0.17	1.40	27.0	12.8	..	..	..
187	South Sudan	1.04	0.95	0.71	0.54	0.93	..	1.24	52.8	26.6	..	..	..
188	Central African Republic	1.03	..	0.76	0.64	1.06	0.43	1.24	29.8	8.6	..	..	..
189	Niger	1.05	1.03	0.86	0.73	0.63	0.48	0.50	50.6	17.0	..	..	..
OTHER COUNTRIES OR TERRITORIES													
..	Korea (Democratic People's Rep. of)	1.05	1.01	..	1.01	0.89	..	0.73	43.4	16.3	..	..	..
..	Monaco	..	..	..	..	..	..	..	..	20.8	..	..	..
..	Nauru	..	1.05	1.03	1.03	..	..	..	..	10.5	..	..	..
..	San Marino	..	1.02	0.99	1.03	..	..	..	..	26.7	..	..	..
..	Somalia	1.03	..	..	..	1.03	..	1.16	12.1	24.3	..	..	..
..	Tuvalu	..	0.99	0.99	1.27	..	..	..	..	6.7	..	..	..
Human development groups													
	Very high human development	1.05	0.99	1.00	1.00	1.01	0.99	1.09	44.8	26.7	—	—	..
	High human development	1.10	1.00	1.00	1.02	1.05	0.92	1.15	41.4	22.3	—	—	..
	Medium human development	1.08	0.96	1.06	1.01	1.07	0.72	1.44	27.0	21.8	—	—	..
	Low human development	1.04	1.00	0.94	0.84	1.10	0.60	1.42	45.1	21.7	—	—	..
Developing countries		1.07	0.97	1.01	0.99	1.07	0.83	1.31	36.2	21.9	—	—	..
Regions													
	Arab States	1.05	0.96	0.96	0.93	1.15	0.83	2.37	16.6	18.0	—	—	..
	East Asia and the Pacific	1.11	0.98	0.99	1.02	0.96	0.90	0.85	42.5	19.8	—	—	..
	Europe and Central Asia	1.06	0.97	1.00	0.98	1.08	0.91	1.15	39.8	20.7	—	—	..
	Latin America and the Caribbean	1.05	1.01	0.98	1.05	1.15	1.01	1.35	43.5	28.8	—	—	..
	South Asia	1.10	0.94	1.09	1.00	1.05	0.66	1.53	17.9	17.5	—	—	..
	Sub-Saharan Africa	1.04	1.00	0.96	0.87	1.11	0.73	1.25	47.1	23.5	—	—	..
Least developed countries		1.04	1.00	0.96	0.92	1.08	0.73	1.56	36.5	22.4	—	—	..
Small island developing states		1.06	..	0.94	1.02	1.18	0.97	1.44	46.6	23.4	—	—	..
Organisation for Economic Co-operation and Development		1.05	0.99	1.00	1.01	0.99	0.97	1.07	44.6	28.9	—	—	0.99
World		1.07	0.98	1.01	0.99	1.05	0.88	1.24	38.6	23.5	—	—	..

DASHBOARD 2 Life-course gender gap

DASHBOARD 2 LIFE-COURSE GENDER GAP

NOTES

Three-colour coding is used to visualize partial grouping of countries and aggregates by indicator. For each indicator countries are divided into three groups of approximately equal size (terciles): the top third, the middle third and the bottom third. Aggregates are colour coded using the same tercile cutoffs. Sex ratio at birth is an exception—countries are divided into two groups: the natural group (countries with a value of 1.04–1.07, inclusive), which uses darker shading, and the gender-biased group (all others), which uses lighter shading. See *Technical note 6* at http://hdr.undp.org/sites/default/files/hdr2018_technical_notes.pdf for details about partial grouping in this table.

a The natural sex ratio at birth is commonly assumed and empirically confirmed to be 1.05 male births to 1 female birth.
b Data are annual average of projections for 2015–2020 based on the medium-fertility variant.
c Data refer to the most recent year available during the period specified.
d Refers to the population ages 10 and older.
e Refers to the population ages 20–74.
f Refers to the population ages 12 and older.
g Refers to 2016.
h Refers to the population ages 6 and older.
i Excludes the 36 special rotating delegates appointed on an ad hoc basis.
j Refers to 2013.
k Refers to the population ages 5 and older.
l Refers to 2015.

DEFINITIONS

Sex ratio at birth: Number of male births per female birth.

Gross enrolment ratio, female to male ratio: Total enrolment in a given level of education (pre-primary, primary or secondary), regardless of age, expressed as a ratio of the official school-age female population to the official school-age male population for the same level of education.

Youth unemployment rate, female to male ratio: Ratio of the percentage of the female labour force population ages 15–24 that is not in paid employment or self-employed but is available for work and is actively seeking paid employment or self-employment to the percentage of the male labour force population ages 15–24 that is not in paid employment or self-employed but is available for work and is actively seeking paid employment or self-employment.

Population with at least some secondary education, female to male ratio: Ratio of the percentage of the female population ages 25 and older that has reached (but not necessarily completed) a secondary level of education to the percentage of the male population ages 25 and older with the same level of education achievement.

Total unemployment rate, female to male ratio: Ratio of the percentage of the female labour force population ages 15 and older that is not in paid employment or self-employed but is available for work and is actively seeking paid employment or self-employment to the percentage of the male labour force population ages 15 and older that is not in paid employment or self-employed but is available for work and is actively seeking paid employment or self-employment.

Share of employment in nonagriculture, female: Share of women in employment in the nonagricultural sector, which comprises industry and services activities.

Share of seats in parliament: Proportion of seats held by women in the national parliament, expressed as a percentage of total seats. For countries with a bicameral legislative system, the share of seats is calculated based on both houses.

Time spent on unpaid domestic chores and care work: The average daily number of hours spent on unpaid domestic and care work, expressed as a percentage of a 24-hour day. Unpaid domestic and care work refers to activities related to the provision of services for own final use by household members or by family members living in other households.

Old-age pension recipients, female to male ratio: Ratio of the percentage of women above the statutory pensionable age receiving an old-age pension (contributory, noncontributory or both) to the percentage of men above the statutory pensionable age receiving an old-age pension (contributory, noncontributory or both).

MAIN DATA SOURCES

Column 1: UNDESA (2017a).

Columns 2–4: UNESCO Institute for Statistics (2018).

Columns 5 and 7: HDRO calculations based on ILO (2018a).

Column 6: HDRO calculations based on UNESCO Institute for Statistics (2018) and Barro and Lee (2016).

Column 8: ILO (2018a).

Column 9: IPU (2018).

Column 10: United Nations Statistics Division (2018a).

Column 11: HDRO calculations based on United Nations Statistics Division (2018a).

Column 12: HDRO calculations based on ILO (2018b).

DASHBOARD 3

Women's empowerment

Country groupings (terciles)

Top third | Middle third | Bottom third

Three-colour coding is used to visualize partial grouping of countries by indicator. For each indicator countries are divided into three groups of approximately equal size (terciles): the top third, the middle third and the bottom third. Aggregates are colour coded using the same tercile cutoffs. See Notes after the table.

		SDG 3.1	SDG 3.1	SDG 3.7	SDG 3.7, 5.6	SDG 5.6	SDG 5.3	SDG 5.2	SDG 5.2		SDG 5.5		SDG 1.3
		\multicolumn{6}{c}{Reproductive health and family planning}	Child marriage	\multicolumn{2}{c}{Violence against girls and women — Violence against women ever experienced[a]}	\multicolumn{3}{c}{Socioeconomic empowerment}	
		Antenatal care coverage, at least one visit	Proportion of births attended by skilled health personnel	Maternal mortality ratio	Adolescent birth rate	Contraceptive prevalence, any method	Unmet need for family planning	Women married by age 18	Intimate partner	Nonintimate partner	Share of female graduates graduating in science, mathematics, engineering, manufacturing and construction at tertiary level	Female share of employment in senior and middle management	Women with account at financial institution or with mobile money-service provider	Mandatory paid maternity leave
		(%)	(%)	(deaths per 100,000 live births)	(births per 1,000 women ages 15–19)	(% of married or in-union women of reproductive age, 15–49 years)		(% of women ages 20–24 who are married or in union)	\multicolumn{2}{c}{(% of female population ages 15 and older)}	(%)	(%)	(% of female population ages 15 and older)	(days)
HDI rank		2007–2017[b]	2012–2017[b]	2015	2015–2020[c]	2007–2017[b]	2007–2017[b]	2003–2017[b]	2005–2018[b]	2005–2018[b]	2007–2017[b]	2009–2017[b]	2017	2017
\multicolumn{15}{l}{VERY HIGH HUMAN DEVELOPMENT}
1	Norway	..	99.1	5	5.6	..	..	..	27.0	..	10.4	35.4	100.0	..
2	Switzerland	..	..	5	3.0	72.9	..	..	..	..	11.4	34.0	98.9	98
3	Australia	98.3	99.7	6	12.9	66.9	..	..	16.9	..	9.7	32.6	99.2	0[d]
4	Ireland	..	99.7	8	9.7	..	..	..	15.0	5.0	13.7	31.1	95.3	182
5	Germany	..	98.7	6	6.5	68.7	..	..	22.0	7.0	..	28.1	99.2	98
6	Iceland	..	97.9	3	6.8	..	..	..	22.4	..	10.3	34.8	..	90
7	Hong Kong, China (SAR)	..	..	..	2.7	74.8	..	..	..	..	..	..	94.7	70
7	Sweden	..	..	4	5.2	..	..	..	28.0	12.0	14.2	39.5	100.0	0
9	Singapore	..	99.6	10	3.7	..	..	..	6.1	..	..	..	96.3	105
10	Netherlands	..	..	7	4.0	73.0	..	..	25.0	12.0	6.3	24.5	99.8	112
11	Denmark	..	94.4	6	4.1	..	..	..	32.0	11.0	12.2	28.6	100.0	126
12	Canada	100.0	97.9	7	9.4	..	..	..	..	..	..	..	99.9	105
13	United States	..	99.1	14	18.8	72.7	9.0	..	..	..	9.9	..	92.7	..
14	United Kingdom	..	..	9	12.5	84.0	..	..	29.0	7.0	17.4	33.8	96.1	42
15	Finland	..	99.9	3	6.8	85.5	..	..	30.0	11.0	13.5	34.1	99.6	147
16	New Zealand	..	96.3	11	20.0	..	..	..	..	..	..	12.5	99.3	112[e]
17	Belgium	..	..	7	4.9	66.8	..	..	24.0	8.0	7.7	32.0	98.8	105
17	Liechtenstein	..	..	..	..	..	..	..	..	..	..	..	..	..
19	Japan	..	99.9	5	4.1	39.8	..	..	..	..	..	..	98.1	98
20	Austria	..	98.4	4	6.9	65.7	..	..	13.0	4.0	14.3	29.5	98.4	112
21	Luxembourg	..	..	10	5.2	..	..	..	22.0	8.0	5.3	14.9	98.2	112
22	Israel	..	..	5	9.2	..	..	..	..	..	..	34.3	93.7	105
22	Korea (Republic of)	..	100.0	11	1.6	79.6	..	..	..	..	15.4	..	94.7	90
24	France	..	97.4	8	8.6	78.4	..	..	26.0	9.0	14.1	31.1	91.3	112
25	Slovenia	..	99.8	9	4.2	..	..	..	13.0	4.0	14.0	41.8	96.9	105
26	Spain	..	..	5	8.6	70.9	..	..	13.0	3.0	12.7	30.3	91.6	112
27	Czechia	..	99.8	4	10.0	86.3	4.3	..	21.0	4.0	13.2	23.1	78.6	196
28	Italy	..	99.9	4	6.1	65.1	..	..	19.0	5.0	16.0	22.0	91.6	150
29	Malta	..	99.8	9	16.6	..	..	..	15.0	5.0	8.6	29.0	97.0	126
30	Estonia	..	99.4	9	12.6	..	..	..	20.0	9.0	16.3	31.6	98.4	140
31	Greece	..	..	3	7.2	..	..	..	19.0	1.0	19.5	24.7	84.5	119
32	Cyprus	99.2	97.4	7	4.6	..	..	..	15.0	2.0	10.4	27.0	90.0	126
33	Poland	..	99.8	3	12.7	50.6	..	..	13.0	2.0	15.3	38.1	88.0	140
34	United Arab Emirates	100.0	99.9	6	28.4	..	..	..	..	..	17.3	..	76.4	45
35	Andorra	..	..	..	..	..	..	..	..	..	..	..	..	..
35	Lithuania	..	100.0	10	10.7	..	..	..	24.0	5.0	11.4	38.8	81.0	126
37	Qatar	90.8	99.9	13	9.9	37.5	12.4	4	..	..	15.8	..	61.6[f]	50
38	Slovakia	..	98.5	6	22.0	..	..	..	23.0	4.0	12.0	34.3	83.1	238
39	Brunei Darussalam	99.0	100.0	23	10.3	..	..	..	..	..	23.6	32.5	..	91
39	Saudi Arabia	97.0	98.0	12	7.8	24.6	..	..	..	..	17.4	..	58.2	70
41	Latvia	..	99.9	18	13.5	..	..	..	32.0	7.0	10.0	46.3	92.5	112
41	Portugal	..	98.8	10	9.4	73.9	..	..	19.0	1.0	18.3	32.2	90.6	..
43	Bahrain	100.0	99.7	15	13.4	..	..	..	..	..	12.6	..	75.4	60
44	Chile	..	99.7	22	45.6	76.3	..	..	..	..	6.5	..	71.3	126
45	Hungary	..	99.2	17	19.7	61.6	..	..	21.0	3.0	11.7	37.7	72.2	168

DASHBOARD 3 WOMEN'S EMPOWERMENT

		Reproductive health and family planning (SDG 3.1, 3.1, 3.7, 3.7/5.6, 5.6)						Violence against girls and women			Socioeconomic empowerment (SDG 5.5)			SDG 1.3
								Child marriage	Violence against women ever experienced[a]					
		Antenatal care coverage, at least one visit	Proportion of births attended by skilled health personnel	Maternal mortality ratio	Adolescent birth rate	Contraceptive prevalence, any method	Unmet need for family planning	Women married by age 18	Intimate partner	Nonintimate partner	Share of female graduates graduating in science, mathematics, engineering, manufacturing and construction at tertiary level	Female share of employment in senior and middle management	Women with account at financial institution or with mobile money-service provider	Mandatory paid maternity leave
		(%)	(%)	(deaths per 100,000 live births)	(births per 1,000 women ages 15–19)[c]	(% of married or in-union women of reproductive age, 15–49 years)	(% of married or in-union women of reproductive age, 15–49 years)	(% of women ages 20–24 who are married or in union)	(% of female population ages 15 and older)		(%)	(%)	(% of female population ages 15 and older)	(days)
HDI rank		2007–2017[b]	2012–2017[b]	2015	2015–2020[c]	2007–2017[b]	2007–2017[b]	2003–2017[b]	2005–2018[b]	2005–2018[b]	2007–2017[b]	2009–2017[b]	2017	2017
46	Croatia	..	99.9	8	8.9	..	..	..	13.0	3.0	16.0	29.5	82.7	208
47	Argentina	98.1	99.6	52	62.8	81.3	..	..	..	..	9.1	39.8	50.8	90
48	Oman	98.6	99.1	17	7.1	29.7	17.8	..	..	..	39.8	..	63.5[f]	50
49	Russian Federation	..	99.7	25	21.6	68.0	8.0	..	..	..	..	48.5	76.1	140
50	Montenegro	91.7	99.0	7	11.8	23.3	21.8	5	..	..	..	..	67.6	45
51	Bulgaria	..	99.8	11	39.5	69.2	..	..	23.0	6.0	12.3	39.3	73.6	410
52	Romania	76.3	95.2	31	33.1	..	..	..	24.0	2.0	20.3	32.4	53.6	126
53	Belarus	99.7	99.8	4	17.2	63.1	7.0	3	..	..	15.5	47.0	81.3	126
54	Bahamas	98.0	99.6	80	26.7	..	..	..	..	..	..	..	..	91
55	Uruguay	97.2	99.9	15	54.7	79.6	..	25	..	..	10.8	33.7	60.6	98
56	Kuwait	100.0	99.9	4	9.0	..	..	..	..	..	..	..	73.5	70
57	Malaysia	97.2	99.4	40	13.4	52.2	..	..	..	..	23.2	20.8	82.5	60
58	Barbados	93.4	99.0	27	37.3	59.2	19.9	11	..	..	..	..	..	84
58	Kazakhstan	99.3	99.4	12	27.5	55.7	11.6	7	..	..	13.7	..	60.3	126
HIGH HUMAN DEVELOPMENT														
60	Iran (Islamic Republic of)	96.9	99.0	25	25.0	77.4	5.7	17	..	..	32.1	..	91.6	270
60	Palau	90.3	100.0	..	..	..	..	..	25.2	15.1	..	..	..	..
62	Seychelles	..	99.0	..	56.9	..	..	..	..	..	9.7	39.9	..	98
63	Costa Rica	98.1	90.0	25	53.5	76.2	7.6	21	..	..	6.9	36.6	60.9	120
64	Turkey	97.0	97.4	16	25.8	73.5	5.9	15	38.0	..	14.2	16.7	54.3	112
65	Mauritius	..	99.8	53	26.6	63.8	12.5	..	..	..	..	29.7	87.1	98
66	Panama	93.4	94.6	94	81.8	62.8	16.4	26	..	..	12.7	43.4	42.3	98
67	Serbia	98.3	98.4	17	18.9	58.4	14.9	3	..	..	18.2	30.3	70.1	135
68	Albania	97.3	..	29	20.7	69.3	12.9	10	24.6	..	13.4	29.3	38.1	365
69	Trinidad and Tobago	95.1	100.0	63	30.1	40.3	24.3	11	30.2	19.0	..	..	73.6	98
70	Antigua and Barbuda	100.0	100.0	..	43.5	..	..	..	..	..	..	..	..	91
70	Georgia	97.6	99.9	36	45.9	53.4	12.3	14	6.1	2.7	16.0	..	63.6	183
72	Saint Kitts and Nevis	100.0	100.0	..	..	..	..	..	..	..	..	..	..	91
73	Cuba	98.5	99.9	39	43.6	73.7	8.0	26	..	..	6.1	..	..	..
74	Mexico	98.5	97.7	38	60.3	66.9	13.0	26	14.1	..	16.6	36.4	33.3	84
75	Grenada	100.0	99.3	27	29.2	..	..	..	..	..	11.0	..	..	90
76	Sri Lanka	95.5	..	30	14.1	61.7	7.5	12	..	..	..	24.0	73.4	84
77	Bosnia and Herzegovina	87.0	99.9	11	10.0	45.8	9.0	4	..	..	14.7	24.2	54.7	365
78	Venezuela (Bolivarian Republic of)	97.5	96.2	95	85.3	75.0	..	..	..	..	..	..	70.0	182
79	Brazil	97.2	99.1	44	61.6	80.2	6.0	26	..	..	8.7	38.8	67.5	120
80	Azerbaijan	91.7	99.8	25	53.5	..	..	11	13.5	..	15.2	..	27.7	126
80	Lebanon	..	..	15	11.8	54.5	..	6	..	..	18.0	..	32.9	70
80	The former Yugoslav Republic of Macedonia	98.6	99.9	8	16.2	40.2	17.2	7	..	..	15.7	27.3	72.9	270
83	Armenia	99.6	99.8	25	23.2	57.1	12.5	5	8.2	..	7.3	..	40.9	140
83	Thailand	98.1	99.1	20	51.9	78.4	6.2	23	..	..	14.1	29.5	79.8	90
85	Algeria	92.7	96.6	140	10.1	57.1	7.0	3	..	..	26.9	6.9	29.3	98
86	China	96.5	99.9	27	6.4	..	..	..	..	..	..	..	76.4	128
86	Ecuador	..	96.7	64	73.9	80.1	8.8	22	37.5	..	8.3	35.2	42.6	84
88	Ukraine	98.6	99.9	24	23.8	65.4	4.9	9	13.2	1.3	14.6	42.4	61.3	126
89	Peru	97.0	92.4	68	47.5	76.2	6.0	22	33.2	..	..	..	34.4	98
90	Colombia	97.2	95.9	64	47.5	81.0	6.7	23	..	..	14.2	..	42.5	126
90	Saint Lucia	96.9	98.7	48	40.5	55.5	17.0	8	..	..	..	..	..	91
92	Fiji	100.0	99.9	30	43.9	..	..	..	64.1	8.5	..	38.6	..	84
92	Mongolia	98.7	98.9	44	23.6	54.6	16.0	5	..	..	12.4	36.7	95.0	120
94	Dominican Republic	98.0	99.6	92	95.0	69.5	11.4	36	20.4	..	6.6	47.4	54.1	98
95	Jordan	99.1	99.6	58	22.4	61.2	11.7	8	23.6	..	18.4	..	26.6	70
95	Tunisia	98.1	73.6	62	7.7	62.5	7.0	2	..	..	37.2	..	28.4	30
97	Jamaica	97.7	..	89	52.8	72.5	10.0	8	19.7	..	..	..	77.8[g]	56

HUMAN DEVELOPMENT INDICES AND INDICATORS: **2018 STATISTICAL UPDATE**

		SDG 3.1	SDG 3.1	SDG 3.7	SDG 3.7, 5.6	SDG 5.6	SDG 5.3	SDG 5.2	SDG 5.2	SDG 5.5			SDG 1.3
		\multicolumn{6}{c	}{Reproductive health and family planning}	\multicolumn{3}{c	}{Violence against girls and women}	\multicolumn{3}{c	}{Socioeconomic empowerment}	
							Child marriage	\multicolumn{2}{c	}{Violence against women ever experienced[a]}				
		Antenatal care coverage, at least one visit	Proportion of births attended by skilled health personnel	Maternal mortality ratio	Adolescent birth rate	Contraceptive prevalence, any method	Unmet need for family planning	Women married by age 18	Intimate partner	Nonintimate partner	Share of female graduates graduating in science, mathematics, engineering, manufacturing and construction at tertiary level	Female share of employment in senior and middle management	Women with account at financial institution or with mobile money-service provider	Mandatory paid maternity leave
		(%)	(%)	(deaths per 100,000 live births)	(births per 1,000 women ages 15–19)	\multicolumn{2}{c	}{(% of married or in-union women of reproductive age, 15–49 years)}	(% of women ages 20–24 who are married or in union)	\multicolumn{2}{c	}{(% of female population ages 15 and older)}	(%)	(%)	(% of female population ages 15 and older)	(days)
HDI rank		2007–2017[b]	2012–2017[b]	2015	2015–2020[c]	2007–2017[b]	2007–2017[b]	2003–2017[b]	2005–2018[b]	2005–2018[b]	2007–2017[b]	2009–2017[b]	2017	2017
98	Tonga	99.0	95.5	124	14.7	34.1	25.2	6	39.6	6.3	..	..	..	..
99	Saint Vincent and the Grenadines	99.5	99.0	45	49.0	..	..	..	..	..	..	..	..	91
100	Suriname	90.9	80.0	155	46.0	47.6	16.9	19	..	..	..	..	..	..
101	Botswana	94.1	99.7	129	30.0	52.8	9.6	..	..	..	..	..	46.8	84
101	Maldives	99.1	95.6	68	5.8	34.7	28.6	4	19.5	6.2	..	20.6	..	60
103	Dominica	100.0	96.0	..	..	..	..	..	..	..	..	..	..	84
104	Samoa	93.3	82.5	51	23.9	26.9	34.8	11	46.1	10.6	..	41.6	..	28
105	Uzbekistan	99.4	100.0	36	16.5	..	..	7	..	..	..	..	36.0	126
106	Belize	97.2	96.8	28	63.5	51.4	22.2	26	..	..	11.7	36.4	52.3[g]	98
106	Marshall Islands	81.2	..	..	..	44.6	8.1	26	50.9	13.0	..	..	..	..
108	Libya	93.0	99.9	9	5.7	41.9	27.0	..	..	..	..	..	59.6	98
108	Turkmenistan	99.9	100.0	42	24.4	50.2	12.1	6	..	..	..	..	35.5	..
110	Gabon	94.7	89.3	291	95.3	31.1	26.5	22	48.6	5.0	..	..	53.7	98
110	Paraguay	98.7	95.5	132	55.7	68.4	12.1	22	..	..	..	..	46.0	98
112	Moldova (Republic of)	98.8	99.7	23	22.0	59.5	9.5	12	45.5	..	12.1	45.4	44.6	126
MEDIUM HUMAN DEVELOPMENT														
113	Philippines	95.4	72.8	114	60.5	55.1	17.5	15	16.9	..	17.8	32.7	38.9	60
113	South Africa	93.7	96.7	138	42.8	54.6	14.7	6	..	..	13.4	29.7	70.0	120
115	Egypt	90.3	91.5	33	50.0	58.5	12.6	17	25.6	..	7.7	..	27.0	90
116	Indonesia	95.4	92.6	126	47.4	60.9	14.5	14	18.3	..	14.9	21.5	51.4	90
116	Viet Nam	95.8	93.8	54	27.3	75.7	6.1	11	34.4	2.3	15.4	..	30.4	180
118	Bolivia (Plurinational State of)	90.1	89.8	206	68.1	66.5	20.1	19	..	4.0	..	..	53.9	90
119	Palestine, State of	99.4	99.6	45	56.2	57.2	10.9	15	..	..	12.6	15.4	15.9	84
120	Iraq	77.7	70.4	50	80.1	52.5	8.0	24	..	..	..	..	19.5	98
121	El Salvador	96.0	99.9	54	69.5	72.0	11.0	26	26.3	..	9.5	34.1	24.4	112
122	Kyrgyzstan	98.4	98.4	76	38.1	42.0	18.0	12	25.4	0.1	9.6	..	38.9	126
123	Morocco	77.1	..	121	31.1	67.4	10.9	16	..	..	17.5	..	16.8	98
124	Nicaragua	94.7	88.0	150	85.4	80.4	5.8	35	22.5	..	..	..	24.8	84
125	Cabo Verde	..	91.4	42	73.8	..	..	18	12.6	..	7.0	..	..	60
125	Guyana	90.7	85.7	229	85.8	33.9	28.0	30	..	..	5.2	35.4	..	91
127	Guatemala	91.3	65.5	88	70.9	60.6	13.9	30	18.0	..	5.4	39.2	42.1	84
127	Tajikistan	78.8	90.3	32	36.4	27.9	22.9	12	20.3	..	..	..	42.1	140
129	Namibia	96.6	88.2	265	73.8	56.1	17.5	7	25.0	..	..	..	80.7	84
130	India	..	85.7	174	23.1	53.5	12.9	27	28.7	..	26.9	..	76.6	182
131	Micronesia (Federated States of)	80.0	..	100	13.9	..	..	..	32.8	8.0	..	..	..	..
132	Timor-Leste	84.4	56.7	215	44.0	26.1	25.3	19	58.8	13.9	..	..	..	84
133	Honduras	96.6	82.8	129	70.8	73.2	10.7	34	21.6	..	8.6	41.1	41.0	84
134	Bhutan	97.9	89.0	148	20.3	65.6	11.7	26	26.5	12.5	..	..	27.7[g]	56
134	Kiribati	88.4	..	90	16.2	22.3	28.0	20	67.6	9.8	..	..	..	84
136	Bangladesh	63.9	49.8	176	83.5	62.3	12.0	59	53.3	..	7.9	..	35.8	112
137	Congo	93.2	91.2	442	111.8	30.1	17.9	27	..	..	..	..	21.0	105
138	Vanuatu	75.6	89.4	78	41.9	49.0	24.2	21	60.0	33.0	..	..	..	84
139	Lao People's Democratic Republic	54.2	40.1	197	62.6	49.8	19.9	35	15.3	5.3	5.7	..	31.9	105
140	Ghana	90.5	70.8	319	66.6	33.0	26.3	21	24.4	4.0	6.0	26.7	53.7	84
141	Equatorial Guinea	91.3	..	342	155.6	12.6	33.8	30	56.9	..	..	..	..	84
142	Kenya	93.7	61.8	510	80.5	61.6	15.6	23	39.4	..	..	..	77.7	90
143	Sao Tome and Principe	97.5	92.5	156	94.8	40.6	33.7	35	27.9	..	..	..	..	98
144	Eswatini (Kingdom of)	98.5	88.3	389	77.0[f]	66.1	15.2	5	..	..	..	..	27.4[f]	14
144	Zambia	95.7	63.3	224	82.8	49.0	21.1	31	42.7	..	..	..	40.3	84
146	Cambodia	95.3	89.0	161	50.2	56.3	12.5	19	20.9	3.8	6.0	14.1	21.5	90
147	Angola	81.6	46.9	477	151.6	13.7	38.0	30	34.8	..	9.9	..	22.3[g]	90
148	Myanmar	80.7	60.2	178	28.7	52.2	16.2	16	17.3	..	47.3	28.3	26.0	98
149	Nepal	83.6	58.0	258	60.5	52.6	23.7	40	25.0	..	..	..	41.6	52

DASHBOARD 3 Women's empowerment

DASHBOARD 3 WOMEN'S EMPOWERMENT

		Reproductive health and family planning						Violence against girls and women			Socioeconomic empowerment			
		SDG 3.1	SDG 3.1	SDG 3.7	SDG 3.7, 5.6	SDG 5.6	SDG 5.3	SDG 5.2	SDG 5.2		SDG 5.5			SDG 1.3
								Child marriage	Violence against women ever experienced[a]					
		Antenatal care coverage, at least one visit	Proportion of births attended by skilled health personnel	Maternal mortality ratio	Adolescent birth rate	Contraceptive prevalence, any method	Unmet need for family planning	Women married by age 18	Intimate partner	Nonintimate partner	Share of female graduates graduating in science, mathematics, engineering, manufacturing and construction at tertiary level	Female share of employment in senior and middle management	Women with account at financial institution or with mobile money-service provider	Mandatory paid maternity leave
		(%)	(%)	(deaths per 100,000 live births)	(births per 1,000 women ages 15–19)	(% of married or in-union women of reproductive age, 15–49 years)		(% of women ages 20–24 who are married or in union)	(% of female population ages 15 and older)		(%)	(%)	(% of female population ages 15 and older)	(days)
HDI rank		2007–2017[b]	2012–2017[b]	2015	2015–2020[c]	2007–2017[b]	2007–2017[b]	2003–2017[b]	2005–2018[b]	2005–2018[b]	2007–2017[b]	2009–2017[b]	2017	2017
150	Pakistan	73.1	52.1	178	36.9	35.4	20.1	21	..	..	..	4.0	7.0	84
151	Cameroon	82.8	64.7	596	105.8	34.4	18.0	31	51.1	5.0	..	..	30.0	98
LOW HUMAN DEVELOPMENT														
152	Solomon Islands	88.5	86.2	114	46.4	29.3	34.7	21	63.5	18.0	..	..	..	84
153	Papua New Guinea	..	40.0	215	52.7	32.4	27.4	21	..	..	..	..	..	0
154	Tanzania (United Republic of)	91.4	63.5	398	115.1	38.4	22.1	31	41.7	..	..	..	42.2	84
155	Syrian Arab Republic	87.7	..	68	38.6	53.9	16.4	13	..	..	19.2	..	19.6[f]	120
156	Zimbabwe	93.3	78.1	443	104.1	66.8	10.4	32	35.4	..	20.9	..	51.7	98
157	Nigeria	65.8	43.0	814	107.3	13.4	27.6	44	16.2	1.5	..	..	27.3	84
158	Rwanda	99.0	90.7	290	25.7	53.2	18.9	7	34.4	..	..	..	45.0	84
159	Lesotho	95.2	77.9	487	89.5	60.2	18.4	17	..	..	4.5	..	46.5	84
159	Mauritania	86.9	69.3	602	79.2	17.8	33.6	37	..	..	16.8	..	15.5	98
161	Madagascar	82.1	44.3	353	109.6	39.8	19.0	41	..	..	16.2	24.5	16.3	98
162	Uganda	97.3	74.2	343	106.5	38.4	29.6	40	49.9	..	..	31.5	52.7	84
163	Benin	82.8	77.2	405	86.1	17.9	33.1	26	..	..	19.1	..	28.6	98
164	Senegal	95.0	53.1	315	72.7	25.1	23.6	31	..	..	..	..	38.4	98
165	Comoros	92.1	82.2	335	65.4	19.4	31.6	32	6.4	1.5	..	..	17.9[f]	98
165	Togo	72.7	44.6	368	89.1	19.9	33.6	22	22.1	..	..	..	37.6	98
167	Sudan	79.1	77.7	311	64.0	12.2	26.6	34	..	..	12.8	..	10.0[g]	56
168	Afghanistan	58.6	50.5	396	64.5	22.5	24.5	35	50.8	..	..	..	7.2	90
168	Haiti	91.0	41.7	359	37.5	34.3	38.0	18	20.8	2.0	..	..	30.0	42
170	Côte d'Ivoire	93.2	73.6	645	132.7	15.5	30.5	27	25.9	..	..	..	35.6	98
171	Malawi	94.8	89.8	634	140.2	59.2	18.7	42	37.5	..	..	..	29.8	56
172	Djibouti	87.7	87.4	229	18.8	19.0	..	5	..	..	..	..	8.8[f]	98
173	Ethiopia	62.4	27.7	353	62.5	36.5	22.8	40	28.0	..	7.6	21.1	29.1	90
174	Gambia	86.2	57.2	706	79.2	9.0	24.9	30	20.1	..	..	33.7	..	180
175	Guinea	84.3	62.7	679	135.3	8.7	27.6	51	..	..	..	..	19.7	98
176	Congo (Democratic Republic of the)	88.4	80.1	693	124.2	20.4	27.7	37	50.7	..	..	..	24.2	98
177	Guinea-Bissau	92.4	45.0	549	84.5	16.0	22.3	24	..	..	..	..	..	60
178	Yemen	64.4	44.7	385	60.4	33.5	28.7	32	..	..	..	..	1.7[g]	70
179	Eritrea	88.5	..	501	51.6	8.4	27.4	41	..	..	..	..	..	60
180	Mozambique	90.6	..	489	135.2	27.1	23.1	48	21.7	..	5.9	22.2	32.9	60
181	Liberia	95.9	61.1	725	127.5	31.0	31.1	36	38.5	2.6	..	20.1	28.2	98
182	Mali	47.9	43.7	587	169.1	15.6	17.2	52	34.6	..	..	3.9	25.7	98
183	Burkina Faso	92.8	79.8	371	104.3	25.4	29.1	52	11.5	..	12.5	..	34.5	98
184	Sierra Leone	97.1	59.7	1,360	112.8	16.6	25.0	39	45.3	..	..	..	15.4	84
185	Burundi	99.2	85.1	712	26.8	28.5	29.7	20	..	..	17.1	..	6.7[g]	84
186	Chad	54.7	20.2	856	161.1	5.7	22.9	67	28.6	..	..	..	14.9	98
187	South Sudan	61.9	..	789	62.0	4.0	26.3	52	..	..	..	..	4.7	56
188	Central African Republic	68.2	..	882	103.8	15.2	27.0	68	29.8	..	..	..	9.7	98
189	Niger	82.8	39.7	553	192.0	18.9	21.0	76	..	..	..	..	10.9	98
OTHER COUNTRIES OR TERRITORIES														
..	Korea (Democratic People's Rep. of)	100.0	..	82	0.3	78.2	7.0	..	..	..	22.2	..	..	..
..	Monaco	..	..	..	..	..	..	..	..	..	..	..	..	..
..	Nauru	94.5	..	..	..	35.6	23.5	27	48.1	47.3	..	..	..	..
..	San Marino	..	..	..	..	..	..	..	..	..	..	..	..	630
..	Somalia	..	..	732	100.1	..	..	45	..	..	..	..	33.7[g]	..
..	Tuvalu	97.4	..	..	..	30.5	24.2	10	36.8	..	..	..	..	..
Human development groups														
	Very high human development	..	99.2	15	15.9	66.8	..	..	..	..	12.9	—	88.4	112
	High human development	96.8	99.0	38	26.6	..	..	..	..	..	..	—	68.8	119
	Medium human development	..	79.5	176	41.3	54.2	14.2	25	28.8	..	23.2	—	56.1	94
	Low human development	77.7	55.2	554	98.4	26.3	25.3	39	30.8	..	..	—	26.6	86

HUMAN DEVELOPMENT INDICES AND INDICATORS: 2018 STATISTICAL UPDATE

	SDG 3.1	SDG 3.1	SDG 3.7	SDG 3.7, 5.6	SDG 5.6	SDG 5.3	SDG 5.2	SDG 5.2	SDG 5.5		SDG 1.3
	Reproductive health and family planning					Violence against girls and women			Socioeconomic empowerment		
						Child marriage	Violence against women ever experienced[a]				
	Antenatal care coverage, at least one visit	Proportion of births attended by skilled health personnel	Maternal mortality ratio	Adolescent birth rate	Contraceptive prevalence, any method	Unmet need for family planning	Women married by age 18	Intimate partner	Nonintimate partner	Share of female graduates graduating in science, mathematics, engineering, manufacturing and construction at tertiary level	Female share of employment in senior and middle management	Women with account at financial institution or with mobile money-service provider	Mandatory paid maternity leave
	(%)	(%)	(deaths per 100,000 live births)	(births per 1,000 women ages 15–19)	(% of married or in-union women of reproductive age, 15–49 years)	(% of married or in-union women of reproductive age, 15–49 years)	(% of women ages 20–24 who are married or in union)	(% of female population ages 15 and older)	(% of female population ages 15 and older)	(%)	(%)	(% of female population ages 15 and older)	(days)
HDI rank	2007–2017[b]	2012–2017[b]	2015	2015–2020[c]	2007–2017[b]	2007–2017[b]	2003–2017[b]	2005–2018[b]	2005–2018[b]	2007–2017[b]	2009–2017[b]	2017	2017
Developing countries	90.1	84.5	232	48.0	53.2	14.9	27	..	..	..	—	58.3	99
Regions													
Arab States	86.5	85.2	149	46.3	48.2	14.4	20	..	..	18.1	—	27.0	75
East Asia and the Pacific	95.8	95.5	62	22.4	..	..	..	..	..	..	—	..	86
Europe and Central Asia	97.1	98.6	24	25.5	63.6	8.5	10	26.3	..	14.2	—	53.5	165
Latin America and the Caribbean	97.1	95.5	67	61.5	74.5	9.6	25	..	..	10.5	—	52.2	96
South Asia	..	78.4	176	32.1	53.2	13.5	29	31.7	..	..	—	65.3	110
Sub-Saharan Africa	81.4	59.5	549	101.3	30.5	24.0	36	31.5	..	..	—	36.0	89
Least developed countries	77.4	56.6	434 T	91.0	37.6	22.1	40	38.1	..	..	—	28.4	87
Small island developing states	95.1	74.3	202	56.5	51.1	21.0	23	..	..	..	—	..	..
Organisation for Economic Co-operation and Development	..	98.8	15	20.7	68.7	..	..	..	..	12.5	—	86.2	114
World	..	86.5	216 T	44.0	55.8	14.4	..	..	..	..	—	64.7	107

NOTES

Three-colour coding is used to visualize partial grouping of countries and aggregates by indicator. For each indicator countries are divided into three groups of approximately equal size (terciles): the top third, the middle third and the bottom third. Aggregates are colour coded using the same tercile cutoffs. See Technical note 6 at http://hdr.undp.org/sites/default/files/hdr2018_technical_notes.pdf for details about partial grouping in this table.

a Data collection methods, age ranges, sampled women (ever-partnered, ever-married or all women) and definitions of the forms of violence and of perpetrators vary by survey. Thus data are not necessarily comparable across countries.

b Data refer to the most recent year available during the period specified.

c Data are the annual average of projected values for 2015–2020.

d Refers to 2009.

e Refers to 2015.

f Refers to 2011.

g Refers to 2014.

T From original data source.

DEFINITIONS

Antenatal care coverage, at least one visit: Percentage of women ages 15–49 attended at least once during pregnancy by skilled health personnel (doctor, nurse or midwife).

Proportion of births attended by skilled health personnel: Percentage of deliveries attended by skilled health personnel (generally doctors, nurses or midwives) trained in providing lifesaving obstetric care—including giving the necessary supervision, care and advice to women during pregnancy, labour and the postpartum period, conducting deliveries on their own and caring for newborns. Traditional birth attendants, even if they receive a short training course, are not included.

Maternal mortality ratio: Number of deaths due to pregnancy-related causes per 100,000 live births.

Adolescent birth rate: Number of births to women ages 15–19 per 1,000 women ages 15–19.

Contraceptive prevalence, any method: Percentage of married or in-union women of reproductive age (15–49 years) currently using any contraceptive method.

Unmet need for family planning: Percentage of married or in-union women of reproductive age (15–49 years) who are fecund have an unmet need if they want to have no (more) births, or if they want to postpone or are undecided about the timing of their next birth, yet they are not using any method of contraception.

Child marriage, women married by age 18: Percentage of women ages 20–24 who were first married or in union before age 18.

Violence against women ever experienced, intimate partner: Percentage of the female population ages 15 and older that has ever experienced physical and/or sexual violence from an intimate partner.

Violence against women ever experienced, nonintimate partner: Percentage of the female population ages 15 and older that has ever experienced sexual violence from a nonintimate partner.

Share of female graduates graduating in science, mathematics, engineering, manufacturing and construction at tertiary level: Share of female tertiary graduates in "Natural Sciences, Mathematics and Statistics," "Information and Communication Technologies" and "Engineering, Manufacturing and Construction" programmes.

Female share of employment in senior and middle management: Proportion of women in total employment in senior and middle management.

Women with account at financial institution or with mobile money-service provider: Percentage of women ages 15 and older who report having an account alone or jointly with someone else at a bank or other type of financial institution or who report personally using a mobile money service in the past 12 months.

Mandatory paid maternity leave: Number of days of paid time off work to which a female employee is entitled in order to take care of a newborn child.

MAIN DATA SOURCES

Column 1: UNICEF (2018).

Columns 2 and 7: United Nations Statistics Division (2018a).

Column 3: UN Maternal Mortality Estimation Group (2017).

Column 4: UNDESA (2017a).

Columns 5 and 6: UNDESA (2018b).

Columns 8 and 9: UN Women (2018).

Column 10: UNESCO Institute for Statistics (2018).

Column 11: ILO (2018a).

Columns 12 and 13: World Bank (2018c).

DASHBOARD 4

Environmental sustainability

Country groupings (terciles)

Top third | Middle third | Bottom third

Three-colour coding is used to visualize partial grouping of countries by indicator. For each indicator countries are divided into three groups of approximately equal size (terciles): the top third, the middle third and the bottom third. Aggregates are colour coded using the same tercile cutoffs. See *Notes* after the table.

		SDG 12.c	SDG 7.2	SDG 9.4		SDG 15.1		SDG 6.4	SDG 3.9	SDG 3.9	SDG 15.5
									\multicolumn{2}{c}{Environmental threats}	
									\multicolumn{2}{c}{Mortality rate attributed to}	
		Fossil fuel energy consumption	Renewable energy consumption	Carbon dioxide emissions		Forest area		Fresh water withdrawals	Household and ambient air pollution	Unsafe water, sanitation and hygiene services	Red List Index
		(% of total energy consumption)	(% of total final energy consumption)	Per capita (tonnes)	(kg per 2011 PPP $ of GDP)	(% of total land area[a])	Change (%)	(% of total renewable water resources)	(per 100,000 population)		(value)
HDI rank		2010–2015[b]	2015	2014	2014	2015	1990/2015	2006–2016[b]	2016	2016	2017
\multicolumn{12}{l}{VERY HIGH HUMAN DEVELOPMENT}											
1	Norway	58.5	57.8	9.3	0.15	33.2	−0.2	0.8	8.6	0.2	0.943
2	Switzerland	50.1	25.3	4.3	0.08	31.7	9.0	3.7	10.1	0.1	0.982
3	Australia	93.4	9.2	15.4	0.35	16.2	−2.9	3.4	8.4	0.1[c]	0.828
4	Ireland	85.4	9.1	7.3	0.15	10.9	62.2	1.5	11.9	0.1[c]	0.917
5	Germany	79.8	14.2	8.9	0.20	32.7	1.1	21.4	16.0	0.6	0.983
6	Iceland	11.5	77.0	6.1	0.15	0.5	205.6	0.2	8.7	0.1	0.872
7	Hong Kong, China (SAR)	93.2	0.9	6.4	0.12	..	..	..	..	..	0.823
7	Sweden	26.8	53.2	4.5	0.10	68.9	0.8	1.5	7.2	0.2	0.992
9	Singapore	97.5	0.7	10.3	0.13	23.1	−5.5	..	25.9	0.1[c]	0.862
10	Netherlands	91.4	5.9	9.9	0.22	11.2	9.2	11.8	13.7	0.2	0.943
11	Denmark	65.7	33.2	5.9	0.13	14.6	13.8	10.6	13.2	0.3	0.972
12	Canada	73.6	22.0	15.1	0.35	38.2	−0.3	1.3	7.0	0.4	0.971
13	United States	82.8	8.7	16.5	0.32	33.9	2.7	13.6	13.3	0.2	0.840
14	United Kingdom	80.7	8.7	6.5	0.17	13.0	13.2	5.5	13.8	0.2	0.789
15	Finland	39.7	43.2	8.7	0.22	73.1	1.8	6.0	7.2	0.1[c]	0.989
16	New Zealand	59.4	30.8	7.7	0.22	38.6	5.1	1.6	7.2	0.1	0.634
17	Belgium	75.8	9.2	8.3	0.20	22.6	..	32.8	15.7	0.3	0.986
17	Liechtenstein	..	63.1	1.2	..	43.1	6.2	..	..	..	0.993
19	Japan	93.7	6.3	9.5	0.26	68.5	0.0	18.9	11.9	0.2	0.785
20	Austria	66.0	34.4	6.9	0.16	46.9	2.5	4.5	15.3	0.1	0.896
21	Luxembourg	80.9	9.0	17.4	0.19	33.5	..	1.2	11.6	0.1[c]	0.987
22	Israel	96.3	3.7	7.9	0.25	7.6	25.0	..	15.4	0.2	0.748
22	Korea (Republic of)	82.0	2.7	11.6	0.35	63.4	−3.9	..	20.5	1.8	0.782
24	France	46.6	13.5	4.6	0.12	31.0	17.7	14.1	9.7	0.3	0.875
25	Slovenia	60.9	20.9	6.2	0.22	62.0	5.1	3.6	22.6	0.1[c]	0.937
26	Spain	72.9	16.3	5.0	0.16	36.8	33.2	33.0	9.9	0.2	0.845
27	Czechia	76.0	14.8	9.2	0.31	34.5	1.5	12.6	29.6	0.2	0.971
28	Italy	79.2	16.5	5.3	0.16	31.6	22.5	28.1	15.0	0.1	0.917
29	Malta	97.8	5.4	5.4	0.17	1.1	0.0	44.4	20.2	0.1[c]	0.883
30	Estonia	12.3	27.5	14.8	0.55	52.7	1.2	13.4	25.0	0.1[c]	0.984
31	Greece	85.1	17.2	6.2	0.26	31.5	22.9	14.0	27.6	0.1[c]	0.848
32	Cyprus	92.9	9.9	5.3	0.24	18.7	7.2	28.4	20.1	0.3	0.983
33	Poland	89.9	11.9	7.5	0.31	30.8	6.3	19.0	37.9	0.1[c]	0.970
34	United Arab Emirates	99.8	0.1	23.3	0.36	3.9	31.7	..	54.7	0.1[c]	0.866
35	Andorra	..	19.7	5.8	..	34.0	0.0	..	..	..	0.919
35	Lithuania	68.0	29.0	4.4	0.17	34.8	12.1	2.6	34.0	0.1[c]	0.988
37	Qatar	100.0	0.0	45.4	0.38	0.0	0.0	..	47.4	0.1[c]	0.833
38	Slovakia	64.6	13.4	5.7	0.21	40.3	1.0	1.1	33.5	0.1[c]	0.962
39	Brunei Darussalam	100.0	0.0	22.1	0.29	72.1	−8.0	..	13.3	0.1[c]	0.828
39	Saudi Arabia	100.0	0.0	19.5	0.39	0.5	0.0	943.3	83.7	0.1[c]	0.908
41	Latvia	56.7	38.1	3.5	0.16	54.0	5.8	0.7	41.3	0.1[c]	0.988
41	Portugal	76.9	27.2	4.3	0.17	34.7	−7.5	11.8	9.8	0.2	0.856
43	Bahrain	100.0	0.0	23.4	0.53	0.8	144.1	..	40.1	0.1[c]	0.849
44	Chile	73.3	24.9	4.7	0.21	23.9	16.2	3.8	25.3	0.2	0.763
45	Hungary	69.3	15.6	4.3	0.18	22.9	14.0	4.9	38.8	0.2	0.929
46	Croatia	70.7	33.1	4.0	0.20	34.3	3.8	0.6	35.5	0.1	0.899
47	Argentina	88.5	10.0	4.7	0.25	9.9	−22.1	4.3	26.6	0.4	0.861
48	Oman	100.0	0.0	15.4	0.38	0.0	0.0	..	53.9	0.1[c]	0.885
49	Russian Federation	90.2	3.3	11.9	0.46	49.8	0.8	1.3	49.4	0.1	0.956
50	Montenegro	64.7	43.0	3.6	0.24	61.5	32.1	..	78.6	0.1[c]	0.816

96 | HUMAN DEVELOPMENT INDICES AND INDICATORS: **2018 STATISTICAL UPDATE**

HUMAN DEVELOPMENT INDICES AND INDICATORS: 2018 STATISTICAL UPDATE

		SDG 12.c	SDG 7.2	SDG 9.4		SDG 15.1		SDG 6.4	SDG 3.9	SDG 3.9	SDG 15.5
										Environmental threats	
									Mortality rate attributed to		
		Fossil fuel energy consumption	Renewable energy consumption	Carbon dioxide emissions		Forest area		Fresh water withdrawals	Household and ambient air pollution	Unsafe water, sanitation and hygiene services	Red List Index
		(% of total energy consumption)	(% of total final energy consumption)	Per capita (tonnes)	(kg per 2011 PPP $ of GDP)	(% of total land area[a])	Change (%)	(% of total renewable water resources)	(per 100,000 population)		(value)
HDI rank		2010–2015[b]	2015	2014	2014	2015	1990/2015	2006–2016[b]	2016	2016	2017
51	Bulgaria	71.0	17.7	5.9	0.36	35.2	17.1	26.4	61.8	0.1	0.941
52	Romania	72.8	23.7	3.5	0.18	29.8	7.3	3.0	59.3	0.4	0.947
53	Belarus	92.4	6.8	6.7	0.37	42.5	10.9	2.6	60.7	0.1[c]	0.970
54	Bahamas	..	1.2	6.3	0.22	51.4	0.0	..	19.9	0.1[c]	0.703
55	Uruguay	46.8	58.0	2.0	0.10	10.5	131.3	..	17.5	0.4	0.833
56	Kuwait	100.0	0.0	25.2	0.36	0.4	81.2	..	103.8	0.1[c]	0.868
57	Malaysia	96.6	5.2	8.0	0.33	67.6	−0.8	..	47.4	0.4	0.687
58	Barbados	..	2.8	4.5	0.27	14.7	0.0	..	31.1	0.2	0.914
58	Kazakhstan	99.2	1.6	14.4	0.61	1.2	−3.3	18.4	62.7	0.4	0.873
HIGH HUMAN DEVELOPMENT											
60	Iran (Islamic Republic of)	99.0	0.9	8.3	0.49	6.6	17.8	..	50.9	1.0	0.835
60	Palau	..	0.0	12.3	0.96	87.6	..	..	..	..	0.750
62	Seychelles	..	1.4	5.4	0.22	88.4	0.0	..	49.3	0.2	0.670
63	Costa Rica	49.5	38.7	1.6	0.11	54.0	7.5	2.1	23.3	0.9	0.820
64	Turkey	87.6	13.4	4.5	0.20	15.2	21.8	19.8	46.6	0.3	0.876
65	Mauritius	84.5	11.5	3.4	0.18	19.0	−6.1	..	38.3	0.6	0.401
66	Panama	80.7	21.2	2.3	0.11	62.1	−8.4	0.7	25.8	1.9	0.735
67	Serbia	83.9	21.2	5.3	0.40	31.1	9.9	2.6	62.5	0.7	0.957
68	Albania	61.4	38.6	2.0	0.18	28.2	−2.2	4.3	68.0	0.2	0.855
69	Trinidad and Tobago	99.9	0.3	34.2	1.10	45.7	−2.6	8.8	38.6	0.1	0.816
70	Antigua and Barbuda	..	0.0	5.4	0.27	22.3	−4.9	8.5	29.9	0.1	0.891
70	Georgia	72.2	28.7	2.4	0.28	40.6	2.6	2.9	101.8	0.2	0.863
72	Saint Kitts and Nevis	..	1.6	4.3	0.18	42.3	0.0	51.3	..	..	0.732
73	Cuba	85.8	19.3	3.0	..	30.8	60.5	18.3	49.5	1.0	0.651
74	Mexico	90.4	9.2	3.9	0.23	34.0	−5.3	18.6	36.7	1.1	0.678
75	Grenada	..	10.9	2.3	0.19	50.0	0.0	7.1	45.3	0.3	0.762
76	Sri Lanka	50.3	52.9	0.9	0.08	33.0	−9.4	..	79.8	1.2	0.569
77	Bosnia and Herzegovina	77.5	40.8	6.2	0.59	42.7	−1.5	0.9	79.8	0.1[c]	0.904
78	Venezuela (Bolivarian Republic of)	88.4	12.8	6.0	0.36	52.9	−10.3	1.7	34.6	1.4	0.827
79	Brazil	59.1	43.8	2.6	0.17	59.0	−9.7	0.9	29.9	1.0	0.901
80	Azerbaijan	98.4	2.3	3.9	0.24	13.8	34.6	34.5	63.9	1.1	0.910
80	Lebanon	97.6	3.6	4.3	0.31	13.4	4.8	..	51.4	0.8	0.918
80	The former Yugoslav Republic of Macedonia	79.3	24.2	3.6	0.29	39.6	10.3	8.6	82.2	0.1[c]	0.971
83	Armenia	74.6	15.8	1.9	0.24	11.7	−0.9	42.1	54.8	0.2	0.845
83	Thailand	79.8	22.9	4.6	0.31	32.1	17.1	13.1	61.5	3.5	0.798
85	Algeria	100.0	0.1	3.7	0.28	0.8	17.3	66.9	49.7	1.9	0.904
86	China	87.5	12.4	7.5	0.59	22.2	32.6	20.9	112.7	0.6	0.746
86	Ecuador	86.9	13.8	2.8	0.25	50.5	−4.4	..	24.5	0.6	0.686
88	Ukraine	75.3	4.1	5.0	0.64	16.7	4.1	8.5	70.7	0.3	0.945
89	Peru	79.6	25.5	2.0	0.17	57.8	−5.1	0.7	63.9	1.3	0.723
90	Colombia	76.7	23.6	1.8	0.14	52.7	−9.2	0.5	37.0	0.8	0.740
90	Saint Lucia	..	2.1	2.3	0.19	33.3	−6.9	14.3	30.0	0.6	0.846
92	Fiji	..	31.3	1.3	0.16	55.7	6.7	..	99.0	2.9	0.671
92	Mongolia	94.1	3.4	7.1	0.63	8.1	0.1	1.6	155.9	1.3	0.946
94	Dominican Republic	86.5	16.5	2.1	0.16	41.0	79.5	30.4	43.0	2.2	0.735
95	Jordan	97.6	3.2	3.0	0.35	1.1	−0.6	117.8	51.2	0.6	0.959
95	Tunisia	88.4	12.6	2.6	0.24	6.7	61.9	69.7	56.1	1.0	0.974
97	Jamaica	81.0	16.8	2.6	0.32	31.0	−2.7	7.5	25.4	0.6	0.724
98	Tonga	..	1.9	1.1	0.23	12.5	0.0	..	73.3	1.4	0.711
99	Saint Vincent and the Grenadines	..	5.8	1.9	0.19	69.2	8.0	7.9	47.6	1.3	0.772
100	Suriname	76.3	24.9	3.6	0.24	98.3	−0.6	0.6	56.7	2.0	0.985
101	Botswana	74.7	28.9	3.2	0.20	19.1	−21.0	..	101.3	11.8	0.980
101	Maldives	..	1.0	3.3	0.24	3.3	0.0	15.7	25.6	0.3	0.846
103	Dominica	..	7.8	1.9	0.18	57.8	−13.3	10.0	..	..	0.669
104	Samoa	..	34.3	1.0	0.19	60.4	31.5	..	85.0	1.5	0.819
105	Uzbekistan	97.7	3.0	3.4	0.64	7.6	5.7	..	81.1	0.4	0.970
106	Belize	..	35.0	1.4	0.18	59.9	−15.5	..	68.6	1.0	0.744
106	Marshall Islands	..	11.2	1.9	0.53	70.2	..	..	..	..	0.841

DASHBOARD 4 Environmental sustainability

DASHBOARD 4 ENVIRONMENTAL SUSTAINABILITY

		SDG 12.c	SDG 7.2	SDG 9.4		SDG 15.1		SDG 6.4	SDG 3.9	SDG 3.9	SDG 15.5
									\multicolumn{2}{c}{Environmental threats}	
									\multicolumn{2}{c}{Mortality rate attributed to}	
		Fossil fuel energy consumption	Renewable energy consumption	Carbon dioxide emissions		Forest area		Fresh water withdrawals	Household and ambient air pollution	Unsafe water, sanitation and hygiene services	Red List Index
		(% of total energy consumption)	(% of total final energy consumption)	Per capita (tonnes)	(kg per 2011 PPP $ of GDP)	(% of total land area[a])	Change (%)	(% of total renewable water resources)	(per 100,000 population)		(value)
HDI rank		2010–2015[b]	2015	2014	2014	2015	1990/2015	2006–2016[b]	2016	2016	2017
108	Libya	99.1	2.0	9.2	0.56	0.1	0.0	822.9	71.9	0.6	0.971
108	Turkmenistan	..	0.0	12.5	0.87	8.8	0.0	..	79.3	4.0	0.974
110	Gabon	24.2	82.0	2.8	0.17	89.3	4.5	..	76.0	20.6	0.961
110	Paraguay	33.7	61.7	0.9	0.10	38.6	−27.6	0.6	57.5	1.5	0.949
112	Moldova (Republic of)	88.7	14.3	1.4	0.29	12.4	28.2	8.7	78.3	0.1[c]	0.968
MEDIUM HUMAN DEVELOPMENT											
113	Philippines	62.0	27.5	1.1	0.16	27.0	22.7	17.0	185.2	4.2	0.648
113	South Africa	86.9	17.2	9.0	0.72	7.6	0.0	30.2	86.7	13.7	0.778
115	Egypt	96.0	5.7	2.2	0.22	0.1	65.9	126.6	108.9	2.0	0.914
116	Indonesia	65.6	36.9	1.8	0.18	50.2	−23.2	..	112.4	7.1	0.763
116	Viet Nam	69.8	35.0	1.8	0.34	47.6	65.6	..	64.5	1.6	0.740
118	Bolivia (Plurinational State of)	85.2	17.5	1.9	0.31	50.6	−12.8	0.4	63.7	5.6	0.871
119	Palestine, State of	..	10.5	0.6[d]	0.13[d]	1.5	1.0	..	..	..	0.787
120	Iraq	97.3	0.8	4.8	0.32	1.9	3.3	..	75.1	3.0	0.819
121	El Salvador	48.4	24.4	1.0	0.15	12.8	−29.7	..	41.9	2.0	0.829
122	Kyrgyzstan	69.3	23.3	1.6	0.52	3.3	−23.8	32.6	110.7	0.8	0.984
123	Morocco	88.5	11.3	1.7	0.24	12.6	13.7	35.7	49.1	1.9	0.886
124	Nicaragua	40.9	48.2	0.8	0.17	25.9	−31.0	0.9	55.7	2.2	0.854
125	Cabo Verde	..	26.6	0.9	0.16	22.3	55.7	..	99.5	4.1	0.881
125	Guyana	..	25.3	2.6	0.38	84.0	−0.8	0.5	107.8	3.6	0.922
127	Guatemala	37.4	63.7	1.2	0.16	33.0	−25.4	2.6	73.8	6.3	0.722
127	Tajikistan	54.9	44.7	0.6	0.24	3.0	1.8	51.1	129.3	2.7	0.984
129	Namibia	66.7	26.5	1.6	0.16	8.4	−21.0	..	145.0	18.3	0.966
130	India	73.5	36.0	1.7	0.32	23.8	10.5	33.9	184.3	18.6	0.684
131	Micronesia (Federated States of)	..	1.2	1.4	0.46	91.8	..	..	151.8	3.6	0.691
132	Timor-Leste	..	18.2	0.4	0.06	46.1	−29.0	..	139.8	9.9	0.889
133	Honduras	52.5	51.5	1.1	0.25	41.0	−43.6	..	60.7	3.6	0.744
134	Bhutan	..	86.9	1.3	0.18	72.3	34.7	0.4	124.5	3.9	0.799
134	Kiribati	..	4.3	0.6	0.31	15.0	0.0	..	140.2	16.7	0.770
136	Bangladesh	73.8	34.7	0.5	0.15	11.0	−4.4	2.9	149.0	11.9	0.766
137	Congo	40.5	62.4	0.6	0.11	65.4	−1.7	..	130.7	38.7	0.984
138	Vanuatu	..	36.1	0.6	0.21	36.1	0.0	..	135.6	10.4	0.665
139	Lao People's Democratic Republic	..	59.3	0.3	0.05	81.3	6.3	..	188.5	11.3	0.810
140	Ghana	52.3	41.4	0.5	0.14	41.0	8.2	..	203.8	18.8	0.844
141	Equatorial Guinea	..	7.8	4.7	0.15	55.9	−15.7	..	177.7	22.3	0.813
142	Kenya	17.2	72.7	0.3	0.11	7.8	−6.6	10.5	78.1	51.2	0.801
143	Sao Tome and Principe	..	41.1	0.6	0.20	55.8	−4.3	..	162.4	11.4	0.788
144	Eswatini (Kingdom of)	..	66.1	0.9	0.12	34.1	24.2	..	137.0	27.9	0.818
144	Zambia	10.6	88.0	0.3	0.08	65.4	−7.9	..	127.2	34.9	0.879
146	Cambodia	30.7	64.9	0.4	0.14	53.6	−26.9	0.5	149.8	6.5	0.823
147	Angola	48.3	49.6	1.3	0.21	46.4	−5.1	..	118.5	48.8	0.936
148	Myanmar	39.3	61.5	0.4	0.09	44.5	−25.9	..	156.4	12.6	0.807
149	Nepal	15.8	85.3	0.3	0.13	25.4	−24.7	4.5	193.8	19.8	0.825
150	Pakistan	59.7	46.5	0.9	0.20	1.9	−41.7	74.4	173.6	19.6	0.862
151	Cameroon	29.9	76.5	0.3	0.10	39.8	−22.6	..	208.1	45.2	0.836
LOW HUMAN DEVELOPMENT											
152	Solomon Islands	..	63.3	0.4	0.16	78.1	−6.0	..	137.0	6.2	0.769
153	Papua New Guinea	..	52.5	0.8	0.22	74.1	−0.2	..	152.0	16.3	0.839
154	Tanzania (United Republic of)	14.4	85.7	0.2	0.09	52.0	−17.6	..	139.0	38.4	0.691
155	Syrian Arab Republic	97.7	0.5	1.6	..	2.7	32.1	..	75.2	3.7	0.953
156	Zimbabwe	29.1	81.8	0.8	0.41	36.4	−36.6	17.9	133.0	24.6	0.789
157	Nigeria	19.0	86.6	0.5	0.10	7.7	−59.4	4.4	307.4	68.6	0.874
158	Rwanda	..	86.7	0.1	0.05	19.5	50.9	..	121.4	19.3	0.849
159	Lesotho	..	52.1	1.2	0.43	1.6	22.5	..	177.6	44.4	0.966
159	Mauritania	..	32.2	0.7	0.18	0.2	−45.9	..	169.5	38.6	0.978
161	Madagascar	..	70.2	0.1	0.10	21.4	−8.9	4.0	159.6	30.2	0.795
162	Uganda	..	89.1	0.1	0.08	10.4	−56.4	1.1	155.7	31.6	0.752
163	Benin	44.4	50.9	0.6	0.31	38.2	−25.2	..	205.0	59.7	0.910

HUMAN DEVELOPMENT INDICES AND INDICATORS: 2018 STATISTICAL UPDATE

	SDG 12.c	SDG 7.2	SDG 9.4		SDG 15.1		SDG 6.4	SDG 3.9	SDG 3.9	SDG 15.5
								Environmental threats		
								Mortality rate attributed to		
	Fossil fuel energy consumption	Renewable energy consumption	Carbon dioxide emissions		Forest area		Fresh water withdrawals	Household and ambient air pollution	Unsafe water, sanitation and hygiene services	Red List Index
	(% of total energy consumption)	(% of total final energy consumption)	Per capita (tonnes)	(kg per 2011 PPP $ of GDP)	(% of total land area[a])	Change (%)	(% of total renewable water resources)	(per 100,000 population)		(value)
HDI rank	2010–2015[b]	2015	2014	2014	2015	1990/2015	2006–2016[b]	2016	2016	2017
164 Senegal	53.7	42.7	0.6	0.27	43.0	−11.5	..	160.7	23.9	0.945
165 Comoros	..	45.3	0.2	0.14	19.9	−24.5	..	172.4	50.7	0.764
165 Togo	17.2	71.3	0.4	0.28	3.5	−72.6	..	249.6	41.6	0.854
167 Sudan	31.8	61.6	0.3	0.10	8.1	−37.5	71.2	184.9	17.3	0.934
168 Afghanistan	..	18.4	0.3	0.16	2.1	0.0	..	211.1	13.9	0.837
168 Haiti	22.0	76.1	0.3	0.16	3.5	−16.4	10.3	184.3	23.8	0.721
170 Côte d'Ivoire	26.5	64.5	0.5	0.16	32.7	1.8	..	269.1	47.2	0.889
171 Malawi	..	83.6	0.1	0.07	33.4	−19.2	..	115.0	28.3	0.806
172 Djibouti	..	15.4	0.8	0.20[e]	0.2	0.0	..	159.0	31.3	0.822
173 Ethiopia	6.1	92.2	0.1	0.08	12.5	−17.8	8.6	144.4	43.7	0.840
174 Gambia	..	51.5	0.3	0.17	48.2	10.4	..	237.0	29.7	0.981
175 Guinea	..	76.3	0.2	0.12	25.9	−12.4	..	243.3	44.6	0.896
176 Congo (Democratic Republic of the)	5.4	95.8	0.1	0.08	67.3	−4.9	..	163.9	59.8	0.891
177 Guinea-Bissau	..	86.9	0.2	0.11	70.1	−11.0	..	214.7	35.3	0.960
178 Yemen	98.5	2.3	0.9	0.23	1.0	0.0	..	194.2	10.2	0.881
179 Eritrea	22.3	79.8	0.1[e]	0.09[e]	15.0	..	..	173.7	45.6	0.909
180 Mozambique	12.6	86.4	0.3	0.29	48.2	−12.5	0.7	110.0	27.6	0.830
181 Liberia	..	83.8	0.2	0.26	43.4	−15.2	..	170.2	41.5	0.890
182 Mali	..	61.5	0.1	0.04	3.9	−29.5	4.3	209.1	70.7	0.982
183 Burkina Faso	..	74.2	0.2	0.10	19.6	−21.9	..	206.2	49.6	0.989
184 Sierra Leone	..	77.7	0.2	0.11	42.2	−2.4	..	324.1	81.3	0.913
185 Burundi	..	95.7	0.0	0.06	10.7	−4.5	..	179.9	65.4	0.921
186 Chad	..	89.4	0.1	0.03	3.9	−27.3	..	280.1	101.0	0.920
187 South Sudan	72.2	39.1	0.1	0.07	..	..	1.3	165.1	63.3	0.932
188 Central African Republic	..	76.6	0.0	0.11	35.6	−1.7	..	211.9	82.1	0.944
189 Niger	24.1	78.9	0.1	0.12	0.9	−41.3	..	251.8	70.8	0.939
OTHER COUNTRIES OR TERRITORIES										
.. Korea (Democratic People's Rep. of)	81.4	23.1	1.6	..	41.8	−38.7	..	207.2	1.4	0.913
.. Monaco	..	..	..	..	..	..	..	..	..	0.753
.. Nauru	..	0.1	4.0	0.32	0.0	0.0	..	..	..	0.773
.. San Marino	..	..	..	..	0.0	0.0	..	..	..	0.992
.. Somalia	..	94.3	0.0	..	10.1	−23.2	..	212.8	86.6	0.902
.. Tuvalu	..	0.0	1.0	0.32	33.3	0.0	..	..	..	0.832
Human development groups										
Very high human development	82.6	10.4	10.7	0.28	33.1	1.1	6.1	23.6	0.3	—
High human development	85.8	14.6	6.1	0.46	31.5	−1.7	4.8	86.2	0.8	—
Medium human development	71.2	35.8	1.7	0.28	30.5	−9.7	..	156.2	15.6	—
Low human development	..	81.0	0.3	0.12	23.1	−14.5	..	200.2	45.9	—
Developing countries	80.5	23.5	3.4	0.38	26.6	−6.7	..	133.1	14.0	—
Regions										
Arab States	97.2	4.0	4.9	0.32	3.0	−23.7	..	101.2	7.0	—
East Asia and the Pacific	..	15.9	5.8	0.50	29.8	3.8	..	114.4	2.2	—
Europe and Central Asia	87.2	9.1	5.1	0.35	9.1	8.3	14.3	66.5	0.5	—
Latin America and the Caribbean	74.5	27.7	3.0	0.21	46.3	−9.3	1.6	39.3	1.7	—
South Asia	76.7	31.1	1.8	0.32	14.7	7.6	23.8	173.7	17.1	—
Sub-Saharan Africa	39.2	70.2	0.8	0.24	28.2	−11.7	..	186.4	47.7	—
Least developed countries	..	73.2	0.3	0.13	26.8	−12.4	..	166.5	34.3	—
Small island developing states	..	26.4	2.4	0.29	69.5	1.3	..	100.1	10.0	—
Organisation for Economic Co-operation and Development	80.0	12.0	9.5	0.25	31.3	1.5	8.6	18.9	0.4	—
World	80.6	18.2	4.6	0.33	30.8	−3.2	7.2	114.1	11.7	—

DASHBOARD 4 Environmental sustainability

DASHBOARD 4 ENVIRONMENTAL SUSTAINABILITY

NOTES

Three-colour coding is used to visualize partial grouping of countries and aggregates by indicator. For each indicator countries are divided into three groups of approximately equal size (terciles): the top third, the middle third and the bottom third. Aggregates are colour coded using the same tercile cutoffs. See *Technical note 6* at http://hdr.undp.org/sites/default/files/hdr2018_technical_notes.pdf for details about partial grouping in this table.

- **a** This column is intentionally left without colour because it is meant to provide context for the indicator on change in forest area.
- **b** Data refer to the most recent year available during the period specified.
- **c** Less than 0.1.
- **d** Refers to 2013.
- **e** Refers to 2011.

DEFINITIONS

Fossil fuel energy consumption: Percentage of total energy consumption that comes from fossil fuels, which consist of coal, oil, petroleum and natural gas products.

Renewable energy consumption: Share of renewable energy in total final energy consumption. Renewable sources include hydroelectric, geothermal, solar, tides, wind, biomass and biofuels.

Carbon dioxide emissions: Human-originated carbon dioxide emissions stemming from the burning of fossil fuels, gas flaring and the production of cement. Carbon dioxide emitted by forest biomass through depletion of forest areas is included. Data are expressed in tonnes per capita (based on midyear population) and in kilograms per unit of gross domestic product (GDP) in 2011 purchasing power parity (PPP) dollars.

Forest area: Land spanning more than 0.5 hectare with trees taller than 5 metres and a canopy cover of more than 10 percent or trees able to reach these thresholds in situ. It excludes land predominantly under agricultural or urban land use, tree stands in agricultural production systems (for example, in fruit plantations and agroforestry systems) and trees in urban parks and gardens. Areas under reforestation that have not yet reached but are expected to reach a canopy cover of 10 percent and a tree height of 5 metres are included, as are temporarily unstocked areas resulting from human intervention or natural causes that are expected to regenerate.

Fresh water withdrawals: Total fresh water withdrawn, expressed as a percentage of total renewable water resources.

Mortality rate attributed to household and ambient air pollution: Deaths resulting from exposure to ambient (outdoor) air pollution and household (indoor) air pollution from solid fuel use for cooking, expressed per 100,000 population. Ambient air pollution results from emissions from industrial activity, households, cars and trucks.

Mortality rate attributed to unsafe water, sanitation and hygiene services: Deaths attributable to unsafe water, sanitation and hygiene focusing on inadequate wash services, expressed per 100,000 population.

Red List Index: Measure of the aggregate extinction risk across groups of species. It is based on genuine changes in the number of species in each category of extinction risk on the International Union for Conservation of Nature Red List of Threatened Species. It ranges from 0, all species categorized as extinct, to 1, all species categorized as least concern.

MAIN DATA SOURCES

Columns 1–5: World Bank (2018a).

Column 6: HDRO calculations based on data on forest area from World Bank (2018a).

Column 7: FAO (2018b).

Columns 8 and 9: WHO (2018).

Column 10: United Nations Statistics Division (2018a).

DASHBOARD 5

Socioeconomic sustainability

Country groupings (terciles)

Top third | Middle third | Bottom third

Three-colour coding is used to visualize partial grouping of countries by indicator. For each indicator countries are divided into three groups of approximately equal size (terciles): the top third, the middle third and the bottom third. Aggregates are colour coded using the same tercile cutoffs. See Notes after the table.

	Economic sustainability						Social sustainability				
	SDG 17.4					SDG 9.5	Education and health expenditure versus military expenditure		SDG 10.1	SDG 5	SDG 10.1
	Adjusted net savings	Total debt service	Gross capital formation	Skilled labour force	Concentration index (exports)	Research and development expenditure	Military expenditure[a]	Ratio of education and health expenditure to military expenditure[b]	Overall loss in HDI value due to inequality	Gender Inequality Index	Income quintile ratio
	(% of GNI)	(% of exports of goods, services and primary income)	(% of GDP)	(% of labour force)	(value)	(% of GDP)	(% of GDP)		Average annual change[c] (%)		
HDI rank	2006–2016[d]	2006–2016[d]	2011–2017[d]	2011–2017[d]	2016	2005–2015[d]	2010–2017[d]	2010–2015[e]	2010/2017[f]	2005/2017[f]	2005/2017[f]
VERY HIGH HUMAN DEVELOPMENT											
1 Norway	15.8	..	28.8	82.4	0.315	1.9	1.7	11.6	3.0	−3.6	−0.7
2 Switzerland	16.4	..	23.3	85.7	0.288	3.0	0.7	25.6	1.5	−3.9	..
3 Australia	5.3	..	24.2	78.3	0.244	2.2	2.0	8.0	0.6	−1.8	0.4
4 Ireland	20.6	..	24.3	82.8	0.242	1.5	0.3	32.0	−0.3	−3.6	−0.6
5 Germany	13.6	..	19.8	86.5	0.106	2.9	1.2	13.5	0.1	−3.2	1.0
6 Iceland	21.8	..	22.2	73.4	0.441	2.2	0.0	..	−1.3	−4.2	−1.2
7 Hong Kong, China (SAR)	..	..	22.3	76.9	0.268	0.8	..	..	..	..	..
7 Sweden	20.2	..	25.7	84.9	0.091	3.3	1.0	16.5	1.2	−1.4	1.1
9 Singapore	32.7	..	27.6	81.7	0.240	2.2	3.2	2.2	..	−5.0	..
10 Netherlands	16.5	..	20.2	77.4	0.072	2.0	1.2	14.0	−0.3	−3.9	0.0
11 Denmark	18.3	..	21.0	76.6	0.097	3.0	1.2	15.6	2.4	−3.2	1.1
12 Canada	5.3	..	23.7	90.8	0.138	1.6	1.3	..	−1.1	−2.5	0.5
13 United States	6.1	..	19.7	96.3	0.100	2.8	3.1	6.2	3.0	−2.4	0.5
14 United Kingdom	3.3	..	17.0	83.2	0.108	1.7	1.8	8.3	−0.5	−3.6	−0.9
15 Finland	7.8	..	22.8	88.3	0.143	2.9	1.4	11.4	−3.6	−2.9	0.0
16 New Zealand	12.0	..	24.4	82.8	0.162	1.2	1.1	14.3	..	−2.3	..
17 Belgium	9.5	..	24.6	83.3	0.095	2.5	0.9	17.4	0.5	−4.5	−0.3
17 Liechtenstein	..	..	..	..	..	..	..	..	..	..	..
19 Japan	6.0	..	23.6	99.9	0.141	3.3	0.9	14.9	..	−2.4	..
20 Austria	12.7	..	25.1	86.1	0.062	3.1	0.7	21.0	1.0	−3.3	1.3
21 Luxembourg	18.8	..	17.3	65.4	0.102	1.3	0.5	24.4	2.1	−4.8	0.3
22 Israel	15.9	..	20.5	88.6	0.255	4.3	4.7	2.2	0.3	−3.6	0.3
22 Korea (Republic of)	19.0	..	31.1	84.6	0.144	4.2	2.6	4.7	−2.0	−3.4	..
24 France	7.1	..	23.5	82.6	0.098	2.2	2.3	7.5	1.6	−3.9	1.4
25 Slovenia	7.9	..	19.3	90.6	0.106	2.2	1.0	14.2	−2.6	−5.1	0.4
26 Spain	7.9	..	21.2	62.9	0.107	1.2	1.2	10.7	8.2	−2.6	2.6
27 Czechia	4.6	..	26.3	95.2	0.124	1.9	1.0	12.0	−1.7	−1.6	−0.6
28 Italy	5.1	..	17.3	67.5	0.052	1.3	1.5	8.9	0.3	−4.2	1.0
29 Malta	..	..	23.1	60.6	0.336	0.8	0.5	33.2	..	−2.4	..
30 Estonia	12.6	..	25.4	89.2	0.110	1.5	2.1	6.0	−1.4	−3.6	−0.3
31 Greece	−8.6	..	11.7	76.7	0.234	1.0	2.6	..	4.6	−2.8	1.6
32 Cyprus	2.2	..	20.4	84.2	0.234	0.5	1.8	8.4	−0.1	−3.3	1.9
33 Poland	10.5	..	20.0	94.5	0.067	1.0	1.9	5.9	−2.3	−1.6	−1.1
34 United Arab Emirates	..	..	24.8	53.5	0.227	0.9	5.6	..	..	−5.1	..
35 Andorra	..	..	..	..	0.199	..	..	..	..	..	..
35 Lithuania	17.5	..	17.5	95.7	0.112	1.0	1.7	12.1	0.3	−2.8	0.8
37 Qatar	25.8	..	45.2	44.0	0.400	0.5	1.5	..	..	..	..
38 Slovakia	5.1	..	22.4	93.7	0.195	1.2	1.2	10.2	0.2	−0.4	−0.6
39 Brunei Darussalam	34.1	..	34.8	79.1	0.629	..	2.9	1.8	..	..	..
39 Saudi Arabia	12.2	..	28.2	60.5	0.593	0.8	10.2	..	..	−5.4	..
41 Latvia	1.9	..	21.5	91.2	0.093	0.6	1.7	13.9	−0.8	−0.8	−2.2
41 Portugal	2.4	..	16.3	52.0	0.071	1.3	1.7	7.9	2.0	−4.3	−0.7
43 Bahrain	8.0	..	29.6	..	0.320	0.1	4.0	1.7	..	−2.6	..
44 Chile	5.1	..	22.1	69.2	0.306	0.4	1.9	6.8	−2.5	−1.5	−1.9
45 Hungary	9.7	95.5	22.5	87.2	0.123	1.4	1.0	13.6	−1.2	0.0	−1.6
46 Croatia	9.0	..	20.5	90.5	0.066	0.9	1.4	7.2	−5.9	−2.0	..
47 Argentina	5.9	34.9	19.1	63.4	0.195	0.6	0.9	15.0	−3.9	−0.3	−3.1
48 Oman	−6.0	..	36.4	..	0.506	0.2	12.0	0.5	..	−2.7	..
49 Russian Federation	6.7	19.2	23.9	96.1	0.305	1.1	4.2	2.5	−2.5	−2.4	−1.8

DASHBOARD 5 Socioeconomic sustainability | 101

DASHBOARD 5 SOCIOECONOMIC SUSTAINABILITY

		Economic sustainability					Social sustainability				
		SDG 17.4				SDG 9.5			SDG 10.1	SDG 5	SDG 10.1
								Education and health expenditure versus military expenditure			
		Adjusted net savings	Total debt service	Gross capital formation	Skilled labour force	Concentration index (exports)	Research and development expenditure	Military expenditure[a]	Ratio of education and health expenditure to military expenditure[b]	Overall loss in HDI value due to inequality	Gender Inequality Index	Income quintile ratio
		(% of GNI)	(% of exports of goods, services and primary income)	(% of GDP)	(% of labour force)	(value)	(% of GDP)	(% of GDP)		Average annual change[c] (%)		
HDI rank		2006–2016[d]	2006–2016[d]	2011–2017[d]	2011–2017[d]	2016	2005–2015[d]	2010–2017[d]	2010–2015[e]	2010/2017[f]	2005/2017[f]	2005/2017[f]
50	Montenegro	..	24.0	29.3	90.1	0.212	0.4	1.6	..	–1.4	..	0.3
51	Bulgaria	12.5	23.6	20.9	87.6	0.085	1.0	1.5	7.4	1.8	–1.1	..
52	Romania	4.8	23.3	24.4	80.0	0.112	0.5	1.9	6.1	–0.5	–1.1	–0.5
53	Belarus	14.1	19.4	26.3	98.6	0.168	0.5	1.2	8.5	–4.3	..	–0.6
54	Bahamas	10.0	..	27.0	73.0	0.510	..	..	..	..	–0.4	..
55	Uruguay	10.3	..	15.7	25.6	0.228	0.3	2.1	..	–1.6	–2.3	..
56	Kuwait	4.5	..	27.0	39.8	0.627	0.3	5.7	..	..	–2.3	..
57	Malaysia	11.7	4.9	25.5	67.3	0.174	1.3	1.1	5.9	..	–1.0	0.2
58	Barbados	–9.8	..	17.8	..	0.171	..	..	..	..	–1.5	..
58	Kazakhstan	–2.3	44.3	27.8	75.1	0.506	0.2	0.8	6.0	–5.9	–3.8	–4.8
HIGH HUMAN DEVELOPMENT												
60	Iran (Islamic Republic of)	..	2.7	34.3	..	0.560	0.3	3.2	3.9	..	–0.8	–2.1
60	Palau	..	..	25.2	..	0.717	..	..	..	..	..	..
62	Seychelles	..	5.7	35.3	94.3	0.512	0.3	1.5	..	..	..	..
63	Costa Rica	15.5	14.8	18.0	40.2	0.258	0.6	0.0	..	–1.8	–1.1	0.2
64	Turkey	11.8	39.3	30.9	44.0	0.078	1.0	2.1	4.6	–4.9	–3.6	–0.8
65	Mauritius	–9.2	18.2	16.9	61.9	0.203	0.2	0.2	57.9	..	0.1	..
66	Panama	29.2	21.8	43.8	52.5	0.151	0.1	0.0	..	–3.6	–0.2	–2.0
67	Serbia	–3.8	30.0	21.0	60.3	0.087	0.9	1.8	6.9	5.9	..	–3.1
68	Albania	6.9	15.2	25.2	55.9	0.232	0.2	1.3	8.8	–3.0	–2.3	–0.8
69	Trinidad and Tobago	–4.9	..	..	71.8	0.317	0.1	0.9	..	..	–0.7	..
70	Antigua and Barbuda	..	..	..	..	0.558	..	..	..	..	..	..
70	Georgia	8.2	37.6	31.9	94.4	0.198	0.3	2.2	3.3	–3.7	–0.8	–0.8
72	Saint Kitts and Nevis	..	..	..	..	0.289	..	..	..	..	..	..
73	Cuba	..	..	9.4	69.8	0.249	0.4	3.1	..	..	–1.0	..
74	Mexico	12.5	19.4	23.2	40.0	0.123	0.6	0.5	16.7	0.2	–1.7	–2.6
75	Grenada	..	5.7	..	..	0.186	..	..	..	..	..	..
76	Sri Lanka	23.0	17.9	36.5	36.0	0.201	0.1	2.1	2.0	–2.7	–1.6	–0.4
77	Bosnia and Herzegovina	..	41.4	20.5	84.1	0.104	0.2	0.9	..	–3.4	..	–0.6
78	Venezuela (Bolivarian Republic of)	7.4	59.5	24.8	55.8	0.612	..	1.2	..	–3.2	–0.4	–5.1
79	Brazil	5.6	51.2	15.5	62.0	0.126	1.2	1.4	10.8	–1.7	–1.1	–2.3
80	Azerbaijan	1.7	8.1	24.2	93.0	0.677	0.2	3.8	1.8	–3.9	0.0	0.0
80	Lebanon	–10.7	20.9	21.8	42.4	0.113	..	4.7	2.4	..	..	..
80	The former Yugoslav Republic of Macedonia	13.0	15.9	31.6	80.5	0.218	0.4	1.0	..	–3.5	..	..
83	Armenia	0.0	34.1	19.0	94.6	0.269	0.3	3.9	3.1	–1.2	–2.9	–0.7
83	Thailand	16.4	5.0	21.7	37.4	0.073	0.6	1.4	5.4	–3.7	1.1	–1.7
85	Algeria	19.3	1.0	47.8	59.2	0.489	0.1	5.9	..	..	–1.8	..
86	China	22.4	5.3	43.6	..	0.105	2.1	1.9	..	–5.3	–2.8	..
86	Ecuador	13.1	26.8	25.4	46.6	0.348	0.4	2.4	5.2	–0.3	–1.2	–3.7
88	Ukraine	2.8	29.3	20.8	98.1	0.144	0.6	3.2	4.0	–2.8	–2.0	–1.8
89	Peru	7.9	15.1	20.9	83.6	0.281	0.1	1.0	5.3	–5.3	–1.5	–3.0
90	Colombia	6.4	28.9	23.4	58.2	0.281	0.2	3.1	3.4	–2.5	–1.8	–1.1
90	Saint Lucia	–1.9	4.2	..	..	0.501	..	..	..	..	..	..
92	Fiji	4.8	5.7	20.0	63.2	0.205	..	0.9	5.3	..	–1.2	–1.3
92	Mongolia	5.4	28.5	36.2	80.0	0.401	0.2	0.7	9.3	–1.4	–2.2	–0.5
94	Dominican Republic	17.1	20.9	21.8	50.2	0.217	..	0.7	..	–2.2	–0.3	–2.0
95	Jordan	14.3	17.2	20.6	..	0.164	0.4	4.8	..	–2.3	–1.5	–1.6
95	Tunisia	–8.6	10.7	19.7	58.4	0.134	0.6	2.1	5.9	–1.8	–1.0	–0.8
97	Jamaica	15.6	40.4	21.8	..	0.441	..	0.9	13.0	0.3	–1.1	..
98	Tonga	13.5	16.2	33.4	..	0.320	..	..	..	..	–1.2	–0.6
99	Saint Vincent and the Grenadines	..	10.9	..	..	0.373	..	..	..	..	..	..
100	Suriname	30.3	..	56.5	44.6	0.489	..	..	..	–1.0	–0.8	..
101	Botswana	29.9	1.9	24.3	..	0.876	0.5	3.1	..	..	–1.5	–2.1
101	Maldives	..	3.7	..	32.3	0.769	..	..	..	7.1	–1.5	–0.2
103	Dominica	..	9.1	..	..	0.412	..	..	..	..	..	..
104	Samoa	..	8.7	..	84.6	0.323	..	..	..	..	–1.7	..

HUMAN DEVELOPMENT INDICES AND INDICATORS: 2018 STATISTICAL UPDATE

DASHBOARD 5 Socioeconomic sustainability

		Economic sustainability (SDG 17.4)			(SDG 9.5)		Social sustainability		Education and health expenditure versus military expenditure		(SDG 10.1)	(SDG 5)	(SDG 10.1)
HDI rank		Adjusted net savings (% of GNI)	Total debt service (% of exports of goods, services and primary income)	Gross capital formation (% of GDP)	Skilled labour force (% of labour force)	Concentration index (exports) (value)	Research and development expenditure (% of GDP)	Military expenditure[a] (% of GDP)	Ratio of education and health expenditure to military expenditure[b]	Overall loss in HDI value due to inequality	Gender Inequality Index	Income quintile ratio
										Average annual change[c] (%)		
		2006–2016[d]	2006–2016[d]	2011–2017[d]	2011–2017[d]	2016	2005–2015[d]	2010–2017[d]	2010–2015[e]	2010/2017[f]	2005/2017[f]	2005/2017[f]
105	Uzbekistan	..	..	24.9	..	0.386	0.2	..	..	..	..	..
106	Belize	0.8	10.1	19.0	39.8	0.356	..	1.2	11.7	−3.2	−1.4	..
106	Marshall Islands	..	..	16.0	..	0.630	..	..	..	..	..	..
108	Libya	41.5	..	29.8	..	0.542	..	9.1	..	..	−3.1	..
108	Turkmenistan	..	..	47.2	..	0.722	..	..	..	−4.3	..	..
110	Gabon	..	..	32.4	..	0.761	..	2.1	4.5	0.9	−0.8	0.0
110	Paraguay	7.7	11.0	19.5	43.8	0.336	0.1	1.2	9.6	0.5	−1.1	−1.7
112	Moldova (Republic of)	13.8	13.0	23.3	60.7	0.165	0.4	0.4	51.4	−3.3	−1.9	−3.8
MEDIUM HUMAN DEVELOPMENT												
113	Philippines	28.4	12.6	25.0	30.6	0.287	0.1	1.4	..	−0.8	−0.7	−0.6
113	South Africa	−0.1	13.2	18.6	47.2	0.121	0.7	1.0	12.6	1.0	−0.7	0.4
115	Egypt	2.3	18.9	15.3	58.1	0.154	0.7	1.4	..	0.9	−1.9	−0.1
116	Indonesia	16.0	39.6	33.5	40.8	0.128	0.1	0.8	7.8	0.9	−1.3	..
116	Viet Nam	18.4	3.9	25.8	32.8	0.173	0.4	2.3	5.5	0.8	−0.3	−0.3
118	Bolivia (Plurinational State of)	..	9.3	22.2	45.2	0.324	0.2	1.8	6.9	−4.6	−1.6	−5.4
119	Palestine, State of	..	..	22.8	47.6	0.185	0.5	..	..	..	..	−0.4
120	Iraq	−13.0	..	17.4	28.4	0.937	0.0	3.8	..	..	..	..
121	El Salvador	4.1	19.9	16.9	38.5	0.221	0.1	1.0	9.7	−2.8	−1.6	−4.0
122	Kyrgyzstan	−1.0	18.6	32.2	92.1	0.316	0.1	2.9	4.1	−5.0	−3.5	−2.2
123	Morocco	21.0	10.9	33.2	20.3	0.175	0.7	3.2	..	..	−1.5	0.0
124	Nicaragua	15.1	16.0	29.0	27.7	0.219	0.1	0.6	..	−1.0	−1.3	−0.9
125	Cabo Verde	8.6	5.8	37.3	47.7	0.325	0.1	0.5	18.2	..	..	−2.1
125	Guyana	18.0	5.3	30.1	..	0.491	..	1.6	6.8	0.0	−0.5	..
127	Guatemala	2.3	22.3	12.1	19.0	0.133	0.0	0.4	21.9	−2.3	−1.1	−2.7
127	Tajikistan	−6.5	28.1	31.1	80.2	0.349	0.1	1.2	9.9	−4.1	−0.9	0.4
129	Namibia	2.7	..	17.7	31.4	0.275	0.3	3.3	..	−3.1	−0.9	−1.1
130	India	15.5	17.3	30.8	18.5	0.120	0.6	2.5	3.1	−1.4	−1.3	..
131	Micronesia (Federated States of)	..	..	..	..	0.835	..	..	..	..	..	−0.3
132	Timor-Leste	21.2	..	16.2	38.8	0.579	..	0.9	..	−2.4	..	−2.9
133	Honduras	18.5	15.4	23.8	27.9	0.212	..	1.6	9.1	−2.3	−0.9	−4.4
134	Bhutan	23.6	11.6	47.2	21.1	0.372	..	..	..	..	..	−2.7
134	Kiribati	..	..	..	..	0.892	..	..	..	..	..	..
136	Bangladesh	26.0	4.7	30.5	27.2	0.406	..	1.5	3.5	−2.6	−1.2	0.0
137	Congo	−22.6	1.8	26.6	..	0.669	..	5.6	..	−4.1	−0.6	1.6
138	Vanuatu	22.9	1.8	26.4	..	0.532	..	..	..	..	..	..
139	Lao People's Democratic Republic	−1.0	12.9	29.0	33.2	0.204	..	0.2	31.1	0.7	−1.3	1.9
140	Ghana	−14.8	10.5	16.1	24.8	0.428	0.4	0.4	17.2	2.0	−0.5	−0.4
141	Equatorial Guinea	..	..	12.1	..	0.681	..	0.2	..	..	..	..
142	Kenya	0.8	10.6	19.3	..	0.196	0.8	1.3	8.0	−2.4	−1.3	0.0
143	Sao Tome and Principe	..	2.9	..	..	0.593	..	..	..	..	..	−0.7
144	Eswatini (Kingdom of)	12.3	2.1	12.4	15.8	0.229	..	2.0	7.7	−2.4	−0.6	0.7
144	Zambia	10.9	8.6	38.2	..	0.664	0.3	1.3	..	1.2	−1.3	2.3
146	Cambodia	6.2	6.0	22.9	9.7	0.286	0.1	2.1	4.9	−4.7	−1.3	..
147	Angola	−38.4	26.5	7.8	11.2	0.934	..	2.5	..	−2.7	..	..
148	Myanmar	23.9	0.8	32.9	17.7	0.289	..	2.5	..	..	..	..
149	Nepal	32.5	8.9	42.5	24.7	0.147	0.3	1.6	6.3	−2.8	−2.2	−3.3
150	Pakistan	14.7	15.4	16.1	28.3	0.214	0.2	3.5	1.5	−0.2	−0.8	−0.6
151	Cameroon	2.3	6.3	21.6	21.1	0.407	..	1.2	6.3	0.1	−1.1	4.1
LOW HUMAN DEVELOPMENT												
152	Solomon Islands	−6.4	3.9	14.6	..	0.713	..	..	..	..	..	−3.5
153	Papua New Guinea	..	49.1	..	27.2	0.286	..	0.3	..	..	0.7	..
154	Tanzania (United Republic of)	13.3	5.4	24.8	5.1	0.322	0.5	1.1	9.4	−1.8	−0.8	−0.5
155	Syrian Arab Republic	..	3.1	27.8	..	0.165	..	4.1	..	..	0.1	..
156	Zimbabwe	−20.7	13.4	16.9	13.4	0.366	..	1.9	7.1	..	−0.8	..
157	Nigeria	3.3	6.3	15.3	..	0.734	0.2	0.4	..	−2.4	..	1.1
158	Rwanda	−6.7	8.3	23.4	6.8	0.327	..	1.2	11.9	−2.7	−1.8	−1.3

DASHBOARD 5

DASHBOARD 5 SOCIOECONOMIC SUSTAINABILITY

		SDG 17.4				SDG 9.5		SDG 10.1	SDG 5	SDG 10.1
		Economic sustainability						Social sustainability		
							Education and health expenditure versus military expenditure			
		Adjusted net savings	Total debt service	Gross capital formation	Skilled labour force	Concentration index (exports)	Research and development expenditure	Military expenditure[a]	Ratio of education and health expenditure to military expenditure[b]	Overall loss in HDI value due to inequality	Gender Inequality Index	Income quintile ratio
		(% of GNI)	(% of exports of goods, services and primary income)	(% of GDP)	(% of labour force)	(value)	(% of GDP)	(% of GDP)		Average annual change[c] (%)		
HDI rank		2006–2016[d]	2006–2016[d]	2011–2017[d]	2011–2017[d]	2016	2005–2015[d]	2010–2017[d]	2010–2015[e]	2010/2017[f]	2005/2017[f]	2005/2017[f]
159	Lesotho	6.5	4.2	28.3	31.2	0.278	0.1	2.0	..	−1.3	−0.6	1.1
159	Mauritania	−12.7	13.2	56.8	6.0	0.360	..	2.9	2.6	−0.9	..	−2.4
161	Madagascar	6.5	3.7	15.2	38.4	0.300	0.0	0.6	9.0	−1.6	..	2.0
162	Uganda	−10.8	18.8	24.0	..	0.170	0.5	1.8	5.4	−1.7	−1.1	−0.7
163	Benin	3.8	3.5	28.6	17.9	0.312	..	1.3	7.6	0.6	−0.6	13.3
164	Senegal	8.0	10.5	28.5	11.8	0.215	0.5	1.9	7.0	−1.4	−1.5	0.4
165	Comoros	2.1	0.6	20.9	..	0.683	..	..	..	0.5	..	−2.5
165	Togo	−31.0	3.2	26.4	7.2	0.204	0.3	1.9	6.9	−0.5	−0.9	..
167	Sudan	−5.2	6.4	18.9	..	0.648	0.3	3.5	..	..	−1.3	..
168	Afghanistan	−28.5	3.5	17.7	..	0.319	..	0.9	13.6	..	−1.0	..
168	Haiti	22.2	5.2	43.4	..	0.509	..	0.0	..	−0.6	0.3	..
170	Côte d'Ivoire	25.9	6.4	22.6	8.8	0.376	..	1.2	6.0	0.3	−0.3	0.5
171	Malawi	−19.1	5.0	13.4	11.7	0.415	..	0.8	23.4	−0.8	−0.4	3.3
172	Djibouti	..	7.1	50.4	..	0.224	..	3.6	..	−0.6	..	2.9
173	Ethiopia	4.0	21.0	39.0	7.3	0.302	0.6	0.7	10.6	−2.5	−1.5	6.3
174	Gambia	−16.9	15.2	19.2	12.9	0.353	0.1	1.5	7.7	−0.7	−0.4	−4.2
175	Guinea	..	2.6	43.1	..	0.448	..	1.6	3.0	−1.9	..	−3.3
176	Congo (Democratic Republic of the)	−12.4	4.3	20.8	44.4	0.509	0.1	0.8	5.1	−2.3	−0.2	0.3
177	Guinea-Bissau	−18.7	0.7	10.5	..	0.876	..	1.6	3.3	−1.0	..	10.0
178	Yemen	−10.0	18.8	1.7	30.9	0.349	..	4.0	..	−1.0	0.2	1.1
179	Eritrea	..	..	10.0	..	0.402	..	..	..	..	..	..
180	Mozambique	−15.8	12.6	35.6	8.0	0.270	0.3	0.8	11.3	−4.0	−1.0	3.9
181	Liberia	−39.3	2.9	20.1	19.8	0.331	..	0.6	13.8	−2.2	−0.3	..
182	Mali	−5.0	4.2	19.9	5.2	0.737	0.6	3.0	4.1	−1.6	−0.5	−2.7
183	Burkina Faso	−8.4	4.4	25.5	4.0	0.750	0.2	1.5	6.8	−1.6	−0.4	−3.4
184	Sierra Leone	−29.5	6.6	20.1	16.3	0.658	..	0.8	23.0	−1.0	−0.3	−2.4
185	Burundi	−28.9	16.7	16.9	..	0.445	0.1	1.8	6.1	−1.4	−0.9	..
186	Chad	..	..	21.4	..	0.738	..	2.1	1.4	−0.4	..	3.2
187	South Sudan	..	..	17.3	..	..	..	4.6	0.4	..	..	..
188	Central African Republic	..	..	17.7	..	0.460	..	1.4	..	0.0	−0.2	8.6
189	Niger	2.6	6.3	33.7	1.9	0.297	..	2.5	7.1	−2.0	−0.6	−3.5
OTHER COUNTRIES OR TERRITORIES												
..	Korea (Democratic People's Rep. of)	..	..	..	..	0.399	..	..	..	..	..	..
..	Monaco	..	..	..	..	..	0.0	..	..	..	..	..
..	Nauru	..	..	..	..	0.693	..	..	..	..	..	..
..	San Marino	..	..	..	..	..	..	..	..	..	..	..
..	Somalia	..	..	..	..	0.448	..	0.0	..	..	..	..
..	Tuvalu	..	..	..	..	0.536	..	..	..	..	..	..
Human development groups												
	Very high human development	8.1	..	21.5	86.1	—	2.4	2.4	7.4	−0.5	−2.4	—
	High human development	18.0	13.1	36.1	..	—	1.6	1.8	..	−4.2	−1.5	—
	Medium human development	13.0	16.7	27.2	25.8	—	0.4	2.0	4.3	−1.2	−1.2	—
	Low human development	0.1	9.8	21.1	..	—	..	1.3	..	−1.9	−0.7	—
Developing countries		15.5	14.1	32.7	33.3	—	1.2	2.1	..	−2.3	−0.9	—
Regions												
	Arab States	8.4	12.5	27.5	47.6	—	0.6	6.0	..	−1.2	−1.1	—
	East Asia and the Pacific	21.6	7.2	41.0	..	—	..	1.8	..	−4.1	−0.8	—
	Europe and Central Asia	8.5	34.0	29.1	71.0	—	0.8	2.0	4.5	−3.9	−2.4	—
	Latin America and the Caribbean	8.0	29.6	19.8	55.0	—	0.7	1.2	..	−2.0	−1.2	—
	South Asia	16.3	16.2	30.1	20.7	—	0.5	2.6	3.1	−1.7	−0.7	—
	Sub-Saharan Africa	−2.2	11.3	19.8	..	—	0.5	1.1	8.8	−1.8	−0.7	—
Least developed countries		3.3	9.6	25.7	19.7	—	..	1.8	5.2	−2.1	−0.9	—
Small island developing states		..	21.5	19.1	..	—	..	..	..	−2.4	..	—
Organisation for Economic Co-operation and Development		8.0	..	21.3	81.0	—	2.5	2.1	7.8	−0.6	−2.4	—
World		10.7	16.2	25.5	47.9	—	2.0	2.2	7.2	−2.1	−0.9	—

NOTES

Three-colour coding is used to visualize partial grouping of countries and aggregates by indicator. For each indicator countries are divided into three groups of approximately equal size (terciles): the top third, the middle third and the bottom third. Aggregates are colour coded using the same tercile cutoffs. See *Technical note 6* at http://hdr.undp.org/sites/default/files/hdr2018_technical_notes.pdf for details about partial grouping in this table.

a This column is intentionally left without colour because it is meant to provide context for the indicator on education and health expenditure.

b Data on government expenditure on education and health are available in tables 8 and 9 and at http://hdr.undp.org/en/data.

c A negative value indicates that inequality declined over the period specified.

d Data refer to the most recent year available during the period specified.

e Data refer to the most recent year for which all three types of expenditure (education, health and military) are available during the period specified.

f The trend data used to calculate the change are available at http://hdr.undp.org/en/data.

DEFINITIONS

Adjusted net savings: Net national savings plus education expenditure and minus energy depletion, mineral depletion, net forest depletion, and carbon dioxide and particulate emissions damage. Net national savings are equal to gross national savings less the value of consumption of fixed capital.

Total debt service: Sum of principal repayments and interest actually paid in currency, goods or services on long-term debt; interest paid on short-term debt; and repayments (repurchases and charges) to the International Monetary Fund. It is expressed as a percentage of exports of goods, services and primary income.

Gross capital formation: Outlays on additions to the fixed assets of the economy plus net changes in inventories. Fixed assets include land improvements (such as fences, ditches and drains); plant, machinery and equipment purchases; and construction of roads, railways and the like, including schools, offices, hospitals, private residential dwellings and commercial and industrial buildings. Inventories are stocks of goods held by firms to meet temporary or unexpected fluctuations in production or sales as well as goods that are work in progress. Net acquisitions of valuables are also considered capital formation. Gross capital formation was formerly known as gross domestic investment.

Skilled labour force: Percentage of the labour force ages 15 and older with intermediate or advanced education, as classified by the International Standard Classification of Education.

Concentration index (exports): A measure of the degree of product concentration in exports from a country (also referred to as the Herfindahl-Hirschmann Index). A value closer to 0 indicates that a country's exports are more homogeneously distributed among a series of products (reflecting a well diversified economy); a value closer to 1 indicates that a country's exports are highly concentrated among a few products.

Research and development expenditure: Current and capital expenditures (both public and private) on creative work undertaken systematically to increase knowledge, including knowledge of humanity, culture and society, and the use of knowledge for new applications. Research and development covers basic research, applied research and experimental development.

Military expenditures: All current and capital expenditures on the armed forces, including peacekeeping forces; defence ministries and other government agencies engaged in defence projects; paramilitary forces, if these are judged to be trained and equipped for military operations; and military space activities.

Ratio of education and health expenditure to military expenditure: Sum of government expenditure on education and health divided by military expenditure.

Overall loss in HDI value due to inequality, average annual change: Percentage change in overall loss in Human Development Index (HDI) value due to inequality over 2010–2017, divided by the respective number of years.

Gender Inequality Index, average annual change: Percentage change in Gender Inequality Index value over 2005–2017, divided by the respective number of years.

Income quintile ratio, average annual change: Percentage change in the ratio of the average income of the richest 20 percent of the population to the average income of the poorest 20 percent of the population over 2005–2017, divided by the respective number of years.

MAIN DATA SOURCES

Columns 1–3, 6 and 7: World Bank (2018a).

Column 4: ILO (2018a).

Column 5: UNCTAD (2018).

Columns 8 and 11: HDRO calculations based on data from World Bank (2018a).

Column 9: HDRO calculations based on the Inequality-adjusted HDI time series.

Column 10: HDRO calculations based on the Gender Inequality Index time series.

Developing regions

Arab States (20 countries or territories)
Algeria, Bahrain, Djibouti, Egypt, Iraq, Jordan, Kuwait, Lebanon, Libya, Morocco, Oman, State of Palestine, Qatar, Saudi Arabia, Somalia, Sudan, Syrian Arab Republic, Tunisia, United Arab Emirates, Yemen

East Asia and the Pacific (24 countries)
Cambodia, China, Fiji, Indonesia, Kiribati, Democratic People's Republic of Korea, Lao People's Democratic Republic, Malaysia, Marshall Islands, Federated States of Micronesia, Mongolia, Myanmar, Nauru, Palau, Papua New Guinea, Philippines, Samoa, Solomon Islands, Thailand, Timor-Leste, Tonga, Tuvalu, Vanuatu, Viet Nam

Europe and Central Asia (17 countries)
Albania, Armenia, Azerbaijan, Belarus, Bosnia and Herzegovina, Georgia, Kazakhstan, Kyrgyzstan, Republic of Moldova, Montenegro, Serbia, Tajikistan, The former Yugoslav Republic of Macedonia, Turkey, Turkmenistan, Ukraine, Uzbekistan

Latin America and the Caribbean (33 countries)
Antigua and Barbuda, Argentina, Bahamas, Barbados, Belize, Plurinational State of Bolivia, Brazil, Chile, Colombia, Costa Rica, Cuba, Dominica, Dominican Republic, Ecuador, El Salvador, Grenada, Guatemala, Guyana, Haiti, Honduras, Jamaica, Mexico, Nicaragua, Panama, Paraguay, Peru, Saint Kitts and Nevis, Saint Lucia, Saint Vincent and the Grenadines, Suriname, Trinidad and Tobago, Uruguay, Bolivarian Republic of Venezuela

South Asia (9 countries)
Afghanistan, Bangladesh, Bhutan, India, Islamic Republic of Iran, Maldives, Nepal, Pakistan, Sri Lanka

Sub-Saharan Africa (46 countries)
Angola, Benin, Botswana, Burkina Faso, Burundi, Cabo Verde, Cameroon, Central African Republic, Chad, Comoros, Congo, Democratic Republic of the Congo, Côte d'Ivoire, Equatorial Guinea, Eritrea, Kingdom of Eswatini, Ethiopia, Gabon, Gambia, Ghana, Guinea, Guinea-Bissau, Kenya, Lesotho, Liberia, Madagascar, Malawi, Mali, Mauritania, Mauritius, Mozambique, Namibia, Niger, Nigeria, Rwanda, São Tomé and Príncipe, Senegal, Seychelles, Sierra Leone, South Africa, South Sudan, United Republic of Tanzania, Togo, Uganda, Zambia, Zimbabwe

Note: All countries listed in developing regions are included in aggregates for developing countries. Countries included in aggregates for Least Developed Countries and Small Island Developing States follow UN classifications, which are available at www.unohrlls.org. Countries included in aggregates for Organisation for Economic Co-operation and Development are listed at www.oecd.org/about/membersandpartners/list-oecd-member-countries.htm.

HUMAN DEVELOPMENT INDICES AND INDICATORS: 2018 STATISTICAL UPDATE

Index to Sustainable Development Goal indicators

Global Sustainable Development Goal and target	Indicator for measuring progress in human development	Indicator table
Goal 1. End poverty in all its forms everywhere		
1.1 By 2030, eradicate extreme poverty for all people everywhere, currently measured as people living on less than $1.25 a day	Population living below income poverty line, PPP $1.90 a day (%)	6
1.2 By 2030, reduce at least by half the proportion of men, women and children of all ages living in poverty in all its dimensions according to national definitions	Population living below income poverty line, national poverty line (%)	6
	Population in multidimensional poverty, headcount (%)	6
	Population in multidimensional poverty, headcount (thousands)	6
1.3 Implement nationally appropriate social protection systems and measures for all, including floors, and by 2030 achieve substantial coverage of the poor and the vulnerable	Old-age pension recipients (% of statutory pension age population)	11
	Old-age pension recipients (female to male ratio)	D2
	Mandatory paid maternity leave (days)	D3
1.5 By 2030, build the resilience of the poor and those in vulnerable situations and reduce their exposure and vulnerability to climate-related extreme events and other economic, social and environmental shocks and disasters	Internally displaced persons (thousands)[a]	12
	Refugees by country of origin (thousands)[a]	12
	Homeless people due to natural disaster (average annual per million people)[b]	12
1.a Ensure significant mobilization of resources from a variety of sources, including through enhanced development cooperation, in order to provide adequate and predictable means for developing countries, in particular least developed countries, to implement programmes and policies to end poverty in all its dimensions	Government expenditure on education (% of GDP)[c]	9
Goal 2. End hunger, achieve food security and improved nutrition and promote sustainable agriculture		
2.1 By 2030, end hunger and ensure access by all people, in particular the poor and people in vulnerable situations, including infants, to safe, nutritious and sufficient food all year round	Depth of food deficit (kilocalories per person per day)[d]	12
2.2 By 2030, end all forms of malnutrition, including achieving, by 2025, the internationally agreed targets on stunting and wasting in children under 5 years of age, and address the nutritional needs of adolescent girls, pregnant and lactating women and older persons	Child malnutrition, stunting (moderate or severe) (% under age 5)	8
Goal 3. Ensure healthy lives and promote well-being for all at all ages		
3. Ensure healthy lives and promote well-being for all at all ages	Life expectancy at birth (years)	1
	Life expectancy at birth, female (years)	4
	Life expectancy at birth, male (years)	4
	Mortality rate, female adult (per 1,000 people)[e]	8
	Mortality rate, male adult (per 1,000 people)[e]	8
3.1 By 2030, reduce the global maternal mortality ratio to less than 70 per 100,000 live births	Maternal mortality ratio (deaths per 100,000 live births)	5, D3
	Proportion of births attended by skilled health personnel (%)	D3
3.2 By 2030, end preventable deaths of newborns and children under 5 years of age, with all countries aiming to reduce neonatal mortality to at least as low as 12 per 1,000 live births and under-5 mortality to at least as low as 25 per 1,000 live births	Mortality rate, infant (per 1,000 live births)	8
	Mortality rate, under-five (per 1,000 live births)	8
3.3 By 2030, end the epidemics of AIDS, tuberculosis, malaria and neglected tropical diseases and combat hepatitis, water-borne diseases and other communicable diseases	Malaria incidence (per 1,000 people at risk)	8
	Tuberculosis incidence (per 100,000 people)	8
	HIV prevalence, adult (% ages 15–49)[f]	8
3.4 By 2030, reduce by one third premature mortality from non-communicable diseases through prevention and treatment and promote mental health and well-being	Suicide rate, female (per 100,000 people)	12
	Suicide rate, male (per 100,000 people)	12
3.7 By 2030, ensure universal access to sexual and reproductive health-care services, including for family planning, information and education, and the integration of reproductive health into national strategies and programmes	Adolescent birth rate (births per 1,000 women ages 15–19)	5, D3
	Contraceptive prevalence, any method (% of married or in-union women of reproductive age, 15–49 years)[g]	D3
3.9 By 2030, substantially reduce the number of deaths and illnesses from hazardous chemicals and air, water and soil pollution and contamination	Mortality rate attributed to household and ambient air pollution (per 100,000 population)	D4
	Mortality rate attributed to unsafe water, sanitation and hygiene services (per 100,000 population)	D4
3.b Support the research and development of vaccines and medicines for the communicable and non-communicable diseases that primarily affect developing countries, provide access to affordable essential medicines and vaccines, in accordance with the Doha Declaration on the TRIPS Agreement and Public Health, which affirms the right of developing countries to use to the full the provisions in the Agreement on Trade-Related Aspects of Intellectual Property Rights regarding flexibilities to protect public health, and, in particular, provide access to medicines for all	Infants lacking immunization, DPT (% of one-year-olds)	8
	Infants lacking immunization, measles (% of one-year-olds)	8
3.c Substantially increase health financing and the recruitment, development, training and retention of the health workforce in developing countries, especially in least developed countries and small island developing States	Current health expenditure (% of GDP)	8
Goal 4. Ensure inclusive and equitable quality education and promote lifelong learning opportunities for all		
4.1 By 2030, ensure that all girls and boys complete free, equitable and quality primary and secondary education leading to relevant and effective learning outcomes	Gross enrolment ratio, primary (% of primary school–age population)	9
	Gross enrolment ratio, secondary (% of secondary school–age population)	9
	Programme for International Student Assessment (PISA) score in mathematics	D1
	Programme for International Student Assessment (PISA) score in reading	D1
	Programme for International Student Assessment (PISA) score in science	D1
	Gross enrolment ratio, primary (female to male ratio)	D2
	Gross enrolment ratio, secondary (female to male ratio)	D2
4.2 By 2030, ensure that all girls and boys have access to quality early childhood development, care and pre-primary education so that they are ready for primary education	Gross enrolment ratio, pre-primary (% of preschool-age children)	9
	Gross enrolment ratio, pre-primary (female to male ratio)	D2
4.3 By 2030, ensure equal access for all women and men to affordable and quality technical, vocational and tertiary education, including university	Expected years of schooling (years)	1
	Expected years of schooling, female (years)[h]	4
	Expected years of schooling, male (years)[h]	4
	Gross enrolment ratio, tertiary (% of tertiary school–age population)[h]	9

Global Sustainable Development Goal and target	Indicator for measuring progress in human development	Indicator table
4.6 By 2030, ensure that all youth and a substantial proportion of adults, both men and women, achieve literacy and numeracy	Mean years of schooling (years)	1
	Mean years of schooling, female (years)[j]	4
	Mean years of schooling, male (years)[j]	4
	Population with at least some secondary education, female (% ages 25 and older)[j]	5
	Population with at least some secondary education, male (% ages 25 and older)[j]	5
	Literacy rate, adult (% ages 15 and older)[j]	9
	Literacy rate, youth, female (% ages 15–24)[j]	9
	Literacy rate, youth, male (% ages 15–24)[j]	9
	Population with at least some secondary education (% ages 25 and older)[j]	9
	Population with at least some secondary education (female to male ratio)[j]	D2
4.a Build and upgrade education facilities that are child, disability and gender sensitive and provide non-violent, inclusive and effective learning environments for all	Proportion of schools with access to the Internet (%)	D1
4.c By 2030, substantially increase the supply of qualified teachers, including through international cooperation for teacher training in developing countries, especially least developed countries and small island developing States	Primary school teachers trained to teach (%)	D1
Goal 5. Achieve gender equality and empower all women and girls		
5. Achieve gender equality and empower all women and girls	Gender Inequality Index, average annual change (%)	D5
5.2 Eliminate all forms of violence against all women and girls in the public and private spheres, including trafficking and sexual and other types of exploitation	Violence against women ever experienced, intimate partner (% of female population ages 15 and older)	D3
	Violence against women ever experienced, nonintimate partner (% of female population ages 15 and older)	D3
5.3 Eliminate all harmful practices, such as child, early and forced marriage and female genital mutilation	Child marriage, women married by age 18 (% of women ages 20–24 years who are married or in union)	D3
5.4 Recognize and value unpaid care and domestic work through the provision of public services, infrastructure and social protection policies and the promotion of shared responsibility within the household and the family as nationally appropriate	Time spent on unpaid domestic chores and care work, women ages 15 and older (% of 24-hour day)	D2
	Time spent on unpaid domestic chores and care work (female to male ratio)	D2
5.5 Ensure women's full and effective participation and equal opportunities for leadership at all levels of decision-making in political, economic and public life	Share of seats in parliament (% held by women)	5, D2
	Female share of employment in senior and middle management (%)	D3
5.6 Ensure universal access to sexual and reproductive health and reproductive rights as agreed in accordance with the Programme of Action of the International Conference on Population and Development and the Beijing Platform for Action and the outcome documents of their review conferences	Unmet need for family planning (% of married or in-union women of reproductive age, 15–49 years)	D3
	Contraceptive prevalence, any method (% of married or in-union women of reproductive age, 15–49 years)[g]	D3
Goal 6. Ensure availability and sustainable management of water and sanitation for all		
6.1 By 2030, achieve universal and equitable access to safe and affordable drinking water for all	Population using improved drinking-water sources (%)	D1
6.2 By 2030, achieve access to adequate and equitable sanitation and hygiene for all and end open defecation, paying special attention to the needs of women and girls and those in vulnerable situations	Population using improved sanitation facilities (%)	D1
6.4 By 2030, substantially increase water-use efficiency across all sectors and ensure sustainable withdrawals and supply of freshwater to address water scarcity and substantially reduce the number of people suffering from water scarcity	Fresh water withdrawals (% of total renewable water resources)	D4
Goal 7. Ensure access to affordable, reliable, sustainable and modern energy for all		
7.1 By 2030, ensure universal access to affordable, reliable and modern energy services	Rural population with access to electricity (%)	D1
7.2 By 2030, increase substantially the share of renewable energy in the global energy mix	Renewable energy consumption (% of total final energy consumption)	D4
Goal 8. Promote sustained, inclusive and sustainable economic growth, full and productive employment and decent work for all		
8.1 Sustain per capita economic growth in accordance with national circumstances and, in particular, at least 7 per cent gross domestic product growth per annum in the least developed countries	GDP per capita, annual growth (%)	10
8.3 Promote development-oriented policies that support productive activities, decent job creation, entrepreneurship, creativity and innovation, and encourage the formalization and growth of micro-, small- and medium-sized enterprises, including through access to financial services	Share of employment in nonagriculture, female (% of total employment in nonagriculture)[j]	D2
8.5 By 2030, achieve full and productive employment and decent work for all women and men, including for young people and persons with disabilities, and equal pay for work of equal value	Gross national income (GNI) per capita (2011 PPP $)	1
	Estimated gross national income per capita, female (2011 PPP $)[k]	4
	Estimated gross national income per capita, male (2011 PPP $)[k]	4
	Unemployment, total (% of labour force)	11
	Unemployment, youth (% ages 15–24)	11
	Youth unemployment rate (female to male ratio)	D2
	Total unemployment rate (female to male ratio)	D2
8.6 By 2020, substantially reduce the proportion of youth not in employment, education or training	Youth not in school or employment (% ages 15–24)	11
8.7 Take immediate and effective measures to eradicate forced labour, end modern slavery and human trafficking and secure the prohibition and elimination of the worst forms of child labour, including recruitment and use of child soldiers, and by 2025 end child labour in all its forms	Child labour (% ages 5–17)	11
8.9 By 2030, devise and implement policies to promote sustainable tourism that creates jobs and promotes local culture and products	International inbound tourists (thousands)[l]	13
Goal 9. Build resilient infrastructure, promote inclusive and sustainable industrialization and foster innovation		
9.2 Promote inclusive and sustainable industrialization and, by 2030, significantly raise industry's share of employment and gross domestic product, in line with national circumstances, and double its share in least developed countries	Employment in agriculture (% of total employment)[m]	11
	Employment in services (% of total employment)[m]	11
9.4 By 2030, upgrade infrastructure and retrofit industries to make them sustainable, with increased resource-use efficiency and greater adoption of clean and environmentally sound technologies and industrial processes, with all countries taking action in accordance with their respective capabilities	Carbon dioxide emissions, per capita (tonnes)[n]	D4
	Carbon dioxide emissions (kg per 2011 PPP $ of GDP)[n]	D4

HUMAN DEVELOPMENT INDICES AND INDICATORS: **2018 STATISTICAL UPDATE**

Global Sustainable Development Goal and target	Indicator for measuring progress in human development	Indicator table
9.5 Enhance scientific research, upgrade the technological capabilities of industrial sectors in all countries, in particular developing countries, including, by 2030, encouraging innovation and substantially increasing the number of research and development workers per 1 million people and public and private research and development spending	Research and development expenditure (% of GDP)	D5
9.c Significantly increase access to information and communications technology and strive to provide universal and affordable access to the Internet in least developed countries by 2020	Mobile phone subscriptions (per 100 people)	13
Goal 10. Reduce inequality within and among countries		
10.1 By 2030, progressively achieve and sustain income growth of the bottom 40 per cent of the population at a rate higher than the national average	Income quintile ratio, average annual change (%)[o]	D5
	Overall loss in HDI value due to inequality, average annual change (%)	D5
Goal 11. Make cities and human settlements inclusive, safe, resilient and sustainable		
11.5 By 2030, significantly reduce the number of deaths and the number of people affected and substantially decrease the direct economic losses relative to global gross domestic product caused by disasters, including water-related disasters, with a focus on protecting the poor and people in vulnerable situations	Internally displaced persons (thousands)[a]	12
	Refugees by country of origin (thousands)[a,p]	12
	Homeless people due to natural disaster (average annual per million people)[b]	12
Goal 12. Ensure sustainable consumption and production patterns		
12.c Rationalize inefficient fossil-fuel subsidies that encourage wasteful consumption by removing market distortions, in accordance with national circumstances, including by restructuring taxation and phasing out those harmful subsidies, where they exist, to reflect their environmental impacts, taking fully into account the specific needs and conditions of developing countries and minimizing the possible adverse impacts on their development in a manner that protects the poor and the affected communities	Fossil fuel energy consumption (% of total energy consumption)	D4
Goal 13. Take urgent action to combat climate change and its impacts		
13.1 Strengthen resilience and adaptive capacity to climate-related hazards and natural disasters in all countries	Homeless people due to natural disaster (average annual per million people)[b]	12
Goal 15. Protect, restore and promote sustainable use of terrestrial ecosystems, sustainably manage forests, combat desertification, and halt and reverse land degradation and halt biodiversity loss		
15.1 By 2020, ensure the conservation, restoration and sustainable use of terrestrial and inland freshwater ecosystems and their services, in particular forests, wetlands, mountains and drylands, in line with obligations under international agreements	Forest area (% of total land area)	D4
	Forest area, change (%)	D4
15.5 Take urgent and significant action to reduce the degradation of natural habitats, halt the loss of biodiversity and, by 2020, protect and prevent the extinction of threatened species	Red List Index (value)	D4
Goal 16. Promote peaceful and inclusive societies for sustainable development, provide access to justice for all and build effective, accountable and inclusive institutions at all levels		
16.1 Significantly reduce all forms of violence and related death rates everywhere	Homicide rate (per 100,000 people)	12
	Perceptions of individual well-being, feeling safe, female (% answering yes)	14
	Perceptions of individual well-being, feeling safe, male (% answering yes)	14
16.3 Promote the rule of law at the national and international levels and ensure equal access to justice for all	Prison population (per 100,000 people)[q]	12
16.9 By 2030, provide legal identity for all, including birth registration	Birth registration (% under age 5)	12
Goal 17. Strengthen the means of implementation and revitalize the Global Partnership for Sustainable Development		
Finance		
17.2 Strengthen domestic resource mobilization, including through international support to developing countries, to improve domestic capacity for tax and other revenue collection	Net official development assistance received (% of GNI)	13
17.3 Mobilize additional financial resources for developing countries from multiple sources	Foreign direct investment, net inflows (% of GDP)	13
	Remittances, inflows (% of GDP)	13
17.4 Assist developing countries in attaining long-term debt sustainability through coordinated policies aimed at fostering debt financing, debt relief and debt restructuring, as appropriate, and address the external debt of highly indebted poor countries to reduce debt distress	Total debt service (% of exports of goods, services and primary income)	D5
	Total debt service (% of GNI)	10
Technology		
17.6 Enhance North-South, South-South and triangular regional and international cooperation on and access to science, technology and innovation and enhance knowledge-sharing on mutually agreed terms, including through improved coordination among existing mechanisms, in particular at the United Nations level, and through a global technology facilitation mechanism	Internet users, total (% of population)[r]	13
17.8 Fully operationalize the technology bank and science, technology and innovation capacity-building mechanism for least developed countries by 2017 and enhance the use of enabling technology, in particular information and communications technology		

NOTES

a The same indicator is used for Sustainable Development Goals (SDGs) 1.5 and 11.5.

b The same indicator—number of deaths, missing persons and directly affected persons attributed to disasters per 100,000 population—is used for SDGs 1.5, 11.5 and 13.1.

c SDG indicator 1.a.2 is proportion of total government spending on essential services (education, health and social protection).

d SDG target 2.1 indicators are on prevalence of malnourishment. In addition, SDG target 2.1 includes ensuring safe, nutritious and sufficient food all year round, which is typically measured by depth of food deficit.

e SDG 3 has 13 targets and 27 indicators; mortality rates are considered summary indicators of overall health.

f SDG indicator 3.3.1 is number of new HIV infections per 1,000 uninfected population, by sex, age and key populations.

g The same indicator is used for SDGs 3.7 and 5.6.

h SDG indicator 4.3.1 is participation rate of youth and adults in formal and non-formal education and training in the previous 12 months, by sex.

i SDG indicator 4.6.1 is proportion of population in a given age group achieving at least a fixed level of proficiency in functional (a) literacy and (b) numeracy skills, by sex.

j SDG indicator 8.3.1 is proportion of informal employment in non-agriculture employment, by sex.

k SDG indicator 8.5.1 is average hourly earnings of female and male employees, by occupation, age and persons with disabilities.

l SDG indicator 8.9.1 is tourism direct GDP as a proportion of total GDP and in growth rate, and SDG indicator 8.9.2 is proportion of jobs in sustainable tourism industries out of total tourism jobs.

m SDG indicator 9.2.2—manufacturing employment as a proportion of total employment—is a complementary indicator.

n SDG indicator 9.4.1 is CO_2 emission per unit of value added.

o SDG indicator 10.1.1 is growth rates of household expenditure or income per capita among the bottom 40 per cent of the population and the total population.

p SDG indicator 11.5.1 is number of deaths, missing persons and directly affected persons attributed to disasters per 100,000 population.

q SDG indicator 16.3.2 is unsentenced detainees as a proportion of overall prison population.

r SDG indicator 17.6.2 is fixed Internet broadband subscriptions per 100 inhabitants, by speed. The same indicator is used for SDGs 17.6 and 17.8.

Statistical references

Barro, R. J., and J.-W. Lee. 2016. Dataset of Educational Attainment, February 2016 Revision. www.barrolee.com. Accessed 8 June 2018.

CEDLAS (Center for Distributive, Labor and Social Studies and World Bank). 2018. Socio-Economic Database for Latin America and the Caribbean. www.cedlas.econo.unlp.edu.ar/wp/en/estadisticas/sedlac/estadisticas/. Accessed 15 May 2018.

CRED EM-DAT (Centre for Research on the Epidemiology of Disasters). 2018. The International Disaster Database. www.emdat.be. Accessed 17 April 2018.

Eurostat. 2018. European Union Statistics on Income and Living Conditions. Brussels. http://ec.europa.eu/eurostat/web/microdata/european-union-statistics-on-income-and-living-conditions. Accessed 15 June 2018.

FAO (Food and Agriculture Organization). 2018a. FAOSTAT database. www.fao.org/faostat. Accessed 6 June 2018.

———. 2018b. AQUASTAT database. www.fao.org/nr/water/aquastat/main/index.stm. Accessed 17 April 2018.

Gallup. 2018. Gallup World Poll Analytics database. https://ga.gallup.com. Accessed 10 April 2018.

ICF Macro. Various years. Demographic and Health Surveys. www.measuredhs.com. Accessed 15 July 2018.

ICPR (Institute for Criminal Policy Research). 2016. "World Prison Population List (11th edition)." London. www.prisonstudies.org. Accessed 2 July 2018.

IDMC (Internal Displacement Monitoring Centre). 2018. Global Internal Displacement Database. www.internal-displacement.org/database. Accessed 16 May 2018.

ILO (International Labour Organization). 2018a. ILOSTAT database. www.ilo.org/ilostat. Accessed 13 April 2018.

———. 2018b. *World Social Protection Report 2017–19*. Geneva. www.social-protection.org/gimi/gess/ShowWiki.action?id=594. Accessed 13 April 2018.

IMF (International Monetary Fund). 2018. World Economic Outlook database. Washington, DC. www.imf.org/en/Data. Accessed 15 June 2018.

IPU (Inter-Parliamentary Union). 2018. Women in national parliaments. www.ipu.org/wmn-e/classif-arc.htm. Accessed 24 April 2018.

ITU (International Telecommunication Union). 2018. *ICT Facts and Figures 2018*. www.itu.int/en/ITU-D/Statistics/Pages/stat/. Accessed 18 July 2018.

LIS (Luxembourg Income Study). 2018. Luxembourg Income Study Project. www.lisdatacenter.org/data-access. Accessed 15 July 2018.

OECD (Organisation for Economic Co-operation and Development). 2017a. *Education at a Glance 2017: OECD Indicators*. Paris. www.oecd-ilibrary.org/education/education-at-a-glance-2017_eag-2017-en. Accessed 15 June 2018.

———. 2017b. *PISA 2015 Results in Focus*. Paris. www.oecd.org/pisa/. Accessed 1 July 2018.

Palma, J. G. 2011. "Homogeneous Middles vs. Heterogeneous Tails, and the End of the 'Inverted-U': The Share of the Rich is What It's All About." *Cambridge Working Papers in Economics, 1111*. Cambridge University, UK. www.econ.cam.ac.uk/research-files/repec/cam/pdf/cwpe1111.pdf. Accessed 15 September 2013.

Syrian Center for Policy Research. 2017. *Social Degradation in Syria: The Conflict Impact on Social Capital*. http://scpr-syria.org/publications/social-degradation-in-syria/. Accessed 15 July 2017.

UNCTAD (United Nations Conference on Trade and Development). 2018. Data Center. http://unctadstat.unctad.org. Accessed 16 April 2018.

UNDESA (United Nations Department of Economic and Social Affairs). 2011. *World Population Prospects: The 2010 Revision*. New York. www.un.org/en/development/desa/population/publications/trends/population-prospects_2010_revision.shtml. Accessed 15 October 2013.

———. 2017a. *World Population Prospects: The 2017 Revision*. New York. https://esa.un.org/unpd/wpp/. Accessed 10 May 2018.

———. 2017b. *Trends in International Migrant Stock: The 2017 Revision*. New York. www.un.org/en/development/desa/population/migration/data/. Accessed 19 July 2018.

———. 2018a. *World Urbanization Prospects: The 2018 Revision*. New York. https://esa.un.org/unpd/wup/. Accessed 17 May 2018.

———. 2018b. *World Contraceptive Use 2018*. New York. www.un.org/en/development/desa/population/publications/dataset/contraception/wcu2018.shtml. Accessed 16 April 2018.

UNECLAC (United Nations Economic Commission for Latin America and the Caribbean). 2018. *Preliminary Overview of the Economies of Latin America and the Caribbean 2017*. Santiago. https://repositorio.cepal.org/bitstream/handle/11362/42002/155/S1700699_en.pdf. Accessed 15 July 2018.

UNESCO (United Nations Educational, Scientific and Cultural Organization) Institute for Statistics. 2018. Data Centre. http://data.uis.unesco.org. Accessed 15 June 2018.

UNESCWA (United Nations Economic and Social Commission for Western Asia). 2018. *Survey of Economic and Social Developments in the Arab Region 2017–2018*. Beirut. www.unescwa.org/publications/survey-economic-social-development-arab-region-2017-2018. Accessed 15 June 2018.

UNHCR (Office of the United Nations High Commissioner for Refugees). 2018. *UNHCR Global Trends 2017*. Geneva. www.unhcr.org/globaltrends2017/. Accessed 20 June 2018.

UNICEF (United Nations Children's Fund). 2017. *The State of the World's Children 2017 Statistical Tables*. New York. https://data.unicef.org/resources/state-worlds-children-2017-statistical-tables/. Accessed 10 July 2018.

———. 2018. UNICEF Data. https://data.unicef.org. Accessed 16 April 2018.

———. Various years. Multiple Indicator Cluster Surveys. New York. http://mics.unicef.org. Accessed 15 July 2018.

UNICEF (United Nations Children's Fund), WHO (World Health Organization) and World Bank. 2018. Joint Child Malnutrition Estimates Expanded Database: Stunting. May 2018. New York. https://data.unicef.org/topic/nutrition/malnutrition/. Accessed 11 July 2018.

UN Inter-agency Group for Child Mortality Estimation. 2017. Child mortality estimates. www.childmortality.org. Accessed 13 July 2018.

United Nations Statistics Division. 2018a. Global SDG Indicators Database. https://unstats.un.org/sdgs/indicators/database/. Accessed 20 June 2018.

———. 2018b. National Accounts Main Aggregates Database. http://unstats.un.org/unsd/snaama. Accessed 15 July 2018.

UN Maternal Mortality Estimation Group (World Health Organization, United Nations Children's Fund, United Nations Population Fund and World Bank). 2017. Maternal mortality data. http://data.unicef.org/topic/maternal-health/maternal-mortality/. Accessed 16 April 2018.

UNODC (United Nations Office on Drugs and Crime). 2018. UNODC Statistics and Data. https://dataunodc.un.org. Accessed 18 June 2018.

UNOHCHR (United Nations Office of the High Commissioner for Human Rights). 2018. Human rights treaties. http://tbinternet.ohchr.org/_layouts/TreatyBodyExternal/countries.aspx. Accessed 29 June 2018.

UNRWA (United Nations Relief and Works Agency for Palestine). 2017. "UNRWA in Figures 2017." Amman. www.unrwa.org/sites/default/files/content/resources/unrwa_in_figures_2017_english.pdf. Accessed 15 July 2018.

UN Women (United Nations Entity for Gender Equality and the Empowerment of Women). 2018. UN Women Global Database on Violence against Women. New York. http://evaw-global-database.unwomen.org. Accessed 19 April 2018.

WHO (World Health Organization). 2018. Global Health Observatory. www.who.int/gho/. Accessed 8 June 2018.

WHO (World Health Organization) and UNICEF (United Nations Children's Fund). 2018. Estimates of national routine immunization coverage, 2017 revision (completed July 2018). https://data.unicef.org/topic/child-health/immunization/. Accessed 17 July 2018.

World Bank. 2018a. World Development Indicators database. Washington, DC. http://data.worldbank.org. Accessed 6 July 2018.

———. 2018b. World Development Indicators database. Washington, DC. http://data.worldbank.org. Accessed 28 July 2018.

———. 2018c. Gender Statistics database. Washington, DC. http://data.worldbank.org. Accessed 26 April 2018.

WSIS (World Summit on the Information Society). 2014. *Forum Report 2014*. Geneva.